been there, done that!

been there, done that!

Unique experiences of a missionary kid

Philip R. Fogle

XULON PRESS

Xulon Press
2301 Lucien Way #415
Maitland, FL 32751
407.339.4217
www.xulonpress.com

© 2022 by Philip R. Fogle

All rights reserved solely by the author. The author guarantees all contents are original and do not infringe upon the legal rights of any other person or work. No part of this book may be reproduced in any form without the permission of the author.

Due to the changing nature of the Internet, if there are any web addresses, links, or URLs included in this manuscript, these may have been altered and may no longer be accessible. The views and opinions shared in this book belong solely to the author and do not necessarily reflect those of the publisher. The publisher therefore disclaims responsibility for the views or opinions expressed within the work.

Unless otherwise indicated, Scripture quotations taken from the King James Version (KJV)–*public domain*

Paperback ISBN-13: 978-1-6628-5020-2
Hard Cover ISBN-13: 978-1-6628-5021-9
Ebook ISBN-13: 978-1-6628-5022-6

PREFACE

Life brings to everyone a variety of opportunities and changes, but how often do we really expect these to be part of our own lives when we can say "been there, done that"? There are times when we seek certain prospects or when we plan to go in a different direction. Just when we think we have it all figured out, a new situation develops, which modifies our plans and goals into what we assume would be our new "normal". However, God does not always work in our lives in ways that we anticipate or desire. Rather, His "mysterious" ways often shower us with blessings far beyond our imagination. Such are the unique and unbelievable stories of my life.

These memoirs reveal many of my experiences, with some in more detail than others. I have enjoyed being a risk taker, adventurer, and a server throughout my life. Some of my life's events are categorized, so everything in my memoirs is not in chronological order. In general, the last part of the book combines portions of my life by subject rather than by sequence. My pre-military life, education, military experiences, ministries, and extensive travels make up the other parts of the book. May you revel in God's rich blessings to me through the many seemingly unreal events and even numerous and sometimes incredible adversities in which He provided direction and safety through my eighty years. I am thankful to the Lord for every aspect of my life!

My life has been anything but "normal". Besides, what is normal for a missionary kid from the southern Sahara Desert region in Africa? Many missionary kids can say "been there, done that" when others share their life's experiences. What do you do when your bucket of "to dos" is already mostly "dones"? Let me briefly share a few "been there, done that" events in my life: parachuting, parasailing, intentionally free-falling off a 630-foot tower, climbing on top of the steel girders of the Sydney Harbor bridge, serving as an infantry commander in combat operations, mountain climbing, cliff-rescue training, rappelling down from or climbing vertical or overhanging cliffs, whitewater rafting, distance bicycle riding, flying in a glider, traveling (as of this time) in about eighty-five countries, going in a tunnel under the Demilitarized Zone in Korea, staring a North Korean soldier in the eye at Panmunjom, editing four years of an annual publication for the Secretary of Defense to send to the White House and to Congress, visiting Israel and its elite military, touring Egypt's Giza pyramids, walking on the Great Wall of China, seeing the terracotta soldiers in China, exploring Machu Picchu in Peru, touring the amazing Galapagos Islands, hunting and photographing big game in Africa, landing on a Navy aircraft carrier at sea, piloting a F-16 fighter jet simulator (yes, I crashed a couple of times!), serving as a church music minister and choir director, facilitating strategic planning for several organizations, walking where Christ walked in Israel, being interviewed on national Christian TV and radio programs, interacting with national public electronic and print news reporters, and the list could go on and on! What a life! Yes, I've truly "been there, done that" and much more—and enjoyed it all!

Did I expect all of these blessings? No! But many circumstances were placed in my life whereby God brought these activities to occur. I have learned to expect the Lord to bring unique and unexpected blessings, for which there is not time or space to share details of them all.

Does it sound like an exciting life? It has been! But what is left to do or where to go? Hot air ballooning, paragliding off a mountain, touring Petra in Jordan, going to the shores of Normandy in France, writing and publishing my memoirs (well, I guess that is what I am doing now!), stepping on the ice of the world's seventh continent (Antarctica—I have been on the other six), returning to the central highlands of Vietnam, and visiting islands of the Eastern Caribbean and the South Pacific. This is just a short list of a few "to dos" still on my bucket list, and my time on earth may run out before most of these can be accomplished.

Many of these opportunistic events have been due to issues beyond my personal control. Some have come through the educational, political, social, cultural, military, family, or religious environments at the time. Examples include when I was separated from my missionary parents to attend boarding schools, when I took the oath of office to become a commissioned officer in the US Army, when I was given orders to serve in combat in Vietnam, when children came into our lives, when I was wounded severely and physically could not go back to lead soldiers on a battlefield, when I retired from active military service, and when doors were open or closed in ministries in which I have been involved. My unique life began as a child of missionaries. I thank God for choosing a missionary family for me and for directing my life rather than leaving it up to me!

The Lord's guidance has led me to establish core values for my life. They are identified in Appendix A at the back of this book. I developed these many years ago even while I was in the military and have made only slight modifications in them since I initially wrote them. I try to use them in my daily living.

I have constantly been reminded that human life is incredibly fragile due to all the dangers of war, drought, political upheavals, health issues, and even religious persecutions, all which exist in our world. But I have been taught to trust in God's promises in His Word and not to fear bombardments of varied threats. As a child, I learned Psalm 91 from the Scriptures, and with David the author, I have been satisfied with the refuge I have found in the Lord. However, I do believe that my guardian angel has had a real workout! Scripture references throughout my text are primarily from the King James Version since I grew up with that translation and memorized many verses from it.

Over the years, countless individuals have encouraged me to "Write a book!" I have slowly taken their advice, and for about fifteen years, I have jotted down brief one-liners as various aspects of my life have come to my memory. Constantly, as I would relate to others an incident from my past, I was challenged to put that in writing. These memoirs are of my life as I remember them.

I am indebted to hundreds of people from many states, provinces, and countries that have enriched my life through a variety of interactions in homes, military service, ministries, and cultures. I have found connectivity of heart, soul, and joy in life even during trials and changes defined in our distinct human journeys.

Several people have helped me while writing my memoirs by checking my facts and helping me organize the myriad of details of my stories into some semblance of unity. I thank them for enduring with me in this process. I could have included many additional pictures but unfortunately have had to limit them due to space. Although some of the pictures are from long ago and may not be of today's quality from digital and professional cameras, I feel they help to give a glimpse of many special aspects of my life.

My parents, long deceased, instilled in me a biblical faith to never give up and at my college graduation told me to "endure as a good soldier of Jesus Christ". They gave me experiences I never could have planned, and I am more than grateful for the rich and biblical model they provided for me. Houseparents and teachers at varying times in boarding schools (from age eighteen months through college) helped me to establish disciplines of dependence, independence, and interdependence in my life that I might not have learned otherwise. I am grateful for each person whom the Lord has used to enrich my life.

My family has always been supportive in my various activities of life—even when it may have been somewhat of a detriment for them. I thank them for enduring with me.

Every individual has stories of their lives that are different from those of other people. But sometimes I wonder if they have had as great a life as I have had, been to as many places, and done such a great variety of activities. What you'll read in the following text is about my life that has been influenced by my extended family and so many other individuals.

My dear wife, Betty, has encouraged me to stick with this writing project in times when I most likely would have set it aside. The isolation due to the coronavirus pandemic of 2021–2022 took away any excuse about not having time to compile my reflections of my past. Betty has been a wonderful help in processing some of the computerized details while I was preparing the manuscript and pictures.

Betty has been with me as we have walked together through many of these stories, and she has heard many people say that I should write down my memories so that others may enjoy my blessings. Betty has persevered through many of life's joys and hardships with me and other times by herself in separations due to war or ministry. I thank her for being like that little energizer bunny in TV ads and for being a "real trooper" as many have called her.

DEDICATION

These memoirs are dedicated to my wife, Betty, who was my instant love at first sight in 1961 and is my generous partner for almost fifty-eight years of married life! She has traveled with me to about 55 nations, tasted innumerable strange foods (to her!), served as a wonderful and loving mother and grandmother in our family, and remained extremely strong in times of separations due to my military duties and ministry opportunities. Betty has endured her own trials in life and marched through them with her strong faith and trust in our mutual love for Jesus Christ. She has been a special blessing in my life!

TABLE OF CONTENTS

Preface..vii
Dedication... xi

Part 1—Pre Military 1

Chapter I—Early Life—Before Africa 3
  Parents' Background 3
  Government Regulations Change Plans 5
  Westervelt Home 7
    A Personal and Difficult Decision 8
    Sunday—Letters from Africa..............................9
    Food for All 12
    Sunburn and Snowman 14
    Mother Picks Up Lois and Me.............................15
    Reunion of the Westervelt MKs...........................17
  1948 Furlough with My Parents...............................20

Chapter II—Africa 23
  Baggage Tag on the Train 23
  My First Flights 24
  Welcome to a New Homeland 24
  Boarding School at Fort Crampel 26
    Mouse in the Classroom!.................................27
    The Dorm..27
    My Salvation 28
    Food Poisoning 29
    Dorm Life and Activities 30
    Abandoned?..34
  Troubles on the Dirt Roads 35
    Stuck in a Mud Hole 36

    Breaking Through a Bridge 38
    Other Road Experiences 39
  Home Life in Fort Archambault. 40
    Foot Pumping the Dentist Drill 41
    My Escape and Hike 42
    Ants in My Pants 43
    "Me Too" Juice 45
    Don't Get Behind a Donkey. 45
    Beginning My Personal Devotions 46
  Home Life in Kyabe 46
    Disc Lips and Pointed Teeth 47
    Kyabe's Mission Station 49
    Temperature Was 163 Degrees Fahrenheit 52
    Welcoming Dad Back from Villages 52
  Lessons from My Early Life 53

Chapter III—Back In America. 55

  1954 Furlough 55
    I'll Stay to Watch the Accidents. 56
    New House. 56
  Mid-Maples—Home for Teenage MKs 58
    Summers at the Lake 59

Chapter IV—Education 61

  Learning on a Typewriter. 61
  Too Young for My Grade 61
  Junior High School 62
    "Free" Throws 62
    "Dumb" Gym Teacher 63
  High School at Wheaton Academy 63
    Great Teachers 63
    Co-Alumna of Year in 2019 65
  Life at Wheaton College 67
    College Dorm Life 67
    Academics and Changing Majors 68
  ROTC as a College Cadet 70
    Pershing Rifles 70
    Traffic Guide for Billy Graham Crusade 70
    Extracurricular Activities 71
    Competitive Drill Team 73
    ROTC Summer Camp 74

    Cadet Battalion Commander 75
  Graduation and Commissioning 76
    What is an Infantry Soldier? 76
  God's Special Financial Provision. 78

Chapter V—The Fairer Gender 81

  Socially Shy Before College 81
  Dating While in College 82
    Love-Stricken at First Sight 83
    Shyness Turns to Boldness. 84
    Engagement 84
  The Wedding Schedule. 85
  Our Short Honeymoon. 87
  First Home at the End of a Runway. 88

Part II—American by Birth—Soldier by God's Choice 91

Chapter VI—Military Training and Education 93

  "Turtle" Time 93
  Infantry Officer Basic Course 95
    An Exploding Latrine 96
  Ranger School 97
    Phase 1—Permission to Drop 97
    Phase 2—Saddened—Yet Happy. 100
    Phase 3—Where's the Ship? 102
  Airborne School 108
  Other Schools. 111
    Public Affairs Schools 112
    Harvard University. 114

Chapter VII—Military Unit Assignments 115

  Fort Lewis, Washington. 115
    Rifle Platoon Leader 115
    Weapons Platoon Leader 116
    Trial and Defense Counsel. 117
    Yakima Firing Center Exercise 117
    A Lost General Officer. 118
    Heavy Mortar/Davy Crockett Platoon Leader 120
  Orders to Vietnam 121
    Deployment—Where Should Betty Live?. 121

Chapter VIII — First Tour in Vietnam 123

Two Broken Airplanes 123
Reporting to a Four-Star General 124
52nd Aviation Battalion 125
52nd Security Detachment Commander 127
      The Growing Organization 129
      Method of Operations 131
      Difficult Soldiers 131
      Rhade Tribal Initiation 134
      Agent Orange 136
      Arrival of 1st Cavalry Division (Airmobile) 137
      Attack on Camp at Plei Me 137
      Confrontation with a Senior Officer 138
      Battle of the Ia Drang Valley 139
Letters to and From Home 140
Lessons from First Combat Tour 142

Chapter IX — Wheaton College ROTC 143

Teaching Military History 143
Sponsoring Conguer Rifles 144
Anti-War Protests 145
Survivor Assistance Officer 145
Military Funeral Service 147
Reassigned Back to Vietnam 149

Chapter X — Second Tour in Vietnam 151

Division Operations Team 151
Company Command 152
      Jungle Environment 155
      Soldier Casualties 157
      Watch out for Helicopter Blades! 159
      Missed by Inches 159
      Invisible Wounds in Combat 161
      A Delayed Mission 163
      Follow Me! 163
      The Dark Valley 165
      Village Raids 167
Final Battles — Wounded in Action 169
      Hammer and Anvil Operation 170
      Shell-Shocked Lieutenant 171

    My Leg Pointed in Wrong Direction 171
    Refuge in My God 172
    Medical Evacuation 173

Chapter XI — Hospitalizations 175

"Wounded, Hawaii Cancelled, More Later" 175
Awakened by Knocking in Japan 176
Back in the USA! 177
    Betty's Visits to Valley Forge 179
    My "Earthquake" 180
    Questioning God 180
    Guinea Pig for a Hinged Cast 181
Convalescent Leave at Home 182
    Relieving My "Girdle" 183
    Family and Church Support 184
Snapshots of Combat Duty 185

Chapter XII — A Different Career Pattern 189

What Is Next? 189
Pentagon — Public Affairs 190
    Defense Department Briefer 190
    Vietnam Veteran Status Awareness 191
    Army Public News 193
    Medal of Honor Ceremonies 194
    Special Day with VP Gerald Ford 194
    A Reincarnated Blackbird 195
    Army Research with LSD 197
    An Unusual Interview 198
    Explosion in the Pentagon! 199
From the Army to the Defense Department 200

Chapter XIII — Transition to Army Reserve 201

CIOR — A NATO Organization 202
Office of the Assistant Secretary of Defense (Reserve Affairs) 202
Reserve Forces Policy Board 203
    Exciting RFPB Study Trips 204
    Editor of RFPB Annual Report 208

Chapter XIV — Military Retirement 211

Take Aways from Military 212

Part III—Enjoyment in Ministry 215

Chapter XV—USA Ministries 217

    Christian Service Brigade 217
        Herald of Christ Badge 217
        Gil Dodds Mile Race Trophy 218
        Battalion Activities in 1970s 219
        Memorization of Scripture Passages 221
        End of a Great Ministry 222
    Moody Keswick Conference Center 223
        Conference Center Campus 223
        Were We Just Volunteered? 224
        Meeting the Banquet Speaker 224
        Volunteer Assignments 225
        Getting to Know Everyone 226
        Meeting at Moody in Chicago 226
        Serving as Interim Director 227
        My Hat Is in the Ring 228
        Bible Conference Experiences 229
        Radio and TV Interviews 232
        "You No Like Ducks?" 233
    Travels for the Conference Center 234
        Canadian Atlantic Provinces 235
        ATVs to the Rescue 235
        Eastern Canada Meetings 237
        Ontario 242
        Upper Midwest USA 243
        Manitoba to British Columbia 243
        West and Southwest USA 245
    Moody Closes Conference Center 246
    D&D Missionary Homes, Inc. 247
        Board Membership 248
        Effects of Change 250
        "Preach It, Brother!" 251
        Other Unusual Church Opportunities 252
        Funding of the Ministry 253
        Benefit Sales 255
        D&D's Great Staff 256
        Beginning of a Downward Spiral 257
        Divisiveness Brings on Demise 258
    Baptist Mid-Missions Elected Council 260

Chapter XVI — Overseas Ministries........263

Missionary Encouragement in Germany..........263
PEP Ministry Trips..........264
India and Nepal..........264
   My Ticketed Flight Is Invalid..........265
   Mountain Road in North India..........265
   Hike up to the Shimla Church..........266
   Extra Teaching in Nepal..........267
   Trek to Sunkhani Church..........268
Myanmar..........269
   A Country Opening Up..........270
   First White Man in Church..........271
   Bible College in Yangon..........272
   Church in Middle of a Rice Paddy..........273
Bahama Islands..........274
   Start of a Bible Institute..........274
   Touring Blackbeard's Cave..........275
   Bad Fishing—Again!..........275
Central African Republic..........278
   Cell Phone Works!..........276
   Three Great Conferences..........278
Chad..........281
   MAF Flight to Koumra..........281
   Meeting Friends in Sarh..........282
   Martyrdom of Former Pastor..........283
Welcome Home to Kyabe, Chad..........284
   Big Contrasts to the Past..........286
   "Yoo Hoo, Lesta"..........287
   Finding My Sister's Footprint..........288
Effect of PEP Ministry..........289

CHAPTER XVII — Short-Term Mission Trips..........291

Colombia..........291
   Blackmailed?..........293
   Flying off the Amazon River..........294
   Arrival at Our Jungle Site..........296
   Answered Prayer for Drinking Water..........297
   Plane Crash Through Triple-Canopy Jungle..........298
   The Hole in the Clouds..........299
   Racing for the Last Flight..........300

       Jungle Underwear Found! 300
   Cambodia..301
       Back of Pickup Truck to Border 302
       Medical Missions in the Village......................302
       Teeth for Sale 304
       Gospel Outreach Opportunities 304
   Argentina 306
       Construction Project..............................307
       Church Ministries................................307
   Romania..308
       The Roma People................................308
       Medical Clinics in Church Buildings..................309
       Ministry in the Roma Communities...................310
   Ukraine...310
       Ministry in Yuzhny...............................311
       Work at Country Churches.........................312
       Church Replaces Radio Jamming Tower 312
   Cayman Islands 314
       Serving with Former D&D Guests 314
       Swimming with Stingrays 315

Part IV—Travels 317

Chapter XVIII—Personally Planned Trips.......................319

   Alaska..319
       Exciting Modes of Transportation 320
       Gee and Haw—Dog Sled.........................321
       Paraglide Weathered Out Again.....................322
       A Rough Catamaran Ride 322
       Bear Watching—Float Plane 323
       Flight Around Mt. Denali—Ski Plane 324
       North of the Arctic Circle—Wheeled Plan 324
       Ice Hotel in Fairbanks 326
       Visit in a "Russian" Village 326
       Our First Cruise 327
   Galapagos Islands 328
       Cruising the Galapagos Islands 329
   Peru..330
       Machu Picchu and Inca Ruins 330
       Ministries in Trujillo and Lima 331
   Sailing Penobscot Bay, Maine........................332

  Schooner *Heritage* 332
 Seeing the USA! 334
  9,200 Miles in Twenty-One Days 334
  Near Arrest in Las Vegas 335
  Patience Needed at Canadian Border. 335
 Glider Flight in Tennessee 336

Chapter XIX — Tours and Cruises 339

 Egypt, Israel, and Switzerland. 339
  Wonders of the Ancient World. 340
  Walking Where Christ Walked. 340
  Jungfrau in the Alps 341
 China and Hong Kong. 342
  Beijing — Picking up a Stone 342
  The Great Wall. 343
  Sunday Morning Service Crowd 343
  Terracotta Army. 344
  Geological Karsts of South China 345
  Trolleys and Buses in Hong Kong. 346
 Cruising the Mediterranean 346
  Starting in Rome 347
  Biblical Places — Mars Hill and Ephesus. 347
 Scandinavia and Russia 348
  Lost Baggage. 348
  Disturbed by Gay Pride Flag 349
  Architectural Beauty in Russia 350
  Finland and Sweden. 351
  Exhilarating Speedboat from Stockholm. 351
 Australia and New Zealand 352
  Paraglide Flight Missed Again. 352
  Glowworm Cave 353
  Rubbing Noses with Maori People 354
  Tour of Hobbiton 354
  Jump from Auckland's Sky Tower. 355
  Zip Lines over the Rainforest 357
  Uluru in Australia's Outback 358
  Walking atop Sydney Harbor Bridge. 359
 Caribbean Region 360
  Mayan Culture Ruins. 360
  Engineering Feature in Panama 361
  Port Building in Costa Rica. 361

Thailand 362
    Temples and Buddhas Everywhere 363
    Using Toes to Swing Hammocks 365
    Interesting Evening Shows 365
The Danube River and Czech Republic 366
    River Cruising Is Different 366
    Oldest Working Astronomical Clock 367
    John Hus's Bethlehem Chapel 368
Uganda 368
    Visit with Granddaughter in Uganda 369
    Tricked at the Equator? 370
South Africa Tour 370
    Victoria Falls 371
    Three-Day, Narrow-Gauge Rail Journey 372
    Soweto 372
    Thornybush Game Reserve 373
    Up Early, Out Late for Game Drives 374
    The Big Five and Others—Up Close! 374
    Fast Reactions by Our Driver 375

Part V—Miscellaneous Interests in Life 377

Chapter XX—Hobbies 379

Biking 379
    Watch Where You Are Going 379
    Dad's Green Bike—Answer to Prayer 380
    My Own Schwinn Bike 381
    130-Mile Bike Journey to College 382
    150-Mile Bike Trip on Skyline Drive 384
    184-Mile Ride on Chesapeake & Ohio Canal Towpath 385
    Home Stationary Exercise Bike 386
Stamp Collection 387
Hymnbook Collection 388
    Unusual Hymnbooks 389

Chapter XXI—Work Experiences 391

High School 391
    A Homeless Person in an Unusual Place 392
    Landscaping at the College 392
    Upholstery and Carpet Cleaning 394

College	394
Lumber Yard—Phuzzy Phil's Nails	394
Heating Plant Shift Work and Dating	395
Night Switchboard	397
Changing the Flag in the Tower	397
Other Work Experiences	398
US Army's Professional Association	399
Indy 500 Track's Brickyard	399

Chapter XXII—Interesting Birthday Facts **401**

Don't Blame Me	401
Red Cross Notification Is Wrong	402
Thanks for a Sprained Ankle	402
Another Wrong Birth Announcement	404
The Kids Today—2021	405
Celebrating Betty's Fiftieth Birthday	406
Black Balloons Covered My Ceiling	407

Chapter XXIII—Sports **409**

Africa—Kick Balls Made from Intestines!	409
High School	410
Football—Undefeated 1957 Team!	410
Basketball—A Great Bench Warmer	411
Track—Team Captain	412
Slow Pitch Softball	414

Chapter XXIV—My Vehicles **417**

Bees in the Back Seat	417
Coal Ash Covered the Car	418
Clunk, Clunk, Clunk on the Highway	420
Engine Rebuilt for $67	421
VW Bug Meets a Deer	422
The Rally-Red Dasher	423
My "Toys" Go to the Kids	423

Chapter XXV—Wildlife Vignettes **425**

Animals	425
Don't Look in Those Holes!	427
My Red Ryder BB Gun	428
Fun Inside an Elephant	427

Where's Our Buddy? Ask a Tiger 430
Rats in the Market 430
Leopard 431
    Oh, Does It Stink! 432
Snakes Alive 433
    Snake in the Bedspring Coils 434
    The Spitting Cobra 435
    Mala, Mala Coral Snake 435
Crocodile Hunt 436
    Oh, Oh! Wrong Group of Indians 437
    Snake Instead of Crocodile 437
Silence Broken Due to a Bamboo Viper 439
Learning to Handle a Snake 439
Done in by Its Own Greed 440
Chased by a Snake 440
Another "Tall Tale" 442
Hawks at My House 442
    Get it back in the Nest 443
    Feeding the Babies 444
    Remember, I'm Bigger 444
    Hawk in the Firebox 445
    Attack! You Looked at My Babies 447
Proud Hawk Hunter 448

Chapter XXVI—"Phil Will Eat Anything!" 451

African Foods—Rancid Beef 451
Ants off the Wall 452
Other Delicious African Menus 452
    How to Eat an Elephant 453
    Lizard in the Gravy 454
I Like Variety 454
    Banquet Food from Eighteen Countries 455
Dog and Stinky Nuoc Mam 455
"You Are a True Indian Brother" 456
Other Nations' Unusual Food 456
    "No, Phil, from a Bull!" 458
    An Expensive Fish Head 459
Fresh Seafood—Right from the Water 459
I'll Never Say That Again 461
Lipstick on My Coffee Cup 461
Normal Foods? 462

Chapter XXVII — Places Where I Have Slept 465

Pine Cote Cabin. 465
Bricks in the Bed 465
Dorm in Africa. 466
The Clock That Couldn't Keep Time 467
Hyenas and Elephants Really Close 468
High School and College Bunks 468
Hanging in a Tree to Get a Nap. 469
Scritch, Scritch — Mattress Deflates 470
An Aircraft Carrier at Sea 471
Hiding Our "Evil" Doings. 471
Two in a Narrow Bed — Without Roaches! 473
Back of a Pickup Truck in a Mud Hole 473

Chapter XXVIII — Christmas Celebrations 475

The Big Coloring Book 475
Popcorn, Cranberries, and Raisins. 476
Unique Christmases in Africa 476
    One-Page Spiral Notebook Gift. 477
    Used Tea Bags and Melted Candy 477
    In Everything Give Thanks 478
Sixty-Two-Inch Waist Used Pants 478
Shooting out Our Christmas Lights 478
Lonely Christmases in Vietnam. 479
In a Cast at Home for Christmas 481

Chapter XXIX — Climbing Experiences 483

Racing up the Washington Monument. 483
Real Mountain Climbing 484
Climbing in Vietnam 484
Agony on the Temple of the Dawn 485
Mountaineering with Teenage Boys 486
View from the Crow's Nest 488
Spiritual Climbing 488

Chapter XXX — A Brief Life Summary 491

APPENDIX A — Phil Fogle's Core Values (Philippians 4:8). 495
APPENDIX B — Military Biographical Summary 497

APPENDIX C—General Biographical Summary...................505
APPENDIX D—Maps **509**

    Central African Republic and Chad...........................510
    Vietnam 511

****

Front cover picture: Phil Fogle on top of the steel girders of the Sydney Harbor Bridge in Australia

Back cover picture: Captain Phil Fogle (US Army) with Montagnard men in village in Central Vietnam

PART 1—PRE-MILITARY

CHAPTER I

EARLY LIFE—BEFORE AFRICA

PARENTS' BACKGROUND

My parents' lives (and mine also) certainly were changed in 1941 while on furlough from missionary service in the heart of Africa. Prior to their desired return to Africa in 1942, the US State Department issued a ruling that families could not cross the oceans together lest the entire family be destroyed by enemy activity on the high seas in World War II. By then, my folks had two young children. Would their call to missions overseas be diverted? What modifications of their plans might be necessary due to this unexpected governmental restriction?

And so begins the saga of my life! A little background is important for better understanding. Both of my parents, Lester and Martha Fogle, were from northern Indiana. Dad's father died when he was two years old. He was the baby of eight children. Because of spousal deaths, his mother married four more times during his lifetime. She had a strong spiritual influence on his life.

Mother was one of ten children from a poor family that became very involved in support of the City Rescue Mission in South Bend, Indiana. At an early age, she learned to play the piano and enjoyed playing for the various services at the mission. Because of the value of her family to the mission's programs, she and her siblings were permitted to occasionally bring to their home any soup or leftover food not consumed by the men who went to the mission from their downtown street living.

In those days, blood tests were required of the man and woman planning to be married. Mother had been a sickly girl in high school. The story is told that when she went to the doctor's office to get her blood test, that Mr. B., the City Rescue

been there, done that!

Mission director, was praying that she would not pass so that she could stay and help the mission rather than go with Dad to an overseas ministry. Meanwhile, Dad was praying just the opposite!

After that medical appointment (which she passed), the doctor told Dad that Mother should never leave the US because she would always need medical help. Bottom line? Mother served in the middle of undeveloped Africa for forty years with Dad, she bore seven children, had cancer twice, had several other major surgeries, and outlived Dad by eighteen years! Doctors don't always know the true future story of their patients—but the Lord sure does!

My parents had accepted God's call, beginning in 1937, to serve in French Equatorial Africa—divided in 1960 into the four independent nations of Chad, Central African Republic, Republic of Congo, and Gabon. Separately, as single people, they had attended a Bible institute at the First Baptist Church in Mishawaka, Indiana. Without much of a strong initial love for each other, they both knew God wanted them in Africa, so they decided to get married and go together! Their love for each other was not a demonstrated romantic love but there was never a hint that they did not own each other and supported each other with deep, loving commitment through their long lives. Their marriage lasted from 1937 into 1994 when Dad was taken to heaven.

Now, to the 1937 wedding ceremony itself: when my parents decided to get married, they chose the venue of the rescue mission because of the influence it had in Mother's life and because of her long, musical service there. The ceremony was unusual and very cheap! The regular gospel preaching service at the City Rescue Mission for the men was held with Mother playing the piano. Following that service, Mother went to the rear of the room and was then escorted by her father down the aisle to the front where Dad was waiting. The mission director performed the ceremony in front of the homeless men who were anxiously waiting for their food. What a simple ceremony it was! But now, Mother and Dad could finalize plans to be commissioned by their home church in Indiana, serve with Baptist Mid-Missions, and leave for Africa together!

In those days, travel across the seas by airplane was not economically feasible; so much of overseas travel was by boat—especially for missionaries! In two weeks following their marriage in 1937, they boarded a Portuguese freighter, the *SS West Lashaway*, in New York and spent forty-six days getting to Africa's west coast. What a honeymoon that must have been! Four other missionaries and one of their daughters were also on the ship. My parents tried to keep it a secret that they were newlyweds, but I'm not sure how that turned out!

After numerous days traveling inland from the coast, they finally reached the heart of steaming Africa where they would spend their careers serving the Lord, preaching the gospel, planting churches, and training believers. In their first term of ministry, my older sister, Lois, was born. Most of their time was in the southern Sahara Desert region of French Equatorial Africa with many years among the Sara Kaba tribe, characterized by its disc-lipped women.

GOVERNMENT REGULATIONS CHANGE PLANS

My parents' first term of missionary service was complete in the early summer of 1941. They returned to the US, settling in the South Bend, Indiana, area where they had grown up and near their home church. Their faith in God was demonstrated by the fact that they left for Africa in 1937 with $25/month of promised financial support, but God had met all their needs! They immediately began their traveling ministry to raise additional support for their continuing ministries in Africa to which they planned to return after one year of furlough. However, the world's situation was becoming extremely tense with the conflicts in Europe and with the rising power and influence of Japan in the Pacific.

Mother's second pregnancy and managing a little, two-year-old girl at home occupied most of her time, and on December 3, 1941, I was born at Memorial Hospital in South Bend, Indiana. (You can do the math to figure out where I was conceived!) Four days later, the horrible attack on Pearl Harbor brought the US into World War II, for which members of both Mother's and Dad's families were called to go and serve our country.

News of enemy submarines and other ships began to tell of significant losses on the high seas. In fact, some of our Baptist Mid-Missions missionaries were coming back for a furlough from Africa on a ship which was torpedoed by the German forces. This was the same *SS West Lashaway* ship on which my parents had first sailed to Africa. Three missionary adults and one of their young daughters perished in that disastrous enemy attack. However, one missionary lady and four young children managed to get on a small, open, 8x10-foot life raft and spent twenty days on it before being rescued! Missionaries became more personally aware of the potential dangers of crossing the oceans in 1942.

Although I never discussed this with my parents, I can imagine the depth of anxiety this must have caused them as they anticipated their own return to Africa— now with two children. Because of the war, instead of remaining on furlough for just one year, they extended their time in the US and planned to go back to the field in the late spring of 1943. Changes of plans often cause delays in what we may perceive to be God's timing, but He always knows what is best!

In the meantime, the US State Department announced that no families would be approved to cross the oceans due to the potential of their ships being sunk and entire families eliminated. What a dilemma missionaries with families now faced! It was one thing for a family with older kids to leave them in the US for college, but what was a family to do when they had only younger children? God had selected some people to take the Gospel to the world, and our government was saying they were not permitted to go with their children.

In the era of the early 1940s, many, many missionaries determined to follow the Lord's call and find accommodations for their kids to remain in the United States—hoping the war would soon end and they could be reunited quickly with their children. So missionaries headed off to the far reaches of the earth, leaving their young children in the care of relatives, an open and inviting home, or a place specifically designated to be a home for these separated missionary kids. One such place was the Westervelt Home in Batesburg, South Carolina.

WESTERVELT HOME

The Westervelt Home was a group home for missionary kids whose parents were serving the Lord in foreign lands during a period of history when the children were not permitted to travel across the oceans to mission fields with their parents. Originally, Mr. and Mrs. Westervelt had served as missionaries in Angola, but because of health issues, they stayed in the United States in the late 1920s and kept their college-age son with them. When a few other missionaries learned of the Westervelts' decision to stay in America, they asked the Westervelts if their sons could also live with them while going to college. Because a couple of the boys wanted to go to John Brown University in Arkansas, the Westervelts moved there from their previous home in the Western US. The Westervelts' hospitality ministry for missionaries' college-age men soon expanded and the group moved to Columbia, South Carolina, so that the students could attend Columbia Bible College (now Columbia International University).

As I understand the story, the Westervelts, with these college-age boys, moved into a large home very near to where the Hampden and Dubose families were caring for teenage girls from missionary families. That home was somewhat of a "finishing" school for the girls to prepare them for life in America. The Hampden and Dubose leaders felt strongly about keeping their place for girls only, but the Westervelts believed that siblings (boys and girls) should be in the same home, even though prior to this they had only kept older boys. The philosophical differences caused the Hampden and Dubose group to move to Florida, but the Westervelts stayed in South Carolina.

As the US became heavily involved in World War II, more and more missionaries felt they could not take their children overseas with them because of the dangers in sailing the waters and the threats of enemy action against Americans. Missionaries now had to make a very challenging decision—do they continue to follow God's call in their lives to take the gospel to other lands and leave their children in the US with other guardians? Or, do they abandon God's call and promises of protection and remain in the US with their children? Transportation

been there, done that!

and communications were very limited in that era, and missionaries lived by faith for God's provisions for their immediate needs. Therefore, it was not wise to even think of a quick trip back to America if an emergency situation would arise regarding their separated children. Fiscal policies and support (as we know it today) had not been developed by mission organizations for their missionaries in those early pioneering years.

A PERSONAL AND DIFFICULT DECISION

My parents, like others, now had to make a personal and very testing decision about God's direction for their lives. They now had two children, my sister, Lois (who was about twenty-six months older than me), and me. Would they return? Yes! Would they leave us in someone else's care in America? The decision was "Yes" and they determined to believe God's promises for His care for themselves and for Lois and me.

More and more missionaries trusted the Westervelts' loving custody and wanted to leave their children with them while they went to their overseas fields of ministry. This influenced Mr. and Mrs. Westervelt to also accept younger children, rather than just college-age students. In some cases, missionaries left their kids because there was no available boarding school for them in the remote areas where the parents served, and home schooling was not as good an option as it became in later years.

When my parents learned about the Westervelt Home, they asked the Lord if they should leave my sister and me there and felt special peace in God's answer to do that. Lois was about three and a half years old, and I was less than eighteen months old. Mother and Dad took Lois and me to live at the Westervelt Home in the spring of 1943 so that they could then return to Africa. Arriving at the "campus," they learned that I would be the youngest child there. I was placed in a small cabin for the babies. It was called Pine Cote, and Lois stayed in Grey Cote.

Mother and Dad told us later that they were invited to stay in town with a couple that first night after they said goodbye to us, but they turned down the offer and went to a hotel instead. Why? They were really struggling and said they spent most of the night crying, not in grief for their decision, but rather in emotional distress due to the family separation and not knowing when we would all be reunited again.

God had asked them to go to Africa, and now they were leaving their kids in the US. However, they knew and had confidence that God had promised to care for us and them in those troubled war years. This was a trial of their spiritual dedication, commitment, and discipleship, and they wanted to pass the test. Jesus said in Luke 9:23, "If any man will come after me, let him deny himself, and take up his cross daily, and follow me." My parents chose to do that. Mother said that some people in churches heavily criticized them for their decision to leave their young children behind and go off to Africa, but in their hearts, Mother and Dad did not waver. They were confident that God knew what He was doing. Their call to Africa was firm! For me, I look back on all this and have learned the lesson they demonstrated to me through their sincere dedication to follow the Lord — regardless of what He might require of us beyond our human comprehension.

Because so many missionary families wanted to leave their children at the Westervelt Home, it outgrew its facilities in Columbia and moved west in the very early 1940s to a farm of more than 200 acres in Batesburg, South Carolina, which is where the home was when I arrived. It had a large, two story brick building which initially could be the dormitory. The dining room was in the walk-in basement. Before long, there were approximately 200 missionary kids (MKs) in residence! Another dorm, a one-room schoolhouse, a small gymnasium, and small cabins were constructed to accommodate the needs of this extended family.

Some MKs attended Columbia Bible College, some were in high school, some in elementary school, and some of us were preschool. Older children — those in Columbia Bible College and those in high school — did the majority of the farm work, housekeeping, kitchen work, and even care of the younger ones. The MKs were from many different evangelical mission agencies and many nations.

SUNDAY — LETTERS FROM AFRICA

I have many memories of those Westervelt Home years when I was there from 1943–1948. Although I don't remember anything about church services or even where they were held, I distinctly and vividly remember Sunday dinners. Everyone was dressed up, and we ate at designated tables in the dining room in the basement of the main administrative building. In those days, we had breakfast, dinner, and supper. The food was always good — at least to me — and that has been true all my life! We usually had some kind of dessert on Sunday!

been there, done that!

After Sunday dinner, my sister would come to my table, and one of the older teens would also be there. They had been given one or more letters from our parents to read to us. Letters were often delayed coming from the heart of Africa because of the war environment, the lack of air or sea mail scheduling, or rudimentary transportation within the country. I learned later that the houseparents were very wise in handling the letters because sometimes they would arrive in bunches since mail service from the heart of Africa was not an everyday service. The houseparents would take that packet of letters and put them in chronological order for one of the older missionary kids to read to us. And they also ensured that we would have a letter read to us each Sunday. We may have had repeats, but what difference would it make to a young child like me?

To us youngsters, the timing didn't matter even though we often received letters that were more than two months old! But the letter reader also clearly explained that the letter was from our parents who were serving the Lord in Africa. And I think most importantly, they showed us a picture of our parents to help us remember that we would be rejoining them someday.

They always reminded us that these were our real parents and that we were temporarily under the care of others until Mother and Dad would come again to us from Africa. I even remember, in late 1945, being told that I had a new baby sister whom we would see when our parents came to get us. We had an expectation and something to look forward to that we would then live with them. This is a wonderful reminder of our Lord's return for us someday!

> Usually, Mother wrote the letters and Dad would sometimes make a note or two in the margins. However, I do have a letter—handwritten solely by Dad to me on April 8, 1948, before they returned to America. It is a treasure. It starts out "Dear Son, Philip." That title reminds me that regardless of separation that I am still in Dad's family—just as my Lord has given me that same son and father relationship in His family.
>
> Here are some excerpts from that letter: "…I sold our horse 'Tony.' We also sold the donkeys. Our chickens we gave to [some missionaries] and our rabbits we gave to the new missionaries at Kyabe, and we ate the pigeons that were left…we left the cats there also.
>
> "Mother and I are going to take a trip for about a week to tell about Jesus and His love for them to some people that have heard this good news so few times and some of them perhaps have never heard how Jesus died to save them from their sins.
>
> "Live for Jesus day by day. Read the Bible, God's Word, and pray. Have you accepted Jesus as your Savior? Has Jesus washed your sins away with His blood? Remember 1 John 4:19. Everybody ought to love Jesus." (Dad's heart for evangelism reached out not only to the African people but also to me in his own family. What a wonderful example this was to me.)

All of us little boys lived in Pine Cote, which was just a small cabin apart from the bigger dorm for older kids. Mr. and Mrs. S. had been missionaries with the Africa Inland Mission in the Congo and had followed Mr. S's own pioneering parents to that region. Now the Lord led them to be houseparents in the cabin for little boys. I was the youngest—at about eighteen months old—of the approximately 200 missionary kids at the Westervelt Home who were away from their parents.

been there, done that!

I remember the old swimming hole that was a short distance from the main campus. To get there you had to pass thorny berry bushes beside the dirt path. When the blackberries were ripe, we often got our fill before going swimming and usually came back with several scratches. (And yes, there was a rope swing hanging from a tree limb over the water which we all really enjoyed!)

Once a year, pictures were taken of the entire group of us at the Westervelt Home. For a little kid sitting cross-legged on the ground in the front row, it seemed to take forever to get a good group picture of approximately 200 people so that most everyone's faces could be seen. I thought: "Why couldn't those bigger people just get it right at the beginning so we young ones would not have to sit there so long in the sun?" The pictures were then printed out—black and white, of course in those days—and sent to the parents. You would need a magnifying glass to identify anyone in the picture! But it was not too hard to find me since I was one of the smallest kids with all the curly hair in the front row!

FOOD FOR ALL

I guess we had enough food to feed the crowd. It seemed like we had a lot of baked mush strips—I think made from grits—and syrup for our breakfasts. I still like them! I assume we must have had meat, fowl, or fish—at least occasionally—but I don't recall that except for big turkeys on the table at Thanksgiving. We had plenty of vegetables that grew in our gardens, fruit, pecans from our trees, and potatoes from our own land.

At potato harvest time, the potatoes were stored under the gymnasium floor because it was cooler there. We little kids were "privileged" to crawl under the gym floor—raised slightly on blocks or stones—through little screened windows (to keep the critters out) and scatter the potatoes around. One night, our gym—although one would hardly call it that today—burned. No one knows how the fire started.

Realizing that the year's potato harvest was under the floor which had not burned completely through, it was quickly decided to let the fire cool and then have us little kids go under the remaining floor to pull the potatoes out. We were the only ones who could fit under the floor joists! We had to be careful because the potatoes were now baked and much softer than when we put the freshly-harvested potatoes under the floor. Some were still even a bit warm! Needless to say, we ate a lot of baked potatoes in the next few weeks! Our year's harvest had to be consumed quickly before it rotted.

I have a personal story about the pecans. We did not have a pecan grove, but there were a few pecan trees scattered out in the fields. I think I was about five years old at the time and was told to go out and fill a little red wagon with pecans and bring them back to the kitchen. I picked a lot of pecans off the ground and proudly piled the pecans in the wagon but didn't think about how to keep them all in the wagon. When I started pulling the wagon across the bumpy field, the pecans started falling from my carefully crafted pile. I would stop and pick them up one-by-one and pile them in the wagon again. This happened several times until finally I just sat down on the ground and cried! Leaving the wagon in the field, I went to the kitchen and told the cook that the pecans didn't want to come to the kitchen because they knew that they would get broken and eaten! Ultimately with the help of a big burlap gunny sack in the wagon, I was able to bring the pecans in from the field.

Speaking of bags—we grew a lot of cotton on the farm. All of us missionary kids (MKs), older and younger, picked the cotton. I distinctly remember that the cotton bag was about as tall as I was. I think that I spent more time wrestling with that bag and pulling it off the cotton plants lapping over the rows than putting cotton in it. I do know that a lot of the cotton had my red blood on it from the stiff and sharp, open casings surrounding the cotton ball on the plant.

been there, done that!

SUNBURN AND SNOWMAN

Two older MKs from South America, H and L, seemed to be in charge of the young boys' activities. I got one of the worst sunburns of my life on one little trip they had planned for our fun. We hiked barefoot in our bib overalls and no shirt on a hot day in South Carolina to a little grass airstrip to watch a small plane land and take off. After getting a little talk about this flying machine, we hiked back home. I have no idea how far away the airstrip was, but I do know that it was too far in the sun for this little guy. The next few days were miserable for me as that sunburn healed.

On the opposite end of things, I remember the *one* time that it snowed. I never remembered seeing snow before, and if I had, it would have been within the eighteen months right after I was born in northern Indiana. I don't think this snow in the southland was more than a half-inch deep, but H and L taught us how to make a snowman! We rolled those snowballs all over the grounds, picking up leaves and everything else, trying to make them big enough for a real snowman. Obviously, it didn't last very long in Batesburg, South Carolina!

In 1944, most of the boys who were of draft age went off to serve our country in the war. This left the older girls with more work and responsibility since they had to pick up many of the home's duties of these boys who were now gone. The farm still had to continue its production. This extra work for some of the girls was one element which caused bitterness and eventual rebellion against the home's leaders and even their own parents who had placed them at the Westervelt Home. For some MKs, this was used as an excuse for rejection of the Lord and all that their parents were doing in the Lord's work overseas.

Discipline at times at the Westervelt Home seemed rather harsh, and favoritism of some kids over others caused additional anguish for a few. However, rules are especially important in a group environment. Rebellion against rules needed to be handled appropriately and with fairness to all. You can imagine the burden on those in charge when you think about the heavy responsibility for more than 200 young folks from Bible college age down to us who were preschoolers. In most cases, our parents were far away overseas with very little chance of immediate communication if that would be needed.

Decisions by the Westervelts and staff needed to be made quickly, and to several kids at the home, some of the discipline did not seem appropriate. I personally didn't experience anything that was abusive, but in today's era, the type of discipline used at that time may be considered to be outside of accepted limits. That was a different era with different laws and different social norms than exist in the US today. I have heard that many of the letters the kids sent out from the home were censored, so it is likely true that oftentimes parents may not have known the full story about some of the discipline issues. Some of those MKs still talk about the harsh discipline they endured.

I have only positive memories of my years at the Westervelt Home, although that is not true of some of the other MKs—particularly those who were in their teen years. Some of the kids went to the public high school and were often ridiculed for their long, worn-out dresses or their hair styles. And, the older kids had heavy burdens with their schoolwork and the requirements to help around the home—whether it was working in the farm fields or on the main campus, cleaning the facilities, working in the kitchen, and at times doing personal care for the aging houseparents. Some did not respond well to the group home rules, environment, and discipline, which resulted in developing some bitter and long-lasting feelings.

In 1947, there was a major change at the Westervelt Home. The war was over, and many parents had come back from their fields of ministry. The MK population at the home dwindled. It became harder and harder to keep up the farm in Batesburg since Mr. and Mrs. Westervelt were no longer physically able to cope with the responsibilities. Their married son assumed the leadership and found a large home in Columbia for those few of us who remained. Moving day in 1947 was memorable as each person garnered strength to move furnishings and equipment on an old stake-bodied truck to the new facility. The home was now back in the town where it had really blossomed at the beginning of the decade!

MOTHER PICKS UP LOIS AND ME

My sister, Lois, and I began living at the Westervelt Home in the late spring of 1943. Finally, in the summer of 1948, our parents returned to the US for a furlough period. Upon coming back stateside, Dad went to pick up a vehicle from somewhere in the Midwest US while Mother and our new sister, Maribeth, who was born in 1945, came to South Carolina to pick up Lois and me.

Although I don't remember this portion, I am told that I was in a parlor playing, when one of the older boys was sent to tell me that Mother and my new little sister were in the front room. Apparently this announcement did not connect with me as I continued to play. Someone again came to get me and upon arriving

been there, done that!

at the living room door—this part I do remember!—I saw Mother and Maribeth sitting on the piano bench in front of a big upright piano across the room.

I immediately knew this was my mother and sister from the pictures I had seen many times at the Sunday dinner table. I ran over and hugged her and would not leave her side. She had returned for me! I often think of this in reference to when our Lord comes back to take all of His children to be with Him. We will recognize Him and want to be with Him forever! He will return as He has promised! Shortly, we left for Indiana where Dad was waiting for us.

Those years at the Westervelt Home were valuable for me because of some of the lessons I learned there. I learned what it means to be dependent on others but I also learned that independence and interdependence were important to be able to accomplish certain things in life. One cannot always rely on others to provide for you, so there are many times in life when you have to look out for yourself. Interdependence is also of value in learning to work and serve together to sustain sanity and an ability to perform tasks. Everyone is gifted differently, and jointly using our gifts is a biblical principle. Older MKs at the Westervelt Home could do things I could not do, but I could help in areas that would free them up to do their other work.

We were also taught the triangle principle where God was at the top of the triangle and our parents and we MKs were widely separated physically on the bottom of the triangle. The lesson was that as the parents and MKs moved upward in their relationship with God, the closer the parents and MKs came to each other.

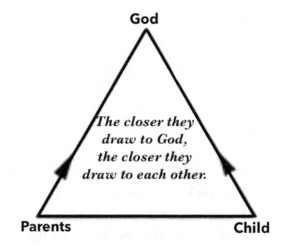

Also, I saw the value of communications when being separated from a loved one. Some of the MKs rarely heard from their parents, and in many cases, they were the ones who seemed to have problems in varying degrees.

Mother wrote letters to us kids almost every week—even after my wife and I were married! Most of the time, the letters from Africa were handwritten on onion skin paper or on an airform with Dad's notes on the side. Other times in later years, they were typed with multiple carbon copies as the family scattered. (What a difference the computer has made for missionaries now in situations such as this!) My folks wanted to insure that each of us seven kids received the same news each week! I will say that sometimes the seventh "carbon" was a little hard to read! When we were separated and in the US, we would also use special airforms to write to them in Africa.

I am so thankful that my five years at the Westervelt Home were good learning years for me and that I have no regrets. Of course, I have to remember that I was the youngest one in the crowd and did not have all the duties of older MKs. The home finally closed in about 1950 after serving hundreds of missionary kids.

REUNION OF THE WESTERVELT MKs

Almost forty years later, some of the former missionary kids (MKs)—who were now in their late fifties and sixties—from the Westervelt Home, planned a reunion in Columbia, South Carolina. About eighty of us, who had lived at the Westervelt Home, and many spouses made the big return! MKs, like me, wore gold badges with our names, and our spouses wore blue badges. Often I would get asked by some of the other gold badge kids if I had the right color badge. I had been the youngest MK at the Westervelt Home—besides the daughter of our little boys' houseparents—and apparently, I still looked young even though I was forty-seven! When I mentioned why I qualified for the gold badge, memories for them seemed to flood back about this little, red-and-curly-haired baby who had been there. Most of us at the reunion stayed in the dorms of Columbia Bible College (now is Columbia International University) where some of the MKs had gone to school.

Several of the ladies recalled being my babysitters, and the men told stories about me and some of my growing-up years. I heard stories about things of which I had no recollection! One of these "girls" was recalling some of those incidents in caring for us. She explained that they were involved in my potty training. Apparently, there were others going through that training at the same time. Portable, enamel-coated potties were lined up against the wall and we little boys were placed on them. As she told the story to me, she said that when one would tinkle in their potty that I would jump up and say: "All Done!" I guess that I just didn't like sitting on that cold, little, round potty and wanted to go back to playing! Well, fortunately, I don't remember that aspect of life at the Westervelt Home, but it was part of group living. It was a little strange for me to meet this lady later in life, who had changed my diapers and pulled up my pants!

One day of the reunion, we went out to the old Batesburg site of the Westervelt Home. What a difference! It didn't seem near as big now as it had seemed to me as a young child. The administrative building was now a county seniors' center, and we were not permitted into the basement where the dining hall had been. One of the big dormitories had been torn down. The long driveway with its formerly manicured hedges was almost grown over. Our farm fields were now filled with streets and houses, and my pecan tree was nowhere to be found. The swimming hole now was just a dent in the ground from all the brush and erosion of the sides that had taken their toll over the years.

I desperately wanted to find the spot where our little Pine Cote cabin had been. After rummaging around through the bramble bushes and dense growth in the general area where I remembered it to be in relation to the big building, I found the remnants. All that was left were some rotting boards laying on the ground and some deteriorating cement blocks which still marked where a couple of the corners had been. It had been just a little temporary "shack" built on block stilts, and forty years later, we could not expect too much. Fairly close by, we found the site of Grey Cote, where my sister, Lois, had lived.

Lunch time that day was interesting. Most of us managed to crowd into the little one-room, brick school building that was still standing but apparently had not been used for decades. Some of the original furniture was still there, and it was surprising how many kids found their initials after turning over a number of those school desks. Others shouted with glee upon finding their own carvings on the desks' writing surfaces. A few even found their initials scratched on the aging, faded, and now useless blackboards still hanging on the walls. I had only been in pre-school, kindergarten, and first grade there in Batesburg, and the one-room school house was mostly used by the older kids. They sure had some exciting stories about some of their classroom antics and about some of their teachers while they were students in that old building!

Our time at that Batesburg site ended with our dedication of a plaque to be permanently displayed near the school house. The legacy of that place would tell many others about the value of the Westervelt Home to the effective spread of the gospel around the world. In closing our visit, the oldest MK (my former houseparent) there that day led in prayer, and I, as the youngest MK to have lived there away from parents, also gave a dedicatory and thankful prayer. Tears were evident in many of our eyes as we left the place that gave us so many memories—some of difficult days and hardships. Other tears, however, expressed the joy of many of us about God's goodness and protection in the days we were separated from our parents due to World War II.

We often hear of the military casualties from the war, but we rarely hear or read of the casualties in missions and missionary kids who often, even today, consider that their parents abandoned them during a critical period of their youth. The reunion did help some of these now-adult MKs in their later years to overcome much of their resentment as they came to understand how so many of us had found great happiness in serving—in our own ways—the same God whom our parents had served. Other tears of repentance were shed as some confessed their extreme bitterness, rebellions, and criticisms over the years. Before the reunion, no one could have anticipated the lasting effects of their release of some of their innermost secrets, which had kept them in bondage for so many years. Praise the Lord for the work He accomplished in hearts through that reunion weekend.

Also during that reunion, we took a tour of the large house in Columbia into which the Westervelts had first moved when they brought several college boys with them from Arkansas. The house was now a historical home that still showcased some of the Westervelts' original furnishings. There was a plaque next to the street denoting it as the former Westervelt Home.

A couple of docents were assigned to show us through the house. As the docent would begin to explain about a room or its furniture, someone from our group would say something like this: "I remember dusting that furniture." "What did they do with the black-painted silver doorknobs that were in the house?" (They had been painted so that the silver would not be confiscated to support the war effort.) "That wall wasn't there when we lived here." "A doorway here has been closed off." Finally, the docent with our group said that she should just be quiet and listen and learn from those who had actually lived there! That was a very interesting tour—not only because of the memories it evoked but also for the surprised docent!

been there, done that!

The entire reunion was very special for me—and for my wife, Betty, who learned so much from the other MKs about a significant part of my early life. The reunion perhaps had more meaning for me because I had been so young at the Westervelt Home and did not know some of the important aspects of the ministry for MKs and their parents. Several of the MKs brought letters and pictures, and I was included in some of them. We borrowed a lot of their materials and spent most of an afternoon at a local library copying this permanent part of the history of my life. I am blessed, first of all, to be an MK and then blessed to have been cared for in the Westervelt Home!

1948 FURLOUGH WITH MY PARENTS

During my parents' missionary furlough year in 1948–1949, after leaving the Westervelt Home, we stayed in the home of my dad's sister, Aunt Helen, in South Bend, Indiana. For some reason, out of all the places where I have lived, that address (617 Rush Street) remains inscribed in my brain. If I ever met a saint here on this earth, it was Aunt Helen. She was a widow whose husband had served in World War I, but the government never admitted that his death—probably from war gases—may have been due to his military service, so she lived in poverty most of her life. She took in clothes to wash and iron, and she sewed dresses and aprons to make a little money. In those days she had only an icebox— not a refrigerator!—to keep things cold, and I remember the iceman coming with his big blocks of ice for the icebox. It was cheaper than an electric refrigerator!

But the Lord always provided for Aunt Helen—I think because of her consistent prayer life for missionaries, her faithfulness at church, her weekly Good News Clubs for neighborhood kids in her backyard or basement, and her sacrifices in letting our family stay with her in her home. To make room for us, she moved from her second floor room into a room on the first floor that was a parlor type of room with a heavy, velvety maroon curtain, separating it from the living room. Our family of five was upstairs. Also in the house were another widow lady, Mrs. Y., and her son, who was about my age. We did a lot together—learning to ride a bike and learning to roller skate—mostly on the sidewalk out front with its big cracks and humps from tree roots raising it up. We used a lot of Band-Aids and bandages as a result!

It was on this furlough that I met many of my relatives—grandparents, uncles and aunts, and cousins. I was six and a half years old but had never met most of them because of my earlier years at the Westervelt Home. I remember the Fogle family and the McCuen (Mother's side) family reunion picnics in Potowanami Park in South Bend in 1948 where we three Fogle missionary kids were introduced to all these strange people called relatives. We did not see most of them again until the next furlough in 1954, but a few of them did seem to take special interest in us. Connecting with relatives has been and always will be a difficult issue for missionary kids since we never really got to know them due to our absence for extended periods overseas. In contrast, my wife's extended family is very close knit, and mine seems so foreign.

My dad's father had died when he was just two years old, so I never did meet him. His mother ended up being married five times, and I never met any of her husbands. Her main characteristic was a nice strong hug but also her constantly moving head. It was almost always bobbing, and for a little kid, it was hard to watch her. But she really loved us. I also never met my mother's mother but did meet her dad and stepmother during that furlough.

One of my mother's brothers and his wife and two children did make a special connection with me for some reason. One event with them always comes to mind. Before we went to Africa in 1949, Lois and I had to get some special medical shots or vaccinations, which were only available in Chicago. Uncle E and Aunt R offered to take us to the big city since my dad and mother could not go due to some other commitments. It seemed to be such a long trip from South Bend, Indiana, especially since we were going to get shots. But the trip went well, and we finally made it home with some very sore arms!

During that 1948–1949 furlough year, we made many trips to the City Rescue Mission that had meant so much to Mother as a young girl. And remember, it was also the place where she ministered at the piano and where she and Dad were married. Dad would often preach at the mission services, and we kids would sit there with all the drunks and homeless, smelly men who had to be in the service if they wanted a meal.

The City Rescue Mission held a camp every summer for inner-city kids, and I was given a week of camp in the summer of 1949. It was sort of a typical camp: cabins with bunks and a counsellor, common bath and shower away from the cabin, activities at the pool, a camp speaker, archery range, BB gun shooting range, and cabin competitions. I had never experienced the camp "life" before, but I did have a great time. One night, I walked down the dusty, sawdust center aisle of the outdoor chapel pavilion as a response to the speaker's invitation to accept

Christ into my life. At the time, it seemed that was the thing to do. In all honesty, as I look back, that was probably just a reaction to some of the other kids going forward, and that night did not make any difference in my spiritual yearnings.

Before the camp week, we had said goodbye to Dad who left with his new 1948 Chevrolet, short-bed, two and a half-ton truck to go with it on a boat to sail to Africa. Dad had found an old Army truck bed with side benches and bows and canvas over the top and he put it on the Chevy's short chassis. The truck cab was dark green, so it sort of looked like an Army truck with the olive-drab, canvas covering. When he left Indiana, the truck was loaded to the top with not only our family's goods but also shipments for other missionaries who were already in or were going to Africa.

Camp ended and I went home to Mother who shared some sad news. My grandmother had died while I was at camp, and Dad would not be back for his mother's funeral. The funeral was to be the next day, and I remember some discussion between adults whether or not this young seven-year-old boy should see his grandma in a casket. I guess they agreed that going to the funeral would be good for me. Frankly, I really didn't understand what it meant to be dead, and I just envisioned that grandma would be laying there with her head still bobbing as it always seemed to do. I was quite surprised at how still she was in the casket and that God had healed her body because now she was with Him in heaven. The idea of living with God in heaven was an intriguing thought to me at the time. That was my first, but certainly not the last, funeral I would attend.

Within a few days of that funeral and in late July, Mother told Lois and me that we were going to leave soon for Africa to get us out there in time for the beginning of school. Mother was going to stay in South Bend for a while since she was pregnant with twins who were due to be born in about one month, and she was not permitted to travel. Maribeth, my younger sister at almost four years of age, would also stay with Mother. Initially, all that meant little to me, but life began to unravel a bit when we started attending "going-away" parties with relatives and at church. We were going somewhere, and I really didn't know where. Nor did I comprehend long airplane flights or crossing an ocean!

CHAPTER II
AFRICA

BAGGAGE TAG ON THE TRAIN

Departure day came in early August 1949 and our family, some relatives, and people from our church headed off to the train station in South Bend. A whole bunch of people were on the platform to say goodbye. I don't think I realized that Lois and I were the only ones leaving from that group! We hugged and kissed and cried.

Then one of the porters came and tied a string with a manila-colored baggage tag to a button hole on my shirt. On the tag were my name, the place where Lois and I would get off, and the names of the people we would meet on the other end. (Fortunately we were not put in the baggage car!) The porter then took Lois and me by our hands and led us up the steps to our seats on the train, and off we went, waving to all the people still on the platform. As a seven-year-old, I wasn't sure what to think of all this, but I soon let it turn into a little adventure. The porter then brought meals to us and at dark brought us some blankets so we could sleep right there in our seats.

I really don't know how long the ride was, but the porter finally told us that we were to get off the train—in New York City! That train ride (as a seven year old without a known adult) was one of those "been there, done that" experiences of my life.) The porter stayed with us and introduced us to the proper people. They were two missionary ladies who would be our escorts to Africa. "Aunt" M was taller than "Aunt" A so they were easy to tell apart. Both were very sweet ladies and really looked after Lois and me. (Missionary kids usually call the adult missionaries aunts and uncles as a way to show respect to them.) They bought us little

been there, done that!

toys that we could take on the plane when we flew the next day. I still remember that my toy was a little car about four inches long with a roof that retracted back into its trunk! I thought that was really unique!

MY FIRST FLIGHTS

I had never been on a plane before, so this added to my adventure—and what an adventure it was! The plane was a TWA (Trans World Airlines), four-engine, propeller-driven plane. I remember nothing of the trip except that it was long and that I was airsick most of the way. One of the aunts kept a barf bag in front of me all the time. They kept trying to get me to drink juices and eat, but you know what happened when I did! I did get some sleep, but it seemed that it was not very much. We finally landed in Paris, and I felt fine on the ground. I think we spent one or two nights there and met some other missionaries who were studying the French language before going to minister in former French colonies in Africa. The aunts took us on a little tour around Paris, and I remember seeing the Eifel Tower.

I dreaded getting back on the plane as we were headed south toward Africa. Again, I was very airsick as we flew. We landed in a town in southern France to refuel before crossing the Mediterranean Sea. I was still sick when we landed in Tunis, Tunisia, on the north coast of Africa. Then it was across the Sahara Desert to Douala, Cameroon, a port city on the west coast of Africa. But with thanks to the Lord, I stopped getting sick while flying over the Sahara Desert and actually felt very well by the time we got off the plane!

WELCOME TO A NEW HOMELAND

Who was there in Douala to meet us? My Dad! The boat with him and his truck had arrived in the port a couple of days before, and he was working to get the truck and baggage through customs. How perfect God's timing was in his being there in the Cameroon when we arrived! The missionary ladies and we kids would not spend long there, however, as we needed to keep moving to get to school in the Oubangui Chari (in later years this portion of French Equatorial Africa became an independent nation and was renamed the Central African Republic). It was interesting to watch actions on the parking ramp in Douala as we prepared to take off. Men came out and pulled on the propeller blades of the two-engine plane to get the motors started! I was hoping they got out of the way before the blades really started spinning—and they did!

It was quite a bumpy ride on that smaller plane, but we finally arrived in Bangui, the capital of that area, where some of our missionaries lived and ministered. It was almost unbearably hot as we exited down the steps from the plane and stepped on to the packed and cracked, deep-red clay and crushed red stone turf! All I saw were black people which no one had told me about—some in bright, colored robes and others in white robes and almost all wore some type of "beanie". Going inside the terminal, which was basically just a wooden frame with bent corrugated aluminum sides and roof, I saw a few other white men in short pants and long socks, and some had pith helmets to ward off the searing sun. After gathering our bags, other missionaries met us and took us to their pickup truck. The two aunts, who were our escorts, got in the cab, and Lois and I got in the back with some missionary men and their helpers.

We were finally in Africa but not to our destination yet! At least we would not have any more plane rides, and a new part of my adventure was beginning! I expected big changes because now I was on another continent where roads were not paved and were full of muddy potholes, there were very few white adults or kids around, it was hot, and almost everyone spoke a language which I didn't understand! What a different world I was facing!

After a couple of nights in Bangui, we headed north. Our trip in the back of that pickup truck was about 120 miles and seemed to take forever. The vehicle had a canvas top and sides but that sure didn't keep the dust out. To avoid some of the road's potholes, the driver was constantly swerving from one side of the road to the other, and every time he seemed to take his foot off the gas pedal, the dust caught up with us and covered us. I had never experienced that before, and in a way, it was sort of fun and exciting. It was one of those "been there, done that" experiences!

We arrived at Sibut, another mission station with more missionaries to meet. The station had been built on a high hill, and the pickup labored a little getting up to the top. We were warned right away that it was stink bug season and to try and avoid crushing the little critters because they would leave a horrible odor—and that was an understatement! On a return trip to Sibut more than sixty years later, I didn't see one stink bug. The big house on the hill was no longer occupied and, in fact, missionaries no longer lived at the station.

been there, done that!

BOARDING SCHOOL AT FORT CRAMPEL

We spent the night there and then continued on our way the next day to Fort Crampel (now called Kaga Bandoro) where the boarding school was. This was a little shorter ride of about seventy-five miles, but it took a little longer because of the extremely poor road conditions. Upon arriving, they dropped Lois off at one house, and I went to another home called the Camp/Houston House. Those were the last names of the two aunts who had escorted us from New York. They had lived there previously, but now the house was the home of the mission station nurse (a different Aunt M) and Miss M. There were two other MKs already staying there—David and Danny. David was in the same grade with me, and Danny was a little younger. There were other boys on the station also attending the school, but they lived with other missionaries.

Aunt M was wise and knew how to deal with mischievous little boys. One day, we tried to pull a trick on her—but she didn't go along with it. Outside the house was a bush that had little red berries on it. We found out that when they were crushed, the juice looked just like blood. We got a white enamel dishpan and crushed a bunch of berries and added a little water so that we probably had more than a quart of liquid. Then we smeared a little of that on one of our arms and carried the pan in to Aunt M, the nurse, and showed her the "scratch" on our arm and that we had captured the blood from the cut in that pan. She showed no sympathy at all! Of course, there was no way that much blood could have come from a little scratch! She just said to throw that juice out and get it washed off our arm. That nurse was just too smart for us! Aunt M was a wonderful and loving woman who later in my life became like a second mother to me.

The Milner School at Fort Crampel was a one-room schoolhouse. It was named for a major donor to Baptist Mid-Missions. The building had an attached apartment for the main missionary kids' school teacher, Miss A. We didn't call any of our teachers "aunt" because of their role as our teachers. We had American-style school desks and used the Calvert Course, a home-schooling curriculum from the United States. Each morning, all of us kids would line up outside before school started to enter our class in an orderly fashion.

During my five years at the Fort Crampel MK school, I had two other teachers besides Miss A. Miss M taught in the same building where David, Danny, and I had lived initially, while Mrs. D and Miss A taught classes in the main school building. I did not really enjoy school, even though I always did well in my studies. The classes that I liked most were the grammar class with its diagramming of sentences, spelling, and the geography class. Arithmetic was OK; but the art class (I just wasn't creative, I guess), reading class, and history class—well let me just say, "Ugh!"

MOUSE IN THE CLASSROOM!

Occasionally, our school classroom was disrupted by little critters (frogs, lizards, insects, and sometimes snakes) also wanting to get an education. One day, a mouse was spotted scurrying around, and as you would expect, there were immediate shrieks and rustling of desks as some of the girls climbed up on their chairs or desks so that the mouse could not come near them. Miss M tried to gain a semblance of control, which utterly failed! And then we boys took over the situation and picked up our wooden rulers and started chasing the mouse—sometimes with glee as we headed it toward one of the girls. We stationed D, with the biggest feet at the doorway so that if it tried to escape, he could stomp on it. Eventually, the mouse came to its end with its entrails spewed from one side of the classroom to the other! What a hoot! D's big foot had hit it squarely, and our plan was successful! Class was dismissed temporarily while the mess got cleaned up, but for some reason, the girls didn't think the class interruption was quite as funny as we boys did. Where else could we have such a great experience—especially during class hours?

THE DORM

Because of the increasing population of missionary kids (MKs) in the country, the mission built a new dormitory building for the MKs to live in rather than the kids living with other missionaries on the station. Lois was living with one of those missionaries, and I only saw her during the school periods and on Sunday at church.

The dorm was not yet completed when we arrived in early August of 1949, but by October, it was done enough for at least David, Danny, and me to be the first MKs to live in it. Aunt M and Aunt A, the two with whom we had flown to Africa, were designated as houseparents. So we three boys pretty much had the cavernous dorm to ourselves with its five big bedrooms, a living/dining room open area, two shower rooms, and a large front porch. The houseparents had their own apartment in the building. There was a small indoor kitchen and a larger cooking kitchen building a few yards behind where there was also some storage and laundry space. No ceilings had yet been installed so we would often try to fly paper planes up over the walls and through the trusses into the next rooms. When other kids moved in, we could send notes over the walls! Oh, what fun—especially during siesta time when we were supposed to be sleeping!

When we moved in, there was running water only in the shower cubicles where the water ran off in a drain to the ground outside. For washing up, in the bathroom we had a fifty-five-gallon barrel of water with a scoop to put the water in a basin. Our toilet facility was initially a two-holer outside. To brush our teeth, we took a cup of water outside where we found a tree with a big hole in it for spitting out the toothpaste. I don't know how long that tree survived but it sure had a lot of toothpaste down in that hole! It is a wonder that the tree's leaves were not white from all the toothpaste in the trunk! As the dorm and its regular bathrooms became finished, other kids began to move in, with the boys living in one end and the girls in the other. Within a year or so, a missionary couple, Uncle F and Aunt E, became the houseparents for all the MKs in the dorm.

MY SALVATION

I can vividly remember the day that I accepted Christ into my life—October 26, 1949—shortly after moving into the dorm. After breakfast and before heading off to school, we always had a brief devotional time. On that day, Aunt M read the scripture and gave us some thoughts from it. The other kids left, but I stayed to talk with her. I said that I knew my parents were going to heaven some day and that they could not take me with them. I needed to ask Jesus to forgive my sins and come into my heart so I could also go where they would be. I don't know what inspired my thinking that day, but she gladly explained biblical salvation to me, and I took Jesus into my heart that morning. It was a momentous day of decision for me although I was a shy kid and headed off to school without telling anyone what I had done. At our evening devotions, I couldn't restrain myself any longer and went to Aunt M and asked if I could tell the others that I had accepted Christ into my heart. That was my first testimony of my salvation!

> In 2012, my brother, Larry, and I were in the Central African
> Republic for a teaching and preaching ministry, and I took a side

trip to Fort Crampel to visit the mission property with the school and dormitory. The mission compound was severely deteriorated after many years of neglect following the missionaries' departure in the 1990s. It was very disappointing to me to see the walls of the school badly cracked and the dormitory walls crumbled and its roof completely gone. However, the cement dorm floor was intact, and I took time to thank the Lord as I stood on the very spot where He had accepted me into His family. What a great experience that was! It was one of my most memorable "been there, done that" events.

FOOD POISONING

In the next months and years, more kids came to the dorm. We all ate together at a huge table that accommodated about twenty-five people and had to eat everything given to us on our plates. We had a lot of foods that were new to me: papaya, gozo (manioc/yucca/cassava), mango, rice, babalo (white sweet potato), wild meat, palm chop, couscous, and others. I like food, so I had no problem enjoying whatever was put before me.

One night, a few of the kids began to get sick and then more also fell ill. It became a mess in the bedrooms and in the bathrooms and the stench became horrible. Everyone seemed to be awake all night. The situation became very serious with some of the kids having temperatures over 106 degrees and becoming delirious. I can remember one of the bigger boys tearing at his chest and saying: "Get these brake shoes off of me. They are too tight!" The nearest missionary doctor was about twelve hours away at another mission station.

By morning, someone was sent off to get the doctor because we didn't have telephones, telegrams, or radios between the stations. Within a day or so, one of the doctors did arrive and determined that the cause of the illness was food poisoning—probably a potato-like salad. Thankfully, no one died, and it is difficult to tell what long-lasting effects the poisoning may have had on some of the kids.

There were only two of us who didn't get sick. Arnie and I were sent out of the dorm to another missionary's house—just to get us out of the way, I think. But why did Arnie and I escape getting sick? That was never determined even though we both had big helpings of the salad along with the other food. How thankful I was that it didn't affect me after having seen and heard and smelled the quick impact on my dorm mates that first night. Often people say that I have an iron stomach, and maybe I do because I can eat almost anything—and like it!—including very hot peppers. Yes, I have eaten foods some would call very weird, but more on that later in another chapter.

DORM LIFE AND ACTIVITIES

Overall, dorm life was wonderful for me. I guess the enjoyment factor started back when I was always with other kids at the Westervelt Home because although I was quite shy, I liked being with others. In Africa, we had lots of places to ride our bikes on little trails all over the big station. After school, we often played softball or tag football. Our quarterback was Uncle F who had been a quarterback for his high school in Indiana. In those days, many of the quarterbacks threw the ball underhanded, but it still had the nice spiral characteristic of football passes today. We knew nothing about competitive tackle football, basketball, tennis, swimming, gymnastics, or other such sports common to a kid in America. We did play some kickball but never was it organized as soccer is today. Dodge ball was also a favorite.

Just outside the dorm was a big swing set made from heavy-duty pipe. We often dared each other to swing so hard that we could wrap the chains over the top bar which was probably eight or ten feet above the ground. No one ever made it over, but some were close before the weight on the seat would collapse the chains as it was getting near the top of its arc. We could swing so hard that at our uppermost height, we were nearly parallel to the top bar of the swing set! Sometimes we had little competitions to see who could "parachute" off the swings and jump the farthest. Usually, the person who could swing the highest was the winner. Thankfully, no one broke any bones when landing!

Life at the dorm was always interesting. One time, one of the taller boys was to be disciplined and little Aunt A—I doubt if she was five foot tall—told him to go out and get a switch for her to use on him. He came back in with a long branch which may have been about two inches in diameter. That seemed to infuriate her and she sent him out to get a small one which she could use to "paddle" him. You guessed it—he brought in a long piece of jungle grass. That ended the potential of a paddling, but another form of discipline was found that lasted longer.

All of us boys made our own slingshots out of a small forked branch and strips from old inner tubes to shoot at birds, lizards, snakes, bats, and mice. There were a lot of small stones around, so ammunition was not a problem. Sometimes we would try and shoot little sticks at targets pretending they were darts. One boy found a porcupine quill and decided to try and shoot it from his slingshot. He pulled the sling back grasping the quill and "fired". The quill never made it past the fork of the slingshot he was holding in his hand but instead hit the web of flesh between his thumb and his forefinger, penetrating about three inches through into his palm's side. Our first reaction was to try and pull it back out the way it went in but that didn't work so well because porcupine quills have little barbs on them. We ended up cutting the quill right near the outside of his thumb and pulling it on through in the direction he had been shooting. No one else tried shooting porcupine quills after that!

The mission station was surrounded with jungle and tall elephant grasses. At the end of the dry season, that dry vegetation was intentionally set afire by the Africans to clear out all the underbrush. Usually, there was very little wind, which prevented sparks from igniting buildings on the mission station compound. As the fire burned, local natives would be near it to catch any mice or other small animals trying to escape the flames. They would later eat them.

When the fires burned down, the remaining forest was thoroughly charred into a deep, black color. Most of the trees would survive because of their thick cork-like bark. As the first rains came, green grass sprouts grew up through the deep-black ash and created a gorgeous reminder of the new life that we all can enjoy in Christ after sin had caused it to be so black. It didn't take long for brilliant flowers to also dot the jungle floor. Some of these were large, bright red, pom pom–like balls approximately eight inches in diameter and standing about eighteen to twenty-four inches tall. Because of their size, they were easy to spot through the jungle, which was now cleared of most of the underbrush.

Occasionally, we would all go for a picnic to a "lando". That is a meadow-like field which is normally covered with short grasses and has many ant hills scattered around. These ant hills looked like big, overgrown mushrooms about two feet tall and with a cap about eighteen inches wide. We would play some fantastic games of tag with certain of the ant hills being a safe base when we jumped up on them. Most of them looked almost alike and were about the same size, so you had to remember which ones were the safe bases and not get on one which was not safe.

been there, done that!

Another place where we liked to picnic was the Citron Falls, a few miles away from the mission station. As I remember, the falls were probably no more than thirty or forty feet tall, but they were unique and special to us. It was a beautiful, almost serene environment where we climbed on the rocks and enjoyed the coolness of the mist from the water tumbling over the small cliff and short rapids.

On Easter Sundays, we went about a half hour east to the barren, wind-swept Bandoro Hills. There we held a sunrise service, which was primarily for the missionaries and the MKs at the school. As we watched the sun come up on our little gathering, we sang acapella hymns such as *"He (Christ) Arose," "Christ the Lord Is Risen Today,"* and *"He Lives"* in that very worshipful outdoors environment while sitting on the dry rock. One of the missionaries shared Easter thoughts from the Scriptures.

Every Sunday afternoon, all the missionaries and kids on the station gathered together for prayer meeting. I certainly understood the need for a devotional and prayers for God's work there at Fort Crampel, but as a kid, I always wondered why the prayer meeting had to be so lo-o-ong! For most of the devotional time we sat on hard or wicker chairs in a big circle, but for the prayer time, everyone got on their knees.

The rug was a heavy, very coarse, braided hemp mat. I didn't have any long pants and after just a couple of minutes kneeling on that mat, I became one constant wiggle worm. It seemed there was no mercy for us kids! I'm not sure how the heavier adult missionaries endured the times on their knees! At the end of the time, my knees were red and heavily indented from the rug. My knees would hurt so bad which made those missionaries' prayers seem all the longer. And believe me; some of their prayers seemed to go on forever!

I'm not sure how much of their prayers I heard, but I know that the Lord heard every word people said—in spite of my agony. I will admit that I occasionally got an afternoon siesta during those long prayers! An occasional loud "Amen," indicating an agreement with what someone had prayed, would wake me up. To this day, I am convinced that their prayers, whether spoken in boldness or in silent sobbing, provided the sustainment for the ministries of the local church and the Bible school, for God's protection over His people, for the salvation of the African people, and for the care and education of all of us MKs. But wow, those adults could really pray! They had unbelievably strong faith that God's work was going to go forward and would overcome obstinate obstacles and the devil's resistance!

The church was on the other end of the station from the dorm. Perhaps it was two to three blocks away from the dorm. There was a nice footpath that led from the dorm toward the church building, and usually the houseparents would be at the back of the file of us kids headed to church. One day, as we were headed down the path, someone noticed a large beehive in a tree near the path. I'll not name anyone, but a couple of boys near the front picked up some stones and threw them at the hive without thinking that the bees would attack. The bees didn't like that and swarmed, and the ones who got the worst of the swarm were Aunt M and Aunt A at the back of our line. They could not run like most of us kids. Being typical kids, at first we thought it was funny, but soon we realized the seriousness of it and contacted some other missionaries who came to help the aunts and insure that most of us moved on to church. Instances like this are regrettable, although it seemed like an innocent incident at the time. Boys will be boys!

been there, done that!

ABANDONED?

The primary disadvantage of living at a boarding school is the separation for long periods from our parents. We would be at school from August through November and then again from late January to June. In between school semesters, we would be with our parents at the mission station where they ministered. Some of the kids had real problems with this kind of life and in later years rebelled against the Lord. A common term used by some MKs who had been at boarding schools in various countries is "abandonment". They felt like their parents had abandoned them to someone else's care. For many MKs, this separation started when they went to boarding school in first grade and continued even after middle school when some were left in America for high school.

In high school, many MKs did not see their parents for three or four years, resulting in increased bitterness against their parents and the Lord. This issue cannot be belittled and has changed the course of life for many missionary families. It is a different era today than when I grew up, having been first separated from my parents at the age of eighteen months. Altogether, counting individual months and years, I have only lived under my parents' roof a <u>combined total</u> of no more than five and a half years, with the longest period being with them was when I was first born in those initial eighteen months of my life. Thankfully, I never had a problem being separated from Mother and Dad since it started so early in my life. I have no regrets.

It is an entirely different situation for those who have lived with their parents for most of their lives. Some adults later in life are called into missions, and for their kids who may now be in their early teens, separation may be extremely difficult for both the parents and the children. Each MK's situation is different and may depend on the personality of both the MK and their parents, the nature of the country of ministry, with whom they stay in a separated environment, and a support structure they may or may not appreciate. However, I wouldn't trade my life for that of anyone else. I have been very satisfied with the life God has allowed me to have. MKs need prayer just as much as their parents do! Hopefully, MKs will not be a detriment to the effectiveness of their parents' ministries but rather will be considered as an enhancement to the furthering of the gospel outreach in the world.

Some MKs may feel like the Israelites in the wilderness after leaving Egypt. They sense that God had also abandoned them, and they have developed increasing bitterness against God and their parents. They see the prosperity and satisfaction of other friends who have always had the physical support of their own families and adopt an attitude that God may have forgotten them. But that is never the case. God has promised in Isaiah 49:15 that He will not forget us! Shortly after those comforting words, the Scripture tells us in Isaiah 55:8, 9 "For my thoughts are not your thoughts, neither are your ways my ways, saith the Lord. For as the heavens are higher than the earth, so are my ways higher than your ways, and my thoughts than your thoughts." These passages (among others) have been a source of great assurance to me in my life of separations as an MK, and I pray they also will be of help to other MKs who may tend to think they have been "abandoned" from their parents and from God.

MKs are not abandoned! Yes, life has given us human difficulties to endure. Our backgrounds have caused some to lose their marriages or even some of our closest family members. Our strange desires for continuing mobility have forced job changes and loneliness in new environments. Some forced their own sense of abandonment by denying their spiritual backgrounds and venturing into the world's allurements—which in turn, built high walls and barriers between them and their families and longtime missionary kid friendships. God's love can still supersede all of that. He has promised His forever presence with us. He will never forget or abandon us!

TROUBLES ON THE DIRT ROADS

Transportation to and from our home mission station to school was often a real adventure. Our home in Chad was about 200 miles from the school in Fort Crampel. At least one trip a year was in the rainy season, and that can wreak havoc on the mud roads—from the staggering size of potholes, to weakened or washed-out bridges, to the rivers of water covering the road's course.

Normally, some type of advance communication was established between both ends of a trip so that if an arrival didn't happen within a certain time frame, then the presumption was that something was wrong and a "hunt party" should be sent out to find out what happened and help the stranded persons get to their destination.

On one trip, two missionary ladies were taking my sister and me on the 200 mile trip from the school to my parents' mission station. It was not unusual for missionary women to take some African help along for the journey so an African

been there, done that!

man was with us. Lois and I and the helper rode in the back of the canvas-covered pickup truck. Our first incident was a blowout on the left side of the vehicle, and we ended up in a ditch beside the road, leaning against a bank. We were able to winch our way out of the ditch and get the tire changed and back on our voyage. Praise the Lord that no one was hurt, although the left side of the pickup did show considerable evidence of the incident.

We soon came to a stretch of the road, which was completely under water for almost a quarter of a mile. Our African helper got out and started wading ahead of the pickup truck to make sure we stayed on the road and did not veer off into an unseen ditch. He would walk from side to side to identify the edges of the road as we followed in the vehicle. The water was up over the running boards and, although in some places the water was deeper, we are thankful that the engine was never drowned. We did some praying during that segment! In several other places, the road was also covered, but we could identify the road's path and didn't need our guide out front. As a result of these two episodes, we were already being delayed in arriving at our projected time and hoped there would be no more interruptions as we traveled.

STUCK IN A MUD HOLE

Those two incidents didn't compare, however, with what was to come. Around 4 p.m., we came upon a huge mud hole in the middle of the road. It was probably thirty to forty feet long. We noted that some big trucks had negotiated their way through or around it by cutting down some small trees and using them to help keep them from being stuck and move through the mess. After evaluating the situation, we tried to follow their path, but about halfway through, we got stuck. We tried to back out but with no success. Our vehicle would not move backward or forward. Now what? We had no cell phones—they hadn't even been invented in 1951!—no radio, and no extra person to send forward by foot to our destination! All we could do was wait for help from either direction to arrive. Within an hour, a truck full of Arabs came up behind us and saw our predicament. There must have been fifteen or twenty men on that truck. Some of them tried to help and even lift our pickup to get us out of the way, but all of those men were not successful and gave up. They got back on their truck, turned around, and left us there. We did ask them to let others behind us know that we were there and maybe, just maybe, some would come to help us.

Near the equator, when the sun goes down, it gets dark quickly, and that night the blackness seemed to suddenly surround us. The mosquitos thought we had good blood, and they were swarming. The buzz became very annoying, and we couldn't swat them all away. Even using a lot of mosquito repellant didn't keep them from us! We prayed for the Lord's protection through the night and that help would arrive soon. The missionary ladies put Lois and me in the back and fastened down the canvas as tight as possible to try and keep some bugs away. We tried to use some of the murky water from the mud hole to rinse away most of the muck from our feet before trying to go to sleep.

In the meantime, the ladies and our helper stayed awake to see if they could hear any assistance coming our way. I remember getting a little sleep but waking occasionally due to the strange sounds of nightlife in the jungle. I could only imagine what might be lurking nearby! I don't think I was scared, although I was very curious about what was making the various noises. In a way, it was just a part of my bigger adventure in life.

On our destination's end that evening, Dad realized something was amiss when we did not arrive at the estimated time. He knew if he headed out in our direction that we couldn't be missed since there was only one road to travel. About two in the morning, I heard the others chatting and asked if help had arrived. They said "no" but that they heard a truck's engine ahead of us. Soon they saw lights against the dark sky and began to flash our pickup's lights on and off. The far-off sound of the engine stopped, and we initially lost hope, although we could see an occasional small, dim light seeming to get closer. Occasionally, we yelled out to see if we could get a response. Before long, Dad responded in the African Sango language with "Ani yeke ga na mo!" ("We're coming to you!"). Excitement built quickly, and I crawled out of the back of the truck to be part of the welcoming party.

Dad and five tall, strong Sara Madjingay tribesmen arrived out of the blackness and said that they had come as far as they could in Dad's truck without getting themselves stuck. Seeing our lights flashing, they walked the last couple of miles to get to us. Assessing the problem, they soon found that a limb from a cut tree branch in the mud hole had become jammed near the truck's rear axle and thus prevented the vehicle from moving in either direction. Those five men then lifted our small truck up enough to pull the branch out. Earlier that whole truckload of men couldn't help, and now just five, strong men got us out of our trouble. Dad then drove us—with the men pushing—to the other side of the mud hole, and

been there, done that!

we were on our way! All of the men could not fit in the small pickup truck—both for weight and space—so they walked back to Dad's truck. Sleeping in a mud hole—yes, in the back of a pickup truck—was just another unique adventure for this missionary kid. I have "been there, done that"! What an experience! Thank goodness for advance planning that had my dad come looking for us when we didn't arrive on time. God had again answered prayer!

BREAKING THROUGH A BRIDGE

On one other trip going to school from our home in Chad we had some unusual excitement. Dad had a big load of stuff on our Chevy truck since he was helping a missionary move from the Chad to a mission station in the Central African Republic. We came to a rather rickety-looking bridge only about twenty-five feet long down in the bottom of a gorge. The people in the village preceding the bridge had cautioned us that it was not in good shape and that the water was rushing at a strong pace. When I say "bridge," don't think about a steel bridge or even a strong trestle-type crossing. Rather, think about a few long tree trunks laid across the water with smaller logs crossing them to provide the bridge decking. The bridge was rather old and since we had been warned, Dad figured before driving across that he had better unload the truck to make it as light as possible. Some of the villagers came to help unload and then carry the things to the other side after the truck had crossed the bridge. And just in case there was trouble, Dad tied a heavy rope and pulley to the truck and to a tree high up on the far bank where Lois and I and one other missionary kid with her mom were located. The Africans would pull the rope through the pulley as the truck inched forward to ensure that it could not be washed away if the bridge completely collapsed.

Dad slowly drove the truck down the hill to the edge of the embankment and put the front wheels on the bridge. So far, all was good, and Dad carefully moved the entire truck on the log bridge. Just as the front wheels were about to reach the far side, CRACK!!! From our hilltop advantage, we heard Dad race the engine to try and drive off the bridge quickly. Then we saw the back left side of the truck drastically tip, pulling the whole truck sideways toward the water.

Fortunately, Dad's foresight with the rope kept the vehicle from tipping all the way into the water. We were worried about Dad's safety as he began crawling out the passenger door to assess the problem, so we had a quick hilltop prayer meeting!

I have to confess that this ten-year-old boy was more interested in watching the struggles on the bridge than praying at that moment, and I did do some peeking through my fingers at the precarious situation unfolding before me! After several hours and with the help of local men, Dad finally got the truck to our side of the heavily-damaged, rickety bridge. The men then helped us load the truck again. That was quite a job because they had to carry everything across the bridge and up the hill so it could be loaded in the truck that was sitting on quite a slant, facing upward. Finally, the truck was loaded, and we were "on the road" again. Prayers were answered and did we ever have a story to share!

OTHER ROAD EXPERIENCES

Other memorable times with this Army-looking truck included getting on and off the bacs (ferries) to cross rivers. Sometimes the bacs were not anchored very well, and as Dad would start driving on or off the ramps, the bac would move and start floating away as our truck's wheels fell into the water. That was a little scary! At other times, the opposite bank was steep and slippery, and it required several of the bac's men to help push the truck to get up the hill. My job was to put a big block behind the wheel as the truck inched forward.

On occasion, as we were heading toward our home, we would come across a flock of guinea hens in the middle of the road. They were great eating, so Dad would stop and shoot his double-barreled shotgun into the flock to bring some fresh fowl meat for us to eat or give to the local villagers. The meat would never be wasted. After a couple of quick shotgun shots, most of the birds would fly away, but the men in the back of the truck and I would jump out to chase and catch those that were wounded and flopping about. We would then wring their necks so that we could put them in the truck. I remember one time that we got twelve of them from one flock! By eating the guinea hens, we didn't have to buy chickens or use our own for dinner! Now that's economy!

HOME LIFE IN FORT ARCHAMBAULT

Our school at Fort Crampel was divided into two semesters, so we were normally at the boarding school for four months and then two months at home with our parents. At the end of the fall semester, a field conference with all the missionaries from that region was held at the property where the school was located. After the conference, we school kids would return with our parents to their ministry areas.

In 1949, when I first went to Africa, Lois and I had gone directly to the school, so I did not know anything about the place where my folks were. Mother had come to Africa in the Chad region after my twin brothers were born in Indiana in August, and I saw her and my new brothers three months later at the field conference that year. We all then went to Fort Archambault (now renamed Sarh) to our home.

I remember some specific things about my time at Fort Archambault. Mother was very musical and played the accordion. But she also wanted us kids to learn to play the piano—except we didn't have one! Instead we had a little pump organ that we used for lessons. The organ was stained sort of a deep orange color! To make any sound, you had to pump two foot pedals and keep pumping while you were playing. It was a unique instrument in that you could also raise or lower the musical key you were playing merely by lifting up the whole keyboard and shifting it to certain notches right or left. Therefore, it wasn't necessary to transpose the printed music—just move the entire keyboard! I have never seen another organ like that. I took sufficient lessons over a few years to be able to read music and play a little for my own enjoyment. However, my fingers did not cooperate well with the keyboard, and I found that I would rather be doing something other than practicing, so I gave up the music lessons—which I often regret.

Dad was responsible for the construction of the big church in town. It was designed as a cross if you were looking at it from above. The pulpit area was near the top of the cross with two wings and a long center section with cement benches (with no backs) emanating from there. The side wings had wooden benches which could be moved around to allow for various activities and small classes. When full, the church would seat about 2,000 people—not counting the window sills! Several Sunday School classes could be held at one time without severely interfering with each other, simply by dispersion within the cavernous building or by a group meeting outside in the shade under a mango tree. I think the church in town was probably next in size after the government's big hospital building.

The hospital grounds had many, many mango trees with their deep shade. It was only a few blocks from our house. Every evening, big black-and-white crows (which looked like they were wearing sleeveless undershirts!) would fly in from all directions to roost in those hospital trees. There seemed to be thousands of crows, and what a racket they would make as they headed back to their night's roost. Of course, you can imagine what the ground looked like under those trees each morning! I won't describe it.

FOOT PUMPING THE DENTIST DRILL

Another thing I remember about the hospital is that a dentist was there. I only visited him once, but that was one time too many! I had a couple of cavities which needed fixing. The dental chair was a very crude, antique thing and frankly, I don't know the last time when those drill bits were sharpened. There was no electricity to power the dental drill, so a man came in, sat down near the chair, and became the power, as he pumped with his feet some billows from which hoses came to make the drill go around! Also, the dentist did not use Novocain or any other anesthetic, so another assistant held my head in one position. I have never liked to go to a dentist since—but then who does like to go for a dental visit?

been there, done that!

MY ESCAPE AND HIKE

One time, another missionary, Uncle B, was visiting our station. He had a five-ton, red Dodge truck that I liked to climb into the back of and play as it was sitting there. It was much bigger than our truck. One morning, Uncle B came and got in the truck, and I thought he was just going to move it out of the sun. I was surprised when some other Chadian men got in back with me. I suppose they all figured that I was going with them. Soon, we were headed off the mission property, and I was told that we were going to the river to get sand for the church construction. I had not told my parents that I was gone and began to plot my escape. While they shoveled the sand into the truck, I would sneak away to get back home as quickly as I could. At that time, I was only eight and a half years old.

As soon as we arrived at the river, the men all started shoveling sand into the truck and I snuck off to head back to town. None of them saw me leave as I ran as fast as I could, knowing that my dad would not be happy when he found out I was gone. It was probably about three miles back home, but I knew my way without any problem. Every time I would hear a vehicle go by, I would hide in case it was a missionary out looking for me or Uncle B coming back with his load of sand. I never asked any of the men that went to the river that day with us what they did or thought when they realized I was not at the truck when it was full of sand and ready to go back into town. I imagine they spent some time looking for me.

Getting back to my house, I saw that Dad's truck was not there. My parents had told me earlier in the day they were going out to Balimba, a separate mission area, to have lunch with other missionaries. That place was another three-plus miles away, and I had already walked and run three miles. But rather than tell anyone in Fort Archambault where I was going, I secretly headed on foot out to Balimba.

More than an hour later, I casually walked into a missionary's house in Balimba as though nothing had happened. The people were all eating, and I sort of remember Dad's piercing eyes as he said to sit down and eat and he would talk to me later. I knew what that meant! But thankfully, I don't remember anything about that conversation or any discipline that took place. Later, missionaries would often talk about this little white boy running around by himself in that area of southern Chad. They marveled that I knew my way around enough to get from the river back to town and then out to Balimba.

ANTS IN MY PANTS

The Balimba station had a long driveway, which was lined by huge mango trees. They were very productive in their season, and as the fruit fell and smashed on the ground, lots of bees found the sweet fruit. Usually, the bees were not a bother, and if we could find a freshly fallen piece of fruit, we would eat it right there just as the local people did. Sometimes, we would see ladies (and even young kids) gathering up fruit and neatly piling it in big pans (up to two feet across and six-to-eight inches deep), and heading back to their homes or to the market to sell the fruit. Often, it would take two people to lift the heavy loads to place them on a lady's head—without spilling the fruit!

Of course, ants loved the fruit also. Underneath these mango trees, there were ant hills, which were very common in that whole region. These were not the mushroom-type of anthills but instead they were built like a tower. I think the tallest one near the driveway at that time was probably about four feet tall but out in the woods, you could find them much bigger.

been there, done that!

Speaking of ants, there were many different kinds. Some were the carpenter variety that would eat wood, some were red ants that had a fierce sting and infested fruit trees, some were the builders like those in the ant hills, some were termites, some made little tunnels for them to move through, and some were big black driver (or "army" ants) so named because they would move three or four ants wide in trails. These latter ones let nothing deter them from going where they wanted.

The missionaries had a garden a couple of hundred yards behind the mission station at Balimba. I liked to go back to the garden with one of the missionaries. One day, I was invited to get on the back of Aunt M's bike and go with her to the garden. (There were a lot of missionary Aunt Ms—Mary, Margaret, Martha, Melba, Marjorie.) In the garden, we gathered a bunch of vegetables, and I was to carry them in a big pan (no plastic grocery sacks then!) as we headed back to her house. Unfortunately for me, some big black, "army" ants had decided that the bike, just laid over in the garden, was in their way, and they decided to go up and over the bike—right over the back wheel and the carrier where I would sit. Neither Aunt M nor I saw the ants on the bike as I took my seat to ride back to the house.

Just a short distance down the footpath toward home, the ants thought I was in their way and they began to bite. Aunt M stopped the bike, and I jumped off almost dumping the vegetables. Aunt M saw all these ants on my legs and clothes. Rather than pick each off individually, she thought it best to strip me right there of all (yes *all*!) my clothes and pick the ants off that were biting my flesh. Most of them were biting and clinging from my waist down! I guess that I did not get too embarrassed because I knew we had to get those ants off of me! She then shook out my clothes, got rid of any ants on them, and I put them back on. For an eight-year-old, this was a painful and humiliating experience! I sure do not want to go through that again!

"ME TOO" JUICE

A couple of second-generation missionary single ladies were at Balimba. One was a nurse, and one was a teacher. Their parents had been pioneers there back in the early 1920s. These ladies made a special blend of juice from tropical fruits— and who knows what else—that all of us missionary and local African kids really liked. Occasionally, we would go to their house, and they would give us a little drink of it. When one of us wanted seconds, the rest would all call out: "Me Too! Me Too!" That special drink became known as "Me Too" juice, and to this day, I have no idea what was in it. But it was only available on the front steps of their house and nowhere else. I can almost taste it even now, seventy-plus years later!

DON'T GET BEHIND A DONKEY

I learned a good lesson about donkeys there at Fort Archambault. Those grey donkeys with the dark stripe running over their front shoulders seemed to be everywhere, and they often roamed onto our property in town. The lesson was that I should never walk behind one of those animals! Once I saw a man get kicked back about ten feet when he got too close to the wrong end of the donkey. He was hurt quite badly and quickly warned me not to get near the back side of any donkey! The donkeys were cute as a baby animal but were taught by older

been there, done that!

donkeys how to protect themselves. I often saw a donkey give a swift kick to anything or anyone that was close by, and many times it was with both hind legs.

BEGINNING MY PERSONAL DEVOTIONS

Fort Archambault was where I learned to have a personal devotional time with the Lord every day. Dad required us to read three chapters of the Bible each day and five on Sundays in order to read through the Bible in one year. And we also had to memorize a verse of scripture from one of those chapters and quote it to Dad or Mother before we could go out and play or do other chores. I will say that reading became a tedious task for me, and I always seemed to pick out a very short verse to memorize! My sisters read much faster and were often gone long before I finished my reading. On occasion, Dad would assign a particular verse to learn and to me, it seemed that he always picked out the longest verse in the reading! I still remember many of those verses but for others, I really didn't learn them. I just reviewed them several times so that I could quote them at the moment. By the end of the day, I had forgotten them, and that is really the wrong way to have an effective and enduring devotional experience! However, I am so thankful for Dad's example in teaching me the value of spending personal time with the Lord. Although I can't always recall where certain scriptures are located, some of the phrases or portions of those "memorized" verses often become meaningful to me.

HOME LIFE IN KYABE

In the "winter" vacation of 1950, our family moved east to the little village of Kyabe, about thirty miles from Fort Archambault in southern Chad where I had first lived with my parents for just a few months. To get to Kyabe, we had to cross a river on a crude bac (ferry), which was "poled" by several men to get to the other side. Later the bac was "modernized" and held in its course by a cable which the Chadians pulled on to slowly move from one side to the other. Occasionally, when the water was moving swiftly, the drive onto or off the bac could be quite precarious as the riverbank could be quite steep or slick. It seemed that most often when we wanted to cross the river, the bac was always on the other side, and we would have to wait for lengthy times for it to be brought to our side. They never seemed to be in a rush. Fun, fun!

DISC LIPS AND POINTED TEETH

Kyabe was in the area occupied by the Sara Kaba tribe. The women of this people group were distinguished by the wooden discs they wore in their lips. Additionally, raised dot markings of scar welts identified both the men and women as permanent Sara Kaba tribal members. In this tribe, the dots were in three or four parallel rows four to six inches long on their foreheads, cheeks, arms, back, and chest. Other tribes in the area had different kinds of markings. For example, the Sara Madjingay tribe had several large stripes (rather than dots) of scar welts on their foreheads and cheeks. The tribe's people received these identities during initiation rites in the bush during their preteen years. As the individual grew, so did the scars!

The initiation rites were very pagan and cruel. The cuts and skin punctures to make the tribe's markings were packed with mud and kept from healing to make the raised welts. To accommodate the crudely carved wooden discs in a girl's lips, the four top and four bottom front teeth were pulled and both upper and lower lips punctured and pegs and later small discs were inserted into these new holes. As the lips eventually stretched and the girls matured, larger and wider discs were needed. Unfortunately, occasionally a lip would break and without any method to put it together again, the remaining pieces of the lip would just dangle. Because the mouth could not be closed, the women with broken lips constantly drooled over their chests. It was terrible to see! Also, to watch a women take her discs out was an ugly scene as the drooling would begin, and the stretched lips would shrivel a bit.

To drink and eat with the discs, the woman would put her hand under the lower disc, place the food or water on the disc and tip her head back so it would roll into her mouth. The largest discs that I have personally seen were a thirteen-inch diameter disc in the lower lip and a nine-inch wide disc in the upper lip. Sometimes, the upper disc was decorated with very small beads. I never saw any of these ladies kissing their husbands!

been there, done that!

You may be thinking: How did this habit get started? From what I have learned through traditional tribal stories, men from North Africa came south across the Sahara Desert and the Sara Kaba tribal folk were the first really black—almost blue black!—people they encountered. The lighter-skinned North Africans thought the Sara Kaba women were very beautiful and would steal the ladies and take them back to their northern homes. The Sara Kaba chiefs, witch doctors, and other village leaders got together to develop a way to stop this decimation of their tribe. They decided to make their women ugly so that the northern, camel-caravan merchants would not want them. Placing discs in their lips was the answer! I sometimes wonder if the women had any say in this decision. I doubt it! The stealing of the women did stop for the most part, but the disc-lips tradition was carried on for many years. With the passing of time, now only small decorative discs are permitted in the upper lips.

It was extremely disgusting to me to hear that a few of these Sara Kaba, disc-lipped women were brought to the United States and used in side shows of traveling circus organizations. They were identified as "oddities," along with others of God's creations. One woman eventually came back to Kyabe to live in the village. She often expressed that it was much better to live in a rural village in the burning heat of Chad than in the conditions she was placed in when traveling with the circus. How demeaning that must have been for her!

The boys of the Sara Kaba tribe also underwent extreme torture of various types in their initiation rites to change them from boys to participating men of the tribe. In addition to undergoing the pains of the tribal skin markings, one of the characteristics of the men was their pointed front teeth. During the initiation rites, tribal leaders would take a piece of metal—normally from an old fifty-five-gallon gasoline drum—and use it to file each of the four front top and bottom teeth to a sharp point. I can hardly imagine the pain those boys endured at the initiation camp in the bush. These Sara Kaba and other Sara tribes were the ones to whom my parents ministered for many years in the very heart of Africa.

KYABE'S MISSION STATION

The mission station in Kyabe is memorable to me because it was my main home in Africa. Just before arriving at our station from Fort Archambault, we passed the little village of Kyabe and then the cemetery. These were the keys for me to know that we were almost home. The cemetery was small but had many graves, which were all marked by a three-forked stick about four feet tall. In the upward facing fork of the stick was a clay pot in which the family placed offerings to their gods and, I think, food for their witch doctor.

Near the entrance of the mission property from the main "road" (which was all sand), was the dispensary on one side and the mud-brick, grass-roofed church building on the other. Along the long driveway—maybe 200 or 300 feet to our house—was a nice mulberry-bush hedge. In season, the huge mulberries were delicious and made wonderful fruit desserts! Our hand-dug well was about halfway down the driveway, and our big vegetable garden was by the well. We grew almost all of the vegetables we ate. Moving on toward the house was a large fig tree with a circular drive around it. A nice bougainvillea-covered arbor with beautiful desert rose plants on each side connected the circle to a brick path leading to a large, half-moon-shaped cement terrace immediately in front of our house. We had a family picture taken on that terrace after my youngest brother was born right there in our Kyabe home.

been there, done that!

    The roof of our house was about a foot thick and made of long blades of jungle grass, although Dad did replace that later with a corrugated aluminum roof. A nice, wide porch provided shade for the house on two of its sides.

    We had four bedrooms in the house, a living room, dining room, two bathrooms (but only one with a shower), a small kitchen for our kerosene-powered refrigerator, and a good-sized back porch. Behind the house, about thirty to forty feet away, was a building with a charcoal-and-wood cooking kitchen and storage rooms. A chicken coop, large carpenter shop, and garage with a pit for repairing vehicles were beyond the kitchen. There was one other missionary home on the property.

    Dad had also built a small 4x4-foot prayer house that had a small bench in it, which he used for reading his Bible and for kneeling to pray. And what a prayer warrior he was! The little prayer house was not too far from my bedroom window, and I would often wake up before six in the morning and hear him praying aloud for so many specific requests. He went straight from there to have devotions with the workmen, and then he would come in to eat with us and lead our family devotional time. Dad was only a couple of inches over five feet tall at that time but certainly was a spiritual giant!

Our gardener's name was Kibagi. He was a wonderful, tireless worker as he prepared the vegetable beds for planting and then protected the tender plants as they grew. The hand-dug well was at the edge of the garden, and he would manually pull buckets of water from the well to water the plants. Kibagi would get very discouraged if the monkeys or antelope got into the garden and ate some of the young plants or the produce. But there was hardly anything that would keep the animals out. He was very proud when he could bring a basket full of vegetables, fruits, or spices to Mother for our meals.

But the main thing I remember about Kibagi was when he was riding his donkey from the village to our station. He was a tall man and sitting on the haunches of the donkey, his feet almost dragged the ground! I don't think he could have ridden in the middle of the donkey's sway back. He always wore a long World War II–era, heavy wool, Army overcoat, and as he was riding, the coat trailed out behind with the donkey's tail flopping between the coat's flaps. I don't think the coat had ever been washed—except by the rain! The coat stank anyway, but when it got wet, that wool seemed to send its strong odor over the entire area. Whew! Stay away!

The hand-dug well was only about twenty to thirty feet deep, and the drawn water was always milky in color. That was caused by the white clay through which the water leached. It looked like water would if you left a half inch of milk in the bottom of a glass and then filled it with water. We had to filter the water through ceramic filters four or five times before we could drink it. One of my jobs was to scrape the clay silt off the filters each time we used it, and it became quite a tiresome chore. After filtering, we would boil the water before we could drink it, but it always had a milky look.

The hand-dug well was our only nearby water source besides some rain barrels to collect water off the roofs of buildings in the rainy season. Within the house, we had running water because of two fifty-five-gallon drums that Dad had put up at the roof line on a stand outside the house to give a little gravity water pressure at the faucets. The workmen would draw the water from the well, put it into barrels on a two-wheel cart, push it to the house, and then transfer it to the drums up high. Believe me, we had hot water every day because of the automatic "solar" heater we had! We only needed one faucet since there was no difference between the hot and cold running water.

been there, done that!

TEMPERATURE WAS 163 DEGREES FAHRENHEIT!

The sun was very hot in the southern Sahara Desert. We had a large, bimetal thermometer on our open back porch. The thermometer went from 0 degrees to minus 50°F or going clockwise, the dial went around to plus 150°F degrees. On a particularly hot day, we looked at the thermometer—which was in the sun in the open air—and the pointer was thirteen degrees beyond the 150° mark. We knew it was not minus 37°F degrees there on the porch! But if the thermometer was correct (and it normally seemed to be!), we were in plus 163°F heat when out in the sun!

Even if 163°F was not an exact temperature, the weather was very hot! In those days, all the missionary family members had to wear a pith helmet or double-layered heavy felt hats. We were never outside without some type of head covering to protect us from the intense sun.

WELCOMING DAD BACK FROM VILLAGES

Usually, if Dad had been out in village meetings away from Kyabe, he would take the truck as far as he could travel on a road. He then would leave the truck with a guard and head out on a path by a borrowed horse, his bicycle, or just by foot to get to a remote village where he would introduce the people to Jesus Christ. Often he was the first white man to enter the village. Sometimes he would be gone for several days and then would come home after dark. We could tell when he was coming since we could hear the truck when it was still a few miles away. As he came within a couple miles of our house, we could see the truck lights bouncing off the sand and flat terrain! The area was so flat that sound and light cut through the still nights with unbelievable clarity. Sometimes he would have an antelope that he had shot for our meat, and other times he would have some guinea hens on which he had used his twelve-gauge, double-barreled shotgun so he could get several with just one shell. I was usually allowed to stay up and help some African men hang the antelope or clean the guinea hens for eating.

LESSONS FROM MY EARLY LIFE

There are some specific lessons which I learned from these early years of my life—from birth and early separations until my high school years.

(1) I have learned to roll with the situations of life given to me.
(2) I believe that attitude is a major aspect of happiness in life.
(3) I can always find positive things to help me enjoy my environment.
(4) I can pray for anything and everything if I want results—even though God may not answer according to my desires but in line with His plan.
(5) It may be necessary to sacrifice something for the benefit of others.

CHAPTER III

BACK IN AMERICA

1954 FURLOUGH

After five years in Africa, our family returned to the United States for furlough in 1954. I was ready for eighth grade, and there were now seven kids in our family—with the youngest being one year old. Of the seven of us, only three were born in the United States: Lois, Maribeth, Larry, and Dale were born in Africa while the twins (Tim and Tom) and I were born in Indiana while our parents were on missionary furloughs.

Where would a family of this size live? We did not have a home of our own, and it would be very expensive to rent a home to accommodate us for only a year. One of Dad's cousins and her family with three kids lived on the edge of Mishawaka, Indiana, in a large farm house at a sharp curve of US Highway 20. After the curve going east was a railroad track behind the backyard of their house. These relatives offered us one half of their big house to live in for about six months.

I didn't remember ever having Cheerios before when we were in America, but I got my fill of them on this furlough. In each Cheerio box was a metal plate with the symbol of one of America's railroads, and I wanted to collect at least one of each—especially because of that railroad track right behind us. Besides, I did like the cereal! I think I collected all of the plates by eventually trading with other kids in the general area around that farm house. That is one of my strange memories of living there. I will say that Cheerios putting those railroad plates in each box as an advertising gimmick worked—at least for our missionary family.

been there, done that!

I'LL STAY TO WATCH THE ACCIDENTS

That curve on US Highway 20 provided another important memory item for me on this furlough. Why? Being just outside of town, people driving east would pick up their speed and, although there were warning signs ahead of the curve, sometimes they weren't heeded. I think we had seven significant accidents in our front yard or at that highway railroad crossing beside our property in the six months or so that we lived there. A couple of accidents were motorcycles going head over heels, one was a car hitting a tree in our yard, one was a family in a car at night that rolled over several times in the yard, and some were at the railroad track, running into trains. One day after a severe accident, Dad was going to drive into town and asked if I wanted to go along. My answer? "No, I want to stay home and watch the accidents." What a warped sense of mind I must have had that day!

NEW HOUSE

That winter, in early 1955, my parents bought a big house in town just a couple of blocks from our home church and less than a block from an elementary school, which my younger siblings would attend. This house was very convenient for us all when Dad would be out of town in meetings because now we could walk to church, I could ride my bike to the junior high school in town, and Lois could walk to the high school. It was an old home, and I had to learn to care for the coal-fired furnace in the basement.

One section of the basement had footings for a room but the room hadn't been dug out yet. That became a major project for me to dig it out and help Dad put a foundation and walls in for that room. The dirt had to be thrown out little casement-type windows and taken from there to the alley behind the house.

I really enjoyed our church, the First Baptist Church in Mishawaka, Indiana. Uncle R, who had been a missionary with us in Africa and who was one of the early missionaries sent out from that church, became the pastor and took me under his wing. In my mind, he was probably the best expositional Bible teacher I ever knew, and I have known a lot of them! Also, he could draw any message to a close, when the radio broadcast or allocated time was concluded, and tie an invitation in response to the message at that point. The next week, he would then pick up again from the verse where he left off and continue the message. He was an outstanding preacher/teacher and a wonderful pastor! I believe it was he who baptized me and ensured that I was in a good Sunday school class and integrated into the youth group. He had four boys of his own, so he thoroughly understood the practical needs of missionary kids.

The church had an excellent summer Vacation Bible School (VBS) for all teenagers in addition to the younger kids. In our teen classes, we studied the little booklet *Rightly Dividing the Word of Truth* by C. I. Scofield—which I still have. It was a valuable study that helped me understand the important outlines of the Scriptures which revealed consistent truth, ordered beauty, and symmetry in the Word of God. In the VBS, the teachers also carefully analyzed doctrines in the Bible and taught about cults and religions in the world which severely distort God's Word. That VBS for teens was a real Bible School!

As in many good churches of that era, the youth group meetings were not just a time for social interaction. They were designed to help us grow in the Lord and receive real biblical training and practical leadership. Under a volunteer youth sponsor, we had teams of teenagers which had responsibility for the entire youth meetings. We, the youth, led the singing; gave devotionals; interacted with missionaries; planned social functions; and encouraged development of each other's skills and platform confidence. The church wanted us to be prepared for our generation's future church leadership. We teens did the work, and the youth sponsors were there to help and guide us as needed. This was excellent training for me. I will say that the youth group did help me get over some of my shyness. The social activities kept us engaged with each other in a variety of ways that tried to avoid cliques within the group. Unlike many groups I have been in or seen since then, missionary kids at this church were welcomed by both the other teens and the youth sponsors.

I lived in that house near the church the rest of that furlough until my parents went back to Africa. Then following my high school graduation, I was there for the summer before I went to college. My folks kept that house for fourteen years before selling it and buying another one in South Bend. When my younger sister and I were in Mishawaka many years later, we drove by the old house and noticed the front door was open. We built up courage to go to the door and tell of our history in the house and asked if we could walk through it for nostalgia sake. The lady welcomed us in and gave us a quick tour. It seemed basically the same, except that the kitchen had been modernized and new paint was on the walls. It

been there, done that!

had been about forty-five years since I had been in the house. The last time had been a week before Betty and I were married in 1964.

MID-MAPLES — HOME FOR TEENAGE MKs

After my eighth grade schooling in Indiana, my parents were preparing to go back to Africa where there was no high school available for Lois and me. Again, Mother and Dad had to make a very difficult decision about our schooling needs versus the Lord's call in their lives to serve in missions. In 1955, Baptist Mid-Missions (BMM) decided to open a home for MKs who needed to stay in America for their high school education. Missionaries in other nations had the same high school education problem as in Africa. So, BMM bought a large home in Wheaton, Illinois, and asked Uncle F and Aunt E to be houseparents. They had been houseparents at the dorm in Africa for a few years when I was there, so my family knew them. My parents decided to leave us at this BMM home called Mid-Maples.

Again, I was one of the first occupants — as I had been at the dorm in Africa. Fifteen or sixteen MKs from several countries were residents in the home that first year. The house had four bedrooms upstairs and two on the main floor for us MKs, a separate living area for the houseparents, three and a half bathrooms, a big dining room, porches, a good-sized living room, a kitchen, and a full basement where we added one more bedroom later. It was on a large property a couple of miles outside the city limits of Wheaton, Illinois.

Each of us MKs had chores, which varied from week to week. Mid-Maples was coed and for one of my years there, the houseparents were responsible for fourteen teenage boys and ten teenage girls! I will say that some "close" relationships developed within the "family" and certain places in the house were discreetly used for these friendships. I have often thought of how God had gifted our houseparents with wisdom and patience — well, most of the time in some kids' view! — as they provided guardianship for us in those years. Our houseparents survived, and we MKs did also! I lived at Mid-Maples four years, and all of my six siblings also spent portions or all of their high school years there.

SUMMERS AT THE LAKE

Uncle F and Aunt E had some good contacts and provided some great summers in vacation spots away from Mid-Maples. One summer, we went to Big Sandy Lake, west of Duluth, Minnesota. Uncle F loved to fish, and he enjoyed reeling in northern pike and walleye, which were great eating! The lake had a dark rust color to it from the iron in the soil in the area. When we would come out of the water after swimming, we all looked like we had a great tan, and our swimming suits never did get back to their original color! The mosquitos at Big Sandy Lake were horrendous! I don't remember them being that bad out in Africa—although out there, many of them weigh a pound! (Ha, Ha. Anywhere in the world it takes a lot of mosquitos added together to weigh a pound.) This was one of Dad's favorite jokes!

Other summers we went to Gull Lake Bible Conference in Hickory Corners, Michigan, where we had a big cabin so all of us MKs could be together. I particularly remember the Luke Cabin where we lived a couple of summers. It was fairly close to a dock on the lake where Uncle F kept a boat. I learned to water ski there. I've never really enjoyed swimming, but the skiing was fun, especially when I learned to weave back and forth behind the boat and jump the wake.

I met some great speakers and musicians at the summer conferences—S. Franklin Logsdon, Lehman Straus, Vance Havner, David Allen, and Merrill Dunlop at the organ were among some of those I particularly remember. Little did I know it then, but that Bible conference sort of set the stage for me about thirty-five years later when I would become the director of a similar Bible conference ministry in Florida. God has a way of using the past to prepare us for the future!

CHAPTER IV

EDUCATION

LEARNING ON A TYPEWRITER

My education has varied from the mundane and routine to the exciting and inconceivable. Did all this really happen for a missionary kid from the heart of Africa? It started in a very small class of preschool kids at the Westervelt Home in South Carolina. The primary tool for learning our ABCs and numbers was an old Underwood or Royal upright typewriter. The teacher would call out a letter, and we had to find it and hit the key several times to mark on the paper.

I loved hearing the peck, peck, peck on those machines and the bell dinging when we came to the end of the typed row. It was rather fun to slam that roller back to the right side to start another row—at least it was an amusing way for this three-year-old to begin his schooling! The strange thing about my early use of the typewriter is that when I got to high school, typing was the only subject in which I ever got a grade lower than a C. No, I didn't quite make it to an F grade! My two middle fingers on each hand always seemed to want to go down together. Kids today will have no idea of what an upright typewriter is!

TOO YOUNG FOR MY GRADE

When my folks came home on furlough in 1948, we lived in South Bend, Indiana, and for some reason I was on a school program where I was a half year ahead of my age-group peers at that school. To get me on their public school schedule (age-wise), I was put back a half year in the second grade at that school because I had started school so early as a three year-old. That further aggravated

been there, done that!

my schooling schedule when I arrived in Africa in 1949, where again I was still ahead of my normal year group. So, a decision was made to move me back another semester rather than have me skip a semester and go into the next grade because I already was younger than some of the others. I spent far too long in elementary school—and it wasn't because I was failing in my schoolwork! It was because I started school when I was so young—three years old!

JUNIOR HIGH SCHOOL

School at Fort Crampel in Africa has already been mentioned earlier in these memoirs. I was there from third grade through the seventh grade. I was ready for eighth grade when our family took their furlough in 1954 and lived in Mishawaka, Indiana. My first semester there was at Kennedy Junior High, but for the second half of eighth grade, we moved into town, and I was in a different school district. Thus, I transferred to Main Junior High. A couple of memories stand out. At noon time, the majority of the kids went to the gym after lunch to dance. I had no clue what all that was about. I hadn't seen it before, and I sure didn't like the music, so I just sat around the edges with some of the other kids. I also thought about things my folks had talked about regarding the "evils" of some music and dancing. Having seen a few really wild dances in Africa, I didn't even want to try the activity at the junior high school.

"FREE" THROWS

In Africa we did not play any basketball, but in America, the boys could bounce and shoot the ball and play on teams because they knew what they were doing. I had not even seen the sport so knew nothing about its rules. In my eighth grade gym class one day, the teacher said that today we were going to shoot "free" throws. I was not aware that the boys on the court had paid anything for the fun they seemed to be having. So when I heard "free," I thought that I could join in since I didn't have any money to pay to shoot the ball. That word is always good to a missionary kid!

"DUMB" GYM TEACHER

But I also thought the gym teacher was a little "dumb" when he pointed out in our gymnastics class that we were going to learn how to mount the horse and use it and the pummel for gymnastics. He went over to this leather-covered, five-foot-long cushion with two handles raised off the top and called it a horse. "He'd probably never seen a real horse or even a saddle," I mused. Yes, this thing was leather, but it had no head or tail, and its legs were shiny chrome and fastened together at the bottom. That was no horse—at least not one like I knew! Where did he go to school? Some things in American schools sure were different!

HIGH SCHOOL AT WHEATON ACADEMY

At the end of eighth grade, my parents returned to the Chad area of French Equatorial Africa after they took Lois and me to the Baptist Mid-Missions home (Mid-Maples) for teenage MKs in Wheaton, Illinois. Home schooling in other countries was not as common or as convenient as it is today through use of the computer and internet. We went to high school at Wheaton Academy, a private Christian high school that had been connected with Wheaton College in the past.

Wheaton Academy was the best place for me to go to high school.

(1) Classes were small.
(2) Many of the kids were boarding students and understood the issue of being away from parents.
(3) Some others at the Academy were also MKs.
(4) Subjects were taught from a biblical worldview.
(5) Teachers and coaches were interested in each of the students.
(6) There was a great music program.
(7) I could be involved in sports—whereas if I were in a large public school, I may not have made any of the teams because of my lack of sports experiences.

GREAT TEACHERS

All of the teachers were great in their own disciplines, and I can still remember most of their names! My coaches were dedicated in their efforts to make me always strive for excellence through disciplined training. The practices were tough but resulted in a lot of wins!

I loved the choir and the outstanding leadership of the director. He impressed upon us that the purpose for music was to minister to others while lifting our praise and worship to the Lord. He was a great model of musical leadership and the best choir director under whom I have sung. He taught us to be expressive in our singing through his effective, definitive hand movements and facial animations. Not to brag—but I will say that our choir was good! We sang a wide variety of music: classical, gospel songs, tunes of that era, southern spirituals, and special hymn arrangements. We sang a special arrangement of the *Battle Hymn of the Republic* at every concert, and because it was always such a favorite, the same arrangement has become a tradition and is still sung by the Wheaton Academy choir today. We had fun in practice and in concerts. Besides local concerts, in the spring we went on tour for two weeks and sang in some well-known venues, such as the large, balconied Peoples Church in Toronto, the Park Street Church in Boston, and the Moody Church in Chicago. But, we also sang in small churches and town squares. We traveled in a regular school bus and played a lot of Rook card games while on the roads.

I refer back occasionally to my Bible doctrine notes as taught by our Bible teacher. He explained Bible truths clearly and thoroughly, and his tough, regular quizzes made us want to learn so that we could pass his tests and be able to explain our beliefs to others.

Our biology teacher was also the school headmaster. I really enjoyed his classes with our dissecting animals of varying sizes and the collections of leaves and insects we were required to do. Our leaf collection had to include at least sixty different leaves with their proper identification. He even took the class on field trips to the Arboretum and the Indiana Dunes for us to find greater varieties. It was a wonderful class, and I have often used the information I got there to identify plants wherever I may be. We all loved that teacher. In my opinion, I think it would be good for teens today to learn how to identify plants and insects—but I doubt that will ever happen for the student in a normal high school biology class today.

I will never forget our home-room and social science teacher of my freshman year. In January 1956, he came to class one day and started leading our class devotions—as he always did. Then he nearly broke down as he explained that he had just received word that five missionary men in Ecuador had been martyred by Indians whom they wanted to reach with the gospel. A couple of those missionary men had been our teacher's classmates at Wheaton College. The story is too long to share here but can be read about in *Through Gates of Splendor* by Elizabeth Elliott, the wife of one of the martyred men who sacrificed their lives for the sake of the gospel on a little sandy beach along a river in the Ecuadorian jungle. Today, some members of that Indian tribal group have given their lives to Jesus Christ as a result of the continuing love of the missionary wives to share the gospel with them!

This incident had a positive impact on missions at the time as many people committed themselves to worldwide efforts to proclaim the gospel to people and disciple them. The account of the five men and their martyrdom was a cover story of *Life* magazine in January 1956. Being an MK far away from my own parents, perhaps caused me to have greater feelings about this incident than others, and I was so glad that our teacher provided consolation for me. I got to thank him again when I realized he was with Betty and me on a tour to China in 2010 about fifty-four years after that homeroom devotional time.

Wheaton Academy was just the right place for me at the right time. I was still pretty new at understanding the American way of life, having been out of Africa only a year. The school helped me build social skills, my love for choral music, confidence in my physical abilities, and it prepared me academically for college. I am so thankful for the Lord letting me attend Wheaton Academy.

One thing I never even thought about as a student there was the cost for me to attend this private Christian high school. I never had to pay anything, and our houseparents never mentioned tuition fees. At our Wheaton Academy 1959 class fiftieth reunion in 2009, I asked our former headmaster about how my tuition was paid, and he mentioned that someone had paid for all of us missionary kids to attend the Academy. The man had since died. I felt so bad that I never knew about him to thank him for the great experience in education that he provided for me. Certainly, he will get additional rewards in heaven for his aid to missionary kids' high school education.

CO-ALUMNA OF THE YEAR IN 2019

I was unexpectedly humbled and pleasantly surprised in 2019 to be selected as a co-alumna of the year by Wheaton Academy—sixty years after I graduated!

been there, done that!

Engraving on lamp gift from Wheaton Academy

    The school honored me at several events at the fall homecoming weekend for my Christian ministries and military service. One was in a school chapel program, another at an evening fine arts concert for alumni, and yet a third time at a special reception. At the fine arts concert, as normal at homecoming weekends, all alumni who had been in the academy choir in past years were invited to sing that special arrangement of the *Battle Hymn of the Republic* with the current choir and orchestra. This wonderful arrangement has been used by the choir for years and is always a joy to sing. Wheaton Academy has always meant a great deal to me, and today (because of this alumni honor), my name is permanently engraved on a plaque in the main building. I am thankful to the Lord for blessing me with all I learned there and for the Lord's preservation of this special academic institution since its founding in 1853.

LIFE AT WHEATON COLLEGE

Having graduated from Wheaton Academy, it was sort of a natural migration to go to college in Wheaton. I had heard a lot about Wheaton College because in the academy's early years, it had been a part of the college and a couple of the Mid-Maples kids had gone to the college there. Also, I had been working for the college's Buildings and Grounds Department for two years, so I knew the campus well. I applied and was accepted at Wheaton College, having no idea of what I wanted for my future. The Lord knew, however! I don't remember applying to or even considering any other college during my high school senior year.

COLLEGE DORM LIFE

One of the other missionary kids (MKs) from the Mid-Maples home was also going to Wheaton College, so we chose to room together in Elliott Hall. That dorm was named for one of the five martyrs who died in Ecuador in 1956. This dorm was next to some railroad tracks and a rail crossing, so it took some time getting used to the regular train whistles, the warning bells at the intersection, and the clackety-clack of the trains' wheels throughout the night. Our dorm building was a couple of blocks from the main college campus, and overall, it was a great freshman year, which included several interesting events.

A freshman from Hawaii lived in the room next to ours. We quickly made friends and often made the trek to the main campus together. I could always tell when he received a package from Hawaii because it usually held some special foods which oftentimes would smell up our entire end of the hall. One of his favorites was dried abalone. It was like a hard ball from which he would slice thin slices and chew sort of like beef jerky. Oh, did it ever have a strong fishy smell! But in spite of that, it was good! I'm glad that he was willing to share small bits of it with a few of us who really enjoyed it. Most of the boys in the dorm didn't even want to taste it because of its smell!

As the first semester progressed, we would often hear tremendous vocal harmonies coming from down the hall. It was the beginning of Wheaton's famous '63 quartet, who would get together and sometimes practice in the laundry room! This quartet stayed together all four years and sang at many special occasions of the college and even continued into latter years when our class of '63 had reunions!

been there, done that!

One of the members became a music professor at the college, and another became a world-renowned orchestra and choral conductor.

Pranks of various kinds were not unusual in a dorm of mostly first-year students. One of the students was quite serious and somewhat gullible. One cold and snowy winter night, most of us from our hallway decided to trick him, and we got his roommate to join in on the joke. After the student went to bed, his roommate reset his buddy's alarm for 7 a.m. when he would normally get up. At that time of year it was still dark outside in the early mornings.

Because we had a common bathroom for the hall, the rest of us went there as we did most school mornings. He came in, thinking it was early morning and he had to get ready for classes. Only thing was, the real time was shortly after midnight! He rushed to get done in the bathroom and quickly got dressed and headed out by himself in the snow for his classes—thinking we had already left the dorm and were nowhere to be found.

Upon arriving at his class building, he found it locked and soon a campus cop came up to him and asked what he was doing trying to get into a building so late at night. That is when he looked at his watch (which had not been reset) and realized he had been severely pranked! By the time he got back to the dorm, the rest of us were in bed—and he made sure that we were not asleep with the racket he made. Fortunately, he took it all as the joke it was meant to be, although he was not very happy that he had to get out in the cold at that hour of the morning!

ACADEMICS AND CHANGING MAJORS

College was a faith experience for me—not only for my course of study but also regarding finances. I did not know what I wanted to be, nor did I know what subjects to take. Naturally, some courses were required for all incoming students, but the college had a procedure whereby a new student could take some tests and validate out of some of the required classes and substitute others. I took tests in Mathematics, English, and Bible to avoid some of those basic courses—and passed in each, much to my surprise! Wheaton Academy had prepared me well. So, I never had to take one mathematics class in college—perhaps to my detriment—and I didn't have to take the fundamental English class. But Bible was required each semester—and that was a good thing!

I tested out of two years of the mandatory Bible classes and was put in with some third-year students in an elective course on the book of Psalms. It was great content, and I enjoyed and benefited from the teaching. However, exams were another story! We had to use special "blue books" for testing, and the questions from this Bible professor were way over my head and seemed very philosophical. I was not used to that kind of testing and just couldn't put down in writing what he wanted the answers to be. I dreaded the tests and ended up with a "D" for the semester. I was devastated, partly because I had only gotten one "D" before in my life, and that was in typing in high school! But my disappointment was also because I had declared Bible to be my major. After all, my youth pastor, my college advisor, and others had said that should be my major since Dad was a preacher and a missionary! That "D" didn't sit well with me at all. I didn't want such a low grade in my records—especially in my major field of study. Although I did much better in the second semester, I began to think that I should change my declared major.

By the end of my freshman year, I was convinced that the Lord had something else for me. I had genuinely tried to pursue the Bible major because that is what others wanted me to do. I began to think: "That is what others chose for me, but what is it that I really want?"

Because of my love for choral music generated through the choir director at Wheaton Academy and the fact that I had directed small choirs while I was in high school at our church and for our Mid-Maples ministries, I changed my college major and enrolled in the Music Conservatory. I took piano, choral conducting, and voice classes and really enjoyed them, but I felt the conservatory tried to own me and my time. I had to work to earn money to stay in school, and the music professors wanted me to practice two hours a day for each of those courses—plus I had to study for other subjects! There just wasn't enough time in the day, so at the end of my sophomore year, I decided to switch majors again—although I sure don't regret that year in the conservatory! It was very valuable to me as I would learn later when I became the director of choirs and congregational singing in several churches.

Now what would my major be? I had tried what others wanted for me, and I had tried what I wanted for myself, but each of those did not work out. I then earnestly begged the Lord for direction in my life since I was going into my third year of college. By now, I had thoroughly relished all aspects of the Army ROTC (Reserve Officers Training Corps) program which was mandatory for all male freshman and sophomore students at the college. I was doing very well in the academics there and was participating in the extracurricular activities of the

been there, done that!

Pershing Rifles, such as the drill team, the rifle team, and the color guard. I was good in the marching and performing all the movements with the rifle.

I sensed that the Lord was leading me to become a commissioned officer in the US Army. Then I had to find a major field of study that was compatible with that goal. I ended up choosing a social science major with a concentration in geography, which was an excellent match for an Army career. I had pursued what others wanted, what I had wanted, and now was focused on what God wanted for my life! That gave me great contentment and freedom as I moved forward in college.

ROTC AS A COLLEGE CADET

When arranging my classes at registration time in my freshman year in college, I discovered that all freshmen and sophomore male students were required to take the Army Reserve Officer Training Corps (ROTC) program. I had no idea what that was about since no one in my immediate acquaintances had been in the military. The little bit of information I had was that I knew a commuting MK who wore a military uniform a couple of times a week and played in the ROTC band. That was the extent of my military knowledge! Anyway, I was mandatorily signed up for ROTC.

PERSHING RIFLES

Within the first few days at the college in the fall of 1959, my assigned big brother (who was high-ranking in the cadet corps) introduced me to Pershing Rifles (PR), a military fraternal-type of cadet organization on many campuses across the nation. It was the "elite" element of the ROTC cadet corps! I went through the harassment of pledging the organization and was accepted into its membership. Little did I know then of the value that PR would be in my life. It provided the early professional base for a military career—which I had never anticipated.

TRAFFIC GUIDE FOR BILLY GRAHAM CRUSADE

One of the first activities of PR that year was to direct traffic for the September 27–October 4, 1959 Billy Graham Wheaton Crusade. Billy Graham was a 1943

Wheaton College graduate. Each afternoon and night, PR cadet leaders organized us to ensure smooth vehicle and human traffic flow on the Wheaton campus to and from the crusade site on the north side of the new Centennial Gym. Parking was a big problem as everyone wanted to be as close to the crusade's outdoor seating as possible. Each night, the campus was jammed as the community joined college students at the crusade. On most of the crusade days, several thousand people came to hear Billy Graham speak, sing in the choir with Cliff Barrows, and hear George Beverly Shea's rich baritone voice. I remember one night being privileged to sing with the huge choir but had to leave the choir early to get to my traffic post. What an exciting introduction all of that was to my ROTC, PR, and military experience!

Pershing Rifles gave cadets more training in military affairs and practical exercises than the normal cadet received in the ROTC program. I proudly wore the blue-and-white braid (called a fourragere) on the shoulder of my uniform, distinguishing me as a PR member. Discipline within PR set the example for other cadets, and I loved the spit-and-polish that PR required of its members. That set the standard for my career. If the leader wears the uniform correctly with its highest gloss and carries himself with excellent military bearing, then subordinates will desire to mimic those traits. That same attitude will carry over into operations on the battlefield, which results in more effective accomplishment of missions. To this day, when I wear my uniform for varying speaking engagements and events, I spit-polish my shoes—no plastic or fake leather shoes for me!—ensure that my brass is highly polished, and that all accoutrements, awards, and decorations are properly positioned.

EXTRACURRICULAR ACTIVITIES

Pershing Rifles offered several extracurricular activities, which seemed to fit well with my academic and work schedule in college. We went on several weekend bivouacs (Army campouts and training periods) each year. On these outings, I soon found that I was among the first cadets selected to be on ambush or reconnaissance patrols because of my alleged "expertise" in tracking and camouflage I had learned in Africa while hunting for our meat. I could "read" broken twigs, overturned leaves, footprints, and false camouflage to which most of the cadets had never been exposed. I really benefitted from the tactics we were taught and practiced on these bivouacs. The bam-bam of the blank ammunition being

been there, done that!

fired from our rifles added to the realism of the training. I also enjoyed the military's canned C-rations and the open cooking fires! I was in my element and all of that proved valuable for my future Army career. These activities enticed me to later apply for the Army's Ranger School—and besides, the PR sponsor was an Army Ranger himself!

In addition to the bivouacs, PR provided the color guard for major college events and sports activities. In my freshman year, I quickly volunteered to be a member of the color guard, and the four of us on that team became the best of friends—even long after college!

The color guard was called on for the presentation of the United States and Wheaton Flags at home athletic events, graduations, similar special activities, and even community functions. Wheaton also had a rifle team and most of us on that team were from PR. Our practice rifle range was in the fifth floor attic of Blanchard Hall, the main (and historic!) building on campus. I fired a lot of rounds up there! PR provided the base for much of my social life on campus and in competitions against major schools in the Midwest.

COMPETITIVE DRILL TEAM

One of my greatest delights in PR was to be a member of the sixteen-man competitive drill team. We practiced and practiced the detailed manual of arms with the 1903 Springfield rifle and became experts at spinning and throwing the rifle even while marching in specific movements and formations. Our team uniforms had to have detailed placement of medals, crisply ironed creases, and boots that would reflect like a mirror. Our marching was judged on its precision and the uniqueness of the formations where we marched forward, backward, sideways, and on oblique angles, oftentimes interweaving our rows and columns. The drill competitions were against major universities such as: Purdue, Indiana, Wisconsin, Michigan, Michigan State, DePaul, Iowa, and Illinois, to name a few in the Midwest. Each of these schools had a much larger cadet corps than Wheaton, but we did very well in most of these competitions!

At each of these drill meets for the teams, there was also individual cadet competition in the manual of arms with the rifle and in-place movements—such as Right Face, Left Face, and About Face. The competitions normally started with perhaps a couple hundred cadets. As commands were barked out, judges would look for errors made by the cadets who then had to drop out of further competition. The numbers would dwindle fairly quickly as cadets would lose their focus. In several of the contests, I was within the last ten to fifteen still standing, but mental or physical distractions would then knock me out, and most of the times that would happen because of "trick" commands. I always determined to practice harder and more often.

In one drill meet at Purdue University, I won second place in a huge regional individual competition. The winner of that competition was Wally. He was from DePaul University in Chicago and was one of my best friends, against whom I had competed numerous times. Wally's father had come to America from Germany and earlier in his life had been in the German Army. He had instilled in Wally the values of discipline and precision in life. Wally was almost like a wound-up, mechanical soldier and was so good! Because of our friendship and after graduating from college, we later roomed together in Infantry Officer Basic Course at Fort Benning, Georgia, and went through Airborne and Ranger training at the same time. He was really sharp and was the envy of most of us competitors.

Our college drill team also marched in various community parades in addition to our competitions. I specifically remember one Memorial Day parade in downtown Wheaton, Illinois, when it snowed and really messed up our uniforms. Our starched creases were gone, our shiny boots had slush on them and the salt on the street destroyed our spit shine, and our chrome-plated helmets did not look sharp with the melting snow running off them. And talk about *cold* and miserable! The wet cotton shirts, and soaked white cotton gloves did not stave off numbness and goosebumps! It hurt to slap our weapons for noise effect, but we persisted and made it through the parade.

ROTC SUMMER CAMP

Normally, a cadet—in the last two years of the college ROTC program—attends a military summer camp between the junior and senior year of college. Wheaton's cadets went to Fort Riley, Kansas, for six weeks of Army field exposure and training. I don't know why, but I was chosen as our platoon's commander on the first day. That was a challenge to get cadets from many Midwestern and Southern universities focused on daily routines and military disciplines at camp. For the cadet parade on that first weekend, I was selected to command the color guard for the entire encampment of several hundred cadets and I performed those duties for the parade each of the six weeks.

One Sunday was quite different for me. I was going to go to the 11 a.m. Protestant service, but when I got ready, another guy from our unit was going to the Catholic mass, so I decided to go with him to see what it was all about. We got to the chapel and found it quite full. I saw an empty seat over near the wall but to get to it, I had go around the front pews. There were a lot of soldiers up there that I needed to work my way around. Suddenly, I realized that I was in a line that led to the priest's office for personal confessions! I didn't know what to do, so I just sat down in a nearby empty seat in the front—which was a very bad thing to do when the service finally started.

Soon I heard some mumbling and rustling behind me and turned around to see everyone kneeling. The priest came out and started saying things which I did not understand, and the soldiers all responded with something afterwards. I really felt strange not knowing what to do—and besides, I was in the front row where everyone could see me! Finally the service concluded, and I tried to sneak out between a group of men so that the priest would not have to talk with me. I really didn't know what was going on, but it was an interesting experience in that Catholic service!

The summer camp was good for all of us. Even though we had learned military tactics at college, very few (unless they had been in Pershing Rifles or similar extracurricular training at their school) had been in the field to practice the tactics. We received training in communications, terrain evaluation, use of the compass, map reading, land mine warfare, first aid, bayonet, drill and ceremonies, physical training, and patrolling. We fired many different kinds of weapons—which could not be done back on our college/university campuses! At the end of the six-week camp, we had to take a comprehensive written test on all we had been exposed to and taught. I did very well on that and also received a good rating on my leadership evaluation. The camp was of great benefit to me.

CADET BATTALION COMMANDER

Rather than just completing the mandatory first two years of ROTC at Wheaton, I had enrolled in the program all four years to earn my commission as a second lieutenant in the US Army. The cadet brigade was large because of the requirements for all males to participate in at least the first two years of the program. In my junior and senior years' ROTC classes (which were much smaller), selection for leadership roles in the cadet corps were merit-driven, and I was privileged to command platoons, companies, and in my senior year, one of the three cadet battalions. My selection for the battalion command was partially based on my ratings from summer camp in addition to my college academic grades and other extracurricular activities. Our drill field was just across the street from a couple of the girls' dorms, and that challenged us who were bellowing military commands to wake the girls up early at 6:00 a.m.—since we had to be up early! We would often hear windows slamming shut in the three-story dorms as the girls tried to muffle our drill field commands. What a fun life!

My senior year was very busy. I was still working about forty hours a week, dating a nursing student, Betty, as often as possible, and going to classes. Additionally, I was asked to be on the college's fall homecoming committee with the duties of coordinating all the class displays and floats construction and exhibition. That took a lot of time.

Within the ROTC Department, I had responsibility for the drill and ceremonies training of my cadet battalion. I was also the primary planner and coordinator for the department's ROTC banquet and the special annual banquet for the Pershing Rifles (PR). As the executive officer for the PR, I had the responsibility

been there, done that!

for the pledging of new recruits, the field training activities on bivouacs (Army camping weekends), and the group's monthly programs. In a way, graduation would be a big relief from a strenuous senior year.

GRADUATION AND COMMISSIONING

As senior cadets, we could indicate our preference for the branch of the Army in which we wanted to serve and the military post we wanted. These branches of the Army include such specialties as military police, armor (the tanks), signal, intelligence, medical service, infantry, chaplain, transportation, artillery, and engineers, among others. Several advisors and counsellors said I should apply for the Chaplain Corps since my father was a missionary. But I quickly reminded them that I had gotten a D in Bible in my freshman year and that the Lord had seemed to close the door to a Bible major for me four years earlier. I wanted to be where the action was! You could say that I was really "gung ho". My first choice among the branches of the Army was the Infantry! I got my branch choice but did not get to go to Fort Bragg, North Carolina, which was the post of my choice. I was happy anyway.

WHAT IS AN INFANTRY SOLDIER?

Ernie Pyle, the legendary World War II news correspondent defined the infantry soldier as the "mud-rain-frost-and-wind boys". In today's warfare, he could have added "dust" as a fifth element, as helicopters churn up swirling dirt and debris wherever they land or take off. Over time, I have learned that an infantry soldier sleeps in foxholes, a vehicle, under the stars, and if possible in a cramped pup-tent. Running water for a "bath or shower" comes from a stream and toilet facilities in the field are wherever you dig them. Meals come from a can, plastic-type pouch, or occasionally a hot cooked meal will come from an Army field kitchen via a rectangular, insulated box. Exquisite dining furniture may be a hard ammunition box to keep you from sitting on some unkind stinging bugs or other slinking critters. The helmet in my era was not only for protection but could be used as a wash basin or uncomfortable stool. Our rucksacks carried all we needed for comfort and for fighting since there were no stores in the jungle to purchase goods. News came from an occasional letter from home (pre-cell phone or computer era!) or a rare visitor from higher headquarters. One person said that an infantry soldier "just sort of exists". Ernie Pyle also wrote: "the velvet is all gone from living" for an infantry warrior.

I must admit that I wasn't fully aware of all of this when I chose to be in the infantry. Yes, a junior officer did have it a *little* better than the enlisted soldiers in my infantry days, but when in the field, there isn't a whole lot of difference in how we lived with our troops. We all hurt the same when we caught a dry cuticle or hangnail when reaching into an ammo pouch or pocket. We all ached emotionally when family members were celebrating a special day and we were tromping in the jungle.

But all of us in the infantry learned to value the little things in life, such as fresh water, a perfumed letter from home, or a package with some special goodies. A can of insect spray prevented some of the bug bites, which were part of jungle life, and fresh batteries for a flashlight reduced a bit of rummaging in the dark. We learned to enjoy a clear night when we could look up through the trees at a gorgeous and magnificent starry night. Jungle sounds were broken only by the soft whispers of soldiers talking about their loved ones in between the noise of artillery or bombing on a distant target. An infantry combatant is part of a brotherhood. We support each other in times of good or bad. We live in combat with the constant knowledge that our buddy (or even we ourselves!) may not be there the next day, so we do everything we can to protect those around us. That gives us reason to bond tightly with one another.

At graduation time from college, about twenty-five of us Wheaton cadets were commissioned as officers in the United States Army. Along with two others, I was identified as a Distinguished Military Graduate, which gave me the opportunity to be a Regular Army officer versus a Reserve officer on active duty. That meant that I was in the same basic category as US Military Academy graduates and would be with them in upcoming military schools and training.

The day I received my college diploma, I also received my Army commission. I was in the Army at that moment! I was given ten days of advanced leave to get to my first duty station. I had thoroughly enjoyed my ROTC experiences that prepared me for a career in the US Army. Entering college in 1959, I never would have guessed that the Lord had planned for me to be commissioned in the Infantry four years later.

My parents came home on furlough from Africa shortly before my graduation and attended both my commissioning and the graduation ceremonies. I was delighted they could be there for this important transition in my life. In a

been there, done that!

graduation card they gave me was this Scripture verse from II Timothy 2:3: "Thou therefore endure hardness, as a good soldier of Jesus Christ." I didn't understand at that time what "hardness" I would later "endure" in my career. However, I did want to be a good career military officer but also a shining example of a Christian soldier honoring my Lord and Savior, Jesus Christ, regardless of any "hardness" I may encounter. After twenty-six years of military duty and retirement as a full colonel, I am so grateful that Wheaton required me to take ROTC. It set a pattern for my life.

GOD'S SPECIAL FINANCIAL PROVISION

College was a faith experience for me, and that was evidenced in my finances. I didn't have any money to speak about, nor could my missionary parents help me. I never heard of any scholarships which might be available to me. So, sometimes I worked approximately forty hours a week to pay my bills. In the first year, I worked mainly on the campus grounds and in cleaning buildings—where I had worked in my high school years. Later to make ends meet, I was able to work some school nights in the college heating plant and on Saturdays back on the grounds.

In my last three years of college, my primary job was in the heating plant. For my junior and senior years, I was in the Advanced ROTC program and that paid a monthly stipend, which really helped. Also, between those last two years, I had the ROTC summer camp for six weeks and was paid for that training.

Even so, Wheaton College was continually a financial challenge for me. I had been able to save a little for my registration fees at the beginning of college and was working as much as possible to earn the money needed for tuition, room and board, books, and some required fees. It never seemed to be enough. But somehow the Lord always had sufficient funds in my account to pay the bills at the moment needed! But my question constantly was: "Will I have enough to pay for the next semester?" I had to depend on God every minute and am so thankful that I never had to take out a loan to cover any of my college costs. To this day, I still can't determine where all the monies came from to let me finish college with no debt. My faith was in God and His promises to take care of me.

A college policy was that you could not take a semester's final exams unless your bill was fully paid. Somehow, I always had sufficient funds to pay the bills—except one time! At the end of the first semester in my junior year, I was called to the second-floor business office for a meeting with Mr. A. I really had no idea what the meeting was to be about when I sat down in front of him. He hesitatingly told me that I couldn't take my exams because my final bill wasn't paid. Naturally, I didn't like to hear that and asked how much I owed. He replied that I owed $323. That seemed like an impossible amount to get in a very few days before exams were to start! To me, there weren't even enough hours left for me to work before exams to earn that much money. But I accepted the fact knowing that with God nothing is impossible!

After prayer together that the Lord would work it out, I left his office and started down the long flight of stairs in a dejected mood but with confidence that God knew all about the debt—and the solution to it! In my heart, I had head knowledge of Proverbs 3:5, 6: "Trust in the Lord with all your heart; and lean not on your own understanding. In all your ways acknowledge Him and He shall direct your paths." Also, I knew Philippians 4:19: "But my God shall supply all your need, according to His riches in glory by Christ Jesus." However, I am not sure that I had sufficient faith to apply these texts to my current situation.

As I neared the bottom of the long stairway, I heard my name called from above. I turned around and looked up to see Mr. A at the top motioning for me to come back to his office. I couldn't tell by his voice or by his face what all this could be about, but I slowly went back up the steps with tears welling in my eyes. Arriving at the top, he put his arm over my shoulder as we walked together to his office and there he announced that my bill was now paid! What did I just hear?

Just a few minutes before he had said I had a debt, but now it was paid! I questioned how that could be. He relayed that a lady in an adjacent cubicle in the business office overheard our earlier conversation—and I'm sure God had heard our prayer! He said that after I left his office, she quickly came to him and said she had just opened an envelope with a check. A note was included that said the check should be used for some needy student to help meet their bill. The check was for $323.00! That was my exact need to cover my debt!

The lady and Mr. A then decided on the spot that the Lord had already answered our earlier prayer and that I should be the recipient of that gift. That is when Mr. A rushed to the top of the stairs to call me back. How could anyone but God have orchestrated that kind of scenario? Prayer and believing faith do work! "But my God shall supply all your need according to His riches in glory by Christ Jesus." (Philippians 4:19). He had just done that for me! I couldn't hold back the tears as we prayed together an emotional and grateful response for God's goodness and

been there, done that!

His provision to meet my financial need. Proverbs 3:5–6 was valid and would come back into my life over and over after that incident.

I left college with absolutely no debt. To think about this young missionary kid going to college on a bicycle (see later section on Hobbies) because he had very little money and graduating four years later with all bills paid and a military career ahead is still an incredible statement of God's work on my behalf. College was a unique experience in my life! It still seems like an unbelievable "been there, done that" story!

CHAPTER V

THE FAIRER GENDER!

SOCIALLY SHY BEFORE COLLEGE

Up through high school, I was quite shy when it came to relationships with the fairer gender. My wife says she still doesn't believe that! One girl at the dorm in Africa was particularly liked by several of the boys. She seemed to be an early developer mentally and physically, and that may have been part of the attraction. I, too, took a liking to her and would try to talk to her out on the swings or be on the afternoon ball team she was on.

However, one boy who was older than me—and bigger too!—decided he didn't want me to be friends with this special girl. (Keep in mind that we were all pre-teens at this time.) At breakfast one morning at the big table in the dorm in Africa, he was sitting next to me and somehow this girl's name came into the conversation. He immediately turned to me in a fit of rage and started pounding on my head with his fist and telling me that I should never get near "his girl" again. I don't remember how that pounding was stopped, but I do remember that she would not let him get next to her for a long time. She had been sitting right across the table from us and saw it all. Now you know why I was shy around girls after that! I didn't want another pounding!

At furlough time in 1954, our family home was in Mishawaka, Indiana. It happened that one of the other missionary kids came home on furlough with her family about the same time we did. It was quite convenient that she lived in the same town and within an easy bike ride from our house. I don't know if there was anything special going between us at that time, but we did have a lot in common just coming from Africa, and we enjoyed talking about those things. She and I were in eighth grade and could relate to each other because of our mutual backgrounds. Our church youth group was quite active so there was plenty of opportunity to interact with other girls if I had wanted to.

Through high school, I was interested for a while in one of the girls living at Mid-Maples. But that fizzled by her beginning to favor another one of the guys. I did not attend the junior-senior banquet at Wheaton Academy my junior year because I just didn't want to ask a girl out and waste what little money I had. It was the same in my senior year. However, one of the girls at Mid-Maples had not gotten a date that year, and I was "strongly encouraged" to go to the banquet and take her. She was a nice girl, but I didn't want to waste my limited money on such a social event. Well, we did go and had a good time, but my heart certainly was not in it. I never did ask her to go with me to the banquet. It just sort of happened that we went together. I guess that was my first real date—even though I hadn't planned or wanted it!

After graduating from high school in Illinois, I went to Indiana to live with my parents for the summer. There was a red-haired girl in the youth group who caught my eye for a while, but the only thing we ever did together was attend youth group functions, so nothing ever developed. When I left for college, all thoughts of her were forgotten.

DATING WHILE IN COLLEGE

Through my first two years in college, I rarely dated because I just didn't have time. I was working about forty hours a week and also trying to study. My main interest was in the ROTC program and extra-curricular activities with the drill team, rifle team, the school color guard, and occasional weekend bivouacs (campouts where you practice Army tactics and life).

When I did informally date, it was with girls from my older sister's nursing class at West Suburban Hospital (West Sub) that was twenty-five miles away. I was at West Sub activities with my sister quite a bit, so I also got to meet other guys from Wheaton who were dating the nursing students there. The girls in their starched, white nursing uniforms were always very pretty! They did not have the casual scrubs that so many students wear today in the nursing schools and hospitals! I became rather familiar with the school because of my sister being there three years and my having gone to many West Sub parties and events.

LOVE STRICKEN AT FIRST SIGHT!

Now comes the good part of the story! West Sub was a source of attractive young ladies for the boys from Wheaton College. I had a car in my junior year (1961), and some of the guys wanted to go to West Sub to meet the new class of freshman nurses who would be giving open-house tours of the hospital. I had been to the nursing school often and didn't need another hospital tour, but I offered to drive the guys in with absolutely no intention of staying at the school with them. My married sister lived only a couple blocks away from the hospital, and I could go to her house. She had continued to work at West Sub after her graduation that August.

By the time we arrived at the school entrance, the guys had convinced me to stay with them since they didn't know what time the tours and little reception would be done, and then they would want to leave. Going in the big doors and walking up a couple of steps into the nursing school lobby, my eyes immediately focused on a blonde, blue-eyed, well-dressed, beautiful, freshman nursing student who was waiting for a group to take on the hospital tour. I was awestruck and didn't even look around to see who was leading other groups but went straight to her location!

She introduced herself as Betty Becker from Chicago. I didn't have to think twice about remembering that name! About eight or ten others were in the group. One of them was a guy she had quizzed against in high school Youth For Christ competitions. As we walked the hospital's corridors and wards listening to her explanations at certain spots, she and this guy occupied every spare moment talking together about their past Youth For Christ events.

I remained as close as I could to them to hear every sweet word that came out of her mouth! I was love-stricken from the moment I first saw her and can even give you details of what she was wearing—neither she nor other girls were in their new nurses' uniforms that day! Regretfully, she doesn't even remember that I was in her group. I guess I didn't make as much of an initial impression on her as she had on me! Let me assure you that I was really happy that I had been convinced to stay at the hospital for the tour that day rather than go to my sister's house! This had to be part of God's plan in my life.

A couple of weeks later, I discovered that the nurses were coming by bus to the college to attend an Artist Series concert at the college. My housemate knew one of the girls who was coming and wanted to sit with her, so he suggested that if anyone was with her that maybe I could ask that friend to sit with me. I had done my "intelligence" work and had already found out that Betty and this other girl were roommates, so I quickly responded that I would help him out—hoping that Betty would be with her. The nurses' bus arrived, and we efficiently carried out our plan. Betty was mine that night! By the way, I have no recollection of the concert that night or who the performer was! I wonder why!

SHYNESS TURNS TO BOLDNESS

Without hesitation after the concert, I offered to drive the four of us back to the nursing school. Betty got permission from the bus chaperone, and we were off. On the way, I asked Betty for a date a couple of weeks away, but she said she already had a date pre-arranged by her "big sister" at the nursing school, so I asked her for another day. Then I pushed a little harder and discovered who this Wheaton boy was that she was going to date. Upon hearing the name, I sure wished he wasn't in the picture at all because I knew him and his personality and initially had not gotten along too well with him. But I didn't say anything about that to Betty at the time.

I then boldly and with great confidence told Betty: "That is the last date you will have with anyone except me!" I knew at that point that she was going to be in my future! This was on my first "date" with her! My previous shyness had suddenly turned to unshakeable boldness! Later, Betty said that she felt that my statement was quite presumptuous, but it turned out to be true as we dated and then were engaged during her years in nursing school.

ENGAGEMENT

In December of Betty's second year at West Sub and after dating her for about sixteen months, I asked her to marry me. I popped the question while we were sitting on the front lawn below the Wheaton College tower. (Unfortunately, we never rang the tower bell as was customary for engagement announcements on the campus. I don't know why!) I graduated the following June (1963) and headed off to my Army career. The next February (1964), I took a brief leave after my initial military training courses in Georgia and spent a couple of weeks with her. I later realized that between mid-June 1963 (my college graduation) and late July 1964 (just before our wedding), those two weeks of military leave were the only occasion we were together in that lengthy thirteen and a half month period. Yet our love survived! That could have been part of the Lord's preparation for separations to come due to military duties.

We had a wonderful time in those two weeks in February 1964 and even bought our first car—a new 1964 Chevelle costing only $2,400—with our joint savings. I headed off to Washington state in our new car to my first unit assignment, sadly knowing that the next time I would see her would be just before our wedding in August.

THE WEDDING SCHEDULE

For the next five months, I eagerly anticipated August 8, 1964. Betty and I wanted to ensure that my parents would still be on furlough from Africa so that they could attend the big affair. My younger sister, Maribeth, also wanted me to be at her wedding in Indiana, but I was not going to be able to take another leave from the Army to go to her ceremony unless somehow it was held in the same period of time when I would be nearby for my own wedding in Chicago. I had planned to take a little more than a week's leave just before my wedding so that Betty and I could make our final wedding arrangements. All of us together had decided that Maribeth (via phone calls and letters) should get married on August 1, the week before me so that our whole family could celebrate both events.

I left duty at Fort Lewis, Washington, late on a Friday afternoon to head east for the weddings. Crossing the wide state of Washington and the narrow neck of Idaho throughout the night, I drove into Montana and saw that it had no speed limit. The highway was very straight and mostly level with an occasional knoll, so to keep on the road, I put the hood ornament of the Chevelle on the center line and pushed the gas pedal. When driving across Montana, I averaged around 100 miles per hour, veering into the right lane only when I couldn't see the other side of the little rises in the road and, of course, in the few towns I passed through! Every now and then, I would stop for a very short nap but never pulled off for a good sleep. Altogether, driving by myself the approximately 2,100 miles from Tacoma to Chicago, I took less than forty hours! That little Chevelle got a real workout, and I think it was about as anxious to see its co-owner as I was!

My sister's wedding was August 1, and ours was August 8, and both were beautiful. Ours was a little unusual in its timing. Betty had to work nights in her last week at the nursing school. At the same time, she had to take her National

been there, done that!

League of Nursing comprehensive exams during the day in preparation for later taking the state boards, authorizing her licensure. I was also spending time with her each evening prior to her night work shift, going over final details for our wedding. How she did all that, I'll never know. She has always been such an amazing woman!

Her nursing school graduation was on a Friday evening, eliminating a wedding rehearsal then, so we held the practice on Saturday morning. Her mother had been determined that I should not see Betty on the wedding day until she was walking down the aisle, but we had no option for the time of the practice. Finally, the wedding took place at Central Avenue Baptist Church in Chicago at 4 p.m. that same Saturday as our morning rehearsal.

I wanted to be married in my dress blue Army uniform, and I wanted my groomsmen also to be in uniform. I chose as my best man, Wally, who had been the guy from DePaul University who always beat me in military individual manual of arms competitions when we were in college. He was also the one who beat me academically in a military education course. He was a good friend, and I was happy to have him as my best man. My other groomsman was a classmate from Wheaton College. I was glad that he lived in the Chicago area where he was assigned to an air defense site. I think we looked quite spiffy in our dress uniforms, and other wedding guests supported my perception!

But Betty was the real attraction that afternoon with her radiant smile; long, flowing blonde hair; and her beautiful wedding dress—well, the dress wasn't really hers! It was borrowed from my sister, Lois, and it didn't even need any alterations! There is a story here. Lois had gotten married in 1961 when our parents were only partway through a term of missionary service in Africa. They could not come back for her wedding so Lois asked me to walk her *down the aisle* in her ceremony. With Betty in that same dress for our wedding, I felt so proud to walk her back *up the aisle* as the new Mrs. Philip R. Fogle! How many people have taken a person in a wedding gown down the aisle and walked another person in the same gown back up the aisle—of course, that was three and a half years later! I have "been there, done that"! I suspect that hasn't happened very often. It is just another unique experience in my life!

Our wedding was followed by a great reception/dinner in a banquet hall a little distance outside Chicago. We had wanted just a simple and quick reception at the church, but Betty's dad said it wasn't fair for family and friends to drive a long way to the wedding and get only a church reception. He also wanted to have alcoholic beverages available for those who wanted them. We were quite adamant about not having such at our wedding but negotiated that the alcohol could be available but had to be kept in an adjoining room to the dinner.

To carry out a tradition from Betty's mother's wedding; after a delicious Scandinavian buffet dinner, Betty and I were taken on to a platform with us not knowing what was to happen. Much to our frustration, they took off Betty's veil, tied an apron around her waist, and placed a broom in my hand. We could tell by the reaction of the guests that this didn't seem all that appropriate, and it sort of temporarily stole some of our joy. Because of the lateness, we quickly opened our gifts, stashed them in Betty's dad's get-away car, and headed to their home to get changed into casual clothes.

OUR SHORT HONEYMOON

We had secretly hidden our car in a friend's garage so that nothing could be done to it that might slow us from our departure. It was pretty much already loaded with a top carrier for our trip west. With that car top, it barely fit under the open garage door. We even had Betty's cedar "hope" chest in the back seat! I

been there, done that!

prayed that her hopes and dreams would now come into fruition when we drove away from Chicago.

Now we had to get our presents out of Betty's parents' car and into ours, so they drove us to the garage—which they didn't even know about. While we loaded the presents, they scribbled "Just Married" on the back window and taped some decorations on the car. After some quick goodbyes, we were off. We spent the first night in a local motel, and then left the next morning to head north and west across the country to Fort Lewis in Washington state to continue my military duty. We stopped at the Wisconsin Dells for about a day since it was right on the way and then proceeded on our short honeymoon. But that has turned out to be a long and wonderful "honeymoon" by going many exciting places (87 nations for me and 57 countries for Betty) in all our married years — fifty-eight in 2022!

FIRST HOME AT THE END OF A RUNWAY

It wasn't much to carry a young bride across the threshold into, but I had bought a small, used, but well-kept 8x35-foot house trailer as our first home near Fort Lewis just south of Tacoma, Washington. It was cozy, but it was ours and we had no debt on it! While there, Betty got a job at the local hospital and passed her nursing board exams to become a full-fledged registered nurse.

Our mobile home was at the end of the runway of McChord Air Force Base, which was home to the very large, two story, propeller driven, Air Force C-124 cargo aircraft. The planes had not gained much altitude as they lifted off the runway and rumbled over our trailer early in the mornings, rattling and shaking our place enough to wake us up. We lived in that little home for about ten months prior to my first deployment to Vietnam.

Betty has always made our house into a real home wherever we were! I am so glad that those guys encouraged me to stay with them at West Sub Hospital that day in 1961 when I first saw Betty. I really appreciate my wife for her devotion, resilience, and support when her own family background would not have anticipated such diverse experiences for her. She has always supported me in my military career and in times of separations caused by my military assignments and duties.

She has been a solid rock in places of shifting sands pushed by a variety of trials and raging storms in life. She has endured without complaint two bouts with cancer—separated by twenty-five years! She has been a strong and influential parent to our three, now-married children and our eight grandkids. Together, Betty with our children and their families have provided background and depth to many of my experiences in one form or another. They continually provided encouragement and support to me, even when it may not have been to their advantage. In their own ways, Betty and our family have taught me and helped me become the man that I am.

PART II

AMERICAN BY BIRTH—SOLDIER BY GOD'S CHOICE

II

AMERICAN BIRTH—VOLUME

BY GOD'S CHOICE

CHAPTER VI

MILITARY TRAINING AND EDUCATION

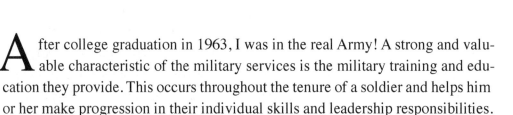

After college graduation in 1963, I was in the real Army! A strong and valuable characteristic of the military services is the military training and education they provide. This occurs throughout the tenure of a soldier and helps him or her make progression in their individual skills and leadership responsibilities. It is available to all ranks of personnel and happens on military bases and in civilian-related industries or schools. I am thankful for the training and education provided to me during my twenty-six-year career.

"TURTLE" TIME

My first assignment after college graduation in June 1963 was to Fort Benning, Georgia, where I would attend the three-month Infantry Officer Basic Course. I had chosen to be commissioned in the infantry because it was the Army branch designated to Find, Fix, Fight, and Finish the enemy—which probably doesn't really fit the image of a missionary kid from the heart of Africa! From there, I would proceed to nine weeks in the Ranger School for special operations training. Airborne School to learn parachuting skills followed and was only three weeks long. While waiting for my schools, I was given some interim duties at the post. Because time seems to go so slow for an individual in a waiting period, a nickname given to these waiting soldiers is "Turtle". A variety of miscellaneous duties are assigned to these individuals.

One day while walking to the office, I had a rather shocking and eye-opening experience. Coming toward me on the sidewalk was a sergeant in the Women's Army Corps (WAC). She was short and a little on the stocky side. As she approached, she snapped up a sharp salute and loudly stated, "Good morning,

SIR!" I guess that I was somewhat stunned and briefly hesitated from what should have been an automatic return salute of acknowledgment. Previously, I had not even seen a woman sergeant, let alone been saluted by one! I had been taught to respect women and had not thought about them being subordinate in the military and that they would salute me. I quickly got my act together, realized that this would be the norm, and saluted. That was the first of many new experiences for this new, "green, butter-bar" lieutenant—as we were often called.

Most of my duties in those days of waiting for my class were fairly routine and administrative. One, however, was rather unique. I was assigned to be the escort officer for four Greyhound busloads of newly-graduated, gung-ho, parachute-qualified, enlisted soldiers to take them from Fort Benning, Georgia, to Fort Campbell, Kentucky, where they were being assigned to the 101st Airborne Division. I made all the detailed plans for the convoy trip: got the buses, arranged the departure time and my return, contacted the mess (dining) hall for box lunches, and set up appropriate communications—this was prior to cell phones! We got off to a good start at 5:00 a.m. and made excellent progress initially. For a couple of the larger towns, I had called ahead for a police escort so that our buses could stay together but in others, stop lights and crossroads temporarily separated our convoy. Then we had to reconnect outside of town.

There were no rest stops along the roads we were traveling or any places big enough to handle the personal needs of about 200 men, so we would stop the buses alongside a heavily wooded road and the soldiers would head into the trees. We were not using any of the few interstate roads, and there were no fences bordering the roads. Some stops became rather lengthy as our bus sergeants had to find and then ensure their troops were all back on the buses.

Shortly before noon when many of the troops had eaten their box lunches, I was notified that a couple of soldiers on one of the buses had gotten very sick—but not with motion sickness. Then others on different buses showed the same symptoms. I contacted the nearest town and found a hospital where I left a couple of the men and a sergeant. As we moved further up the road, more got sick, and I had to leave others at different hospitals. I notified authorities at Fort Campbell that we had a number of sick soldiers and that I had left eleven of them in towns along our route. One of the hospitals reported to me that food poisoning was most likely the cause of the sickness. Apparently the box lunches were the cause, so for those who had not yet eaten, I told them not to eat because of the potential problem. I had already eaten my lunch and wondered if I would end up being one of the sick ones. Thankfully, my lunch did not adversely affect me.

Upon arriving at Fort Campbell after more than a ten-hour trip, senior sergeants at the reception station starting barking orders at "my" troops as they got off the buses. About half of the soldiers were very weak (although not sick enough to leave in a hospital) and stumbled off the buses, yet the sergeants kept pushing them to pick up their duffle bags and double-time away from the area. Because of the sickness, some could hardly walk, let alone carry their bags, and yet the sergeants kept shouting at them to get moving. Finally, this young second lieutenant had to step in and stop the action and explain how sick many of the troops were. I know those crusty, hardened sergeants didn't like these orders from a new, butter-bar lieutenant, but they did respond and began to show some compassion. Welcome to the real Army, Lieutenant Fogle!

My task was not yet complete, however, as I had to account for the sick soldiers whom I had left in hospitals along the way. I got with a representative from the Fort Campbell hospital, gave him all the necessary details, and wrote a report for him. On the plane back to Fort Benning, I wrote a full after-action report to give to the commander there. Fortunately, all the sick troops recovered, but there was quite an investigation into the entire episode. This was my introduction to several new aspects of the Army of which I was neither aware nor trained in ROTC. All of this was in my first month on active duty!

INFANTRY OFFICER BASIC COURSE

The Infantry Officer Basic Course (IOBC), in 1963, was very professional and provided valuable information and training for my career. My class was comprised of ROTC Distinguished Military Graduates from colleges and universities across the US and graduates from the United States Military Academy at West Point, New York. The big difference between the academy lieutenants and the rest of us was that they were all sporting new cars—and some were really top-of-the-line vehicles! (They were obviously paid well while in the Military Academy.) I soon found out that although they were from West Point, they were really no better than those of us who graduated through ROTC. Like in any group of people, some of military academy graduates had excelled near the top of their 1963 class, and others had not done so well! All of us from the colleges and universities were at or near the top of our cadet classes, and some of the West Pointers were from

been there, done that!

the bottom of their class, yet they seemed to be treated as "prima donnas" just because they had a military academy diploma and commission.

My roommate was that robot-like, super soldier, and friend (Wally) from DePaul University against whom I had competed many times in ROTC drill meet events. And again, he beat me as he was number one in the class of almost 200 lieutenants and, much to my disappointment, I ended up in second place. The ROTC students had excelled over the graduates from West Point! Wally was so good in everything military related—academics and field training! He was an excellent friend and military model. The IOBC was a good refresher of what I had been taught so superbly in ROTC at Wheaton, plus it added much more hands-on experience with equipment in the field.

I was very grateful for a couple of the West Point lieutenants in my class who introduced me to the Officers Christian Union (later Fellowship). They invited me to an OCU Bible study and explained that the organization was on many military bases and could provide great spiritual growth and wonderful relationships. This Bible study group was for military officers and their spouses and gave us a real break from our military training. Through that OCU group, I was invited to be a Sunday School teacher at the base chapel and loved that outreach during the time I was at Fort Benning. We always enjoyed the fellowship in OCU groups in several locations where I was assigned, and I keep up with its ministry today.

This initial military course was intense! We had 906 hours of actual training in the nine-week period! On top of that, we had our own personal preparations of shining our brass and spit polishing our shoes and boots although about halfway through the course, most of us paid to have the spit polishing done by some community people. In our allotted "free" time, we had to eat, occasionally shop, get our uniforms to the cleaners for laundering and starching, study, and get some sleep. I averaged about five hours of sleep a night throughout the IOBC, so I guess my four hours average in college was good preparation.

AN EXPLODING LATRINE!

One of the funniest things—at least to those of us not involved—happened on a rifle range at Fort Benning. Our IOBC class had been taken to the range in a "cattle car," an open semi-trailer with bench seats along the sides and down the middle. After our briefing in the bleachers, some of us were on the firing line, getting ready to shoot at variable-range targets when there was a huge explosion behind us. Turning around to look, I saw splinters of wood flying in the air and a lieutenant with his pants down and covered in "filth". He had gone to the latrine (outhouse) and decided to light up and smoke while sitting in there. When he was done, he threw his still-lit cigarette down the hole between his legs and the methane gas in the hole exploded! He was taken to the hospital to be cleaned up and splinters pulled out from his "you know what". Fortunately, he was not seriously hurt and returned to the rifle range later in the morning as a rather embarrassed (and bandaged) lieutenant. Lesson learned and confirmed: Smoking can be dangerous to your health!

RANGER SCHOOL

After graduating from IOBC, the nine-weeks-long Ranger School was next on my military timeline. It is one of the Army's elite training courses. The school's tough, challenging program is designed to ensure that only those individuals with extremely high physical and mental durability supporting their military skills could qualify for the "Ranger Tab" for the uniform and fulfill the missions of a special operations soldier. Ranger school would be a real confidence builder for me. I knew that if I made it through that course, I could probably do most things in an Army career.

PHASE 1 — PERMISSION TO DROP

The first three weeks of Ranger School were at Fort Benning, Georgia. We were assigned a Ranger buddy with whom we would always train together, sleep and eat together, and account to each other during the course. My Ranger buddy was D, a US Military Academy graduate. We made a great team. In these three weeks: we learned and were grilled and tested on the basics of patrolling; training was conducted to push us to our physical limits; we learned how to use explosives for the destruction of bridges or other structures; we practiced fierce, hand-to-hand combat and bayonet usage; instructions were given in swimming in our uniforms and with our rifle; survival skills were taught; and our leadership was confronted and evaluated.

Our confidence was challenged early in the course. On the bank of a large pond, we had to climb a vertical telephone pole to a small platform approximately forty feet above the ground. From there, we had to balance ourselves and walk about thirty feet on a horizontal log at that height over water out to another small platform on another vertical pole in the water. In the middle of that horizontal log were two wobbly steps you had to go up and down without hanging on to anything! From the pole in the water, a long rope with a Ranger sign in the middle extended horizontally toward shore. The object here was to monkey climb on the rope to slap the Ranger sign and then loudly proclaim to a cadre member on shore: "Ranger Fogle requests permission to drop." At the instructor's desire, he could let you hang there a while or give his quick permission at which time you let go of the rope and dropped approximately thirty feet into the deep water and swam to shore.

Think about this: When a Ranger drops from that rope, it causes the vertical pole in the water to wobble, which also causes the horizontal log with the steps to move, and anyone on that log is going to have to be careful that he does not fall off. Yes, it was scary up there on that log with nothing to hang on to! If you touched the log with your hands to gain balance, or if you fell off, you had to start all over again. Thankfully, I made it through that entire challenge on my first attempt, although a number of others took several tries to get to the Ranger sign and drop into the water. If a person could not complete this confidence-building event, he was eliminated from the Ranger program. I recently noted that the telephone poles of my day have been replaced with steel beams, flat surfaces, and a much sturdier structure. How times have changed for military training!

One portion of this phase of Ranger training was a 10,000 meter (about six and a quarter miles) night compass course. Not only did we have to navigate through the dense underbrush and "wait-a-minute" thorny vines, but we had to be stealthy to avoid "enemy" aggressors who were trying to capture us and treat us as prisoners of war! D, my Ranger buddy, and I didn't get caught and were one of the first teams to arrive at the finish line before dawn after having been out in the night's deep blackness for less than eight hours! Some of the teams didn't finish within twelve hours, and one team got completely lost and was found back near the beginning drop-off place. I can brag a little and say that both D and I were good with the compass and the necessary pace counting to find our way to scattered navigation instruction points to get to the next of the ten points during the night.

Because we would be involved in water operations later, we all had to pass a swimming and water survival test. Swimming has never been my thing, and my float level had always been about two feet below the surface of the water. The jellyfish float was one of the tests where we were to be in the water while wearing our field uniform and boots. A large breath was supposed to hold us up where our backs would be just above the water's surface. In my case, my float level was below the surface, and the instructors hollered at me several times to float higher in the water. I remembered that I had the lowest lung vital capacity score in my high school biology class, and it certainly was showing up in this floating test. I just didn't have big lungs. Finally they got the picture that I was not "floatable" but let me pass anyway.

Another water test was to climb up onto the ten-foot high diving board at a swimming pool. In turn, the instructors blindfolded each of us and guided us to walk off the end of the diving board—with all of our equipment on and carrying our rifle! When we hit the bottom of the pool, we could remove the blindfold, get out of our equipment harness, hang on to our weapon, and swim to the edge. That part was not so difficult, but it was rather frightening to walk off the diving board—blindfolded!

One last test was that we were to swim the eighty-foot length of the pool in our uniform and boots while carrying our rifle! The easiest way to do that for most of us was to use the sidestroke. The only problem for me, again, was that I didn't float, so I just swam underwater and would come up for a breath as needed. Every time I surfaced, an instructor would loudly shout at me to stay on top of the water. How could I—especially with the rifle and wet uniform weight added to my own? When I exited the other end, I had to convince the cadre that the requirement was to swim to the other end, and how I did it had not been defined. Anyway, I passed the overall swim test but was designated a weak swimmer—which actually I appreciated because with that designation in luminescent tape on the back of my patrol cap, others would look out for me when in the water.

An unusual aspect of the Fort Benning training was that occasionally in the woods, there were patches of soft, sucking muck! On one patrol, I was designated as the radio-telephone operator, so I was carrying the twenty-six-pound radio in addition to my own pack. Normally, a patrol navigates in a single file and at one point; I slipped off a log and stepped into some of that muck. I could not get out on my own and had to remove my pack and radio. Then trying to get out of the muck, it pulled my boot off. Oh, what fun I had trying to recover my boot and finish the patrol walking in soggy, very muddy boots!

Some of our patrols were quite lengthy. I quote from one of my letters to Betty while in Ranger School: "Talk about tired! Some of us did not have any sleep in over forty-eight hours. We got back here and had a debriefing and critique and after showering and shaving, crawled (almost literally) into the sack. We had been on our feet for fifty-four hours, and our feet are really sore now from going up and down, sideways, and every other direction." We were told that this kind of endurance training was to test our reactions and leadership under adverse and extreme conditions. Thankfully, my Ranger buddy and I made it through this phase to move on to the next phase of training.

PHASE 2—SADDENED—YET HAPPY

Having successfully passed Phase 1 of Ranger School at Fort Benning, our class got in the back of two and a half–ton (deuce and a half) or five-ton trucks for a long, tactical ride to the Dahlonega, Georgia, northern Ranger Camp for another three weeks. Here we would be exposed to mountaineering skills and cold weather operations. We were now into the second week of November and located just south of the Tennessee Valley Divide where we lived in eleven-person tents. A small, oil-fired, pot-bellied stove in the tent gave us a little bit of heat in that cold environment.

Most of our mountaineering training was on Yonah Mountain, a few miles away. There we learned varying kinds of rope knots and their uses. That knowledge was necessary for our cliff-rappelling and climbing exercises as well as our mountain, medical evacuation training. We learned cliff casualty evacuation by riding piggyback, carrying your buddy, or by riding as a litter casualty or guiding a litter down the face of the mountain's steep walls. Rappelling was rather fun, going over the edge, jumping out from the rock face, free rappelling from an overhang, and zipping down to the bottom of the cliff. I did not enjoy the climbing as much as the rappelling. But we had to learn how and where to use pitons (a metal spike hammered into a crack or seam in a rock wall to act as an anchor place) which we would hook into for safety and assistance as we ascended the steep mountainside, traversed overhanging outcrops, and climbed vertical rock faces. These activities were real confidence builders as my Ranger buddy and I increasingly learned to trust each other's abilities and strengths.

Patrolling in the mountains was so very different from the rolling terrain and thorny thickets of Fort Benning. The vegetation was not as dense, and young saplings could cause a real problem. Often a Ranger patrol moves in single file, and most operations are at night. Every soldier in the patrol had a sequential number to help keep track of each other and for use as a control measure when the patrol was stopping or moving at night. Before beginning a move during an operation, the patrol leader would ask for a "count-off" to ensure everyone was awake and ready to go. The last man in the file was usually the assistant patrol leader, and upon getting the count, he would communicate to the leader near the front of the column that all were present and accounted for.

It was common in the darkness to accidently straddle those small, two-to-three-inch-diameter saplings and catch it so that it wouldn't rebound and hit the soldier behind. However, on one of the count-offs, we discovered that one number was missing. After a couple of rechecks, we still were short a man. At that point, the patrol operation was stopped by the cadre member accompanying our patrol until we could find the missing man. Light discipline was negated, and before long we found him unconscious about twenty feet down the mountainside. He had been hit by one of those rebounding saplings and rolled down the mountain! He was evacuated by helicopter, and then we continued our patrol's mission. Everyone was even more careful about those saplings after that scare!

Sometimes our patrols crossed from south to north over the Tennessee Valley Divide, and the temperature dropped 10–15°F into the freezing environment as we crested the ridgeline where we often encountered snow or sleet! Believe me, those were miserable hours in that cold for this soldier who had been raised in the southern Sahara Desert! Our final training patrol in the mountains was to cross over the big divide and destroy a communications site on a mountain across the valley. It was to be a three-day operation with no resupply available. The "hike" to the objective would be more than twenty-five kilometers (fifteen and a half miles) as the crow flies—not counting the additional distance of the ups and downs and on the mountainsides. We would carry three days of rations, a sleeping roll, cold weather gear, C-4 explosives, ammunition, water, our rifle, ropes and climbing gear, plus other smaller items of equipment. This would be a real test of our physical and mental abilities.

But now for some shocking news! Just after we completed our patrol rehearsal in the afternoon, we were given the news that President Kennedy, our Commander-in-Chief, had been assassinated in Dallas, Texas. Although no one was very eager to get on with the patrol, that afternoon was consumed with mock practice training of some of the details of how we would infiltrate to the target destination, destroy the structure with explosives, and silently exfiltrate back to base camp avoiding "enemy" aggressors along the way. There was a mixture of rain, sleet, and hail

been there, done that!

as we returned from this pre-patrol practice exercise to our tents before supper, which would be our last kitchen-prepared, hot meal prior to the intense challenge ahead of us. After supper we had our routine patrol inspection by the Ranger cadre to make sure no one was carrying any "snacks" and that we had all the equipment and rations we would need for the next three days. Morale was low because of the increasingly severe weather and the news of our president's death. We then went back to our tents to wait our departure time.

Then as a huge and unexpected surprise, one of the cadre officers came to our tent shortly before we were to depart on our patrol and announced that all training—military wide!—was cancelled for three days out of respect for our now-deceased Commander-in-Chief! Talk about an emotional swing—we were deeply saddened by the news of President Kennedy's death, but on the other hand, we were so happy and relieved that we didn't have to go on that potentially miserable patrol! It rained and sleeted and snowed on us for almost the entire three training "holidays," and we could hardly imagine what it would have been like out there in that depressing weather and crossing the Tennessee Valley Divide into the colder north country.

That little pot-bellied, oil-fueled stove became a real friend as we huddled around it in our tent to try and stay a little warm from the outdoor environment. We got to know each other quite well through the many stories that were told. Taking away a little of our happiness three days later, we were told that the patrol objectives and time length had been modified and that we would still have to fulfill the training requirement. So—get ready for another patrol inspection. The past and current weather added to our lack of enthusiasm as we climbed up the mountain and felt the sting of the north side of the mountain's bitter cold. The patrol went fine, but no one had their heart in it. I was glad that I was not chosen as one of the patrol leaders for that mission. It would have been a tough leadership responsibility. That training exercise ended our three-week mountain phase of Ranger school.

PHASE 3—WHERE'S THE SHIP?

The next three-week phase of Ranger training was in Florida's western panhandle at Eglin Air Force Base. It was now the beginning of December, and what we thought was going to be warmer weather did not turn out that way! The winter before this 1963 winter, several of the Ranger trainees received severe cold-weather injuries in Florida and had to stop their training and be recycled into another class. The cadre felt this was an anomaly, and by adding some extra precautions, they felt that training could proceed as in previous years. The safeguards didn't prove to be enough, however, as several in my class also suffered cold-weather injuries—primarily because we were wet most of the time! Common sense would have dictated that cold-weather injuries should have occurred in our previous phase in the mountains, but here we were casualties of the cold in "sunny" Florida. Our training now consisted of swamp operations, small boat training, water navigation skills, more survival training, river crossings, and stealthy attacks over the beach from a ship at sea. Most of the time, we would be cold and miserable in our wet, field uniforms!

During the swamp operations, we thought it practical to try and always put the taller guys on point or up front while heading toward an objective through the swamp. That way, the rest of us would know when there was a drop off or deep water if we saw the tall guys' hats start to float away after they stepped into a deep spot! I was glad that I was not one of the tall guys!

Some days were extra cold and I actually appreciated being in the warmer-than-air swamp water. Some in our class were afraid in the swamp because of rumors they had heard about snakes and alligators, but frankly, that was not a significant concern to me. My greater concern was tripping over a root and going under! In the training, we would often traverse several hundred yards of chest-deep swamp water before hitting an objective and then walking several more hundreds of yards to reach a river flowing before us. There we would have to construct a rope bridge or make rafts out of our ponchos and equipment to cross the river to reach our next objective. Sometimes the shivering from the cold—yes, we were in Florida but it was cold!—seemed to be the only thing keeping us awake after days of practicing a combat patrol with very little nourishment or sleep. The Ranger instructors were always conscious of the potential of hypothermia and watched for early stages of it among all the Ranger trainees.

At times the mission was to go through the swamp to get to a small knoll and lie there quietly on a reconnaissance mission. On one operation, my Ranger buddy and I completed our reconnaissance where we had been for several hours on a little "dry" spot in the swamp. We were watching some "aggressor" activity and making reports to higher headquarters. Upon moving we realized that our field uniforms had frozen. We could actually break the ice off our clothes! That is probably the day that my toes became frostbitten. A couple of days later I found my toenails all black and had to get some medical treatment. Thankfully, that did not make me lose any training time, or I would have had to be recycled to a later class. My toes have been extremely sensitive to anything—cold, hot, or rough surfaces—since that frostbite. Others from our class experienced the same or other cold-weather injuries. Because the previous year's winter class suffered similar problems, I learned later that the Army modified both the timing and some of the training for all upcoming winter classes so that such cold-weather injuries would not happen to future Rangers in training.

The river crossing training involved two aspects. One was to build a couple varieties of rope bridges—some at water level and others were from high ground across a ravine. We all had to use each bridge we built to cross over the water or ravine and come back to the original bank. By doing this, we gained confidence in our ropes, knots, and safety procedures.

For the second portion of our river crossing training, each Ranger buddy team was to make a raft out of our ponchos, put *all* of our clothes, boots, equipment, and weapons in that poncho raft and swim down river with it to an exit spot. So, while making our poncho rafts, all of us were working stark naked out in the woods next to the river. Each of the Ranger buddy teams then had to wait with our raft until it was our turn to launch and swim with it in the river. By now, all of us on the river bank, being completely bare, were turning blue with huge goose bumps because the temperature was only 38°F degrees! Brrrr! The river water was actually warm compared to the outside air and it wasn't too bad swimming fifty meters downstream with our raft to the exit point where we quickly dried off and put on our clothes again. Oh, did that ever feel good to be in dry clothes and my warm field jacket! Fortunately, our poncho raft didn't leak as some of the others did!

As part of our survival training, we were taught to identify plants which were edible and how to cook them if necessary, what vegetation could be of medicinal use, and to recognize poisonous or dangerous flora. We also learned how to make various snares and traps for animals and the best places to put those. For practice, we killed snakes and turtles from the swamps and cooked them for eating. We didn't go after the alligators from the swamps—although they would have been delicious and would provide lots of meat! Today, I would not trust my memory of some of those survival skills if I were suddenly alone in the jungle for an extended period of time.

Being a Ranger meant that we could be called upon for a variety of special operations missions. This could involve small boat operations, so some of our training was with large rubber rafts for over-the-shore actions. Our major patrol operation with these rafts was from a ship approximately five miles out in the Gulf of Mexico south of Eglin Air Force Base in Florida's panhandle. Our mission was to launch from the ship, paddle the five miles to a barrier island, cross its large sand dunes carrying our raft, launch again on the north side of the island, make a landing on the mainland and hide our raft, attack inland to destroy a facility, and reverse our course out to the ship.

At night, we loaded our equipment and weapons over the side of the ship into the rubber rafts and tied it all in. Our patrol size needed three rafts with each carrying about ten men. At the particular nighttime hour, our rafts were released from the side of the ship. The gulf was rather rough, and rain was beginning to fall. Suddenly, a wave hit one of our three patrol rafts and it completely flipped,

been there, done that!

dumping all its Rangers into the water. (Fortunately, all their equipment was properly tied in, so none of it was lost.) Our teams in the other two rafts were told to continue on our mission while the ship's crew rescued the soldiers from the water and took them back aboard ship. The next day, we would connect with them when they were brought with their raft to the shore where we were in hiding.

We paddled our raft for a couple of hours with the wind behind us and finally hit the barrier island. We couldn't believe how heavy the raft with all our equipment was as we clamored over the high sand dunes, got back on the water, and eventually landed on the mainland—all at night. We hid and camouflaged our raft and then hunkered down for the day while waiting and continuing to plan our attack for that night.

Everything went fine during the attack. We successfully accomplished our mission and quickly retreated to recover our well-camouflaged raft. Crossing back over the island's dunes, we headed out into the gulf toward the mother ship. This time, the wind was in our faces, and the paddling was much more difficult. It seemed that with every stroke, we lost progress instead of moving forward but in the middle of the night, it was difficult to know. All we could do was to continue rowing and dig deep with our oars, causing extreme fatigue in our arms. The night was pitch black with a heavy cloud cover, but our compasses indicated we were headed in the correct direction toward the ship. In those days, hand-carried GPS didn't exist!

We were supposed to be back to the ship by 5 a.m. and after paddling for three hours, it was now around 4 o'clock, and we could see no sign of the ship. It was on blackout status and could not emit any signals, and we began to doubt our compasses. Where's the ship? That question was constantly on our minds. Here we were way out in the gulf, not knowing exactly where we were, and fearing that the ship would soon leave its position. Yes, we were all concerned as we continued to paddle harder and harder against the wind and the waves. But we were taught to trust our compasses and each other. About fifteen minutes before our deadline, we finally saw a silhouette on the horizon and hoped that it was our ship. Sure enough, when we got closer, we recognized it, got on board, and stowed our raft and equipment. What a relief we felt—but on the other hand, one of our patrol's rafts had not yet arrived! It wasn't until after daylight that a brief helicopter search found the other raft which was still quite a distance from where the ship was anchored. At least in the end, we were all safe with many stories to tell. I have never been a water-loving guy and hope never to have a similar experience again out on the high seas. That was the last patrol exercise of our Ranger School. What a conclusion to the nine weeks of training!

Each patrol throughout Ranger School is designed to enhance leadership development. A Ranger must maintain a calm demeanor, even in the most challenging and probably hazardous mission. Rangers must develop into confident and competent individuals who can undertake timely critical thinking, make decisions, and take action in the most diverse situations. Common sense, employing Army doctrinal concepts, must be used to solve tactical problems in spite of the potential inherent risks of injury or loss. A leader must contemplate the end result and worthiness of the cost in relation to mission accomplishment and victory versus defeat. A person in charge must accept and manage risk while also controlling the use of allocated personnel and other assets.

We learned that care of our men and accomplishment of the mission must be uppermost in our minds, regardless of the tough environment or terrain, the lack of time to sleep or eat, and personality conflicts in leadership challenges. Ranger training clearly taught us that leadership is a critical characteristic necessary in all of life's situations, whether that is in an administrative role or serving in a significant, tactical combat situation. Leadership for each of us in Ranger school was tested in various ways and under varying circumstances as we were rotated through numerous positions within our patrols and larger units. Errors in decision-making by a leader in Ranger School always impacted subordinate personnel, but thankfully in training, this was temporary in nature since a new leader could be designated at any moment by the cadre who were always with us. The instructors were continually evaluating each of us, and in the end, their evaluations determined if an individual would pass the course, be eliminated from the training at any moment in the nine weeks, or recycled into another class. In real life, however, leadership is generally not as temporary, and it may make or break an organization. It is a critical and dynamic element whether in combat, in a civilian organization, in a nonprofit ministry, or in government, as it brings together all the other aspects necessary to accomplish a mission. These Ranger lessons have stuck with me in my leadership roles in the military and in other aspects of life. I can't say that Ranger training was the most enjoyable experience of my life, but it was extremely valuable! I'm pleased to say that I have "been there, done that"!

We were bused back to Fort Benning from this Florida phase for graduation ceremonies. Everyone in our class was somewhat tense because we had not yet

been there, done that!

been told if we were going to get our Ranger Tab indicating that we had passed this nine-week training test. Already, more than ten percent of our class had been washed out of the program for a variety of reasons. The rest of us had to wait for our final individual evaluations by the cadre. When the graduation listing was posted, we noted that at least one third of the class did not pass and were either being recycled to another class or completely failed the course—even though our class had been comprised only of US Military Academy and distinguished ROTC graduates. Ranger School was indeed a tough challenge for the graduated lieutenants that year, regardless of the source of their commissions, and it definitely helped solidify my understanding of leadership.

Just a couple of days after Ranger graduation, I wrote the following in a letter to Betty. "Now I'm fully qualified [as a Ranger] and I have the tab. What a good feeling it is! I can't think of anything else that's been more challenging, difficult, and given me more hardships—such as: cold, wet, hunger, fatigue—than getting the Ranger Tab. But it was worth it and now that I look back and it's over, I think that I learned more than in 15–20 other officer courses. This was all so practical! The Ranger Department claims that we go through *more* than if we had been in three combat campaigns." (I would later be in numerous individual battles and later be in numerous individual battles (See map in Appendix D) and in five combat campaigns in Vietnam!) I was so emotionally and physically fatigued at graduation time in mid-December that a break before Airborne School was a needed welcome. For me, Ranger School was much more than techniques, tactics, operations, and survival skills in a jungle, in the mountains, or in or on the water. Ranger School was a great confidence builder for me! I am so thankful that I met the requirements and passed the course. I wear my Ranger Tab with pride!

AIRBORNE SCHOOL

Following Ranger School graduation in December 1963, I remained at Fort Benning, Georgia, since my next school in January 1964 was at that post to become trained in parachute operations. So much of that training was physical. We did lots of running, pushups, and pullups. For those of us who had just come from Ranger School, the physical exercises seemed like nothing, and our confidence had been developed to a point that we knew we could handle anything put before us. We had some Navy Seal guys in our airborne class and what a bunch of showoffs they were! They would run circles around us while we Army men ran in formation as we were told to do. Sometimes when a Seal was told to "Give me ten" (pushups!), he would respond with "Which hand, Sergeant?" and then would do twenty pushups. They were physically fit!

Airborne School taught all the proper techniques: for a parachute landing fall, for jumping out of the plane, for using the reserve chute if needed, for guiding the parachute, for jumping with equipment, and for preventing injuries. I was full of confidence just coming out of Ranger School and was not hesitant to do the practice jumping (with a static line) from the thirty-four-foot tower which simulated exiting an airplane. Nor was I reluctant to make the jump from the 250-foot tower, which was demonstrating how to steer the free-floating parachute and then make a proper parachute landing fall.

Speaking of that, every morning the school's cadre would raise a dummy (not a person!) to the top of the 250-foot tower to test the effect of wind on the drop. There was a big plowed circle at the bottom of the tower where a little softer landing was to take place. If the dummy landed outside the circle, no live-soldier jump could take place. On "our" jump day, the test dummy landed just inside the circle's edge, which meant that the rest of us could be pulled individually up to the top of the tower and make a practice parachute drop.

I was the first from my group (called a stick) to go up. The cadre was still discussing the wind issue but proceeded to pull me to the top even as the winds were increasing. Upon the release of my free-fall parachute, a gust of wind took me to a landing a few meters outside of the circle in spite of my tugging on one of the parachute risers to steer me back into the circle. I landed on the hard ground rather than on the softened dirt in the circle but nonetheless made a successful parachute landing fall. I was used as a guinea pig! No more jumps from the 250-foot tower were allowed that day since the strong winds persisted.

In our last week of Airborne School, we made our required five jumps to become airborne qualified. Three jumps were without equipment, one was with all our gear and our rifle, and one was a night jump. Except for my equipment jump, all of my jumps were uneventful. On that one jump, however, I happened to land in a small ditch in which I could not execute the proper parachute landing fall. Due to the wind in my chute, I came in backwards and went head over heels, knocking my helmet down over my eyes, and being dragged slightly.

In any landing, you are to immediately get back on your feet and chase down your chute to knock the wind out of it and wrap it up. I really struggled to get up on my feet out of that small ditch and must have looked quite funny in getting up a little, then falling back down a few times as the chute dragged me faster than I could get my legs under me. Finally I caught up with the chute and wrapped it up and ran off the drop zone.

I will forever remember the feeling of getting ready to jump while standing in the open door of an airplane. The wind seemed to push one cheek inside my mouth all the way over to the other cheek! And then taking that big jump out the door put my stomach in my throat as I counted "1001, 1002, 1003, 1004". My parachute opened properly but if the chute had not popped open by then, I needed to start thinking about pulling the cord on my reserve chute! But when my chute did pop, I felt the jerk, placed my hands on the risers, and looking up into the open canopy, I thought, "Oh, you glorious parachute!" Jumping is an exhilarating experience! Unfortunately, I was never assigned to an airborne unit—although I did volunteer several times—so I never parachuted again.

As part of airborne operations, some soldiers are taught how to pack the parachutes. There is a unique way to pack the canopy, all the cords that support it when it is deployed, and the risers that connect the parachute to the jumper. The nylon canopy must be able to fully deploy without any disruptions. The parachute packer must put his/her initials on each parachute they pack. Why? At any time, a senior person may come through the parachute warehouse, select a chute from the shelf, and call out the packer to go and jump with that particular parachute. If the chute should fail to open properly, the packer rather than another soldier would suffer the consequences. That fact keeps the packers honest and carefully paying attention to their work at the long tables where they fold and pack the chutes into their cases. I am not a parachute packer, but it does give a good lesson that we are always to do our best in order to make someone else successful.

Completion of that Airborne School qualified me as an Airborne Ranger, a highly respected, special operations officer because of the rigid and tough requirements to earn the wings and the tab. That training in the Ranger and Airborne schools instilled in me a strong confidence that I could do most anything I put my mind to complete. Challenges require taking risks of varying natures, and I had proven my ability to overcome these intense tests put before me. Becoming an Airborne Ranger certainly is among my most satisfying accomplishments.

I wore my Airborne Wings and my Ranger Tab on my uniform with pride and portrayed that through my constant "spit and polish" to keep my uniform looking sharp. I tried to keep my actions consistent with the honor I felt for my country when in my uniform. Occasionally, a soldier would ask, "What makes you so different, Lieutenant?" This was always a good opportunity to briefly share my faith as I would reply, "It is not what you see that I am wearing on my uniform but it is what is in my heart that makes me different." I tried never to say this in a boastful way but in such a manner that would give me further opportunity to share the Good News of the Gospel with another person.

OTHER SCHOOLS

The Army sent me to many other schools or courses which were all very useful in my career. I was thankful for each one of them, although some were quite challenging and academically competitive.

In the mid-1960s when the new replacement vehicle (M-151) for the old Army Jeep came out, my unit in Fort Lewis, Washington, sent me to a maintenance and driving course for this new vehicle. I was to come back then and train my organization's mechanics and drivers. You may ask: "Why the driving course?" The M-151 Jeep had independent suspension on each of its four wheels and experience showed that it was easy to roll it over if proper driving techniques were not used. Being safety conscious, the Army took precautionary measures to avoid casualties. I am happy that our drivers maintained their excellent safety record as a result of my instruction.

I guess the Army had plans to send me to a hot spot somewhere in the world when they chose me for a special school to learn a unique and classified code to use if I should be captured. The school was in California, at a Navy facility. We were a small class, but the sessions were very intense as we not only learned a specialty, hand-written code and its options, but we also spent a lot of time practicing writing letters and other communications using the code. Thankfully, I never had to use that code training in my Army years, and I certainly have forgotten all the code that I learned and could never use it or even explain it to anyone today. The type of code we were taught in those days preceded the use of all the electronic and ultra-secret technical systems used in the modern military forces. Cyber issues have completely changed some of the communications available and the methods which can be employed to transmit, receive, and analyze messages. Of course, if captured, a soldier will not have access to electronic systems and will have to rely on other communication resources.

After my second tour of duty in Vietnam and my nine months of hospital time after being wounded there (discussed in a later chapter), I was sufficiently recovered to resume assignments on active duty in 1970. I returned to Fort Benning, Georgia, for my next step in professional military education. This was the three-month Infantry Officer Advanced Course that was designed to prepare me for higher positions of responsibility of command and staff work. The Army had already told me that because of my wounds, I would not be assigned in the future to a position with a field infantry unit—yet that is what I was being trained for in this class which was a prerequisite if I ever expected to be promoted! Again, I graduated second in the large class. But now what would be my next step? I was given a three-week course on nuclear weapons employment—probably because I had previously commanded a unit with nuclear weapons and could do nuclear employment planning as a staff member. The class was very technical, and I really didn't enjoy it or ever benefit from it in future assignments, but at least I knew the terminology and procedures for use of nuclear weapons if our military needed me to use them in the future.

I did fine in that course, and while there, I got orders to Tulane University in Louisiana to pursue a master's degree in Operations Research/Systems Analysis. Why that subject? I hadn't had a math or statistics course since high school and really didn't like those subjects. I am not a technical or research-oriented person and wasn't interested in that type of work for the coming years. I told the Army Personnel Office that I could accept schooling in Operations Research/Systems Management at Georgia State University but that I did not want to take the first offer at Tulane. No slots were available at Georgia State University for the management course, so the personnel assignment officers said they would get back to me regarding my next assignment.

PUBLIC AFFAIRS SCHOOLS

Soon I got a notice that I would be going to the Defense Information School (DINFOS) at Fort Benjamin Harrison near Indianapolis. Following that school in 1971, I would be assigned to the Office of the Chief of Public Affairs for the Secretary of the Army and Army Chief of Staff in the Pentagon. That school sounded great to me! It was nine weeks of excellent education and training in news writing, radio and TV broadcasting, grammar (which I was generally quite good at), media relations, developing stories, community and industrial relations, managing media interviews, and communicating the Army story. I was the Distinguished Honor Graduate of this multiservice, multinational course. It was an exceptional school and prepared me very well for future assignments—although I didn't realize at the time that my next eighteen years would be primarily in various public affairs assignments—most of which were at the Pentagon!

In the summer of 1973, the Army sent me and several other officers to the University of Wisconsin in Madison to attend a graduate level Senior Public Affairs Officer School conducted for civilian and military personnel. The school had an excellent reputation, and some former military public affairs officers were on the faculty. However, that university had a history of its students protesting against military issues. Literally, it was a hotbed of anti-military, anti-war protests. In fact, the students had set fire to one of the buildings which housed an Army research contract. As military officers going to the school, we were told that we were to avoid any appearance of being in the military and were given permission to start growing our hair longer, wear beards or mustaches, and wear only casual clothing. I had been wearing my hair rather short and began letting it grow out a couple of months before going to the school and looked and felt somewhat out of place while working in the Pentagon. (When the school was finished, I was wearing quite an Afro hairdo which was changed to a typical military cut as soon as I left the university campus!) I was a captain, and a lieutenant colonel was also in the class. We became strong competitors in the class. He was rather disappointed that I beat him out as the top graduate. When he later became my boss, I began to wonder if I would regret that I had bested him in the class. But he never held it against me, and in fact, we were good friends. He ended up retiring as a major general and the commander of an Army post.

During my eighteen years in Washington, I completed (by correspondence) the Army Command and General Staff College, which took almost three years. Also (by correspondence) I passed a year-long course from the Industrial College of the Armed Forces which was part of the National Defense University. Portions of each of these correspondence courses required physical classes away from my assignments in the Pentagon. Both of these programs were precursors to eventual promotion and were part of the professional military education of the services. I am sure that in today's world, all of these courses can be completed online with the use of internet virtual services, which would eliminate the need for shipping books, other study materials, and in-class tests.

been there, done that!

HARVARD UNIVERSITY

My last significant education through the military was the Senior Officials in National Security (SONS) resident course at the John F. Kennedy School of Government at Harvard University in Massachusetts. Two to five people are selected each year by the Defense Department for this semester-long course. Many other civilians from industry, universities, government agencies, and other nations' leaders also attend the course. I was privileged to be one of those chosen in 1987. The curriculum teaches negotiation techniques and governmental relations between federal departments and with other nations. The primary method of instruction was through case studies, and the school brought in high-level US government and foreign national personnel as professors and guest lecturers. Students become role players in the case studies. Most often our class preparation required reading an average of about 400 pages each night. Knowing this, I had taken some speed-reading courses prior to going to the school so was somewhat prepared. However, what I didn't expect was the rapid deterioration of my eyes! (Upon my return to the Pentagon after the course, I had to get reading glasses to support my contact lenses and then I had to figure out how to carry those glasses around without bulging my pants or shirt pockets. That convinced me to get mono-vision contacts so that I didn't have to use the reading glasses.)

The SONS course proved valuable to me in Washington as I dealt with Congress, other federal departments, and within various offices of the Defense Department. But it has also been a valuable asset in my life in ministries following my military retirement.

The military recognizes the importance of continuing education and training throughout a soldier's career—regardless of an individual's rank or position. Although it is easier to document certain education than it is to quantify training, both are interwoven in the profession of soldiering. I am thankful for all the schools I was privileged to attend and the training I received while I was in the military through the courtesy of Uncle Sam. I am a better person because of it.

CHAPTER VII

MILITARY UNIT ASSIGNMENTS

FORT LEWIS, WASHINGTON

My first troop duty station after my initial infantry officer training was at Fort Lewis, Washington, where I was assigned in early 1964 to the Army's 4th Infantry Division. The post is known for its constant rain. In fact, when I was there, it seemed to rain whenever we were in the field—and that was most of the time since I was in an infantry unit! It seems that the only days we saw the sun were when we came into garrison for classroom training or doing maintenance in the motor pool! At that time, Fort Lewis was the only US Army post where US Navy wet-weather gear was issued to troops who would spend much of their time in the field. I felt somewhat strange running around with US Navy stamped on the rain jacket when I was in the US Army!

RIFLE PLATOON LEADER

My initial assignment was as the 2nd Rifle Platoon leader in B Company of the 1st Battalion, 22nd Infantry Regiment. (The historic regiment's history can be found on the internet.) For this being my first unit, I was very pleased to have a great mentor in my company commander. And I will never forget the excellent counsel of the sergeant major. He was the senior enlisted man in the battalion and liked to take all of us junior officers under his wing to make us better in our leadership roles. His advice was: "Listen to your NCOs (Non-Commissioned Officers). They have more expertise in handling troops than you do and have been around longer. They can help you to be a successful officer!" He also emphasized that I should always <u>strive</u> for perfection (although everyone knows we can never attain that status), be consistent and fair, and be aggressive in decision-making! His guidance concluded with: "Take care of your people, and they will take care of you". All that was wise advice for a new lieutenant, and I will always remember and appreciate his stimulating and passionate words. In my future assignments, I saw many instances of young lieutenants demonstrating their commissioned authority, without accepting the advice of an experienced NCO, to the detriment of the morale and efficiency of their unit. A rifle platoon had forty-two men, organized into three rifle squads and a weapons squad, which included machine guns. The platoon was the basic tactical maneuver element for the larger unit.

WEAPONS PLATOON LEADER

After a few months, I was given the leadership of the weapons platoon in the company. For the company's three maneuvering rifle platoons, this unit provided fire support with its three 81mm indirect fire mortars and a fire-direction center. Because of the weight and bulk of these mortars, the platoon had three-quarter ton trucks. The weapons platoon also had two antitank 106mm recoilless rifles mounted on jeeps. I learned the capabilities of my squads and the operation and tactical use of these weapons fairly quickly because I "listened to my NCOs" and let them train me, rather than me training them on the systems. I had studied the weapons in class and knew their capabilities, but I did not have experience to really know the operations of the weapons. I was to be the leader in the tactical employment of my men and their weapons, but they were the ones who actually fulfilled the mission. My experience in B Company was superior!

While in the infantry company, I was pleased that our higher headquarters would test its infantry soldiers' knowledge of skills needed in the performance of duties both in combat operations and when in garrison. Successful passing of the test's written and practical criterion would be recognized with the award of the Expert Infantryman Badge (EIB). The evaluation was conducted over a three-day period and consisted of a series of about thirty infantry tasks, ranging from land navigation, use of infantry weapons, tactics, casualty care, and completing a twelve-mile road march in under three hours. Out of the approximately two hundred soldiers who took the test, only eighteen of us passed! I was so pleased that my training and education, starting in ROTC, were sufficient for me to qualify for and proudly wear the EIB—a distinctive metal badge depicting a silver musket mounted on a blue field.

TRIAL AND DEFENSE COUNSEL

One of the unique experiences that many officers had in the early days of my Army career was to serve special duty assignments in the military justice system for soldiers in the battalion. The book explaining the justice system, and all the potential violations, is the *UNIFORM CODE OF MILITARY JUSTICE*. Military officers were appointed as judges, the jury, and could be either a defense or trial counsel. I was never a judge or on a jury, but I had the "privilege" to perform either the role of the trial or defense counsellor for several courts-martial of soldiers. Working through investigations, depositions, and prosecution and defense arguments became very difficult in some of the cases. I did not really enjoy those legal duties, which were in addition to my normal platoon responsibilities. Thankfully, in subsequent years, these responsibilities were transferred to appropriate military lawyers, and they are no longer additional duties for officers in the unit. However, a commander still retains authority to administer non-judicial cases and deal out appropriate punishment.

YAKIMA FIRING CENTER EXERCISE

I was recognized for my leadership in the weapons platoon and was selected to manage the entire division's live-fire exercise with the 81mm mortars when we went to the Yakima Firing Center in the heart of Washington state. The exercise was in the winter, and we had to convoy from Fort Lewis, Washington, in the more subtropical, west side of the state through the Snoqualmie Pass of Mt. Rainer to the desert region near Yakima. We were to convoy in a tactical manner, which meant that there would be no canvas overhead on our jeeps or trucks, and the front windshields would be folded down over the hood for the approximately 175-mile trip. Talk about cold! This young lieutenant, who had spent five years in the southern part of the Sahara desert (where the thermometer at our house often read 130-140°F!), was almost an ice block by the time we arrived at the training area. At least there was no snow—initially!

After a couple of nights out under the stars—we didn't use our pup tents—and doing some maneuvers both in the day and at night, we settled in one night

been there, done that!

and crawled into our Army-issued, down-insulated, sleeping bags. Early the next morning, I tried to roll over and found my bag to be very heavy. Poking my head out a little farther, I saw that five inches of snow had fallen overnight. I almost had to laugh as I looked out in the pre-dawn light and saw just a bunch of elongated humps where my troops were still sleeping. The snow had completely blanketed the ground and everything else—including us! It was really difficult getting out of that warm, insulated bag to get dressed and get my boots on! By noon, the sun had pretty much melted all the snow except in some of the lower or shadowed areas. Then the ground became mucky!

The two weeks of training at Yakima was to end with a division-level tactical exercise. From among the many other weapons platoon leaders in the division, I felt honored to be designated as the officer responsible for the live-firing of some of the division's 81mm mortars. Up to this time, I had managed only the three mortars in our platoon, but for this exercise I was in charge of fifteen more of them with their crews from different units! I was to have all eighteen of the mortars properly "laid" (aligned and ready to fire) by 8:00 a.m. for accurate live-fire on the target area. I left our encampment area in a convoy at 4 a.m. to get out to the firing site. I needed plenty of time to guarantee that all the mortars were properly placed and to double-check the proper alignment of the guns with my aiming circle (an instrument used to ensure the weapons are accurately aimed).

Because the terrain was in the desert and had no real roads, you could not easily follow the tire tracks in the sand and mud while it was dark and especially since we were using tactical blackout driving conditions. I had reconnoitered the route the previous day and successfully led my small convoy of around twenty vehicles to the mortars' firing position. Soon after our arrival, an extremely dense fog rolled in over the desert and reduced sight to no more than ten to fifteen feet. I was very thankful that we had beaten the fog to our location.

A LOST GENERAL OFFICER

Now here's the humorous part of this story! Because our mortar firing was a significant part of the exercise, one of the division's one-star generals was to oversee my operation and certify that all safety procedures were being followed, the weapons were properly aligned, and that the target area was cleared. About 7:30 a.m., the general had not yet arrived, and we were supposed to begin firing in a half hour. I knew he would want to check the proper alignment of the mortars and expected him to be at my position early. Soon, I received a call on his jeep radio from his aide. They were lost in the fog and wanted me to direct him in to our location. However, he could not tell me where he was out there in the wide-open desert area! The fog prevented his entourage from identifying any surrounding terrain features, and there were no real roads leading to our position. I could give him our accurate location by map coordinates but that was of no help if neither he nor I knew where he was! His aide and driver would have to figure out how to find us. I could not help the general and sort of laughed internally about the "lost" general officer. Again, in those days there was no GPS to guide them to my position.

Around 8:45 a.m., the general finally showed up—and was not in a good mood and seemed to try and blame me for his problem of being lost in the fog. I was prepared to escort him to my aiming circle (the special instrument used for "laying the weapons") for him to check the accuracy of my positioning of the mortars. Instead of using my aiming circle, he told his aide to get his (the general's) aiming circle out of his jeep. He handed the box to me and told me to set it up for him. I had never seen that model, which was from a previous generation, so I quickly called my experienced platoon sergeant for help. He also had not ever used that obsolete model, so I went to the general's aide and asked him to guide us through the setup of the instrument. The aide pulled me aside and said the general had never showed him that particular piece of equipment! It was an ancient item that the general, as a former junior artillery officer, had used in one of his very early units and had kept it with him all these years while he rose through the ranks.

I finally went to the general and told him my predicament. Somewhat angrily, he came over to "show" me how to set "his" aiming circle up. Underneath my breath, I again snickered as he fumbled with the equipment. Finally in exasperation, he said the time was getting late and he would use my aiming circle to verify that the mortars were properly placed. Whew! The fog lifted and the firing finally took place after 10 a.m. What a show it was when eighteen mortars fired on the designated target, causing white phosphorus plumes, dirt and rock sprays from the high explosive rounds, and smoke to fill the skies about 3,000 meters (1.86 miles) away. The day ended well, but there were moments that morning when I wondered if my career was going to terminate immediately because I couldn't direct the general to my site and could not use his antique aiming circle. I escaped a general's wrath that day!

been there, done that!

HEAVY MORTAR/DAVY CROCKETT PLATOON LEADER

Perhaps because of my successful leadership of the multi-mortar firing at Yakima, I was transferred from B Company's Weapon Platoon up to our battalion's Heavy Mortar/Davy Crockett Platoon. This heavy mortar was a 4.2" diameter tube, indirect fire weapon that could place massive fire upon an enemy from a good distance behind our own front lines. Each mortar was carried in a three-quarter-ton truck and trailer because of the weapon's weight, along with its ammunition. The platoon had four of these weapons. It was the infantry battalion's own "artillery" support. The platoon's fire direction center in its own dedicated truck provided important technical data for the gunners about the target area and appropriate ammunition.

Perhaps the most unusual "gun" ever made for use at the infantry battalion level was the M28 and M29 Davy Crockett Tactical Nuclear Recoilless Guns, a Cold War–era weapon primarily designed to defend against Soviet aggression in Europe. The weapons could provide a devastating blow by an infantry battalion commander should the Soviets cross the line in an attack against our US forces. The 4"-diameter "Little" M28 Davy Crockett had a 1.25-mile range, and its bigger brother, the 6.1"-diameter "Heavy" M29 Davy Crockett, had a 2.5-mile range. Each weapon could be fired from a vehicle or from a dismounted tripod on the ground. The guns could fire sub-kilo-ton atomic fission warheads containing the explosive equivalent of ten to twenty tons of TNT. The guns proved to have poor accuracy in testing, so the warhead's greatest effect would have been its extreme radiation hazard rather than its explosive power. The round would produce an almost instantly lethal radiation dosage within 500 feet, and a probable fatal dose within a quarter mile.

Because these Davy Crockett weapons were nuclear systems, they required unusual security. Movement of the systems demanded a full infantry company to accompany our travel. Going to the field for training with these weapons was always a logistical nightmare. On one training occasion with all the security and adherence to technical procedures, we placed a bulbous dummy practice round on the gun tube. The command finally was given to fire. The practice warhead flew—about twenty-five feet!—and landed with a thud. Were we ever happy that warhead was not the real thing! If so, I would not be here to tell you about it! The Davy Crockett system was removed from the Army's inventory in 1971—having only a short fifteen-year lifespan in the Army.

ORDERS TO VIETNAM

By the late spring of 1965, I had been with my battalion for about fifteen months. I was very pleased with the wide variety of assignments I had experienced so far, culminating as the Heavy Weapons/Davy Crockett Platoon Leader for a few months. In that position, I regularly worked with the battalion operations section to coordinate indirect fire support for the battalion's maneuvering companies. It was great duty and my military professionalism was enhanced.

We were on training maneuvers deep in the Olympic Rain Forest in the northwest corner of Washington state. One day while clamoring through the dense forest to find a firing site with sufficient overhead clearance for my heavy mortars, I received a call to report to the battalion headquarters. I wondered what the urgency was to pull me from the field. But I soon learned the answer as I was handed orders to be transferred to Vietnam. Where is Vietnam? I then recalled from my geography classes that Vietnam was the former French Indo-China in Southeast Asia. Why me? Questions were abundant.

DEPLOYMENT—WHERE SHOULD BETTY LIVE?

Betty and I were married in Chicago in August 1964, and our honeymoon was driving back to my duty station at Fort Lewis, Washington. About four months later, she became pregnant, and we were looking forward to a birth there in Washington. However in May of 1965, Uncle Sam interrupted our plans by issuing me orders to Vietnam. Now we had to expect a major diversion in our lives. Where would Betty stay while I would be gone overseas for at least a year? Would she continue to live in the Northwest US where we had no family? Would she live in the Chicago area near her family? Her extended family was very close knit with almost all of her aunts, uncles, and cousins living within a fifty-mile radius of Chicago where she grew up. They would expect her to settle near them. There was already some angst among her family members because Betty was the first of the family since World War II to marry a military man who took her away from the general homestead region. But now, where would Betty settle to have this newborn?

We drove from Washington state to Chicago to visit her parents. They immediately told Betty that she would live with them and that she could stay upstairs until shortly before the baby was to be born at which time she would move into the first floor den so she wouldn't have to climb steps. The den was very crowded; it only had curtains for doors and was only a few steps from her parents' bedroom door. They also said she would not be driving at night to go to church. Such potential "rules" just seemed to pile up. I believe this was all done because of their love for Betty and their desire to be with their first grandchild. They just wanted to protect her and the newborn. But to us, we knew the seemingly overbearing control wouldn't work.

After spending a few days with them, we went to visit my family in the South Bend, Indiana, area. Before we said anything about the likely difficulty of Betty living with her parents, my older sister suggested that Betty could live with her, her husband, and their two young kids. This would solve some of their babysitting problems because Lois worked evenings as a nurse and Jerry owned a gasoline/service station and often worked into the late evenings. Betty could care for the kids and prepare dinner for them and for Jerry when he came home. This sounded like a very workable solution to Betty and her housing needs. Another factor in our decision for her to stay in South Bend was that my home church was there, and I knew they would be a great support to her. Up to this point, we really didn't have a solution to where Betty would live while I was gone, but God clearly gave us His timely answer!

How could we break this decision to Betty's parents? They would think that we were trying to deny them the necessary care of their oldest daughter and first grandchild. There was already a rift between them and me (because I was a Christian believer, was in the military, and had taken their daughter away from the area) and now this would further antagonize the relationship. We carefully prepared our thoughts and then faced them with our decision and assured them that Betty would be only a couple of hours away and that visits could be as often as desired. This was the right decision for Betty, and we were assured that the Lord had planned this for her while I was gone. I left for Vietnam with great confidence in Betty's comfort and care at my sister's house.

CHAPTER VIII

FIRST TOUR IN VIETNAM

TWO BROKEN AIRPLANES

After tearfully leaving Betty, I flew commercially to San Francisco and transferred to Travis Air Force Base in California. There I waited for my flight to Vietnam, which became very interesting. We were to fly on a charter flight via Pan American Airlines. As the plane was coming in, I looked out the windows and saw firetrucks rushing to the runway where a Pan American plane was landing with an engine on fire. That was to be my plane, and we soon heard an announcement saying that our flight was delayed due to "maintenance" issues. Thankfully, I was not on that plane over the Pacific Ocean somewhere! A different plane was then ordered to come and take us to Vietnam.

We waited for approximately four hours in the passenger area of Travis AFB, and finally it was announced that our replacement plane was coming in. Again, I went to the window and watched. The rear wheels touched down, leaving their wisp of smoke and then the nose gear touched the runway and immediately collapsed! Was I really supposed to go to Vietnam? I began to wonder! Two Pan American planes had come for me, and two planes had major maintenance problems!

We were put up overnight at Travis and flew out the next day with a brief stopover in the middle of the night in Hawaii. Although the airport was empty, some Hawaiian ladies welcomed us and were there doing hula dances and brought leis and draped them over our necks. From there, we flew to Guam and finally to Saigon, the capital of South Vietnam. What waited for me now?

been there, done that!

One of my first surprises when arriving in Vietnam was the busyness of the streets. Motorcycles, mopeds, bicycles, small taxis, three-wheeled pedicabs, and old buses and trucks crowded the city streets. Everyone seemed to be honking their horns and hollering as hordes of pedestrians wove in and out between all the vehicles. Police in white uniforms (jokingly called white mice) tried to control traffic and appeared to me to be causing more confusion. I had not seen such traffic jams as there were in Saigon. What a mess!

A reception center provided accommodations for a couple of days during which I received briefings on the country's "do's and don'ts" and a little background of the developing war. I was also given my field gear and personal weapon, which I zeroed in at a nearby firing range.

REPORTING TO A FOUR-STAR GENERAL

The next day, two other airborne ranger lieutenants and I reported to General Westmoreland's office. The highest-ranking officer I had ever seen before was a two-star general, and now here was a man wearing four stars! General William C. Westmoreland was the commander of all US forces in Vietnam. The three of us first lieutenants smartly saluted as he rose from behind his desk. After putting us at ease, he discussed what our duties would be, and he made a point of telling us that we were the first three Army officers to be assigned to Vietnam in a "direct combat" role assignment with US soldiers. (I suddenly thought that this was the reason I had been sent to that special code school a few months earlier!) Up to this time, Army personnel were in the country as advisors, aviation support, logistics specialists, and other such support personnel for the South Vietnamese military forces.

Our mission would be to provide internal and external security for US Army airfields. Most of these were in the southern three military Vietnamese Corps areas. (See map in Appendix D.) The northernmost military corps was primarily the operational area of the US Marine Corps in those early days of the war. General Westmoreland explained the primary areas where we would have responsibilities—the delta with its rice paddies and rivers, the Saigon area and its urban environment, and the jungles of the highlands in central Vietnam. I knew I didn't want to be breathing through a rice straw while hiding in the waters of a rice paddy nor did I want the urban fighting in a guerilla warfare environment. I had grown up in the jungles in Africa, so I knew right away that if given the choice, I would go to the highlands of Vietnam.

The general asked who wanted to go where. I should have spoken up right then, but frankly, I was a little intimidated in the general's presence, and each of us lieutenants just stood there saying nothing. So, General Westmoreland said he would flip a coin. He reached in his pocket, pulled out a coin, flipped it and said: "Fogle, you call it!" I don't know what my call was but I won, and without any hesitation said that I would go to the jungled highlands. What a relief! Although I knew nothing about the terrain, density of the jungle, the nature of the enemy in that area, or how many Army airfields I would be supporting, I would be going to an environment in which I would be much more comfortable than in the other two regions.

The general emphasized to us that we would be under the operational control of a local aviation unit but that he was counting on us to provide complete physical security of the airfields in our area. The reason we were there, at his request to the Pentagon, was that earlier in the year, a number of our airfields had been attacked, and we had lost a considerable number of aircraft and other equipment. This was primarily due to the fact that basically only military police had provided security for the airfields, and that was all from inside the protective perimeter of barbed wire. The general wanted infantry men to go outside the airfields' perimeter wires and provide other security measures to find and destroy the enemy before they could attack our airfields again. He made it clear to us that he would support any requests through the chain of command from us for qualified personnel and any equipment we felt we needed to accomplish our airfield security mission.

52nd AVIATION BATTALION

I was assigned to the 52nd Security Detachment, which was under the operational control of the 52nd Aviation Battalion. The battalion headquarters was at Camp Holloway Army Airfield (near Pleiku), with some of its aviation elements scattered through the Vietnamese II Corps military region. (See map at Appendix D). At that time, the battalion was primarily in support of Vietnamese national military forces, which were advised by US Army personnel. Our aviation assets backed up the ARVN (Army of the Republic of Vietnam), local tribal Montagnard units (mostly advised by US soldiers in special forces camps), and the local

been there, done that!

regional force and provincial force troops (RF/PF). The aviation unit also provided airlift to clandestine operations since we were the major flying unit near the Cambodian and Laotian borders. Special forces units were scattered at various places in our area of operations. In later months, the battalion supported the Korean Division, which was nearer my east-coast security element. Eventually, my detachment helped build and provided security for two additional Army airfields in the east-coast area of the Vietnamese II Corps military responsibility.

Prior to 1966, the battalion had both fixed wing and rotary wing aircraft. On the fixed wing side, we had small L-19 Birddog spotter/observation planes, single-engine Beaver and Otter planes for carrying limited cargo or small numbers of personnel, Mohawk planes for intelligence gathering, and some Caribou and Buffalo planes for larger cargo and personnel loads. Sometimes I was asked to fly in the back seat of an L-19 to give another set of eyes when trying to spot enemy locations or activities. The L-19s had the capability to call in artillery fire or mark targets with smoke for air support and were an important asset of our team.

Much to our initial dismay, most all fixed-wing planes in the Army inventory were transferred to the Air Force in January 1966. These had all been used in a variety of ways to haul and support our Army troops, but now we no longer had direct control of them. There was a lot of angst about that decision, and it left some big holes in Army aviation capabilities and operational support. But we eventually got used to the new system of getting help from the Air Force and adjusted the use of our helicopters to meet our needs.

At that time, most of our helicopters were UH-1B "Hueys". But we did have a few of the twin-bladed, old H-21 "Flying Bananas" and the H-13 observation helicopters with their bubble cockpit. Later in my tour, we got some CH-47 Chinooks and the updated UH-1D Huey helicopters, which could carry more troops or cargo. Some of our UH-1B Hueys were then converted to have mounted machine guns or rocket launchers on their sides.

The Hueys all had door gunners with machine guns for more firepower going into landing zones (LZs), where it was known or suspected that the enemy might be. Occasionally, my troops were asked to be the door gunners but more often than not, my troops would go in with the first flights into the "hot" LZs (under enemy fire) to provide security for follow-on troop or command elements. On more than one occasion, we flew through the Mang Yang pass in the central highlands where at times, the North Vietnamese forces would shoot at our helicopter. Some of the most heart-thumping and heartbeat-skipping times I had were when the North Vietnamese fired ground-mounted, anti-aircraft fire at our helicopters. As those bullets passed by the helicopter, they looked like big fuzzy softballs. I was thankful that none ever hit an aircraft in which I was riding!

52nd SECURITY DETACHMENT COMMANDER

Upon first arriving at my new support base at Camp Holloway near Pleiku in the central highlands, I was somewhat surprised to learn that I had primary security responsibility for three airfields—the one at Camp Holloway which was my headquarters, one in Qui Nhon on the east coast, and one at Ban Me Thout to the south. I would be spending quite a bit of time flying back and forth to visit my troops at those sites. (See map at Appendix D.) Our aviation battalion had aircraft units at each of these locations. Each place was very different. Qui Nhon was very hot, and the area was not heavily vegetated because the people in this densely populated, coastal area had pretty much stripped the land to provide wood for cooking.

Ban Me Thout was cooler, had a lot of tea plantations, and was closer to the Cambodian border. This was the town where former President Theodore Roosevelt had chosen to build and use a beautiful teakwood hunting lodge. Our airfield there had tea plantations on three sides. These had often been used by the enemy as an attacking avenue of approach to the airfield. Ban Me Thout is also the town from which some Christian and Missionary Alliance missionaries were later captured and taken into the jungle as prisoners of the enemy forces. Some survived, and others died at the hands of the North Vietnamese.

Our airfield at Camp Holloway was in the middle of the Montagnard tribal region and we had good support from the Rhade and Jarai tribal groups. But it was also in the general pathway through which the North Vietnamese wanted to cut South Vietnam in half. The surrounding area was mostly triple-canopy jungle, and unit operations at that time were generally smaller.

I quickly learned that I was the only officer in the detachment of more than one hundred and fifty men almost all of whom were military policemen who were focused on security inside the airfields' defensive perimeter wires. They had little or no infantry training, which my troops would need to conduct patrolling operations outside the perimeter as General Westmoreland had ordered. The men's morale was low and, basically, they had little guidance or support when I arrived. The senior non-commissioned officer (NCO) was an E-7 platoon sergeant who also was a highly trained military policeman but with little infantry experience. There were a few indirect-fire mortars on the compound, but no one was trained to use them. That was the unit which I inherited.

After a few days assessing the situation at Camp Holloway, I flew to the other two airfields and found the same situation.

The aviation assets at each site were subordinate elements of the 52nd Aviation Battalion headquartered at Camp Holloway. Within a couple of days after taking command, I asked for a meeting with the battalion commander and his staff in which I said that even though I was only a lieutenant that I needed to be included in future staff meetings since I was now the primary person responsible for physical security at the commander's airfields. I would need the support of all of the battalion's subordinate leaders (who all outranked me!) to establish an effective security plan. In time, I also became a primary briefer for incoming VIPs, such as the Secretary of Defense and a couple service chiefs of staff, foreign dignitaries, and other civilians or multi-starred officers who came to our area.

I clarified to the battalion staff what my orders were from General Westmoreland and that I needed infantry troops to do infantry operations in the field and qualified mortar men to support my troops outside the wire. I said that I would not be able to provide the security I was ordered to provide if I could not get infantry-trained personnel. The commander supported my request, which was sent to higher headquarters. Within a month or so, infantrymen began to arrive, and the military police were assigned to other locations. We did cross-train a few of the military police to perform infantry duties.

THE GROWING ORGANIZATION

To relieve my infantry men from some of the internal security functions, I asked for a section of sentry dogs and handlers—especially for Camp Holloway. Sentry dogs are trained to viciously attack targets on their handler's command (by hand or voice signals) whereas scout dogs are trained differently to search out and help identify enemy personnel and positions outside the perimeter wire. We had to build appropriate kennels for the twelve dogs and ensure that dog food was ordered and that veterinary support would be available.

The sentry dogs were a great asset to our security operations. They are trained by attacking very heavily padded men in order to take down the person and hold them until their handler tells them to release. Most of my dogs were of the German shepherd breed and were trained to be very vicious. My largest dog could stand in his kennel and reach the top, which was eight feet above the ground. He weighed just over 120 pounds! That is a dog! I turned over most of the internal security patrolling to the handlers and their dogs, and they did a fabulous job! I think the word got out quickly one night when a Viet Cong enemy soldier tried to get through our perimeter's barbed concertina wire and immediately one of my dogs attacked him and tore his foot off. I am sure that his cries and the vicious growling scared off any other Viet Cong that may have been in the area that night!

To better "see" at night, I asked for a ground radar unit to be assigned to me. These radar elements could locate enemy action in both short-range and long-ranges, depending on the terrain and vegetation. I also requested six infrared searchlights (approximately twenty inches in diameter) which we would mount in reinforced towers to more rapidly spot potential infiltrators.

Initially, I had just a couple of 81mm mortars (indirect fire weapons) at each of my three locations. Having commanded a 4.2" mortar unit back at Fort Lewis, Washington, I knew their extended range capabilities and asked for eight of the heavy mortars and additional 81mm mortars. As my mortar men increased their skills, I realized our total security would be more effective if we could immediately

been there, done that!

identify enemy indirect-firing locations, so I asked for a counter-mortar radar unit to supplement my security plan. This radar could identify and pick up the trajectory of enemy incoming, indirect fires, and backtrack an enemy round, thus giving me the exact location of the enemy firing point. We then could react with our own mortars or troops and launch helicopter gunships if needed to destroy the enemy.

Thus, my unit of what had been about one hundred and fifty military police soldiers in three locations had now ballooned to more than two hundred twenty highly qualified men to accomplish our mission. They were all integrated into a tight security plan for each of my three locations.

Keep in mind that I was the only officer (a first lieutenant) in the unit, and my senior NCO was only an E-7 (sergeant first class). I had all the responsibilities for the personnel care, tactical operations, logistical support, clerical record-keeping and reports, training, and general administration, which would normally be required of a rifle company commander. A captain of a typical infantry rifle company (smaller than my command) would have five other officers, an E-8 (first sergeant) senior NCO, and many other well-trained junior NCOs. Normally, his troops would be in one general location—and mine were in three areas initially (separated by many miles)—but by the end of my tour, I had troops at five different Army airfields! I later learned that I was commanding one of the largest tactical detachments—if not the largest!—in the US Army.

Normally, an Army infantry rifle company has three 81mm mortars, and there are three or four companies in a battalion. In addition, a battalion's heavy mortar platoon has four 4.2" indirect fire mortars. For contrast, my 52nd Security Detachment had eighteen of the smaller 81mm weapons and eight of the big mortars. I had considerably more indirect fire power than a whole infantry battalion (about 800 men)—and my infantry capability was only a detachment of 180 men! My detachment also had a searchlight section, a ground radar unit, a counter-mortar radar element with its supporting maintenance, and the sentry dog section of twelve dogs and twenty men—all of these latter elements are not normally in an infantry battalion. My combined forces and equipment made us a highly unconventional unit (in organization but not in tactics). General Westmoreland had told me to ask for what I wanted and I took him up on his word! Obviously, he meant it when he said he would support my requests for people and equipment to meet security needs. I am pleased that during my tenure, none of my airfields were ever physically penetrated by the enemy.

METHOD OF OPERATIONS

My primary mode of operations to generate maximum security was to send reconnaissance and/or ambush patrols each night into different areas within a few thousand meters (one to five miles) outside our airfields' physical perimeters. I would plan irregular patrol routes and define variable times for their operations. A night patrol normally lasted about five hours. I thoroughly briefed and debriefed patrol leaders each day. Occasionally, I would lead patrols, but my routine night duties primarily were to maintain communication with patrol leaders. Usually, I was inside the fortified combat operations center (COC). From there, I could keep abreast of all the other actions in the military corps area and could make patrol adjustments as tactically needed.

If an enemy activity area was spotted, the reconnaissance patrol could instantly become a combat patrol! For example, one night, one of my patrols spotted the enemy setting up mortars to fire against our airfield. We attacked the small team and captured the mortars and some personnel. That night, every other military installation or outpost in the general area was attacked, but we had protected ours! On another night, my troops found a well-camouflaged weapons cache of new AK-47 rifles. The rifles were still packed in a thick, waxy, corrosion-resistant grease and marked with Russian manufacturing data. Apparently they were hidden there for use by some communist North Vietnamese troops in the future—perhaps even against our airfield. Around our area, the enemy did not regularly use land mines. But one day while delivering materials and troops to an outpost, my two-and-a-half-ton truck did hit a mine. Fortunately, no troops were seriously wounded, but the truck had its whole right front quarter blown off.

DIFFICULT SOLDIERS

Soldiering can be extremely difficult and very tiring. Sleep can be elusive, especially in a combat environment. During my first tour in Vietnam, my soldiers were in constant demand. Some would be door gunners for helicopter missions, some would man security posts day and night, some would be on night patrols, some would man our mortars 24/7, and yet others would be on various administrative duties for the unit. I also had to ensure that they were maintaining their infantry skills through regular training. Because of all these time-intensive missions, it was a continual struggle for me to arrange sleep times for my troops since most of our tactical, patrol operations were at night. Daytime sleep was often hampered by the loud and constant whop, whop, whop of the helicopters or the noise of Air Force cargo planes leaving or arriving at our airfields.

A couple of my soldiers could not seem to stay awake on duty, regardless of how much I tried to accommodate them. As I would check on my troops on a regular basis, I would sometimes find certain men repeatedly asleep at their post. When not on patrol, I would assign two soldiers to be together in a foxhole, in a searchlight tower, or in a bunker so that they could alternate sleeping. However, occasionally when one of these soldiers was supposed to be awake, I would find them both asleep. Sleeping on duty is a court martial offense and can be punished severely! Eventually, I had issued enough warnings and had to file charges, which resulted in a couple of my men being sent away to a military prison. I regretted having to do that, but it was necessary when they did not heed warnings and continued to put others in my unit at risk. Besides, it demonstrated to my other troops the seriousness of our mutual mission.

At one point during the year, a new soldier reported to my unit. However, when he came, he had no written orders. This was highly unusual. I questioned him in detail and talked to my higher officers to learn more about him and his assignment. His last name added to the confusion as he told me it was Cxyd—not the actual name but for this story it is very close with four letters and no vowels (except sometimes y). He did have a copy of an award certificate for a Soldier's Medal he claimed was given to him when he was in a unit in Germany. He had helped to rescue other soldiers who had been trapped in an overturned vehicle, and he was appropriately recognized with the award. He told me that one of his buddies had been killed in action in Vietnam and that he had requested to be sent to Vietnam so that he could avenge that killing by fighting the Viet Cong and North Vietnamese Army. His story was strange, and it concerned me but with directives from above, I began to give him duties inside our garrison perimeter. I had doubts about him.

One day, Cxyd was missing. The airfield's gate guards—who were military police and not part of my unit—told me that they had seen him drive off our Army airfield in one of my machine gun jeeps. They thought he had been authorized to leave, although they did think it strange that he was by himself. I did a quick inventory of our weapons and discovered that we were missing a grenade launcher, a rifle, hand grenades, flares, and a bunch of ammunition as well as the jeep with the mounted machine gun. We had no idea where he could be. I sent a couple of men into the nearest town to see if he was there, but they did not find him. Then we sent up a couple of helicopters on a search mission for him but they came back without sighting him or the gun jeep.

Two days later, I received a radio message from a tribal village regional force commander about twenty-five miles away saying that an American soldier had wandered into his village and asked for protection. His clothes were torn and he gave a story that he had fought off some enemy soldiers, lost his weapons, and his vehicle was stuck, so he burned it in a rice paddy where he had supposedly chased the enemy. This soldier had to be Cxyd, and I was very upset because this whole story sounded phony just like his personal background. I told the tribal leader to hold the soldier until I could come.

The next morning, I took a squad of men in an armored personnel carrier and went to the village where Cxyd was. It was potentially a dangerous mission, going through Viet Cong territory, but we arrived at the village safely and the tribal commander brought Cxyd to me. His story was that he "needed" to go after the enemy that killed his buddy. In trying to avoid being seen by our helicopters, he went off the road under the triple-canopied trees and ended up being stuck in the rice paddy. He claimed that some enemy troops fired on him and that they set the jeep and all the weapons on fire. Our investigation concluded that Cxyd himself shot the jeep up, set it on fire, and then went to the village, thinking he could be honored as a hero for keeping the Viet Cong away from the village.

Cxyd was later court martialed and sent to a stateside military prison with charges of AWOL (absent without leave), stealing government property, and destroying government property. He was a difficult soldier!

Another of my men was an alcoholic who stole beer from the airfield's club and would report for duty very drunk. Of course, I could not have him on a patrol or in a foxhole protecting our airfield in that condition. We tried all sorts of methods to keep him away from beer, but somehow he managed to continue to get drunk. I think he must have stashed the alcohol in a stockpile somewhere. As a last resort, I asked our battalion's flight surgeon if he knew of any aids we could use to stop his drunkenness.

He said that there was a pill that when taken would make the soldier sick if alcohol was in his system, so I sent the soldier to him. Well, of course, the soldier didn't like that and would fake taking the pill. My senior sergeant then said the solution would be to bring the soldier into the office twice each day and watch him swallow the pill. It did the job! If the soldier tried drinking any alcoholic

been there, done that!

beverage, he became violently sick because of the "throw-up" pill. This was not a fun thing for a young lieutenant or his sergeant to manage in a combat environment, but it was necessary. Eventually, this difficult soldier had to be dismissed from the service because of his addiction. I had not been exposed to this level of addiction before, but it did teach me that sometimes you have to take extreme or unusual measures to effectively command your unit.

RHADE TRIBAL INITIATION

Speaking of alcohol — I had quite an experience when I was initiated to become a "brother" in the Rhade (Montagnard) tribe. Montagnard is a generic name for more than twenty tribal groups in the west, central highlands of Vietnam. Some of the tribes spilled over into Cambodia and Laos. As a group, these Montagnard tribes were very friendly to our American military and were vicious and strong partners in our efforts to defeat the Viet Cong and North Vietnamese forces. But they also had been suppressed by the South Vietnamese government, which on occasion seemed to be as much against its own people as they were against the North Vietnamese. The Montagnards didn't trust the South Vietnamese, nor did the South Vietnamese trust these tribal members.

Because of my airfield security mission in the central highlands, I often interacted with the Montagnards — and particularly the Rhade and Jarai tribes in my areas of responsibility. (When possible I would try and visit with missionaries reaching out to and ministering with these two tribes.) Most of the men in these tribes wore a brass bracelet as a symbol of tribal identification. Many American soldiers would buy similar fake bracelets in the outdoor markets to demonstrate a friendly connection with the tribes, but those soldiers were not formally initiated into the tribe to become a true "brother".

After I was about two-thirds through my tour in Vietnam, I learned that a brigadier general and I were to be honored for our support to the Rhade tribe's people. After being assured of appropriate security for the area, we went to a village and were taken into a grass-roofed meeting house. We were given seats of honor in front of two big clay pots — about two feet tall and eighteen inches-wide at the middle, narrowing to a four-inch-wide opening at the top. Introductions were made to the audience, and they were told why we were being honored.

Then about eight drummers entered and started dancing around the "room". Long straws were given to the general and me for drinking from the pots and we were told to "drink up" and that men would come with more of the "juice" and keep the pots full. I immediately realized that the beverage was heavily-fermented rice wine. Physically, I could not drink it. I had never drunk an alcoholic beverage, and it tasted and smelled horrible to me. So, I kept the straw in my mouth and pretended to suck on the straw—so that I wouldn't offend the people at this initiation ceremony. The general kept sipping his, and they kept refilling his pot and at the same time urging me to drink out of my pot so they could add more! As his liquid lowered in the pot, I could see some kind of grasses or weeds in his pot but I couldn't see them in mine because they were below the wine level. A Rhade tribesman later told me that the bottom of the pot contained uncooked monkey and water buffalo meat! Yummee! The general soon was wobbling a bit, and I tried to warn him that he may be consuming too much, but he continued to drink.

The drums got louder and louder and other tribal people in the room began a frenzied dance. I was trying to figure out a means of escape but since I had gotten through the "drinking" part safely, I decided to stay. Then the witch doctor (with all his fancy regalia) came in with great ceremonial pomp and honor. In one hand, he had an aluminum quart-sized pan with some very dark, red liquid in it. In the other hand he had a weed which had a brush-like tip. We were instructed to take off our boots and socks and push our feet forward and flat on the ground. The witch doctor than dipped the weed into the dark, red, thick liquid—yes, it was coagulating blood!—and dabbed it on my toenails first and then on the general's toes. (Although I had asked, I never did get an answer about the meaning of the dabbed blood on my toenails.)

The drumming became heavier, and the crowd extremely boisterous before the tribal chief entered, came over to us, and put a brass bracelet on one of our arms. This was to be the sign that we were to be treated as members in the tribe and must have been the clue for the drums to quiet down and people to leave. I only heard of one other initiation of Americans during my first tour in Vietnam. I felt humbled that I had been chosen and now honored to be part of the Rhade tribe, but in reality, I felt a little dirty having been "blessed" by a witch doctor and having faked the wine drinking. The bracelet did give me greater "clout" when dealing with tribal people following my initiation.

been there, done that!

AGENT ORANGE

I have often been asked if I was exposed to Agent Orange, the toxic chemical used to defoliate jungle areas, along roads, and in front of defensive positions. "Yes," unfortunately, is my answer. We used it quite liberally around our airfields and outpost perimeters and especially heavy under the barbed concertina wire. We used commercial sprayers to apply the chemical, and in those days in 1965–1966, certainly we were not too concerned about winds blowing the sprayed mist back on us or getting the agent on our hands or clothes.

As you would expect, we built bunkers and foxholes we would occupy to defend the airfields from inside the perimeter. In that tropical environment, the weeds grew fast and the defoliant helped us keep our fields of fire for our weapons cleared of the brush. As part of our security plan, we used ground-emplaced claymore, anti-personnel mines which could be electrically detonated from our defensive positions about 25 to 30 feet away. To ensure the claymores would be effective, one had to lie down behind each weapon and sight it in properly. These weapons were normally camouflaged in areas where previously we had sprayed the Agent Orange defoliant, so naturally it was all over our field uniforms and boots as well as our skin.

Barrels and barrels (fifty-five-gallon drums) of the chemical were brought in to our airfields where the agent was then transferred into helicopter or hand-held spraying tanks. Spills were not uncommon, and it would get on our boots and clothes—occasionally even splashing on our faces. When going to bed, we would wash in community bathrooms before going to our rooms, but then we had to take off our boots, which had the agent on them. Sometimes we slept in our clothes, depending on the tactical situation. I know there must have been many times when I went to bed with Agent Orange on my hands and with it having soaked portions of my uniform. Frankly, none of us were concerned about the potential effect—short or long-term—on our health.

In those days, the disastrous physical and mental effects of Agent Orange on some soldiers had not yet been identified. I know that the chemical has affected people in different ways. Thankfully, it has not affected me as severely as it has some troops. However, part of my Veterans Administration disability rating is directly attributed to my Agent Orange exposure, resulting in ischemic heart disease. (I had open-chest bypass surgery in 1998, and two stents were emplaced after a heart attack in 2021.) However, I am so thankful that at the time of this writing, I have had few other severely disabling issues pertaining to Agent Orange, although the Veterans Administration is currently evaluating it as the probable cause of other physical issues.

ARRIVAL OF 1st CAVALRY DIVISION (AIRMOBILE)

In the late summer of 1965, the US Army's 1st Cavalry Division (Airmobile) began arriving in Vietnam and established its base at An Khe halfway between Pleiku (Camp Holloway) and Qui Nhon on the coast. (See map at Appendix D.) This division's deployment to Vietnam was the beginning of a huge buildup of US forces to counter the increasing effort of the North Vietnamese and Viet Cong troops' threats to cut South Vietnam in two and change the government. My detachment was tasked to provide some of the security where the new base for the division was being built. The Air Cav Division—as it came to be known—was the first unit of its kind in the Army. Its air mobility allowed for battalion-sized forces to be delivered, supplied, fight, and extracted from a battle area by using helicopters. The concept had been thoroughly studied and its practicality proven in the US, but it had not yet been tested in combat. That would soon change.

ATTACK ON CAMP AT PLEI ME

I was in the combat operations center of Camp Holloway Army Airfield on the night of October 19, 1965, when a desperate call came in from the small, triangular Special Forces camp at Plei Me, several miles to our south. The camp was strategically placed for border surveillance and interdiction of enemy troops. Besides our small twelve-man US Special Forces men, around 350 national Montagnard tribesmen in a military unit were based in that camp. On that horrible October night, the camp came under heavy attack by a large North Vietnamese Army (NVA) unit. Our aviation battalion scrambled to provide some quick support, but the NVA attack continued its viciousness and attempted to overrun our defensive forces. Sadly, some of our aircraft were shot down, and we lost some of our aviation battalion's brave men.

Four days later in a letter to Betty on October 23, 1965, I wrote:

> "Down at Plei Me things are still going hot. The NVA must really want to destroy that place for the price they are paying.

been there, done that!

> Today we (US forces) captured some enemy anti-aircraft weapons and an unbelievable picture was found. Some NVA soldiers were *chained* to their weapons! Morale must be pretty low when you have to start that. The weapons are too big to lug very far, so the troops just had to fire until they could no more because they couldn't run off—that's for sure!"

With the aid of heavy aerial bombardments by our US Air Force and artillery supporting the relief force, the NVA siege was broken late in the month, and its forces withdrew to the west. In the meantime, I put my security detachment's patrols on extra alert, and my searchlight and ground radar forces kept their intense vigil throughout each night. I also told my dog handlers to increase the number of their internal patrols.

CONFRONTATION WITH A SENIOR OFFICER

At the end of October, due to the intelligence indicating a buildup of NVA forces in our area, the Air Cav Division was ordered to go on the offensive to our southwest to block and defeat NVA efforts. A battalion from the division moved to our Camp Holloway airfield to use as a base of operations and the unit's commander attempted to usurp my authority and take over my airfield security responsibility. I told him that I was in charge of the security and if I needed his help, I would ask for it, but my orders were from General Westmoreland, the commander of all US forces in Vietnam. We had a rather heated debate, with him pointing his finger in my chest and using some strong language. I had to be careful to keep in mind that he was three ranks higher than me, even though I felt he was trying to take advantage of his rank!

A leader must find the balance of getting along and getting it right with others. Getting along may not be that difficult in most situations but having the courage to confront a senior person to get things done according to appropriate authority and ahead of any potential problems is challenging. I had an operational security plan for the airfield and I needed to continue to manage that plan even though this senior officer wanted to assume responsibility for it. In spite of some changes in numbers of personnel on my airfield, my security objectives remained the same. However, my leadership would have to be proactive in adapting to inclusion of other soldiers in my plan—simultaneously dealing with unknown commanders of those men. Leadership is about doing the right thing (militarily, ethically, and morally) under challenging circumstances.

There are times when one has to stand up for what is right, and this was one of those times. I don't like confrontation, but I was confident in my security arrangement and that I would be supported by my aviation battalion commander and by General Westmoreland who was five grades higher than the lieutenant colonel! He left our conversation in quite a huff in that he had to yield to a lieutenant. After that, things smoothed out between us, once my authority for security was established and later supported by my battalion commander.

BATTLE OF THE IA DRANG VALLEY

The almost month-long Battle of the Ia Drang Valley, conducted by the Air Cav Division and other forces in the fall of 1965, is well documented and available for study in books, movies, and the internet, so I will not dwell on its action. A few things stand out to me about the overall battle action. It is notable for being the first large-scale, helicopter-borne, air assault maneuver in combat and reportedly was the first major engagement of the Vietnam War between US Army ground combat troops and North Vietnamese regular forces. It also included the first use of B-52 strategic bombers in a tactical support role. The previously untested airmobile concept passed its first operational trial and proved itself valuable for future operations. I was there on the ground to watch the transformation of Army tactics change with the use of the helicopter.

There were some hard lessons learned that have since been written into Army doctrine as a result of this historic Ia Drang Valley battle. In addition to the gallantry and courage demonstrated by the pilots and crewmen engaged in fighting the battles, casualty evacuation brought forth stories of extreme heroism of those bringing back every wounded or deceased soldier from the jungle. I was horrified at the sight of neatly arranged and respected piles of full body bags brought back to Camp Holloway from the intense fighting. It was just awful, profoundly affecting, and terrifying. It was very difficult for me to grasp the physical and spiritual loss of so many soldiers who just a few hours before were loading themselves on helicopters to go into combat—from that very spot on my airfield! Now they were being unloaded in body bags by other soldiers. War is gruesome. I was glad that I had the Lord beside me to lift me up and away from potential depressing doldrums, which could have resulted from that shocking and staggering battle.

been there, done that!

LETTERS TO AND FROM HOME

Recently, I reviewed some of the letters I wrote to Betty and that she wrote to me. The 1965–1966 year in Vietnam actually seemed to go by very fast, and her letters sure helped. Betty's letters sometimes took several days (and sometimes weeks) to arrive, but when they did, my morale certainly was lifted—especially when they smelled so good! But as I read through some of them, I was saddened to think of her with difficulties of raising a new baby and living under someone else's roof. Fortunately, I was kept busy day and night so I could not dwell on those issues. However, there were also significant advantages to having the support of family so close and I was thankful! Following are some things I was reminded of in re-reading some of our letters.

Living conditions for me were really not that bad. I lived in a hooch—a canvas-topped hut with sand bag walls—which was my "home" for the year of my first tour in Vietnam. Showers and bathroom facilities were in other tents several yards away. Initially, when it rained, we had to wade in the muck, going to and from our hooch, but later we put down wooden pallets to walk on and at the end of the tour, we finally had cement sidewalks.

Four of us lived in the hooch, which had curtain dividers between our bunk areas. We slept on foldable Army cots with mosquito nets. Our "rooms" each had a chair and an armoire for clothes and personal items. However, because of the intense humidity, things in the enclosed armoire would often get moldy and green! We finally gained permission to hang a light bulb in our armoire. The bulb generated a little heat to reduce the mold factor. When the generators were down, the mold factor was up! About the only things I brought home out of my armoire were Betty's letters to me. Almost everything else had the detestable smell of mold or was covered in red dust!

My letters to Betty occasionally told of sad situations—particularly of helicopter crashes and the deaths of some of my friends. One casualty is always one too many, and our base took on a very somber feeling as we mourned our losses and held memorial services.

But those times were countered by joyous opportunities for me by occasional meetings with local missionaries and tribal believers. At a hymn sing with them, I was asked on the spur of the moment to sing in a quartet comprised of a missionary, two tribesmen, and me as a soldier! That demonstrated our unity in Christ! English classes were offered at the mission station, and I was suddenly announced as the teacher a couple of times. I loved occasionally going to the mission property and found real spiritual encouragement there. On one Sunday afternoon, I enjoyed watching the river baptism of several Jarai tribal people. Someday in heaven, I'll see those people again!

In those days, troops were paid in cash on payday—once a month. Some of my men had most of their pay sent directly to their bank or families through allotments. Other men wanted their full pay or portions of it provided to them in cash—and unfortunately wasted much of it there in Vietnam. As the pay officer for my dispersed unit, I had to go with other units' pay officers to sign for thousands of dollars, count it (and count it again!) to ensure I had the exact amount needed to pay my troops. Then I had to establish pay times for the soldiers to pick up their monies. If there was any discrepancy raised by a soldier, I had to resolve the problem. It took several days to get everyone paid since I had to schedule helicopter flights to the other locations of my troops, Sometimes those flights were adversely affected by the weather or operational requirements. At the conclusion of the paying cycle, each pay officer had to carefully account for his distribution of the payroll.

The USO (United Services Organizations) brought a couple of shows to Camp Holloway while I was there. Martha Raye was a particular hit with the troops, and all appreciated the manner in which she brought a little "Americana" to our Army airfield. Bob Hope with his troupe (including actress Ann Margaret!) visited us at Christmas time and delighted us with his unparalleled humor, his ever present golf club, and involvement with our soldiers. A couple of other actresses and singers came to the club at the nearby Air Force base, but their performances were not as good or memorable.

In a letter to Betty dated 21 January 1966, I wrote of a dust storm which placed a red cloud over our airfield for a couple of days. It completely shut down all of our aviation activities and also much of our communications because of the density of the dust. The dust penetrated everything and caused a lot of downtime of our activities after the dust had cleared since we had to do a major cleaning and maintenance on our equipment to get it back in good operating shape again.

been there, done that!

LESSONS FROM FIRST COMBAT TOUR

That combat tour in Vietnam from July 1965–June 1966 was one of the most professionally rewarding and satisfying times of my military career. My assignment benefitted my leadership development through many learned lessons:

1. I was required to analyze life-threatening situations and come to rapid, critical decisions.
2. I built an inner confidence through my ongoing interaction with those who ranked above me.
3. Emotions of despair had to yield to taking the next decisive step in accomplishing a mission.
4. Ingenuity was constantly required to outwit enemy actions or diminish the effect of his terror.
5. Fear can be overcome even in the midst of a dangerous environment.
6. Every person must be dealt with by demonstrating compassion with firmness and fairness.
7. An Army sergeant major once stated that leadership requires five Cs: Commitment, Courage, Competence, Candor, and Compassion. I have learned the veracity of that statement and am thankful for the experiences given to me to apply these principles.
8. My knowledge of tactics was enhanced for my benefit in the future.
9. Being a commander requires integrity, responsibility, accountability, and bearing the weight of heavy troop and mission-accomplishment burdens.
10. A leader must constantly strive to help others reach their maximum potential in performance of duties.

I probably would have extended my combat tour in Vietnam if I had not been married and had a new son at home. My leadership skills had been tested and successfully passed, and I did not lose one soldier to enemy action although the ravages of death were always around me. I felt I had contributed to our nation's effort to support the Vietnamese people's real desire for freedom within their own country.

CHAPTER IX
WHEATON COLLEGE ROTC

After my first combat tour in Vietnam (1965–1966), I came home to a military assignment as an Assistant Professor of Military Science in the Reserve Officer Training Corps (ROTC) Department at Wheaton College, my alma mater. I learned that the Army was trying to increase officer recruitment and production by assigning young combat-experienced officers back to the schools from which they had graduated and received their commission since they could probably relate more to the culture of their own schools. I was glad to be there, although my reassignment request had been for me to go to an airborne unit.

Because I arrived back in America in late June, our country was getting ready for July 4th celebrations. I didn't realize that my Vietnam experiences would affect my enjoyment at fireworks demonstrations. Betty wanted to show our new ten-month old son the beauty of fireworks' colors and let him hear the evening's noises so we went to watch a big fireworks show. I did not enjoy it at all having just come from Vietnam where the dropping of bombs and firing of artillery brought disaster on human life. Emotionally, the celebrations and noise were too much for me and we had to leave before the show ended. I would rather have been in a bunker or in a foxhole than sitting out in the open with the explosions in the sky. It took me quite a bit of time to overcome my distress when fireworks and loud pops were being used for a celebration.

TEACHING MILITARY HISTORY

Shortly after arriving at Wheaton, I was promoted to captain and told by the Professor of Military Science that I would be teaching military history and the Army's organization to freshman students in the ROTC (Reserve Officer Training

been there, done that!

Corps) program. In those days at Wheaton, all male students in their first and second years were required to take ROTC. (Females were not permitted to be in the ROTC commissioning program.) Needless to say, some of the young men had no interest in the military, and it showed on the drill field and in the classroom. That in itself was a problem and a challenge for me—especially since I was not a history buff myself! Somehow I would have to show enthusiasm in my teaching, so I had to do extensive study in preparation for my classes and spent many hours in the books each night and weekend. It was surprising what I learned in research for my classes! In the end, it was beneficial to me in my career, but that didn't make me enjoy teaching military history.

In my second year of teaching ROTC at Wheaton, I taught third-year ROTC students—those who were now under contract to complete four years of military training in preparation for commissioning. These students were more highly motivated because they had volunteered to continue ROTC, and they were more disciplined in the classroom. My classes were more in my line of interest as I taught small unit tactics and the purposes of the various branches of the Army such as these: Infantry, Armor, Artillery, Engineers, Aviation, Signal, Intelligence, Medical Service Corps, Military Police, Transportation, and Civil Affairs—to name a few. I am sure I was much more enthusiastic and effective in teaching those subjects.

SPONSORING CONGUER RIFLES

My satisfactions came through helping cadets on the drill field, as the coordinator of the ROTC band, and particularly as the staff sponsor for the counter-guerilla unit (Conguer Rifles) of cadets. The Conguer Rifles succeeded the national Pershing Rifles fraternal organization that was on campus when I was a cadet. This group would focus on field operations with extracurricular training and occasional weekend bivouacs (Army campouts) to prepare those cadets who wanted to learn new techniques and operations to fight in an environment, such as Vietnam. I thoroughly enjoyed working with these cadets and was much more comfortable in the tactics and field environments than I was in the classroom.

In the spring of 1968, the Conguer Rifles had planned a banquet which was to be held in Chicago. This was a formal affair with all the cadets in uniform and their dates in their beautiful gowns. Leaving Wheaton's campus and arriving in the mega city, we soon were faced with road blocks in the streets. Police car lights were flashing everywhere, and sirens were blaring. The police detoured us far out of our way to get to the restaurant where the banquet was to be held. We had no idea what the problem was—this was before cellphones and instant news reporting on the radio. But when we finally arrived at the banquet site, we learned of the riots occurring throughout Chicago because of Dr. Martin Luther King's assassination. I then checked with the police to determine the best route out of the city in order to avoid the worst riot areas. We hurriedly ate our meal but cancelled most of the program that evening to get an earlier start heading back to the Wheaton campus. Thankfully, everyone made it safely.

ANTI-WAR PROTESTS

Across the US, anti-war protests were happening on many college and university campuses and in a number of cities. In the 1967–1968 school year, the University of Wisconsin in Madison was somewhat of a hotbed of these protests, and students had threatened its ROTC department because of its military connections. A Midwest regional drill competition weekend that had been scheduled on the Wisconsin campus would bring in many college and university ROTC drill teams. Wheaton College's drill team was to be part of the competition. Upon arriving on the huge university campus among many other cadets heading toward the competition building, we were met by protestors with verbal and physical threats. Campus police soon arrived and eventually before the competitions actually started, the university leadership canceled the drill meet. This was a great disappointment to all of the contending cadets, but it was certainly an understandable and timely decision. I was glad that nothing serious happened while we were there. It wasn't too long after that when students set fire to the building housing the University of Wisconsin ROTC department. A mathematics building was also bombed because it was the location of some major military research projects.

SURVIVOR ASSISTANCE OFFICER

One of the most difficult assignments I was given by the Army while I was teaching in the ROTC Department at Wheaton College was to be the military's Survivor Assistance Officer (SAO) to several families whose sons or husbands had been killed in the Vietnam War. On the death of an enlisted soldier, a senior non-commissioned officer (NCO) would be designated to personally notify the next of kin that their family member had been killed in action. (An officer would make the notification if an officer had been killed.) Within a short time, another officer would then go to the family to offer the government's assistance in making final arrangements. I was that designated SAO to provide help in this tragic and sad time for several soldiers' families.

This duty was emotionally challenging in that I was dealing with grieving individuals, and even in that era, I was not permitted to offer spiritual encouragement. I had to deliver information regarding the circumstances of the soldier's death, offer aid in bringing the deceased member's body back to his hometown, inform the next-of-kin about financial allotments from the government, assist in military funeral arrangements and burial sites, and provide answers to innumerable questions. As expected, this was not an easy time for families of the soldiers—or for me.

In one situation, the family was strongly against the Vietnam War. When I arrived in my uniform at the individual's home, I had already been told by the notifying NCO that the mother of the deceased was angry and that I needed to be careful at her house. I knocked and a large man, who was a brother to the deceased soldier, answered the door. I introduced myself and asked if I could talk with the mother. He hollered to the back of the house and said, "Another Army guy is here." She angrily answered and said she didn't want to see me. I talked with her son for a while and explained my desire to be of help in this troubling time and could come back with more details at a future time but would really like to introduce myself to his mother.

He went to the back of the house, and I could hear him calmly talking to his mother, but her responses to him were loud, angry words. Finally, she came out to the living room where I was. Her hair was a tangled mess, her robe was wrinkled and torn, and her face was tight and wrathful. She saw me and immediately headed toward me with her hands open and raised to my neck's level. What was I to do? I stood firm and determined to let her attack since I was there to help and not fight. Thankfully, her big son wrapped his arms around her and restrained her and said, "Mom, you don't want to do that." He sat her down in a chair and explained to her why I was there. We had a short, emotional conversation, and I then told her that I would come back at an appropriate time of her choosing. As I left, I was thankful that I (and my uniform) was still in one piece! After a couple of more visits, she had gained her composure but determined that she didn't want any military representation at the funeral. I then worked through her son and the funeral director to deal with all military-related issues to close my assistance to her.

I was happy that none of my other SAO duties were that difficult. One of the deceased soldiers was a medic who had already been recognized with a high military award. I heard that years later, he was awarded the Medal of Honor, our nation's highest award. Another soldier had been a Catholic seminary student there in our Illinois county. He had dropped out of seminary in his last year because he wanted to enlist and serve his country. He had only been in Vietnam a couple of months when he was killed in action. The seminary requested of his family that the funeral service and burial be on the seminary property.

Previously, I had not attended a formal Catholic funeral mass and had to ask several procedural questions of a priest assigned to escort me while I was on the seminary grounds. The service was more than two-and-a-half hours long with incantations and music from different groups in between lengthy orations in Latin, which of course, I did not understand. The service finally concluded and an announcement was made regarding the procession to the burial site on the campus. It was mid-winter and snowing heavily as we walked in the bitter wind and blowing snow to the prepared grave spot. Fortunately, I had my military overcoat and gloves, but to be truthful, I was freezing! My feet were soaked as we walked through the six-inch deep snow and then stood in the open, wind-blown field around the gravesite. My teeth were chattering as another group of seminary students sang and the priest gave a lengthy committal sermon—all in Latin. Finally, after four hours at the seminary, I got in my car to head home. I hoped that I would not have another SAO duty like that, even though all of my responsibilities went smoothly. In each of my SAO cases, I wished so much that the deceased soldiers and members of their families could experience the hope of eternal life that I have because of all that is offered in the Scriptures to those of us who have accepted Christ into our lives.

Joining in an assistance role for the grieving families and at the funeral services of their loved ones was one of the most honorable (but yet most difficult) tasks of my military service.

MILITARY FUNERAL SERVICE

Most family members of a deceased military person desire assistance with a military funeral to honor the love of their soldier for our country. Individuals are not aware of the protocol and meanings of some of the elements of a military funeral. I doubt that most of the readers of these memoirs have attended a military funeral, nor had I prior to my duties as a SAO. Since I would be a participant in the funeral events, I needed to prepare myself for the emotions that are generated in both the chapel and at the gravesite. The conduct and sequence of a military funeral and military honors can be reviewed on the internet, so I will not take space to explain it all here.

However, I'll give you some of my observations at the gravesite of one of those first funerals in which I was involved. After the chaplain/pastor had completed his final words at the burial site, the signal was given to initiate the rifle volley. This consisted of three separate times of simultaneous firings by the rifle salute team following commands of their leader. Although I had briefed the family to expect the sharp noise of the rifles, several of them and their friends jumped at the sound. I knew what was coming next as the smell of the fired blank rounds filled my nostrils, and I steeled myself against showing emotion.

On a military post, Taps are played every night at bedtime, so the tune from the bugle is familiar. However, Taps at a funeral seems to take on an eerie sound as the notes echo over headstones and through the trees of the cemetery. Standing at attention, I couldn't help but look at the young wife and mother dabbing the tears from her puffy eyes. Just seconds before, her body shook strongly as the three rifle volleys had rendered their salute but now underneath the bugle's sounds, she was heaving with sobs. Other nearby weeping friends wrapped their arms around her in consolation. As she cried, I felt my own emotions welling up beneath my collar. I had to take my focus from her to look at the horizon or I would have cried with her. I had to take some deep breaths and gain control of my heart and voice for my next responsibility.

The flag was lifted above the casket and carefully folded into the well-known triangular shape and handed to me. Carrying it at waist high, I moved to a position in front of the grieving young widow, leaned over, and presented the flag to her. Then moving to one knee, I softly expressed for the president, our nation's appreciation of her loved one's service and sacrifice. I then stood up, slowly saluted the flag now in her lap, and backed away. That was a most difficult task that I did not enjoy but was honored to do for the family. I don't remember how many of those funerals I was a part of, but each one was one too many, and the duty never became easier.

I am qualified, as a Purple Heart Medal recipient, to be buried with military honors in Arlington National Cemetery outside of Washington, DC. The cemetery is just across a highway from the Pentagon where I served much of the time from 1971–1989. I trust it will yet be many years before my internment there, but when my day arrives, I will be ready and will be honored to rest among the thousands of other veterans in those sacred grounds.

REASSIGNED BACK TO VIETNAM

After completing my two-year assignment at Wheaton College in 1968, I assumed that I might be assigned to Germany since I had not yet had duty there where thousands of our Army troops were stationed. But I was not too surprised to receive orders to return to Vietnam where the war was still raging. This would have greater emotional impact now that I had to leave my wife and two children behind. In addition to our son, who was born while I was in Vietnam on my first tour, we now had added a daughter born in the summer between my two years of teaching at Wheaton. Thus, a second separated tour was even more difficult.

Again, we had to make a decision about where my family should live. While teaching at Wheaton College, it was convenient to visit with Betty's parents and other family in the greater Chicago area, but we had not developed a lot of other close friends, nor did we feel very connected to the church we were attending. Betty seemed to feel more at home in Indiana where she had stayed through my first tour in Vietnam, so we decided to buy a house in South Bend. We found one only a few blocks from where she had lived with my sister during my previous Vietnam tour. My parents had also purchased a house in that general area and were now on their furlough from their missionary service in the Central African Republic. Betty's parents were not that far away in Chicago, and it had worked out well for visits during my first tour. Betty now had our two children and needed to be in her own space but have support from our family and church nearby.

CHAPTER X

SECOND TOUR IN VIETNAM

Because I had previously been assigned in 1964 to the 4th Infantry Division in my initial duty assignment at Fort Lewis, Washington, I was given orders back to the division that now had been deployed to the central highlands, just south of Pleiku in Vietnam. I was very familiar with this area because that is where I had been on my first tour. I wanted to be a company commander in the 1st Battalion, 22nd Infantry Regiment since I had been with that unit before I had deployed to Vietnam in 1965, but when I arrived in Vietnam in 1968, no company command position was open.

DIVISION OPERATIONS TEAM

Until a command position became available, I asked for duty in the division operations section where I would help develop daily plans for the division's subordinate units. I felt that my interest and expertise was more in tactics and operations, rather than in other venues such as personnel, intelligence, or logistics. My duty hours were from seven in the evening until nine the next morning. The long hours of busy duty made this portion of my tour go very fast!

Each evening at 10 p.m., I briefed the division commander (a two-star general) and appropriate staff on results of the day's combat actions of subordinate units. He then issued his guidance for the next day's operations. Throughout the night, our section then formulated plans for the employment of the infantry brigades, artillery support, and tactical air support for the operations in coordination with the intelligence and logistics folks. In the morning when the general came in at 7 a.m., I again briefed him on the details of plans that our team had developed and informed him of tactical operations, which had occurred throughout the night. This was my duty for about four months. It was very satisfying work for me.

I did not particularly enjoy one aspect of that time period in the plans section. I was designated as the classified documents security officer and was accountable for all the classified documents coming in or going out of the operations department. That meant I had to have a top-secret clearance and initially had to inventory all of those papers. If one was missing, I had to investigate where it might be and write appropriate reports. Someone had to do that job, and being the junior officer in the department at the time, I was given the duty.

There was increased NVA and Viet Cong aggressive activity in the southern part of our operating area, and the division commander put together a task force commanded by a brigadier general (one star) to prevent enemy successes. I was chosen as the operations officer for the task force with its headquarters in Ban Me Thout. (See map at Appendix D.) My hours changed from working through the nights to getting into the new combat operations center at 5:30 a.m. until my duties ended around 9:30 p.m. I continued to be the brigadier general's tactical briefer and often traveled with him to the hot spots of our area of operations. Part of my unit in 1965–66 had been located in this Ban Me Thout area, so I was comfortable operating in that terrain. The area to the west near the Cambodian border was very hostile territory and was an entry point for the NVA into South Vietnam after coming down the Ho Chi Minh Trail from North Vietnam through Laos and Cambodia. Our task force's mission was successfully accomplished in blocking the NVA's advances and after a couple of months, the task force was disbanded. We then returned to the division headquarters at Camp Enari, just south of Pleiku. The experience of serving on the operations staff at the division level was very helpful to me as I anticipated being a commander at higher levels.

COMPANY COMMAND

It was not long after that when a major, who had also been in the division operations section, became the operations officer of the 2nd Battalion, 35th Infantry Regiment (nicknamed Cacti Blue) in the division's 3rd Brigade. This brigade had been part of the 25th Infantry Division but now was under the operational control of the 4th Infantry Division. The major asked for me to come to the battalion to command D Company. We had worked together well in division operations, so I happily accepted the position. I was now doing what I wanted to do—command an infantry rifle company in combat. This is the highlight of an infantry officer's career because you are directly leading and influencing men in the toughest of situations, but unfortunately you also face emotional roller coasters dealing with casualties of your "own" men.

In the field, I came to know some of my men better than others because they were in my company headquarters element. They included my field first sergeant, radiotelephone operators, medic, and field artillery observer. We came to know each other quite well as we worked closely together!

In one of my letters to Betty after I had been in command of my company for a couple of months, I wrote: "You say that in my letters that I sounded completely happy in my command. Well, let me tell you, I AM! This is the best job in the Army. Here I am directly concerned with leadership of soldiers and tactics, and I feel that this is what I'm designed for. If I could get promoted and still keep this job, I sure would! Yep, I'm in my glory now. Only one bad thing—I'm not with you!"

been there, done that!

Even when operating in the field or temporarily sitting on a firebase, a commander must keep up with demanding administration. Letters of condolences needed to be sent out to families of casualties, personnel decorations and promotions must be kept timely, pay had to be distributed, sometimes discipline had to be rendered, and other routine administration needed to be conducted. When feasible, I would build a makeshift desk from ammunition boxes or wooden pallets to provide some protection from the rain or sun and give me a solid writing surface. Today, much of this is done via secure communication networks by field computers.

As foot soldiers in the light infantry, I was always concerned about the weight of personal gear and equipment which we carried. If too heavily burdened, we would not be able to move with the speed we would need to reach an objective. Already we were doing a lot of long-distance movements at night, which naturally decreased our speed, trekking in the jungled terrain. The requirements for my men were heavy with the average individual load (including my own as the commander) being around 60 pounds. Our machine gunners, ammunition carriers, and radio-telephone operators normally carried 80–100 pounds. Our loads usually included sufficient rations, water, and ammunition for three days plus our ponchos, sleeping equipment, extra socks, and other personal items. Demolition items such as explosives, saws, and axes often added to the personal weight we carried. But my men were disciplined and rarely griped, realizing the respect and support that was so necessary for one another. There was little access to drugs or alcohol while we were out in the jungle so that was not a problem in my unit. We seemed to be continually on the move and never wanted to be surprised. I had great soldiers, sergeants, and lieutenants in my company. My men knew the value of always being ready to face an unknown circumstance caused by our tenacious enemy, which constantly tried to disrupt the unity and morale of my company.

JUNGLE ENVIRONMENT

The environment in the jungled highlands of Central Vietnam often became an issue for our operations. Some of the mountains that my company was airlifted to were quite cool after coming from steamy valleys. Clouds often restricted our view. From a March 25, 1969, letter to Betty, I wrote: "We started walking down a ridgeline...we didn't make it to our night position because it started to thunder and lightning and got real dark about 5:15 p.m. I picked a spot for the company to set up for the night, and immediately the skies let loose with a heavy rain." A couple of days later, that same letter to Betty continued: "This hill where we are 'was' covered with huge trees—both mahogany and teak—and we have to take many of them down so our mortars can fire. (The mortars need overhead clearance as they are indirect fire weapons.) We've been using axes, two-man crosscut saws, demolitions, and machetes...We've used close to 800 pounds of explosives already, and everyone's ears are ringing and heads aching from all the powerful blasts...Some of the trees are four to five feet in diameter."

been there, done that!

One day, before we had provided sufficient clearance for helicopters to land, we received a resupply of rations, water, munitions, explosives, and other equipment. Mail also had to be delivered! The helicopters hovered above the trees about 100 feet in the air, and their crews threw everything out the side. My letter to Betty read: "Wow! It was a nice show but a little hard on the mail and containers." One of Betty's wonderful packages was in the mail drop. I continued to write: "The brownies weren't in too bad shape nor was one of the apple pies. But the other one and the berry pie were flattened! I still ate every bit, and they were delicious!" Usually when someone received a "goodie" package, if there was enough, it was shared with others on their team and some of Betty's pies and brownies were enjoyed by others. Betty's packages and letters were always such a morale booster—especially when I was out in the field and when she used perfumed stationery!

If we were on a hilltop for a few days, we had to be careful to ration our drinking water, knowing that we might not be able to be resupplied if helicopters were not available or if the weather was too bad for them to fly. It seemed that water was always scarce. Each of my troops really needed at least five to six quarts per day just for drinking but we averaged only about three quarts per man when in the field. In one of my letters I wrote: "It has rained the last two nights and looks like it again today. Caught water off our poncho tent last night in my helmet so had some to shave with and some more to drink. It is the hard way to get it, but it works."

Our helmets then were two pieces and not like modern soldiers have. The inner liner was wearable by itself but in combat we always used the steel pot over the liner. The steel pot was good for a lot of things like for personal hygiene, cooking, use as a stool for sitting, or just catching water. The liner and steel pot with a camouflaged cloth cover weighed approximately three pounds.

On occasion in the jungle, we would have to cross a large stream or small river. If the situation permitted, I would set up perimeter security and let the men take a bath—especially if we had just come through a swampy or very muddy area. The bath was always very refreshing as we stripped down in order to rinse out our stinky, sweat-soaked clothes and socks and wash the muck from our boots. At times in the dry season, I thought I was getting some tan on my arms but after a rare bath in a creek, I realized I was as white as ever! It was just dust generated by whirling helicopter blades that gave me that great, red-brown tan look!

Our jungle boots were mostly canvas. They dried quickly when wet and were a lot lighter than the leather boots. They also had a special liner for under your foot. This mesh liner was made of a special Kevlar material which was very helpful in preventing serious injury if you stepped into a Viet Cong punji trap. The punji was a sharpened bamboo stick which was heated on the point for hardening. It or several were placed in a hole over a suspected walkway and camouflaged. If a person stepped in that spot, the punji could easily penetrate the boot (and foot!) causing a casualty. The Kevlar boot liner helped prevent the punji stick's penetration. The punji trap was designed in different configurations in or above the ground and could be hastily constructed. In most cases, a punji injury may not be life threatening but it probably was life crippling.

SOLDIER CASUALTIES

I can vividly recall the situation where my first soldier was killed in action (KIA) as we battled up a steep hill with our artillery fire "walking" upward and ahead of my forward troops. In this situation, an artillery round must have hit a rock close by and its shrapnel killed my man instantly. We could not stop our advance because of the casualty, so my medic and a couple of men evacuated him quickly. Seeing his body pulled down the slope shattered my feeling of command and authority as I humbly asked myself—for this the first of future casualties—if I could have done anything differently that would have saved my soldier's life. It was a nagging and enduring feeling, which made me desire to always be a better commander in whatever endeavor I might undertake in my leadership roles. I learned to be courageous in my decisions, even though they could risk the life of one of my troops (or my own) while justly taking the lives of our foes.

In another battle, my men on point duty were attacked as we moved forward. My medic quickly rushed to the aid of one of the men who was hit. Just as he arrived to the wounded man's side, an enemy B-40 rocket hit my medic and instantly took his life. This medic had been a tremendous morale booster and motivator for my company's men, even in the midst of flying bullets and rockets, but now he was suddenly gone. In times like this, I wanted to tell the war to "JUST STOP!" and give us time to grieve when one of my most respected men had given his life in an effort to save another. Whenever I had casualties who were being evacuated, and if the battle situation permitted, I tried to be at the medical evacuation (Medevac) helicopter landing site to encourage and lift up my men who had lost another buddy. In this instance where my medic's disfigured body was being loaded on the helicopter, it seemed like the majority of the company wanted to come to express their sorrowful goodbyes. It was not common for my seasoned and weary soldiers to cry, but that day and for this medic who had treated so many wounded men, many tears dripped down battle-hardened faces to the soggy jungle floor.

I regretted the loss or wounding of any one person under my command, but in combat, you have to expect casualties to occur. When you have been taught to value life and each person's contribution to your team's success, the sight of one or more of my men's blood was tough emotionally. It is an ugly scene which sticks with you. The crucible of combat includes visions of experiences, which are rarely forgotten. These come from war. It is just the nature of it and the memories cannot be undone easily. I found that with God as my refuge and strength, I could and did endure through it all. Perseverance and coping are characteristics that must be demonstrated while engaged in all aspects of arduous combat—and even in civilian-type duties in life.

WATCH OUT FOR HELICOPTER BLADES!

My battalion commander became a casualty while coming to visit my fatigued men after we had fought a long battle up a steep mountain. Our division had a policy that if a helicopter hit a tree while coming in for a landing near a unit, the company commander on the ground would be relieved. Why? Because he (the company commander) had a responsibility to ensure the landing area was big enough to accommodate the diameter of the swirling helicopter blades.

I was on top of the hill, and a helicopter bringing my battalion commander to my location was going to land on the edge of a big bomb crater on the mountain side. Naturally, the blades would be much closer to the ground on the uphill side of the landing zone, which was plenty wide for the chopper. The helicopter pilots often landed in precarious places, and this would not be an unusual landing for this pilot who would have to hold the aircraft with only one skid resting on the side of the bomb crater as the passengers jumped out.

Without thinking about the potential danger, the battalion commander exited the helicopter on the uphill side and walked into the overhead spinning blade. Up top in my location, I heard a loud whack and thought the blades had hit a tree, and I thought I would be relieved of my command on the spot. Then the pilot hollered: "Medic, Medic!" My medic and I rushed down the hill to find our commander in the bottom of the crater with a portion of his skull missing from the strike of the helicopter blade. He was a big man, and to this day, I have no idea how we garnered enough strength to pull his unconscious body up the loose dirt and stones inside the bomb crater and put him on the helicopter. I can only say that the power of adrenaline can do miraculous things. We found his severely damaged helmet more than thirty feet away where it had been propelled by the whirling helicopter blades. My commander was evacuated and did survive, but the last I heard, he was severely disabled. How can a young captain handle such calamitous situations?

MISSED BY INCHES

The Scriptures tell us in Psalm 46 that God is our refuge and strength and that when we are in trouble, He is still there and therefore we should not fear. This promise is further detailed in Psalm 91 where the psalmist writes about deadly pestilence, terror by night, and arrows in the daytime. But he writes that

been there, done that!

God's angels will be with us to keep us in all our ways. Also, in I Samuel 30:6, the Scripture records that David was greatly distressed but he encouraged and strengthened himself in the Lord. I found great comfort in those words numerous times in the war environment. But, I'll assure you that I have experienced fear in the combat zone when I realized how close I was to meeting the authors of those words in the Bible. I know the Bible often tells us to "Fear not" in many circumstances, and we must learn to overcome our fears. With the Lord's help, our natural fears can be short-lived and fleeting because if not, they would build to a point of weakening and defeating us.

I was holding the radio-telephone corded handset to my left ear while giving subordinate units commands in the heat of a battle. Suddenly, my communications stopped so I turned to my soldier who was carrying the radio and asked if it had been hit. He wasn't aware of it so I then reached out the non-working handset to him and realized the cord had been severed just below the mouthpiece of the telephone-like handset. A bullet had passed between my hand holding the handset to my face and through the space in the crook of my arm. I had not even felt the slightest jerk when the bullet severed the cord. A bullet had missed me by only a couple of inches. The Lord was there! Thankfully, I was also!

On another day, we were convoying to a new action area, and our vehicles were ambushed. I was riding in the passenger seat of the truck with my rifle pointed out the right window. As the ambush began, I felt a movement of my rifle and the sound of automatic weapons. I told the driver to "gun it" to get through the ambush. After all the action ceased and looking at my rifle, I saw that a bullet had passed through my rifle's sling leaving a ragged hole. Apparently the bullet had gone right on through the truck cab and out the other side in front of the driver because we didn't find any other holes in the cab. Again, that is too close for comfort, but the Lord was still there with me! I was again missed by inches. Seeing all the bullet holes in the side of the truck made me so very thankful that the Lord had protected my troops from injury except for one man who had been hit in his little finger. Thankfully, the enemy's ambush was not successful!

In the middle of another battle, my artillery forward observer and I were lying on the ground with a map, identifying targets and coordinates where we wanted artillery and air sorties to strike. Our helmets were close to each other so we could hear each other talk over the battle's noise. My head was abruptly jolted to the side, my ears began ringing, and my eyes seemed to spin. I couldn't figure out what was happening. I looked at the lieutenant, and he was also somewhat dazed. Then I noticed a crease on the left side of his helmet and said his helmet had been hit and asked if he felt wounded in any way. He said he didn't think so. He then saw a groove on the right side of my helmet. We determined that because our helmets were very close together as we were talking over all the noise that an enemy bullet had hit his helmet and ricocheted into mine. That is really close! Again, the Lord was there with me! As I reflected on these near misses and other similar situations, I knew that God had spared my life for other unknown events in the future.

INVISIBLE WOUNDS IN COMBAT

Other than the physical wounds in battle, occasionally in the military, there are invisible wounds to the troops. Sometimes these wounds become evident later in life (such as in post-traumatic stress), but sometimes the invisible wounds are immediate. One such particular incident comes to mind. My company had been in the field and in combat for a number of days. We were fighting our way up a hill in the triple-canopy jungle of the central highlands of Vietnam. A battalion senior staff officer was flying overhead in a helicopter to "oversee" the battle from well beyond small arms range from the ground. Sometimes that guidance can be helpful, but in this situation, I felt his helicopter overhead was drawing the enemy's attention to my unit's location, and the helicopter was restricting some of my use of artillery and mortar indirect fires. He seemed to think that he could direct some of my subordinate teams (by looking down through the triple-canopy trees?) better than I could, although I was right on the ground in the battle with my troops. I said nothing back to him at the time but was quite upset that he was trying for no apparent reason to change my tactical plan in the middle of a progressing attack. He had "wounded" me and my company's morale with his lack of trust when we had not failed in any previous mission. I heard later that "someone" had put him in for a highly valued award for his "direction" of the battle. This reduced my respect of him even more.

But that wasn't the end of that situation. When we finally reached our objective by defeating the enemy and conquering the hilltop, I called for a resupply of rations, water, and ammunition for my troops, who had been so engaged and now were battle-weary. The staff officer answered my call but denied my request, saying that we were just going to come down from the mountain the next day and could get water at a stream. My ire rose quickly and intensified. What if the enemy counter-attacked that night? I had very little ammunition in my unit to repel the attack. What if one of my troops collapsed at night from lack of water and food? I told the officer that his answer was not satisfactory and that I was calling our mutual boss, the battalion commander, who was not at the firebase headquarters at the moment.

Finally, I did make contact with the battalion commander while he was still in the air flying back to the base. He said he would resolve the matter and would send a helicopter out with supplies as soon as he got back to the firebase—and he did! I don't know what his conversation with the other officer was at that time, but I imagine that it was not very friendly. However, I was happy that my troops were being cared for. That was decisive and timely leadership from my commander!

In my mind, the senior staff officer failed in his responsibilities to me and my unit and caused significant morale injury—even though for a short period of time. My radio-telephone operator and my company headquarters element all heard the verbal exchanges between me and my higher officers, and word spread rapidly in my company after we were told the officer would not send a resupply. Respect for him dwindled as it appeared that he had turned against my fighting men. His earlier inappropriate action in the combat situation and now his inaction by refusing supplies began to decimate my unit's esprit-de-corps and tear into the willpower and motivation of my troops. At that time, he seemed to be a toxic "leader" who was detrimental to my unit's ability to operate at our full potential to achieve success. He threatened and challenged my personal leadership, but my battalion commander (also the other officer's boss) later came through for my men. Morale injury and invisible wounds caused by one person can sometimes cause more long-term damage to a unit than physical injury. It is a leader's job to minimize such injury and find appropriate cures immediately to sustain the command's effectiveness. One of the most important elements of a unit's success in a combat environment is the morale of its soldiers. Napoleon once said: "Morale makes up three-quarters of the game; the relative balance of manpower accounts for only the remaining quarter."

A sidebar to this story is what was probably most injurious to my own career. Unfortunately for me, our battalion commander was severely injured shortly after this incident and had to be evacuated. In the transition time to a new commander, this senior staff officer became my efficiency rating officer. As a result, I did not get the marks in my rating which, I speculate, could have helped my career to move at a faster rate. I have learned that sometimes in life, you must make decisions that will be best for your organization and your people but yet potentially detrimental to your personal plans. This "conflict" with my senior staff officer was certainly one of those times! I knew that I would have to expect some kind of adverse reaction as a result of the stand I took with and for my troops. I have no regrets for my actions in support of my soldiers and am also confident that the Lord was well aware of all of this and how it fit into His plans for my life.

Other invisible wounds of war include seeing my men falling as a result of enemy action, losing men to jungle disease, failure of an individual or team to perform as trained and expected, memories of rapid bursts of enemy machine gun fire, and even the long-term impact of exposure to the Agent Orange defoliant. Some of these invisible wounds affect troops immediately, and others would have impact on one's life in future years—sometimes resulting in post-traumatic stress.

A DELAYED MISSION

In my company command time, there was only one mission which we did not fulfill in the designated time. My D Company was in a coordinated operation with B Company, moving through a large tea plantation toward our mutual objective when B Company was attacked by a swarm of bees. The bee "venom" attacked the men's nervous systems, and some of them became disoriented and confused. In listening to the company commander on the radio, I could hear increased slurring in his speech and then a lack of clear decision-making. Over half of his company men were disabled to some extent by the bees, and the operation had to be delayed for some time until treatment was received and the men were able to recover from the effect of the bee stings. The company commander and a few of his men had to be evacuated because of their severe reaction to the bee stings. After several hours, the operation continued with success.

FOLLOW ME!

One morning as the company commander in the field, I was awakened by a call from the battalion headquarters giving me orders for another operation. It was fairly routine for me to get my orders for that day's action about 4 a.m.! We had just fought part way up a hill, and I had lost some good men who had been on point out in front of the rest of the company. The difficult role of a commander of troops in combat is that in order to accomplish a challenging and life-threatening mission, we must often choose good men to be out front as point men. They may be our most skilled soldiers, team, squad, or platoon to initially confront the enemy. These may be the men who first give their lives or limbs in the battle. This is the sad memory we commanders live with for the rest of our earthly lives. Those recollections come back to haunt us both during the night hours and quiet times in the day. They never seem to completely disappear.

To be on point was always dangerous because in most situations, the point team is the initial force to spot or be spotted by enemy forces. Because of the losses of some of our best men in the previous couple of days, no one wanted to be ordered to point duty in the hazardous, enemy-infested environment in which we were operating. For this operation, when I selected the next point team, which would lead us out of our night position, there was almost a mutiny among my men. It was a continuing risky mission, and there was almost certainty that we would lose more men in the coming contact with the enemy. But as a young captain, I had learned that it's up to a good leader to ensure that his men know that somebody is in charge.

Somewhat feeling desperation and seeing the hesitancy of my men to "move out," I decided to go to the front and be the point for the company. Some may argue that this was not a wise decision, but I did feel that if I set the example—and yes, I was also fearful—that my men would follow and then assume the role. The infantry motto is "Follow Me!" so I headed to the front of the company and into the thick, mountainside jungle. My soldiers followed. Before long, one of my junior sergeants came to the front and said he would lead his men on the point team. My company was soon moving again into the unknown. I had practiced "sacrificial leadership" and demonstrated some previously learned core values in moving my unit toward its mission accomplishment. I don't say this in a bragging way, but for me on that day, it is what I had to do as the leader in front of my men. I needed to re-instill tactical confidence in my men to do what they were trained to do.

One of those core values taught to me in leadership classes is that the most important place for a leader is to be at the most critical and decisive location of a situation. That is the place or specific time where the threats to your command are the highest and where your presence can make the difference between mission accomplishment and failure. The morale of an entire unit can be impacted by the commander's action or inaction. The tactical planning can be excellent, but if the leader does not demonstrate courage and decisiveness, the planning will be ineffective. A leader must be able to see, hear, and understand his organization's emotional condition in order to make key decisions at a crucial moment to have a positive influence on his subordinates.

Another core value is that leaders must never ask their subordinates to do things that they themselves would not do. How could I have asked some of my best men to be out front to face a hidden enemy if I was not willing to do that myself? Strength of character must be demonstrated in the riskiest and most dangerous of situations. These types of beliefs must be so deeply entrenched in our minds that we live by them and are willing to die for them. They must drive us, regardless of risks in life, to not waste time espousing ideals and living our lives by values or principles to which we really don't believe or adhere. Accomplishment of a mission on a battlefield will depend on the commander's loyalty to these values that impact the very fiber of our being.

One of the Scriptures I found comforting in combat situations such as this scripture from Exodus 14:14 which says that the Lord will fight for us and that we only need to hold our peace and be still or silent. Moses, the commander of the questioning Israelites escaping Egypt, had to get control of a problematical situation and reminded the Israelites that they still had the Lord on their side. The people of Israel often found themselves directly confronting opposition—whether it was an army, the Red Sea, the Jordan River, and even their own tribesmen. Since they could not win under their own power, they needed to remain at peace with God's promise and be still to listen to His instructions. They needed to believe God's promises and trust His power for the nation's salvation. There were times when I found myself in situations entirely beyond my control and capabilities. Those were circumstances when I had to be reminded to remain peaceful and let God give wisdom for winning solutions. As God was there for Moses and the Israelites, He was (and is!) always there for me.

THE DARK VALLEY

Generally I am not fearful in the dark, but one night, things were very different. I was to lead my company of about ninety men cross country through the triple-canopy jungle to conduct a cordon around a suspected Viet Cong village. We needed to be in place at least an hour before daylight. There were no available roads that could be stealthily used to get us to the target area by the next daylight, and the distance as the crow flies was more than ten miles. We were

been there, done that!

used to moving sometimes longer distances by foot, so this would not be a major undertaking even though much of our time on this move would be at night. We had all developed large callouses on our feet from the extensive walking we had done, but callouses only followed the pain of initial blisters! (In fact, later when I was in the hospital, the nurses said that the callouses on the bottom of my feet were almost a quarter of an inch thick!) The map showed that we would have to cross a couple of deep ravines, and hiking there would take ten to twelve hours at night. My battalion commander did not want to give the enemy any hint of our mission so chose to not move us by helicopter—particularly not at night.

We left our current location at 3 p.m. and made great progress until about 10 p.m. It was now pitch black under the jungle's three layers of trees, but our compasses were trustworthy, and my pace men all agreed on the distance we had traveled. Unexpectedly, the map was not agreeing with the terrain or our distance traversed. Were we lost? Where is this hill we should be going over? There should be a rivulet to the right, but it wasn't there. The only choice I had was to follow our compass azimuth (direction) and see if things would begin to match up again, which they did after about another kilometer. I figured later that somehow the map had been misprinted without a 1000-meter section because the contour lines, which we couldn't see clearly under a red light at night, didn't match up. Thank goodness for a trusty compass that guided us through what initially seemed to be a dire situation. This reminds me of the tremendous value of the compass we have in our spiritual lives. The Bible is our trustworthy guide, and its effectual use will carry us through the many frightful journeys in our lives.

But that wasn't the end of our problems that night. My troops were beginning to get restless and somewhat hopeless as we floundered with that map issue. Their impatience and agitation only increased when we got down in the bottom of one of the deep ravines and the compass needle started to waver. We followed it a little this way and then it said we needed to turn and go that way. The compass was apparently being adversely influenced by magnetism in the rocks in the side of that deep ravine. Although it was pitch black and unlikely that enemy forces could possibly be down in that valley, we still had to maintain sound and light discipline.

With my leadership team, we would open a poncho, crawl under it and use the flashlight to read the map. The heat and the stench of our sweaty bodies would become almost unbearable. It was a relief to poke out occasionally from under the poncho to get a breath of "fresh" air—where it seemed there really wasn't any air to breathe in the bottom of that steamy, deep ravine. To resolve our dilemma,

I called for artillery flares to be popped over known grid points (coordinates) on the map. We used the flares as our guiding stars to lead us in the right direction out of that valley—even though we could barely see their light through the trees' canopies. After losing a couple of hours in that ravine, we finally made it out and did get set up in our cordon around our objective village just before the morning nautical twilight. We were surprised to find NVA (North Vietnamese Army)—instead of Viet Cong—soldiers who were trying to use the village as a safe haven. The mission was accomplished, but if we had spent another half hour in that dark valley, this mission would not have been successful, and we may have had to retreat into the valley for another night. I must admit that on that particular mission, I was fearful of that very dense darkness in the depths of that valley when our compasses ostensibly went wacky.

I have learned some great lessons from this experience. In life, we often find ourselves in deep valleys, and we try to work our way out through the use of manmade objects, unfounded reasoning, and human advice. But we get mixed signals, pointing us to try this way or that way, which just lead us to conflicting potential solutions. We have our guidance from previous planning of the way we should be going, but we continue to flounder in our perceived darkness, trying to study our route under the dim light of human reasoning. As a last resort, we call out for help from Someone in whom we have faith to lead us out of the valley—if we pursue what we know is true. The Bible provides my light from above. David says in Psalm 27:1: "The Lord is my light and salvation; whom shall I fear?" and Jesus said: "I am the light of the world: he that follows me shall not walk in darkness, but shall have the light of life." The Lord Jesus is always available for me when I call. When I appeal for help, He will answer with His truth. In turn, I must have faith to accept His provision—even though I may only see a flicker of His light—and follow it to escape the darkness of my valleys in life. As Christians, we can be assured of this fact: Whether we find ourselves on the pinnacle of the mountain or in the darkest depths of the valley, God is there and will give us peace.

VILLAGE RAIDS

Several of our operations were to conduct village raids to gather intelligence from the people. This required us to secretly set up village cordons at night, and at first light, we gathered all the villagers out of their long-houses into the center of the village.

been there, done that!

We then separated the men from the women and children and selected the most suspicious men for interrogation regarding enemy activities in the area. We flew some of the men out to a secure area for questioning.

After we had gathered sufficient intelligence, we returned the men to their villages—unless some of them turned out to be North Vietnamese or Viet Cong soldiers themselves.

In one of our raids, some men—later discovered to be North Vietnamese Army soldiers—tried to escape. In fleeing from our engagement, they left behind a wounded comrade, a rifle, several satchel charges, some Chinese grenades, and a whole lot of blood trails and drag marks, indicating that they took some of their wounded soldiers with them.

In some of the villages, we found caches of food or weapons hidden there for later use by the enemy. These had to be either destroyed or removed. Some of the huge supplies of food were redistributed to other "friendly" locations. Over a three-week period very near the end of the rice harvest, we found an estimated forty to forty-five tons of rice stolen from local villagers and stockpiled by the North Vietnamese. At one place, we also found over two hundred pounds of salt. From our reconnaissance position, we were pondering what to do when three NVA soldiers came to get some food items. I then sent a small unit to follow them back to their unit, but unfortunately, my men lost them and came back empty handed. Being a valuable commodity, we secured the area until a helicopter came in to take the rice and salt away.

FINAL BATTLES—WOUNDED IN ACTION

I will not dwell on other battle casualties or difficult situations while in command of my company except for my personal situation. I was wounded twice in battles. The first was on May 12, 1969, when my company was providing security for an artillery unit. I had established a perimeter defense for the night and had placed listening posts outside the perimeter on potential avenues of approach the enemy could use in an attack against us. Sure enough, the North Vietnamese did come at us that night. It started with incoming artillery that I think was designed to distract us from their movement in a ground attack. During the ensuing battle, we called in air support and thankfully received it. Our artillery guns were leveled to fire directly at the enemy rather than into the air as they would normally do when providing indirect fire support. If you ever want to see real fireworks, observe a battle at night! Our rifles and machine guns, lines from tracer bullets, artillery, bombs and rockets from aircraft, and even grenades provide a tremendous amount of noise and flash directly to your front. The cacophony of sounds is almost debilitating when in direct conflict as we were that night.

While checking on my troops in their perimeter defensive locations, I was hit with enemy artillery shrapnel in the left arm and my right shin. They were just flesh wounds, which later were patched by my medic, and I did not feel that these were serious enough for me to leave my troops. The enemy did not penetrate our perimeter security, but two of my men in an outpost were killed in action. Additionally, three men were killed and nine wounded in the artillery unit. The next day, the artillery moved, and my company was sent on another mission.

HAMMER AND ANVIL OPERATION

My unit continued its normal operations, and on the night of May 17, 1969, I received orders for another mission at daybreak on Sunday. (Combat operations do not stop for a break on weekends!) Little did I know it at the time—but even beyond some of our unit's traumas of the past—this "ordinary" day in war would be riddled with the unexpected. It would be my final battle in Vietnam.

Our fellow B Company had been locked down on a ridge against a sizable North Vietnamese unit. My company was to make an air assault at daybreak farther down the ridge behind the enemy unit and proceed to "hammer" the enemy against the "anvil" of B Company. The assaulting airlift went smoothly, and we pushed along the ridge with extreme caution. At one point, my scouts in my point team could sense by noise, smell, and by reading tell-tale signs on the ground that we were closing in on the enemy.

I called for artillery but was told that because of the rules of engagement—which stated that artillery could not fire over a village unless direct contact already had been made with the enemy—we were prevented from getting indirect fire support either from supporting artillery or my own mortars. I was furious thinking that we may have to sustain casualties before getting the fire support we needed.

Sure enough, the contact and shooting soon began! The enemy turned from their engagement with B Company and brought their wrath on my troops. Now, I could bring massive indirect fire and air support on the North Vietnamese Army troops in front of us, but it was a little late. My men began suffering casualties as we pushed forward in the battle.

SHELL-SHOCKED LIEUTENANT

Unfortunately the day before—as replacements for two of my previously wounded platoon leaders—I received two new inexperienced lieutenants into my 1st and 3rd platoons. In the frustrations and complexities of battle on May 18, one of them failed in his leadership. It appeared to me that he was in shell-shock, just kneeling there in an upright position and not moving. He was a prime target, and I had to have his senior sergeant knock him to the ground and take command of that platoon. The other new lieutenant was leading my reserve platoon, and in the movement of his unit forward to the battle on our right flank, he suffered heat stroke, and his sergeant had to take care of that situation. In the middle of battle, two of my three line-platoon leaders had failed. What a disappointment! Thankfully, I had experienced senior non-commissioned officers in those two platoons. The enemy did not stop its action to let me deal with these difficulties in my subordinate leaders. The North Vietnamese soldiers continued its aggressive attack on my troops.

MY LEG POINTED IN WRONG DIRECTION

In the midst of the ongoing battle, I noted that one of my men had been hit and that my medic was caring for the physical wounds of other soldiers. I went to the individual on the ground and saw that he had a sucking chest wound. Keeping as low as I could while kneeling to apply first aid—there is a certain procedure to treat this kind of wound—I patched him. I was going to pull him to a safer spot away from the direct line of fire, when I noticed my right leg from just above the knee was pointed out to the side when it should have been in front of me. I had been wounded and with all the adrenalin flowing, I hadn't even sensed or felt that I had been hit. I turned over the care of the soldier with the sucking chest wound to another soldier, grabbed my now-useless leg to straighten it, and dragged myself behind a big tree still trying to keep control of my troops and the fierce fighting to my front. I talked with my artillery forward observer and directed that he increase artillery bombardment of the area between my D Company and B Company. I also called for more air support from the Air Force tactical fighters and bombers as I maneuvered my platoons in our effort to defeat the enemy and protect my own troops. I had to keep my company's hammer ferociously pounding on the enemy against B Company's anvil!

been there, done that!

In the meantime, I assessed my wound and figured that I had been shot with a tumbling bullet (or maybe a piece of shrapnel) because of the approximately six-inch tear in the flesh at the entry site on the front of my leg. I saw that the bone, about four-inches above the knee, had been severed and that I was bleeding profusely. After putting a compression bandage on the front of my leg, I soon realized that blood was also pouring out the back of my leg. I had to borrow a couple of bandages from other fighting troops to apply more pressure and reduce that blood loss. I also debated applying a tourniquet to my leg if I couldn't get the blood loss to stop. The bullet had obviously entered the front, hit and shattered and divided the femur bone, and exited out the back of my leg, leaving a gaping hole in my leg. I quickly pulled straps off my rucksack and fastened its frame to my leg as a splint. (In earlier training, we were taught to use our rifle as a splint, but I wasn't about to give up my rifle as a splint at that point!) Thankfully, I was not sensing any pain—much to my surprise.

With all the "whys" and "impacts" on others, time in war also has a way of tearing at the fabric of an individual's soul. I was fully aware of the politically charged nature of this media-covered conflict and the anti-war attitude that had been generated in so many young lives in America. Was I contributing to this by leading my troops into killing zones? Was God taking me out of the middle of this horrific struggle between the generations? Why did I have to be responsible for these young men on the front lines? These were mind-searching matters, but through all these types of questions, I still had to remain focused on the battle at hand to win victory with minimal casualties of my heroic men.

REFUGE IN MY GOD

Knowing that I could never make the world safe, I found that my personal refuge behind that big tree had to be in my God who had given up His life in order to save others. The terrifying life of a soldier was suddenly being described again for me in Psalm 91, which I had learned years before as a kid in Africa. Relentless legitimate fear, enveloping blackness of death of my men, and potential injustice against innocent men was all portrayed before me on that ridgeline in my emotional pain. It could seem overwhelming and gruesome, but as David portrayed in the psalm, there is a place of safety that the field environment of battle cannot eliminate. My haven of safety was in God, and I could confidently and completely trust Him for whatever outcome He chose. I was not afraid to die, but the realism of death's potential was there. In a time like that, I realized that I could still find rest in my Lord even in the midst of spiritual, emotional, and physical suffering. For now, I realized that I had a second chance at life and apparently the Lord still had more for me to do. Perhaps it would be in some other venue than commanding troops in the field in the future.

MEDICAL EVACUATION

After a couple of hours and with the battle still raging, I recognized that because of my loss of blood, I was not thinking clearly. I also recognized that I could not be in the physical places I needed to be in the command of my company as they slowly pushed forward in the conflict. Thankfully, throughout these hours, I was not feeling any pain—although my femur had been severed, muscle destroyed, and nerves damaged. I know that this was a blessing from the Lord!

But I also knew that there was no clearing on that ridgeline we had traveled earlier in the day for helicopters to land to evacuate my wounded soldiers. With the intensity of the battle diminishing due to our relentless push and the effect of our heavy artillery barrages and aircraft bombings, I ordered a few of my men to use explosives we carried to blow down some of those huge trees—at least three feet in diameter—and saw down smaller ones so that Medevac helicopters could come in. There was no way we could clear sufficient space in the dense jungle for them to land on the ground, so they would have to balance their helicopter skids on a fallen tree while loading the casualties. Making a landing hole in the triple-canopy jungle was a huge undertaking, but it had to be done so troops could be lifted out to a hospital. The battalion headquarters sent us some engineers who rappelled from helicopters with their chain saws and additional equipment to help prepare the landing zone.

Then I called the battalion commander and said I was turning over command of the company to the one previously combat-tested lieutenant in the company. Not too much longer after that, the battle eased and evacuation of my company's wounded could begin. I had not been in physical pain to that point, but when my troops started to put me in a poncho to carry me a few hundred yards to the helicopter medical evacuation area, the pain struck with unbelievable fierceness, and I felt that I would soon pass out. (I just learned from the internet that a break in the lower femur is one of the most painful bone breaks.)

been there, done that!

I called for the medic to give me some morphine. After waiting for a brief period of time for it to take effect, they tried again to move me, but the pain was still very intense. I knew the medic could give a maximum of two shots of morphine so I asked for another and then told the men to just go ahead and move me. The poncho "ride" to the evacuation area was rough with my butt often bouncing on the ground. When we neared the landing zone, all of us living and the deceased casualties were put in lines to be put on helicopters as they came in. At that point, the morphine had kicked in and I was one "happy" soldier and pulled my camera out of my pocket and asked that a picture be taken. I sort of leaned up on one elbow and flashed the "V" sign with my fingers along with a big smile. The last I remember was being picked up in my poncho and loaded into the helicopter that was balancing on a big horizontal tree trunk. I was laid on the floor, along with a couple of other wounded men and my "lights" went out.

CHAPTER XI
HOSPITALIZATIONS

"WOUNDED, HAWAII CANCELED, MORE LATER"

From that time of my helicopter evacuation from the field on May 18, I do not remember anything until I was awakened in a field hospital tent in Pleiku where they did some initial cleansing of the wound and put on a more effective splint for further evacuation. I do not know how many days or hours I was there, but I do remember that someone—it may have been the brigade commander or the personnel officer—came in and questioned me regarding a Purple Heart Medal. I told him that I had also been wounded six days earlier on May 12 (from shrapnel), so he gave me two medals. (Interestingly, the clerk typing the orders for one of the medals didn't get my name right although the rest of the information [like my service number] was correct.)

I did ask about my unit and the result of the battle. Sadly, five of my men had been killed in the battle and seventeen of us had been wounded that day. On the other side, in a letter to my wife on May 20, 1969, I wrote: "Found out the results of our contact on Sunday [May 18]. The radio said that we killed 90 NVA [North Vietnamese Army] soldiers. Their wounded numbers were unknown but with all the bullets, artillery rounds, and aerial bombardments poured into that area, I can't imagine that too many of them escaped without injury! We had faced a much larger enemy unit than anticipated. Now, that unit would no longer be a threat in our area of operations! My company's hammer against B Company's anvil had been successful. Mission accomplished!"

At that field hospital on the day I arrived, I asked to send a Red Cross message to my wife. Not wanting to get her too alarmed, I made it rather brief. It read:

been there, done that!

"Wounded. Hawaii cancelled. More later." My wife and I had been scheduled to go to Hawaii for my rest and recuperation (R&R) from the war in just a couple of more weeks, but obviously that was off. That May 18, 1969, started another whole saga of my military career!

In her own words, Betty said: "Expecting a call from the Red Cross about joining my husband in Hawaii, I was excited when the Red Cross called. But that excitement was soon dashed when they said they knew nothing about the trip to Hawaii. They had a message for me. As they read it, I guess I was in a state of shock, but then I remembered what the Lord had impressed upon me when Phil left for Vietnam for his second time that he was coming home to me. God just didn't tell me he would come home wounded. Then I realized the message was from him, and that meant he was still alive! I didn't know the extent of his injury for a week until I finally got a call from him in Japan. That was a most welcomed phone call!"

AWAKENED BY KNOCKING IN JAPAN

From the field hospital in Pleiku in the central highlands, I was evacuated by an Air Force plane to one of their hospitals in Nha Trang on the coast of Vietnam to prepare me for further transport and surgery. I believe I was there only a couple of days where I was put in a more rigid splint outfit and then flown to an old Army surgical hospital in Yokohama, Japan. I don't remember that flight at all as they must have had me pretty well drugged. In that Army hospital, I was put in traction immediately. To do that, a doctor said they were going to insert a pin horizontally through the bone in my leg just below the knee and the traction cords would be fastened to that pin.

The doctor showed me the stainless steel pin that was about eight inches long. Then he said they would sterilize and numb the area and fasten the pin to a drill and quickly drive it through the bone. They would not let me watch, nor was I put out, so I could hear the drill grinding even though I could feel nothing except some pressure against my leg. It didn't take long before they pulled the sheet away so I could see this shiny rod sticking out both sides of my upper tibia shin bone of my right leg! I still have that pin which they gave me when it was removed at Valley Forge Military Hospital in the United States.

After some time in traction in Japan, I underwent surgery to further align the femur bone and close the wound. Already under a light anesthesia, I can remember "floating" down ramps on my way to surgery and hoping the hospital corpsmen would not crash me into walls at turns in the ramps! (The old hospital structure used ramps since there were no elevators to transfer patients from one floor to another.) Before the surgery, the doctor told me that if I was still in a traction contraption after surgery, I would be staying in Japan for another six weeks. I said that if possible, I'd really like to get evacuated to the US where my wife could come see me. He then said that if I woke up with him knocking on a cast on my chest that I would then be going back to America. Was I ever glad to awaken to his knocking!

BACK IN THE USA!

My cast was a full body spica cast, which meant that it went from around my body under my armpits to my hips, down my wounded right leg to the ankle, and down my left leg to the knee. A 1x3-inch board was built into the cast just above my knees to keep my legs apart at about a forty-five-degree angle. Obviously, I could not go anywhere unless I was carried on a stretcher. From Japan, I flew on an Air Force medical evacuation plane back to the United States.

The plane had rows of litter racks down the middle of much of the cargo space, with some rows of seats for walking wounded in the forward area. The stretchers were stacked four high and most were full with patients, but for me on the second level from the bottom, they had to take out the litter just above me so that the flight nurses could come and rotate me every couple of hours. When they put me on my side, they ran straps around the upward leg—remember that board between my legs!—and fastened them to the litter above me so that I would not sway or roll back and forth. The Air Force flight nurses were extremely professional and compassionate as they handled the needs of all of us on that plane.

Our first stop (as far as I know) was at Elmendorf Air Force Base in Anchorage, Alaska. It seemed like many servicemen got off the plane and went in to the terminal, but those of us on litters could only remain where we were on the plane. Before long, we were thankful to see Red Cross ladies come on board with some goodies for us. They welcomed us back to the United States! I was really happy to be back on American soil!

After refueling and reloading, I think that our next stop was McGuire Air Force Base in New Jersey—where we were put on a bus reconfigured to hold stretchers—and driven about sixty miles to Valley Forge Military Hospital in

been there, done that!

Valley Forge, Pennsylvania. (This also was a very old Army hospital—but I'm sure was built long after General George Washington had encamped in the area following his successful crossing of the Delaware River!) It was a long ride in that bulky cast, swaying back and forth on that bus as we sped along weaving in and out of traffic! Why Valley Forge? It was the main Army hospital handling orthopedic cases. Several Army hospitals had been designated to care for special needs, such as for burns at the hospital in San Antonio, Texas, and head wounds at Walter Reed in Washington, DC.

My doctor, Dr. G, had been brought into the Army with a direct commission as a major because of his orthopedic specialty and research at Michigan State University. He treated me very well. The gunshot wound had taken out about three-quarter inch of bone and there were some nerve, tendon, and muscle damages in my right leg. At Valley Forge, my cast was taken off (and was I ever glad to get out of that!). I was given a bed in a private room and put in traction again with about forty pounds pulling on my leg.

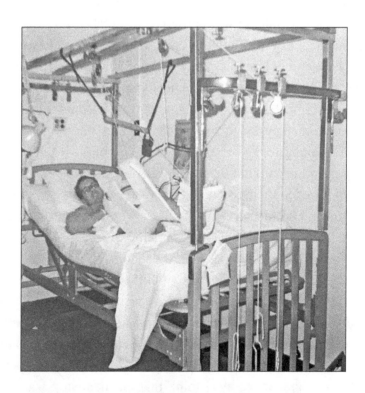

The doctor wanted to keep the bones separated initially so that they could grow calcium off their ends and eventually connect to be one solid bone. My only problem was that the weights kept pulling me to the foot of the bed, and I would wake up sort of scrunched down at the footboard. I was in traction there for about six weeks.

BETTY'S VISITS TO VALLEY FORGE

Betty flew from South Bend, Indiana, to see me very shortly after I arrived at Valley Forge. Her flight went to Philadelphia, but she didn't know how she would get from the airport to the hospital. When she explained her dilemma to my dad, he said he would call some pastors in Pennsylvania to see if they could arrange for some help. Sure enough, one pastor in nearby Norristown agreed to provide whatever transportation was necessary during Betty's brief stay with me at the hospital. How thankful we were for his assistance! This was Betty's first plane ride, and it was very rough as it came through a severe storm. (She didn't realize that most flights were not that rough and wondered if she ever wanted to fly again!) We had a wonderful visit together, but she had to get back home to our three kids in Indiana. (Our third child had been born into our family while I was in Vietnam on my second tour.) She said she'd be back sometime but didn't know when.

One night a couple of weeks later, she popped in on me again! Her sister had driven to Pennsylvania with her because Betty had brought our kids to see me. They were not allowed on the hospital floor where I was so the next day Betty asked the staff to roll my bed with its traction weights down the ramps and around the corners to take me outside. That's where I saw our new, four-month-old son, Todd, for the first time as Betty laid him on my chest! I cried tears of joy as my family was together again! Betty then asked the nurses to roll my bed outside each day during her stay for the week. They felt that was too much work, so they agreed that the kids could come up to my room on the hospital ward since I was not in an open bay with other wounded soldiers. In fact, the nurses would sometimes take the kids to their nurses' station and give them little things to do to keep them entertained while Betty was with me. In the evenings, Betty's sister would keep the kids in their accommodations on the hospital grounds so Betty and I could have more time together.

been there, done that!

MY "EARTHQUAKE"

One night, I woke up with my hospital bed shaking vigorously. I thought we were in an earthquake. I called the nurse, and when she arrived, the weights of my traction were still swinging. My leg was straight but was sort of wobbling back and forth from where the break was. When Dr. G came in the next day, he said that probably what had happened was that the calcium on both ends of the bones had met and connected in previous days, but perhaps my moving that night had caused the calcium to break apart, making the weights to suddenly drop and the bed to shake. He said we had to go back to almost square one but that now he would let the bones stay smashed together and let the calcium create a knot around the former break. The bones did eventually grow together. That soft calcium growth formed the solid knot the doctor wanted, even though the bones grew at a little offset angle, and my leg would be somewhat shorter. He said that it seems a certainty that my right femur bone would never break in that spot again with that mass of bone that had developed!

One highlight for me in those days, was that I remember staying awake throughout the night of July 21, 1969, to watch the first moon landing when Neil Armstrong made that historic step out of the lunar lander onto the moon's surface! The hospital staff had brought a TV into my room just so I could watch that fascinating and historic event.

QUESTIONING GOD

As I lay in my hospital bed in the days, weeks, and months, I began to wonder about the future of my career. Here I was an Airborne Ranger Infantry officer with two tours of combat duty, who had long-range desires to continue levels of commands up the chain. But would I even be able to stay in the Army, and if so, what would the Army let me do? Of course, the hospital personnel could not answer those questions. They just said that they would provide information to a medical board that would make such decisions. I was quite concerned.

Lying in bed in traction for those weeks caused me to question God and His plan for my life. Sometimes I would get angry with Him. I don't know if I ever physically raised my fists at Him or not, but I know that I felt like doing it. Why? Why? Why? were constant questions in my mind. I had given my life to the Lord as a young boy in Africa, and I thought I was fulfilling His will in my life, but had He now laid me aside and forgotten about me? What did I do to deserve this? Why was God allowing these circumstances now to change my plans in my military career? I was in a struggle with the Lord.

One night, the Lord clearly reminded me again of Proverbs 3:5–6: "Trust in the Lord with all your heart, and lean not on your own understanding. In all your ways acknowledge Him, and He shall direct your paths." I had heard a lot of messages about "trusting," but I didn't recall ever hearing any sermons about the "lean not" part of the verse. I was trying to understand God's actions, but I was to stop that and just turn every concern over to Him and He would provide a path ahead. I began to think about other verses pertaining to the Lord's guidance. God says in Psalm 32:8 "I will instruct thee and teach thee in the way thou shalt go: I will guide thee with mine eye." God is always faithful to carry out His word. That night my life was changed. I was now convinced that He had a plan for me that might not be my own plan! I needed to have an attitude of acceptance of what God was doing for and in me and trust His love for me and His perfect timing for my future. It could be that I would be medically discharged from the Army and for sure if I did stay in, I'd not be able to go back to command troops in the field. God had other plans unknown to me at the time, but as I later thought about those long hospital days, I realized that His plans would be much better than I could even dream about. I would need His power and my willingness to follow and fulfill the opportunities He would give me.

GUINEA PIG FOR A HINGED CAST

Following sufficient time in traction, I was again put in a big spica cast, except this one did not have the cast down to the knee on the left leg. Now with the aid of crutches, I could get out of bed! My new cast had some hardware that was really different! Before coming in the Army, Dr. G, my orthopedic surgeon, had been doing original research into the use of hinges in casts which covered joints. If his information was accurate, a hinged cast potentially would increase an individual's joint mobility once the final cast was removed. He told me about his research and felt that I was a good candidate for a cast with hinges at the knee. Without them, he predicted that I would have a stiff leg. I agreed to be a guinea pig for the test, and he proceeded to tell the machine shop downstairs in the hospital how to make the hinges. This was my second time to be a "guinea pig". The first had been in Airborne School on that 250-foot-high jump tower!

been there, done that!

The spica casting table is not comfortable since you lie on what is basically a steel frame with your back on a metal rod which can be easily pulled out after they have wrapped the casting material—which was really warm!—around you. As he finished wrapping my leg and knee, he called for the hinges to be brought up from the machine shop. He fastened a heavy metal hinge piece on each side of the cast with additional casting wrap and plaster above and below the knee and then cut away the cast so that the full knee was exposed. He tried bending my knee slightly but quietly remarked that the hinges weren't right and that he would have to use the cast saw to cut them off, send them back to the machine shop for modification, and re-cast the knee temporarily. In the meantime, I am lying on this very uncomfortable spica table! It wasn't too long until the hinges came back up and were replaced on the cast with more plaster wrap. The cast over the knee was again cut away and the doctor was satisfied! Then I had to get used to walking in that cast with its minimal knee bending and still with no ability to bend at the waist. When I first started walking in that cast, I really wasn't too sure about putting weight on the leg with the hinges, but eventually I gained confidence in it. I sure thank Dr. G for letting me be a guinea pig for his orthopedic research.

CONVALESCENT LEAVE AT HOME

I was permitted now to take convalescent leave at home. But how would I get home since I couldn't sit or even bend at the waist? Betty borrowed a station wagon from a friend, put a twin bed mattress in the back, and she and Dad drove from South Bend, Indiana, to Valley Forge to pick me up. Since I was not "bendable" yet, they picked me up like a log and shoved me in the back of the station wagon! She and Dad took turns driving back to Indiana without taking any time to stop somewhere and sleep. When one was driving, the other slept, and Betty even crawled in the back of the station wagon on the bed with me and got some much-needed sleep! That was so wonderful to have her beside me again!

I was given a pair of "Canadian" crutches to help me get around once I was vertical, but that is where Betty's help was really needed because the cast covered from my armpits down through my hips and on the right side down through my knee hinges to my ankle. I could not bend at the hips to get myself up. Betty had three young children to dress and feed, and now she had one big kid she also had to care for! Also, I could not bend over the table to eat my food but I could sit on a small portion of my left cheek butt on a high kitchen stool with my right leg extended a little to the side. Otherwise, I was pretty much confined to lying on a couch or bed. My cast didn't let me sit in a chair because I was straight as a log. Think about all you cannot do if you are not able to bend at the waist! How do you get out of bed? How do you get dressed and put shoes on? How do you pick up something from the floor? How do you sit? Even at church, I was on a couch in the library where I could hear the message and where people could come and visit me.

RELIEVING MY "GIRDLE"

Betty's cooking was much better than the rations I had in the field in Vietnam and the food provided in the hospitals—although I never found any reason to complain about any of it! I think she pulled out her best menus for me when I was home. It all tasted so good! Soon the cast over my stomach began to get tighter and tighter and was very uncomfortable! I thought that this is how women—in the past!—must have felt when they put their girdles on and cinched their waistline! The resolution? Betty suggested that she cut away some of the cast to give my belly some relief. It worked and did not change the integrity of the cast. I wish I had paid more attention to the nurses' and doctor's reaction when I got back to the hospital! They were probably a little surprised about my newly designed and more practically comfortable cast.

But Betty's cast cutting did not stop at the belly. I was feeling very sharp pains in the area under the cast on the back side of my leg where the bullet had exited. It seemed like something was poking me at the site of the wound closure, and it really hurt, so Betty decided to investigate. To get to the spot, again she had to break away some of the cast without violating its integrity. Then she found the problem. Apparently during my initial surgeries in Vietnam and Japan, a piece of a leaf was hiding and had gotten left inside when they sewed me up to close the wound. That little leaf was now wanting out and was pushing through the skin, causing the pain. Betty got some tweezers and carefully pulled it out without it breaking. That's the skill of my good home nurse! It was less than half of an inch square, but that little thing sure caused a lot of agony.

Throughout life, many small things can have a big impact on us or those around us. In the Scripture in the book of James, we are reminded of how a tiny spark can generate a destructive flame, how a little bridle can control a powerful horse's actions, and how a small rudder can cause a mammoth ship to change directions. In my life, that small piece of leaf—and a small bullet which caused it to be there—turned the course of my career. Removing a small antagonizer provided great physical relief. And a small bullet caused an unimaginable change in my future assignment!

In my convalescence, I would be home for a few weeks then went back to the hospital for a few weeks, back and forth like that into December. It was tough traveling because I had to have two seats on the airplane since I couldn't sit normally. Finally, my bulky hinged cast was removed for good, and more intense physical therapy (PT) began—I call it Pure Torture! It seemed that I spent hours on an exercise table extending, flexing, and strengthening my leg and knee. Although I never did get normal full extension and flexion, I can do almost anything I need or want to do. I have learned to walk without a noticeable limp most of the time, although my right leg is a little crooked and is shorter than my left, and it does have some muscle, tendon, and nerve damage, which affect my lower leg and foot.

I am glad I do not have an artificial leg. A couple years after I was back on duty again in the Army, I met my former brigade commander, and he said: "Fogle, you walk pretty well on that prosthesis." When I told him that I am all flesh and bones, he was surprised and said that when I left Vietnam, he was told that I would lose my leg. I am very thankful for the excellent medical care and rehabilitation I received through the military services and even now through the Veterans Administration.

FAMILY AND CHURCH SUPPORT

I sincerely honor my wife, Betty, for her courage, strength, and care during those Vietnam years and especially at Christmas times. Not only did she endure the responsibility of dealing with normal household functions, but she was alone with one child in 1965, with two children in 1968, but then with three small children and one big "kid" (me!) in 1969. My sister, Lois, and her husband, Jerry, and my parents who lived nearby were all great helps to Betty when I was overseas and then in my "invalid" status. I also thank them for their efforts to aid my family.

In the times when I was home on convalescent leave in the fall of 1969, Betty had to do so much for me since I could not bend at the waist. To accommodate the large knee hinges on my cast, she had to open the right leg seams of all my pants on both sides of my knee and make sure the waist was big enough to go around my cast. She put pants and socks on me every day, tied my shoes, gave me a "bib" when we ate since I could not get up close to the table or bend to eat over a plate due to my cast's restriction. She had to "load" me in and out of the car if we were to go anywhere. At church, she helped me get up the steps and into the library where I lay on the couch during the service. Some of you may say that you would like to have done that—that is, lie on the couch to listen to a message! (Maybe you did that during the coronavirus lockdown of 2021!) Betty was the real trooper in those days—and still is!

In that context, I must also give credit to the pastor and members of First Baptist Church in Mishawaka, Indiana. While I was in Vietnam both times, and when I was nine months in the hospital in Valley Forge, Pennsylvania,—with some of that time on convalescent leave at home—the church as a body of Christ really looked after Betty and provided her with much-needed physical and spiritual support. It also provided great encouragement to me through prayer, cards, calls, and visits.

I was so thankful for my God being my Great Physician. He has been at my bedside from the times of early childhood diseases, gunshot wound, heart surgery, back problems (and later surgery), hip replacement, and many other physical issues. When Bunny, my daughter-in-law, was in nursing school, she had to do a case study and chose me as her subject. She got an A on the project, but there was also a notation below the grade. It read: "Is this really one person?" If she were writing her report today, she would have even more to include. God is always good to me and I am so thankful for His blessings on me in so many ways!

SNAPSHOTS OF COMBAT DUTY

It has been a long time since I left Vietnam's battlefields in 1969, but my recollection of those days remains very clear. I can visualize actual locations and mentally relive specific combat actions and apparently talk of some of them in my sleep. I think Betty is the only person who knows a lot about those strenuous days in my life.

Someone once asked me: "What are some quick snapshots of your combat duty?" It is hard to make them "quick," but here are some of my reflections with no effort to determine priorities: eardrum-shattering sounds of friendly and enemy rifles, machine guns, and artillery fire; blistered and calloused hands from digging foxholes and cutting down trees; smell and sound of C-4 explosives; fear of punji stakes and trip-wired booby traps; constant alertness for enemy action; itch and pain of bug bites; weight on my shoulders of a sixty-pound backpack; sweaty stink of body odor from days of operations with no showers; unending emotions of apprehension and battlefield sadness; increased adrenalin flow in the crescendo of a firefight; smell of gunpowder and exploding grenades; the thunderous, earth-shaking of nearby B-52 bombing; terrible sight of splattered blood from ripped bodies; screams of agony from wounded and dying heroic men; carrying men in ponchos to evacuation helicopters; dragging wounded soldiers out of the line of fire; eerie sounds of a jungle night; daily consumption of canned rations; tremendous struggle to move through an area blasted by massive bombing in the triple-canopy jungle; conducting bomb damage assessments; incessant whop-whop-whop of helicopter blades; trudging in the darkest nights toward an objective; the rapid swish and roaring of our close-by attacking fighter jets; smell of searing flesh from enemy bullets; anxiety about the next mission call from headquarters; never-ending process of making decisions impacting the lives of soldiers; sound of artillery whistling overhead; effect of shrapnel shards impacting the battle area; marking (with colored smoke grenades) the spot you want close combat support aircraft to drop their ordnance or fire their "Gatling" guns or rockets (sometimes very close to our troop positions); sights and sounds at night of Spooky aircraft circling and firing streams of bullets on a specified target; first use of starlight scopes to "see" in the night; sentry dogs and scout dogs; and most of all, the tremendous heroism of my soldiers. Each of these snapshots can be developed into full-length videos, but nothing can portray combat any better than combat itself. If you have never fought in a ground battle against a formidable enemy, you will never fully grasp what combat is. I have "been there, done that!"

Each moment in combat was a learning experience for me, as it taught me how people react under unbelievable, sustained pressure. Some handle it well, and others become shell-shocked and inefficient. To enable victory, the vast majority of my soldiers remembered and applied their training and never broke under the burdens of caring for their fellow men and themselves. I gained a renewed pride in our American soldier!

Combat has been described by an anonymous person as "hours and hours of boredom punctuated by moments of sheer terror". That could well be true if you are in a defensive position or in some types of support units. And I suppose it could be true for a unit on a long road march. However, boredom was never a description of my unit's life. In the jungle, there are many things which attract attention—whether they are the animals or bugs, unusual noises, the intensity of the heat, or the anticipation of a booby trap made with punji stakes (sharpened bamboo stakes placed in a trap to injure a person). My company was in defensive missions for very few nights and in only one of those nights did we face that *sheer terror* following boredom. But *sheer terror* also can come at any moment when being helicopter-lifted into an enemy-infested, hot landing zone or when moving down a ridgeline knowing the enemy is directly in front of you—somewhere! That is *not* boredom!

Effectively leading soldiers in a combat environment is the ultimate test of leadership and the most fulfilling experience for a military leader. From my early days in ROTC, I have tried to internalize the Armed Forces eleven principles of leadership which are:

1. Know yourself and seek self-improvement.
2. Be technically and tactically proficient.
3. Develop a sense of responsibility among your subordinates.
4. Make sound and timely decisions.
5. Set an example.
6. Know your people and look out for their welfare.
7. Keep your people informed.
8. Seek responsibility and take responsibility for your actions.
9. Ensure assigned tasks are understood, supervised, and accomplished.
10. Train your people as a team.
11. Employ your team in accordance with its capabilities.

Those principles have proven timeless and valuable from my experiences in combat. When consistently applied, the principles should lead to success in a person's career. In all aspects of leadership, combat truly tests the determination and resiliency of the commander and the unit. When under dire circumstances, with bullets flying and a demanding mission, it's up to the leader to provide the impetus to keep moving, brave the danger, and accomplish the mission. It's a real test of character on the part of the commander to lead in such conditions. I always look back on how my experiences as a young officer shaped my leadership style, even in civilian or spiritual endeavors.

War is not pretty from whatever perspective you may view it. It is stressful, stinky, loud, agonizing, exhausting, terrible, bloody, emotional, physical, shocking,

been there, done that!

horrific, eye-opening, sleep-depriving, maturing, and scary! Combat can make you witness events that can rock you to your core—the very essence of who you are. The experience of combat can develop a tremendous "hate" for the enemy and sometimes even for those who order the combat operation. Unless you are a true Rambo who loves fighting, you should even hate the whole concept of war itself. It can change your entire personality. But if you have a solid trust in God, war is endurable and can develop a resilience that is unexplainable. I had that belief in my God and am so thankful for all that He sustained me through in my combat periods.

CHAPTER XII
A DIFFERENT CAREER PATTERN

WHAT IS NEXT?

For a while in the hospital, the medical board kept me in suspense as to whether I would stay in the Army or receive a medical discharge. I was super happy when I found out I would be retained in the service. I began working with the personnel office on my next assignment and learned that there was an opening at the US Military Academy at West Point, New York, for an assistant professor in the geography department. I pursued that and traveled from Valley Forge Military Hospital in my cast to the US Military Academy for an interview. I was accepted to teach there, but the Army's personnel office told me that since I had already served in a teaching position (at Wheaton College ROTC), that they would not permit me going to another one this early in my career. Instead, they said I would attend the Infantry Officer Advanced Course at Fort Benning, Georgia. That was fine with me since it was a requirement for career advancement as an infantry officer.

While waiting for the course to begin, I had another period of turtle time (as I had when first entering the Army) and was given a couple of months of temporary duty with the Ranger School. I could have accepted administrative functions there but I asked to be a cadre member with Ranger training patrols in the field. I did have a limited physical profile since my knee was not fully bendable and getting over fallen logs and catching the leg in wait-a-minute vines made tromping in the woods very difficult. But this duty was the best for me because it forced me to continue to use my leg even through pain. I tried to keep others from knowing about my disability when I was in the woods with the Ranger trainees. Gradually I picked up routine Army physical training (PT) and running to pass the future PT tests the rest of my career. That Ranger School duty in the field helped me regain confidence in my physical capabilities after the long nine months of hospitalization and convalescence. I thought that would influence personnel assignment officers to place me in an operational assignment somewhere but that didn't happen because I now had a physical profile which would keep me from a troop assignment in the field.

PENTAGON—PUBLIC AFFAIRS

The Army sent me to schooling to become a Public Affairs Officer (PAO), and my follow-on assignment was with the Office of the Chief of Public Affairs (OCPA) for the Army in Washington. My first duty office was located in the Washington Navy Yard where I was the administration/publications director for OCPA's Command Information Unit. However, I was constantly in and out of the Pentagon to coordinate my work. We produced all the internal information materials going out to Army-wide public affairs offices. Our unit wrote news articles, gathered pictures, and prepared them for use in Army newspapers and magazines. We printed materials in our own print shop, stuffed, and mailed everything from our office. This was in an era before modern, day-to-day computer usage. Our unit also conducted annual competitions for worldwide Army public affairs printed publications.

The Command Information Unit also produced *The Big Picture,* a half-hour national television series giving the American people historical and current information about activities, equipment, and programs of the US Army. *The Big Picture* productions were distributed on 16mm films so we had a lot of bulky film cases going out and coming back to our office on a regular basis. It was aired on 366 TV stations on several networks and ran 828 weekly episodes. All of this was very interesting to me since I had never been around broadcasters and media production folks. I was in that office for two years and then moved into the Pentagon for my everyday duties.

DEFENSE DEPARTMENT BRIEFER

A short, two-month task was given to me when I initially moved to the Pentagon. The Defense Department was changing some of its benefits for military retirees and developed a new Survivor Benefit Program (SBP) which, if they chose, could provide better financial care for a retiree's family after the service member's death. It was a major change for retirees to think about and was quite complicated with its advantages and disruption of the way some policies were being changed from the past.

The Defense Department selected six officers from each service to be thoroughly briefed on the SBP and trained so they could go out to all the major military installations and explain the SBP to the troops. I was an Army selectee, and with another officer, we went to most of the major southeastern US Army posts and also to our troop concentrations in Panama. Panama was particularly interesting to me because of its history of construction of the canal and disease eradication. While there, we got a briefing at the locks and flew from one end to the other in a helicopter since we had Army posts on both the Atlantic and Pacific sides of the isthmus. Overall, it was a tough briefing tour, and on some days we gave two or three two-hour briefings with additional question-and-answer periods. On this briefing assignment, I got on several military posts I would not have otherwise been able to visit in my career.

VIETNAM VETERAN STATUS AWARENESS

Being in Washington and constantly dealing with public news media personnel after moving into the Public Information Division of the Office of the Chief of Public Affairs, I became more conscious of my status as a Vietnam veteran. We had willingly sacrificed portions of our lives and bodies for our nation but were now torn inside emotionally and outside physically. We bore the burden and invisible wounds of a "no respect" attitude—although appreciated respect is being regained at the time of this writing—of a disgruntled American populace who increasingly disapproved of a media-hyped war. Horrific and macabre scenes of combat primarily showed the casualties of war but rarely mentioned victories won both on the battlefield as well as in the hearts and minds of the villagers and people of Vietnam. The American public and media seemed to focus on the disastrous decisions of Lieutenant William Calley and the resulting massacre of villagers at My Lai. We learned of the traitorous actions of Jane Fonda who betrayed our trusting prisoners of war in Hanoi and we were constantly reminded of the tragedy at Kent State University in Ohio.

been there, done that!

I had come home from the war in 1966 to demonstrators hollering, booing, and spitting on me in the airport. The spit showed up in dark spots on my khaki uniform, and I was not happy. (In those days, the military did not travel commercially in our field uniforms as many do today.) It took everything I had within me to resist reacting to these unpatriotic people and to not even look at them. It was as though they were making villains out of us warriors who were serving our nation to protect their rights to speak and do horrific things. What an ugly return from the war that was! In later years, there was "blood" spattered around military facilities, bombings within the Pentagon, fires set to ROTC buildings and military research centers on university campuses, and protestors trying to prevent us from getting into the Pentagon where I was now assigned.

In the early 1970s, we could not even wear our uniforms every day to the Pentagon. Instead, we wore them only one day a week, and sometimes that required law enforcement personnel to provide a safe corridor for us to get into the building. The uniform, of which I was so proud, was a sign of shame to others. Deep down, I was extremely patriotic, but I wrestled with the lack of appreciation showed to our military personnel. We were obeying legitimate orders to protect not only our freedoms—and the liberties of the protesters!—but also the desire for freedom of our compatriots in Vietnam.

I have been in a number of countries where freedoms are or have been severely restricted. When visiting in those places, I am reminded how privileged I am to live in a country where I can live in freedom and pursue my own interests, enjoy an amazing and beautiful America, and especially to see my family living in the blessings of liberty. In my life, I feel that I have made a small (and it is very small) contribution to my country. The baton and torch of freedom is now passing to following generations to continuing the legacy of this great nation. Will they grab the baton or drop it?

Freedom of choice and independence for most Americans is like the air we breathe. We hardly give it a thought. We assume it will always be there, and rarely do we pause to consider the value of all that we have. I am increasingly appalled that many Americans ignore the real reasons we celebrate national holidays, such as Memorial Day, Independence Day, and Veterans Day, or do not even show respect for the flag of the United States of America when it passes by or is recognized at local and national sports events. It is often said that you can't prize something (fully appreciate its worth) until you have lost it. We seem to be on the precipice of losing our freedoms in America. On a hot, steamy May 18, 1969, day in the jungles of Vietnam, in an intense battle not far from the Cambodian border, I began a long, painful lesson on just how valued and sacred my freedom is.

Those Pentagon years in the 1970s were difficult for any of us who wore the uniform of our military services. Perhaps it was even more trying for those who remembered the heroes' welcome for service members who returned from earlier wars. That kind of recognition was not given to our Vietnam War heroes. Our great nation cannot let the Vietnam War disappear from textbooks, classrooms, and the minds of America's younger generations. Forgetting about that segment of the 1960s and early 1970s would be a deep blight for the future because there are important lessons to be learned.

People must always respect those who serve in our military, regardless of personal disagreements with our national policy or leadership. In current days and years, I am delighted to see increased respect awarded to our service personnel who have served so honorably in our nation's recent wars. They have volunteered to be in the military and have fulfilled a tremendous obligation we all have to protect the freedoms provided to us by our constitution. May our good Lord bless with future liberties all who have served and those who actively serve in our Active, National Guard, or Reserve forces. Additionally, I ask for the Lord's enrichment in the lives of the family members of each of our service members. They have endured difficult days when supporting their man or woman who has served our nation.

ARMY PUBLIC NEWS

I was excited to serve in the Public Information Division (PID) of the Army's public affairs office. Whereas my earlier duties had been working with the Army's internal news functions, now it would be my function to respond to public news reporters' questions about the Army. I had certain accounts and subjects for which I was responsible to give accurate and timely answers to TV and radio broadcasters and national news chains and publications. Some of my accounts were Army Operations and Exercises, Medal of Honor Recipients, Special Operations, Chemical/Biological/Nuclear Activities, Environmental Issues, and Research and Development. Each of these subjects brings unique memories.

been there, done that!

MEDAL OF HONOR CEREMONIES

I was the Public Affairs Officer for several Army Medal of Honor presentation ceremonies. Usually in those busy years, if the recipient of the military's highest award was living, the President presented the award. If the recipient was deceased, the Vice President or Secretary of Defense would present the medal to the recipient's family. The ceremonies were very somber, and the recipients and/or their families were treated with great honor, dignity, and respect. We always gave them in-depth tours while they were in Washington. I worked closely with the White House and its press corps and was in some special places in the White House in my media coordination role. Some of the ceremonies for living recipients took place inside the White House, and others occurred outside in the Rose Garden. The honors ceremonies for deceased recipients' families were not routinely held at the White House.

An individual who is honored for their heroic actions should never be called a Medal of Honor "winner". They were never in a competition for an award, but rather, they exhibited extreme valor at an unplanned time and in an unexpected situation. They did not "win" and someone else "lost". Thus, they are officially designated as a *recipient* of the award—and what an honor it is for their battlefield actions to be recognized with the Medal of Honor, our nation's highest award!

I have had the privilege to reconnect with a few of the recipients for whom I was at their ceremonies and am almost in reverence to think of all these heroes have done to protect their fellow soldiers! I am pleased that a Medal of Honor museum is being constructed now to honor Medal of Honor recipients.

SPECIAL DAY WITH VICE PRESIDENT GERALD FORD

One ceremony for deceased Medal of Honor recipients was held in the Blair House, which is immediately across the street from the White House. (Many dignitaries who visit the President stay in the Blair House.) Vice President (VP) Gerald Ford was presenting the Medals of Honor to the families of seven deceased recipients in this early August 1974 courtyard ceremony. The dignified program went smoothly as each recipient was individually recognized and the citation for the award was read. After the ceremony, all family members and special guests were invited inside to personally meet the Vice President and enjoy some refreshments.

As VP Ford was mingling with the families, his aide pulled him aside into a private room. Knowing that the whole Watergate problem was a hot topic, I asked one of his assistants what was happening. He said he would let me know, and soon he came to tell me that the Vice President had to leave and that he did not want to answer any questions from the press while leaving the Blair House.

To get to his limousine, he had to descend two flights of outside canopied stairs. I looked out and saw a horde of reporters who would want to get comments from the Vice President. I told him that I would lead him down the steps and that he needed to stay close behind me because I would have to bat some of the boom microphones up and hopefully over his head. It was a two-handed, necessary action for me as we quickly got down to the sidewalk level where his transportation was waiting. I saluted him and went back in to the Blair House to be at the Medal of Honor reception.

Why did the VP have to leave? On the next day, the public media reported that President Nixon pulled Vice President Ford from a Medal of Honor ceremony at the Blair House to tell him that he (President Nixon) was resigning and that VP Ford would become the President! I assume that I was one of the last few people to be with him as the Vice President prior to him being told he would soon be our nation's President!

A REINCARNATED BLACKBIRD

Most public news items, like a Medal of Honor ceremony, lasted just a few days but other queries from reporters took several days and sometimes longer to satisfy their subject interests. A couple of these stand out in my memory.

One of our Army posts is a major helicopter base. Especially in the winter, flying flocks of blackbirds and grackles caused a potential hazard to our aircraft by occasionally keeping them from landing when coming in from an exercise or training. These birds were also potentially harmful to kids walking home from school, and their purple and white poop would cover playground equipment and walkways. The birds were the greatest problem when they were coming in to roost in trees in the late afternoons and leaving the roosting area in the mornings.

Something had to be done to resolve the problem. The Army tried noise makers of various sorts but that was a very temporary solution. The flocks would fly around for a little while and come right back to their roosts. The permanent solution was to destroy the birds and that couldn't be done by killing them one by one.

Scientists and ornithologists determined that if the oil in the birds' wings could be reduced, they would not be able to fly and would fall out of their roost and be injured and no one wanted that. So then what? If this was done in the winter, the birds would fall, freeze, and die. The professionals identified an oil-dissolving liquid which could be sprayed over the bird's roosting areas while the birds were "at home". But to be most effective, the air temperature would have to be at freezing or below. This was determined to be the best answer to the problem, but that mess of thousands of dead birds would also have to be cleaned up.

This unusual approach was very successful, but after the first couple nights of the mass destruction, local media tried to make the story into a crime scene and got the Humane Society involved. I had to answer all the media questions about the bird eradication: Who authorized the action? How many birds were killed? How did we help injured birds? How did we do the clean up? Did we give them a proper burial? At what other posts did we kill birds? It was almost hard for me to keep a straight face when answering some of the queries when the birds themselves had generated the problem. The Army did reduce these pesky birds at a few of our posts, but it took quite a while to verify the temperatures were just right to ensure the kill rather than just injure birds falling from the roosting areas.

But the worst comments against the Army came from a private citizen who called and said that one of her friends had been reincarnated as a blackbird and that we had killed her friend the previous night. She wanted to know who was responsible and told me that she was going to sue the commander of the military post and his chain of command right on up to the Army itself.

Because of the potential implications of my answers, I had to go to the Army Judge Advocate General (JAG) for an answer to some of her queries! I wonder how she knew that her reincarnated friend was at that post and was one of the hundreds killed that previous night. Did the "reincarnated" bird get a warning call from her friend that the spray was coming? (Public announcements were given in advance!) If so, why did the reincarnated bird hang around its old roost instead of leaving? While discussing the subject with the caller, I had to ensure that I showed respect for the individual even though I was inwardly snickering while sitting at my desk. I could only give her an approved explanation of the reason why we had to destroy the birds and leave the next step up to her. The Army was not sued by this private citizen, but if the suit had moved forward, I believe it would have been denied in the courts. I think her case would have been difficult to prove! If for no other reason, she would have had to positively identify her reincarnated friend, which had probably already been buried with thousands of other birds. That would have been difficult! The bird eradication issue took several winter months to resolve.

ARMY RESEARCH WITH LSD

My longest continuum of public media questions (regarding a single subject) came from a well-known national producer and journalist from CBS. She called just before our normal closing one afternoon and had some tough questions about the Army's previous research and experiments with LSD, the hallucinogenic drug. She queried about our chief scientist and our science research laboratories. She said if she didn't have an answer in a half hour that she was running with her story on national TV.

The subject was too sensitive to give her a rapid response because something of that nature had to have input from many sources. I thanked her for contacting me and said I'd get back to her as soon as I could. I worked into the evening and all the next day to get some preliminary answers for her. When I gave her a response, it generated more questions on a different track in her mind. Her probing went on for almost six months, and her national "news" stories triggered other media to also address the whole topic of Army chemical and biological warfare (much of it being classified), international laws pertaining to its use, and long-lasting effects on those involved in scientific experiments. She also raised issues pertaining to the use of psychedelic drugs at Woodstock a few years before, but I said I could only do my research about the Army's involvement and not civilian usage.

It was true that the Army had worked quite extensively with LSD—primarily to find an antidote for it—since some foreign enemy forces were known to have plans for its use if we were to be entangled in warfare with them in the future. The Army research and experimentation involved voluntary, controlled use of LSD (and its potential antidote) by individual soldiers and small military units, and through a variety of civilian contract organizations. It took a lot of time to provide coordinated responses because I had to work with so many offices within the Pentagon, both at the Army and the Defense levels. It became such an issue that before I could give a reporter any information, I had to get approvals on

been there, done that!

my responses by the Army's Chemical and Biological Laboratories, the JAG, the Surgeon General, each military service involved, Public Affairs, Freedom of Information, Army Operations, civilian organizations (some of our experiments were done through university and corporation contracts), and other offices including some Congressional members.

It was a challenge for me to get all the correct answers—especially since much of the information was classified—and then the approvals. The most difficult issue was to get the information in a timely manner. Each morning, I had to report to our two-star general, who was the Army Chief of Public Affairs, what the media had written or broadcast on the subject and importantly, provide to him the information which I had actually provided to the reporters. Sometimes the public media reports were so incorrect that we would put out our own truthful news bulletin but rarely would any media run corrections. That is as typical today in the media world as it was then.

AN UNUSUAL INTERVIEW

One of our tasks in the Public Information Division was to coordinate interviews, which were requested by various media outlets. All of the major national news outlets had a reporter with a desk in the Pentagon. Because the Rangers were one of my accounts, I was asked by an Associated Press (AP) reporter to find someone who had been a Ranger in World War II and arrange an interview. I identified a brigadier general and set up the time and place for the interview.

As the PAO, I was responsible to explain the ground rules of the interview and what should be on and off the record. When I completed that, the general said he thought this would be his last assignment and that he would never be promoted, so we should just leave everything on the record. The interview went fine and nothing classified was discussed. The AP reporter was satisfied that he had gotten a good news story.

Now for the rest of the story as Paul Harvey would say. Within a few months, the brigadier general was promoted and given his second star and moved to command an Army division. Within a couple of years, I read that he was being promoted to a third star and moved to a higher command position. Wow! His promotions were coming faster than his peers. Because of his performance in these commands, he was back in the Pentagon and received his fourth star and soon became the Chairman of the Joint Chiefs of Staff—the highest-ranking officer in the military and the chief military advisor to the President and Secretary of Defense. I am glad he did not mis-speak in that interview I had coordinated, or this story may have ended much differently. He had been very wrong about never being promoted!

EXPLOSION IN THE PENTAGON!

Each day, one of us in the public affairs office was assigned as the duty officer. In addition to answering any nighttime reporters' queries, we had to ensure all classified material was removed from all desks and placed in safes and coordinate with Pentagon security officers before we left the office. One evening, one of the generals in our office was also working late, so he and I (as the duty officer) were the only people in the office area. This was an era when protestors were constantly working against the military and in fact, had gotten into the Pentagon and had detonated small bombs in unusual places, such as a bathroom.

In making their routine rounds, a Pentagon security officer checking our office area, noted a small aluminum briefcase between a safe for documents and a wall. He asked me what it was. I had no idea, and asking the general about it, he also was not aware of what this briefcase may contain. I will say that the case looked suspicious, especially in the location where it was next to a wall of the general's office. I suggested that we call someone who worked in the room where it was located but the general said to let security handle the situation. Security called for additional support and analysis and made the determination to clear the area and blow the briefcase in place. BAM!

The general and I went into the office following the explosion and found small red blobs all over the place mixed in with pieces of paper, foil wrappings, and the destroyed briefcase. What was in it? The case had contained some samples of a new, dehydrated cherry dessert which the Army's Natick Food Research Laboratory was proposing for Army Long Range Reconnaissance Patrol (LRRP) rations! The laboratory had brought these samples from Massachusetts to us in the metal briefcase so that our office could prepare a news release for the media and provide morsels for those who wanted to taste the new product. Well, it was not quite the type of media announcement that was being planned—but the "bomb" in our office sure got some publicity! Obviously, no one got to taste the dessert! It also was quite an embarrassment that neither the general nor I knew

been there, done that!

in advance about this briefcase filled with cherry dessert until it was plastered all over the room!

FROM THE ARMY TO THE DEFENSE DEPARTMENT

I thought that after serving a few years in the Pentagon, I would be ordered to an overseas assignment. I volunteered to go to Korea as a public affairs officer since I knew I could not be in the field with infantry troops. That didn't happen. Then I tried to go to Germany since I'd never been there, but the Army chose to reassign me within the Pentagon to the Army desk in the Defense Department News Department. What I had done in the Army staff, now I would be doing on the Defense staff—answering media queries but also now helping to prepare briefs for the spokesman for the Secretary of Defense. He gave regular press briefings, and we on the staff had to ensure that he was prepared to answer any potential questions he might be asked from the public media in the Pentagon. In this new assignment, I regularly interacted with many national news reporters from both the electronic and print media whose faces and reports were in daily news sources.

In addition to responding to media queries, I was also responsible for information regarding new contracts for Army equipment. This was very interesting to me since I learned a lot about hardware and communication systems which were just coming into the Army or about items being researched for potential use several years in the future. I was in the Defense News Department for a couple of years.

CHAPTER XIII

TRANSITION TO ARMY RESERVE

Because I had not gained a promotion in the time frame I wanted and needed it, and also felt that maybe the Lord had other options in ministry for me, I left active duty in the Pentagon in 1977 and immediately joined the Army Reserve. I served occasional Reserve short tours in the public affairs office of the four-star Army's Training and Doctrine Command at Fort Monroe, Virginia, for a couple of years and then became the PAO of a two-star Army Reserve Command at Fort Meade, Maryland. I was now a "citizen-warrior" and performed military duties at the reserve center basically on one weekend a month and for a couple of consecutive weeks during the year. Our family continued to live at our home in Virginia, and I took several military correspondence courses to enhance my future in the military. I did seek full-time ministry in a few churches, but the Lord closed those doors. I had to support my family, and I got some civilian jobs until I determined where the Lord wanted to place me.

These assignments in the US Army Reserve gave me a new appreciation for the Reserve Components of our military. Men and women in the National Guard or Reserve are vital to the defense of our nation as they provide many skills, which are not available within the active military forces.

Today, they are part of our operational forces in places around the globe and recently have been instrumental in the US successes in our military actions of the US Central Command in the Middle East region. They are no longer "weekend warriors" as they had been called but are available to be called up for duty as our total defense operational needs are evaluated. In those years, I had to spend many off-duty hours to ensure success in my military reserve responsibilities and had to maintain physical fitness on my own time. This is true for any individuals in positions of leadership in all the Reserve Components of our military services.

been there, done that!

Additionally, I could not have performed follow-on assignments with clarity of understanding if I had not had the experiences of my Army Reserve time.

CIOR — A NATO ORGANIZATION

The Interallied Confederation of Reserve Officers (CIOR is its international abbreviation) is a NATO (North Atlantic Treaty Organization) group that coordinates reserve officer policy within the NATO nations in Europe. Every few years, the CIOR meets in one of its member countries. Besides the CIOR diplomatic and policy meetings and the international medical studies, a military competition for international reserve officers is held in marksmanship, orienteering, and a large obstacle course. In 1984, the CIOR met in Washington, DC, and I was selected by the Defense Department to return to active duty for six months to serve as the PAO for the CIOR activities. My reserve unit in Maryland had a public affairs detachment, and I asked that its personnel also be put on active duty to provide print and broadcast news releases and complete news coverage of all the meetings and military competitions.

There were also many formal and informal social functions at various locations in the Washington area for the international CIOR personnel. I enjoyed these because of the diverse interactions with European cultures. This CIOR PAO duty was valuable experience for me to oversee the public affairs side of an international military organization. As in the United States, the reserve forces of other nations contribute immensely to NATO's defense against aggressive actions taken by other nations in the European theater.

OFFICE OF THE ASSISTANT SECRETARY OF DEFENSE (RESERVE AFFAIRS)

Simultaneously with the ongoing CIOR, the Defense Department was establishing the new Office of the Assistant Secretary of Defense (Reserve Affairs) within the Pentagon. Seeing my work with the CIOR, the Defense Department retained me as a reserve officer on active duty and assigned me as the public services officer for this new office.

My boss, a civilian political appointee, was a fiery, dynamic US Naval Academy graduate who had joined the military as a Marine officer and served with distinction in Vietnam. He had written an award-winning book, which later was made into a very successful movie. (After serving as the Assistant Secretary of Defense for Reserve Affairs, he later became the Secretary of the Navy, a Congressional senator from Virginia, and for a while in 2019, he ran for president of the United States.) I responded to media inquiries for him and the office regarding the military Reserve Components and also coordinated his speeches and got them cleared as required through the Defense Department. He was in high demand as a speaker within the civilian and military National Guard and Reserve communities.

As I was sitting in my office early one morning he came in and began railing on me with language I am not used to hearing. He was very upset that I had sent one of his upcoming speeches for clearance and he didn't feel that was necessary and said I had no authority to do that. I explained the Defense Department policy that I had complied with for his previous speeches, but he didn't want to accept that. I had never been belittled for doing my job as I was that day. He finally stormed away and went into his office.

Shortly, one of his aides, who had been his buddy since their US Naval Academy days, came in and asked what I had done to the boss. He said he had never seen him so mad. After relaying to him the early morning event, I asked if there was anything I could do to reduce the heat. He suggested that I should just keep out of his sight. I also got the feeling right then that I should start looking for another job! Within a few days, I found an opening for an Army Reserve staff officer for the Reserve Forces Policy Board (RFPB) in the Pentagon and was accepted there by the Military Executive two-star general. I hate to think what might have happened to my career if I had not quickly found this new position.

RESERVE FORCES POLICY BOARD

The Reserve Forces Policy Board (RFPB) is an organization chartered by Congress to provide independent insight, advice, and recommendations to the Secretary of Defense. All of this specifically pertained to strategies, policies, and practices, which could improve and enhance the readiness, capabilities, efficiency, and effectiveness of the National Guard and Reserve forces of the military services. It is a very high-level organization that has tremendous potential impact within the Department of Defense.

While I was with the RFPB, the chairman of the board was a civilian from Alabama. He was appointed to the position by the US President. Other board

been there, done that!

members were two and three-star generals and admirals from each of the active military services and each of the seven Reserve Components. Some other political appointees were also included on the board. Altogether, more than twenty of these high-ranking personnel comprised the board that met quarterly for updates and decisions regarding Reserve Component issues and recommendations. Our support staff for the board consisted of the military executive two-star general; colonels from the Army National Guard, Army Reserve, Air Force National Guard, Air Force Reserve, and Marine Reserve; captains from the Navy Reserve and Coast Guard Reserve; some enlisted personnel, and civilian assistants. I was the Army Reserve staff representative.

The staff served throughout the year, lining up keynote speakers for board meetings from within the Defense Department as well as principals from other agencies such as the State Department, Congress, overseas national leaders, industry, and so forth. We also coordinated and prepared itineraries for board visits to major military commands, military forces of cooperating countries, key political and military defense ministers, and sometimes the top governmental leader of a country. Other staff duties included in-depth research and study for the board regarding significant policy issues impacting the National Guard and Reserves. I enjoyed the interaction with key decision makers at a wide variety of levels within and without the Pentagon.

EXCITING RFPB STUDY TRIPS

Our board's study trips were very intense, and our staff was kept extremely busy keeping track of all these high-ranking personnel and the data being gathered. We went to places and did things I could never have believed I would have the privilege of doing in a "normal" infantry career.

Following a major destructive earthquake east of the Andes Mountains in Ecuador, our Defense Department sent Reserve Component military forces to aid in the recovery and reconstruction efforts of the local people. Our board went to the South American country to observe and evaluate the deployment of our military reserves in support of this natural disaster recovery mission in a partnering nation.

We flew out to sea and landed—thanks to the arresting cable and our plane's tail hook!—on the *USS Dwight D. Eisenhower* nuclear-powered aircraft carrier. I was now a certified "Tailhooker"! That sudden stop coming onto and later being catapulted off the carrier sure makes the eyeballs move in your head! We spent a couple of days and nights reviewing the augmentation and integration of Navy Reserve personnel into the operations of an aircraft carrier at sea. One night, we watched a replenishment and refueling mission under blackout conditions. A smaller Navy ship came beside us, and with cables, hoses, and ropes, it transferred needed supplies to the carrier. It was very interesting to observe the efficiency of this operation under the moon and starlit sky. We had quite the experience the next day, standing close to jet fighters being catapulted off the front of the carrier and at the other end being next to the flagmen and lights near the arresting cables bringing jets onto the carrier's surface. Who would have ever guessed that this missionary kid (who was in the Army!) would be at sea on a Navy aircraft carrier? Unbelievable! How many other Army infantry officers have "been there, done that" in their careers? To prove our visit on the carrier at sea, each of us with the RFPB that day were given a "Tailhooker" certificate.

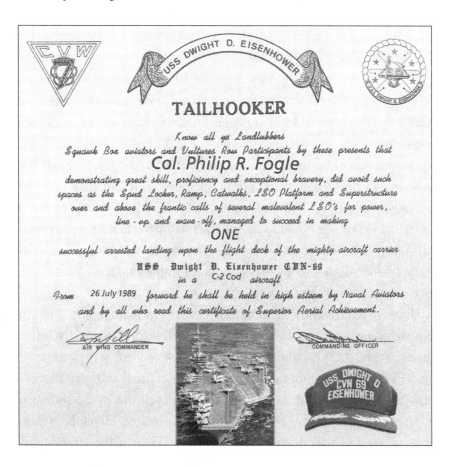

been there, done that!

In 1988, we boarded the recently built *USNS Comfort*, a military medical hospital ship with 1,000 beds. The ship is an amazing structure with its medical wards, surgical suites, modern technology, and the medical specialties as any major land-based hospital would have. We were concerned that at that time it was primarily manned by active Navy personnel and civilians, but in a combat or emergency environment it would need to be augmented by a large medical element from the reserves. These reservists could be called up quickly to sail with the ship anywhere there may be a military conflict, a natural disaster, or to aid partnering nations as a community development facility. (This is the same ship that was sent to New York City for the 2020 coronavirus pandemic.) What an experience this was for an Army soldier!

The board received onsite briefings one year by joint and specific service commands in Hawaii, Japan, and Korea. In Korea, we ensured that we did not cross the red line in a negotiation room at Panmunjom at the DMZ (Demilitarized Zone) between South and North Korea. The North Korean soldiers on their side carefully observed us with their steel-eyed, cold stares. That gave me somewhat of an eerie feeling to realize that I was a very few feet from godless, communist forces. In Korea, we also went into a tunnel which had been constructed under the DMZ by North Korea in their attempts to infiltrate the south. The tunnel was big enough to drive a small truck through, so it was a major feat to dig it out and camouflage all of the extracted dirt. The US and South Korean military forces discovered the tunnel before it could ever be used and, therefore, all the North Korean work was in vain! This was only one of several tunnels which the North Koreans have dug (and still try to use) under the DMZ. From one of our security outposts at the DMZ, we could look into the hostile north with its aggressive military, communist activities and ideology. They even had built a fake city—just with walls facing south—to try and convince people that there was commercial activity on their side of the border.

A visit to Switzerland by the board demonstrated that country's neutrality. It does not maintain a large standing army and, therefore, primarily relies on its reserve forces and their rapid call up if defense is needed.

The RFPB spent considerable time with the Israeli military forces on the northern Golan Heights and down to its military facilities in the southern desert region. The Defense Minister and former Prime Minister, Menachem Begin, was our host and gave us superb support on our trip. (He was the Israeli leader who negotiated the US-led Camp David Accords with President Anwar Sadat of Egypt and therefore the first Israeli Prime Minister to establish peace with an Arab state.) Our RFPB board helicoptered to most places including to the top of Masada where we were briefed by a two-star general on its historic defense and importance to all recruits entering the Israeli Defense Forces. We were given special permission to fly in restricted air space around the old city of Jerusalem. Looking at it and its massive walls from the air gave us a unique perspective on this historic and controversial city. Very few people have had this privilege.

All Israeli Defense Forces personnel keep their weapons with them and are ready at any moment to resist personnel trying to disrupt the peace in the nation. It was unusual for me to see so many uniformed men and women on the streets and in the open markets of the nation. At one base in the desert, we received a demonstration of a no-notice defense drill to see how rapidly (actually in just a few minutes!) the forces can deploy. The Israeli Defense Force is truly amazing and must always be on high alert because of Israel's location and small size, the potential aggressiveness of surrounding nations, and internal or external hostile people groups.

The southernmost military base in the US is a Coast Guard station in the Florida Keys where we were taken out on one of their fast boats—and they are fast!—to demonstrate how they interdict drug runners on the high seas. Those boats are heavily armed, and the active and reserve Coast Guard personnel work together as a great team to prevent drug and people smuggling into our country. They showed us pictures of the "loot" they had confiscated recently. I was shocked to think about the damage all of that could have done in our American population.

On one of our stateside visits, I got to "fly" an F-16 fighter jet simulator—and yes, I crashed a couple of times and only shot down one simulated plane! That twirling around in airspace and trying to keep track of the horizon was very challenging. I now have a much greater feeling for the expertise of our fighter pilots, but I'd much rather be a ground-pounder!

At the time when our new M-1 Abrams main battle tank was being tested and in its initial fielding, our board went to a tank-testing and driving range at an Army proving ground. There, I got to drive the old M-60 main battle tank which was currently in the inventory and then compare it to my driving of the new M-1 tank. What a difference in the ride as well as the capability between the two!

While driving the M-60, the tank commander told me to be very careful that I didn't knock my teeth out going over some of the moguls (much like on a downhill snow skiing course). These are major humps in the roadway to test shock absorbers and controllability of a vehicle on the move. But in the M-1 tank, the tank

been there, done that!

commander said: "Faster, Faster, Colonel. Get this sixty-five-plus ton tank airborne going over this next mogul." I did "fly" it and was surprised at how smoothly that monstrous machine landed! The main gun has a gyroscopic control on it, which allows for very accurate shooting on the run, and the crew of my tank did hit a moving target while I was driving about thirty miles per hour. What a powerful tank the Army has in its inventory! It continues to be upgraded with modern technology.

EDITOR OF RFPB ANNUAL REPORT

Our staff compiled our reports and recommendations regarding the National Guard and Reserves into one annual document, which the board members approved and signed before forwarding it to the Secretary of Defense. He then signed this publication and forwarded it to the President and Vice President of the United States, other cabinet members, Congressional members, major military installations and libraries, and other notable places, which had an interest in the integration of the Reserve Components with the active forces. I was assigned by the Military Executive to be the editor of the report—which I did for four years. Working with the chairman of the board, I also coordinated the rebranding of the RFPB and developed its new logo.

I was told that this RFPB report was one of the most coordinated documents that the Secretary of Defense signed each year. It normally took at least four months to gather and compile the data, prepare recommendations, gather appropriate photographs, coordinate and get approval and agreement from many varied sources, edit it—I used a green ink pen so all would know where the edit came from, and I still have a reputation for editing other documents with green ink!—and then getting the couple-hundred-page report printed and distributed. I was always tremendously relieved when that project was completed early each calendar year.

My duty of four years with the Reserve Forces Policy Board was probably one of my best assignments in the military. I met high-level people in the US and overseas governments, industry, and the military with whom I would never have connected; I visited places where I would never have gone; and I did things I would never have done if I had not been assigned to the RFPB. These were some of the unbelievable experiences of a missionary kid. I couldn't have planned a better conclusion to my military career! I was very thankful for the broadening military knowledge I gained through the RFPB. Those four years gave me more "been there, done that" growth than almost any other period in my life. The experiences there were part of God's preparation for opportunities He was yet planning for me.

CHAPTER XIV

MILITARY RETIREMENT

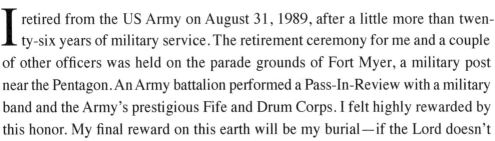

I retired from the US Army on August 31, 1989, after a little more than twenty-six years of military service. The retirement ceremony for me and a couple of other officers was held on the parade grounds of Fort Myer, a military post near the Pentagon. An Army battalion performed a Pass-In-Review with a military band and the Army's prestigious Fife and Drum Corps. I felt highly rewarded by this honor. My final reward on this earth will be my burial—if the Lord doesn't come back for me before then—in Arlington National Cemetery right there within sight of the Pentagon and the Fort Myer parade field where I retired! I had a great but unusual career in both the Army's Active and Reserve Components and the Defense Department.

My planned infantry career transitioned to the majority of my time being spent in public affairs for the Army and Defense Departments. I was privileged to serve in the Pentagon and live in the Washington, DC, area for seventeen and a half years, and in each of my latest four years I was with a joint military forces policy board addressing issues pertaining to the National Guard and the military services' reserve elements. Those years were very satisfying to me. Many military personnel try to avoid service in the Pentagon because of the limited subject matter they would deal with in their small spaces, but my experiences and subjects varied greatly, and I enjoyed my long service in that massive building. God directed my unusual Army career, and I thank Him for doing that for me. So much of my military service was directly impacted by that battle on May 18, 1969, which ended my potential command and service with infantry units in the field. The Lord always knows what He is doing and accomplishes His plan in ways we cannot comprehend! I am sincerely grateful!

been there, done that!

In 1990, after the buildup of US military forces began in the Middle East following the invasion of Kuwait by Iraq, my family fully expected me to re-enter the military. I may have done that except that my wife had just been diagnosed with cancer, and I needed and wanted to be with her during her times of surgery, recovery, and follow-on treatment. The Lord then opened up doors for us to move to Florida, and within a month, I began serving as a volunteer in a ministry at Moody Keswick Conference Center. However, even now I keep up with happenings within the military through professional military magazines and other publications, military-related organizations, and the internet. Except for potential health issues, and with some additional updates, I feel I could again serve my country in the military in a public affairs position.

TAKE AWAYS FROM MILITARY

1. You cannot prepare and train too much to be successful in dealing with potential adversities you may be exposed to in life. Sometime you will face the worst day of your life, and your advance preparation will enable you to deal with it.
2. In combat, you will always confront a brutal enemy who has as much a desire to be the victor as you. His tactics and warfare equipment are always changing, thus requiring continuing education, wisdom, and flexibility in your own thinking and operations.
3. Complacency tends to lurk in the background of some of those in any organization you lead. To overcome this and win in battle (whatever its nature may be), you must be prepared spiritually, morally, mentally, emotionally, and physically. But you also must be tactically and technically proficient at your skill level, always striving to move your organization forward and upward.
4. It is essential that you stay mission-focused. The mission must be clear and effectively communicated to all involved in any military or civilian organization.
5. Identify someone you can set as an example for your own life and leadership.
6. Always strive for excellence in every aspect of your life.

7. Follow this moral principle in an Army ethic: "We lead by example and demonstrate courage by doing what is right despite risk, uncertainty, and fear."
8. Open up with others (particularly with veterans) with discussions of your unclassified military experiences. Dwell on the positives of your service, but don't completely hide the difficult times you have had. Your conversation can help another person overcome depression and a sense of loneliness or feeling when no one else may understand their inner soul.
9. Build trust—never harm—it. Trust is essential for great leadership. Developing trust may take time depending on the circumstance you find yourself inheriting, the cultural environment, and "how you show up" in your initial encounters with your people in your organization.

PART 1II
ENJOYMENT IN MINISTRY

Opportunity, Opportunity, Opportunity—that is the story of my life. I have determined that if I don't accept an opening presented to me in any aspect of my life that God may not give me more opportunities. Opportunities may have a short life span and I would not want to miss any of them if God makes them available. As I look back, the prospects placed before me have challenged me to grow in my spiritual life and have brought me great excitement in my physical life. I've had so many helps and enouragements which have provided unbelievable pathways for me to develop and demonstrate leadership and responsibility. The Lord has continually blessed me with the privilege to serve in varying types of ministries over the years, both during my military career and following

CHAPTER XV

USA MINISTRIES

CHRISTIAN SERVICE BRIGADE

While in high school in Wheaton, Illinois, our church participated in a national program for boys called the Christian Service Brigade (CSB). The CSB Stockade program was for elementary grade boys, and for the junior and senior high boys, the program was called a Battalion. It was somewhat like a Boy Scout program with uniforms, badges, and activities, but it used Scripture as the basis for its principles and instruction. Memorization of Scripture was part of meetings and achieving progress within the organization. Activities and outings were mostly based on the knowledge and background of the leaders who then passed that on to the younger boys—always using the Bible as the basic teaching tool with its guiding tenets and values.

HERALD OF CHRIST BADGE

Our leaders believed in us as teenagers and mentored us in spiritual things as well as in various crafts, skills, and other requirements of the defined program. By progressing through the differing book levels, one could finally achieve the Herald of Christ badge, which is the highest Christian Service Brigade award. Throughout my high school years, I was very aggressive in completing requirements for various badges and desiring to move forward and on to the next level to become a junior leader in the battalion program. After four full years in the battalion, in 1960, I accomplished all requirements for the Herald of Christ badge which can be compared in prestige to the Eagle Scout award. I still value it as a

been there, done that!

great achievement in my teen years. One of the final challenging requirements for the reward was to write an essay regarding a meaningful passage of Scripture. I chose Philippians 4:8 for my passage and was so pleased that my four-page essay was accepted by the national office. (This scripture later became the base for developing my Core Values of Life identified in Appendix A.) Although CSB was formed in 1937, I was the nineteenth (one of the earliest people) to receive the Herald of Christ badge.

GIL DODDS MILE RACE TROPHY

Throughout my battalion years in high school, we did basic camping, hiking, and played sports against other battalions in the greater Chicago area. Every year, we had a Camp-O-Rama gathering with other battalions. It always included a variety of competitions, which included a track meet at the end of each school year. I was on the high school track team as a mile runner, and as a result of that training, I won the Christian Service Brigade mile race three years in a row. Each year, my name was put on a Gil Dodds nineteen-inch-tall trophy, and because I won it three consecutive years, I was presented the trophy to keep permanently.

Gil Dodds (1918–1977), nicknamed "The Flying Parson," was an American middle-distance runner in the 1940s, who held the US and world records in the mile race. He never lost a race in high school and set records in both the Nebraska state mile and half-mile races. Gil Dodds went on to race in college, and after seminary, he set new world indoor mile race records three times with his best time being 4:05.3 minutes. He was the Wheaton College track coach from 1945–1959. After I won my third CSB mile race in the spring of 1960, Gil Dodds was the individual who presented me with the permanent trophy. I was honored to meet Gil Dodds. My best mile time in 1959, while on the Wheaton Academy track team, was 4:36 minutes, but at the CSB meet, after not running competitively for approximately one year, my time was a "slow" 5:01 minutes.

BATTALION ACTIVITIES IN 1970s

All my previous battalion experience in high school was unknown preparation for when I would become the leader (Captain) of a CSB battalion in Northern Virginia from 1971–1980. My goal was to challenge boys to do things in which they had not had the opportunity to be involved. Some of these included distance biking, backpacking, mountain climbing, rappelling, mountain rescue (including medical litter and piggyback rappelling), whitewater rafting, river canoeing, use of ropes and knot tying, survival training (including making traps and eating snake!), orienteering, compass and map reading, winter camping, snow caves, spelunking (caving), horseback riding overnights, capture the flag games at night, first aid, and more. Each school year, we emphasized one or more of these skills and activities. Before the boys engaged in these activities, we provided them with quality training in weekly battalion meetings. I believe that my Ranger training in the Army made me a better leader of the boys because I could teach them skills they would probably never try if I had not been there. The battalion also was a great stress reducer for me to get outdoors and away from my duties in the Pentagon.

The boys did enjoy our spelunking trips. For one of them, the ending was a little unusual. We had gone into one cave which was very dry and in places was difficult to negotiate through some of the small passages. Our clothes were quite dusty. After a couple hours there, we moved to another cave several hundred yards away but in the same ridgeline This cave was extremely wet and we got very muddy and soaked. In a scouting of the cave a couple of weeks earlier, it was not as wet as this day when we were spelunking with the boys. It was winter and when we exited the cave, we became very cold as we headed to our bus. The heater in the church school-type bus was not operating so we had brought along some catalytic camping heaters to use to provide some heat while traveling. But, there was never enough heat to warm up all the shivering boys.

I decided that we should not take the boys back to the church in their filthy, wet, and muddy clothes so we stopped at a laundry mat on the way home. Most of the windows on the bus were all fogged and people could not see in so I had the boys strip down out of all their outer clothes and a few of us took them in and threw them in several washing machines and then into the dryers. Most of the boys stayed on the bus and were just in their underwear until we could bring out their warm and clean clothes. Several parents thanked me for not bringing their boys back in their muddy clothes. However, there were a few who loudly criticized me for having their sons strip down on the bus while we washed their clothes. Sometimes, you can never make everyone happy. I will say that we had to take a garden hose to the inside of the bus to clean it up for further use. We did learn a lesson for future caving experiences: We should always bring a change of clothes and a big garbage bag to use for our caving clothes.

One of the teen boys' favorite activities we did a few times was a lengthy, 10,000 meter (a little more than six miles) treasure hunt in the forest. After weekly training, the boys were divided into three or four-person teams and given a topographic map and a clue to a place in the woods. Using their map reading, compass, terrain orientation, and orienteering knowledge, they had to find a hidden clue in that spot and move on to the next clue. There were at least six clues, which eventually led them to the treasure! This was very time consuming for me and another leader to set the course up as we tromped over acres and acres to find clue sites and make up the clues. These had to be different for each team to ensure that no two teams should arrive at a clue site at the same time. My wife, Betty, even got involved by using strings and the map to make sure that each team's overall distance was the same. The boys loved the challenge, and I enjoyed being in the woods, practicing the skills I was teaching the boys.

The battalion was involved in some type of outdoor activity on the third weekend of every month in the school year. Invariably on that weekend, it would precipitate in some fashion, whether it was rain, snow, sleet, and even hail. It became a joke around the church that people should not plan any outdoor activity on the third weekend of the month because the battalion was going to be on a trip, and it was going to precipitate somehow!

Only once did we have to cut a battalion activity short because of weather—and we got caught in some pretty severe weather on occasion. We were riding our bikes on the C&O canal, a 184-mile-long towpath along the Potomac River from the Harper's Ferry, Virginia, area to Washington, DC. On the second day of the trip, the skies opened up for much of the day, causing the river to begin flooding. I called the rest of the trip off for safety reasons.

Each year, we had a Father-Son Advance—we didn't "retreat"!—to tighten relationships between the boys and their dads. Most of the time, we held this weekend event at River Valley Ranch which was north of Baltimore in Maryland. In addition to preplanned Bible studies between fathers and sons—one or both who may not be believers—we had several competitive events between father-son teams, including stick hockey, can-n-ball, ping pong, and some board games. When there was snow, everyone enjoyed bobsledding, skiing, snowball fights, and sledding at the ranch. One time, we did have a calamity when the ranch's driver of the ten-man bobsled couldn't get the bobsled turned in time and it ended up crashing in a creek. Several men and boys were injured—some with broken bones—but no one complained, and they all realized that sometimes accidents do happen when you are having fun.

At the close of the CSB battalion season, we hosted an end-of-year, Father-Son Steak Fry. Normally, we had about eighty to ninety men and boys attend. We bought premium-grade steaks, and each family grilled their own steaks on the numerous grills we either made or borrowed. My wife baked potatoes and made big pots of vegetables, and we bought rolls and lots of butter. Betty also made huge 2x3-foot sheet cakes and always decorated the cakes with the theme of our battalion year. Then we showed slides (in those pre-Power Point days!) of the year's activities, and sometimes demonstrated what the teenagers had learned during the year—such as rappelling off the roof of the church building! Mothers got upset with me because they wanted to see their boys in action and weren't invited to these steak fry events, so after a few years I gave in and invited them also!

MEMORIZATION OF SCRIPTURE PASSAGES

For a number of years we averaged around fifty junior and senior high boys every Wednesday evening during the school year. A public school gymnasium

been there, done that!

was made available to us for our meetings. In addition to specialized training in skills mentioned previously, we played large canvas ball games, inner tube games, stick hockey, a homemade can-n-ball game, and a lot of regular games such as dodge ball, basketball, and other indoor active games. Like when I was in high school, we competed against other churches' battalions in basketball and often won because of the depth of our team.

At the annual Camp-O-Rama with other battalions from the region, we had Bible quizzing competition, which covered pre-announced passages of Scripture. Our battalion's boys normally memorized the complete passage for the year—sometimes a book of the Bible and other times certain chapters such as the books of James, 1 John, and 1 Peter; several chapters in Romans; or several chapters of Proverbs or Psalms. Because of our boys' diligence in memorizing and practicing quiz questions, they won every Bible quiz in which they competed. As the Captain of the battalion and to be an example, I memorized the passages right along with the boys—although sadly, now I cannot quote those passages as I used to do because I did not continually refresh them in my mind. If I look at them, many of the verses come quickly to mind, but I cannot quote a whole chapter or book as I could in those years. It sure was good for me to memorize scripture each year, even though it always was a stimulating challenge just to stay ahead of the young men.

The boys' parents really appreciated the exposure and training which we gave their sons in such a wide variety of activities, and to this day, some of the boys and their parents still thank me for the leadership I gave to the battalion. One of the boys became a trainer and worker at the climbing school at Yosemite National Park in California. Another was on the mountain rescue team of his university out west. One became a highly respected missionary in a majority Muslim country. Several have been pastors, youth leaders, or other leaders in their churches. One pastor came from South Carolina to Florida to surprise me at my wife's and my fiftieth anniversary celebration. He said that his time in battalion influenced his decision to be a pastor, and he came to let me know that! God was so good to give me such fruit through the battalion ministry.

END OF A GREAT MINISTRY

Unfortunately, a new staff youth leader in the church told me that he believed it was not "healthy" for the church to have a program which segregated the boys and girls. He moved some of his co-ed youth activities so that they were held simultaneously with our Wednesday or weekend battalion programs. Naturally, some boys will want to be with the girls, so they stopped coming to our battalion training and activity times. We men leaders no longer had the privilege of mentoring and challenging these boys as we had been doing. Boys will not risk failure in front of girls by doing some of the extremely difficult activities in which we had them engaged. That church's battalion completely closed down within a couple of years after the new youth leader came, and many parents expressed their regrets that their young men never had the opportunity to participate in the battalion's exciting experiences and leadership training.

MOODY KESWICK CONFERENCE CENTER

After I retired from the Army in 1989 and after supporting Betty for fifteen months through her cancer treatments, the Lord led us to Florida's west coast where our son was teaching in the Keswick Christian School in St. Petersburg. It was part of Moody Bible Institute in Chicago. Betty anticipated doing some nursing part-time, and because I had gotten licensed in insurance and securities sales, I would just work as much as I desired.

When moving into our new home in Largo, Florida, our moving truck broke a small branch off our neighbor's tree. Our son suggested we borrow a chainsaw from a friend of his who lived a couple blocks from his school. With the saw, I could give the broken branch a clean cut. In a couple of days on a Wednesday, Betty and I returned the saw and the lady of the house asked: "Have you signed up to work at the Moody Keswick Bible Conference yet?" It was the first week of January 1991, and we said we hadn't heard about it and really hadn't even considered doing some regular volunteer work. She quickly responded: "Get in your car and follow me on my bike. I'll take you there." Well, that was the beginning!

CONFERENCE CENTER CAMPUS

The Bible conference was thirteen weeks in the winter. It had different speakers and musicians each week. On the campus were a chapel that could seat about 600, a forty-eight-room guest lodge (with eight of the rooms being kitchenettes), a lounge/reception area, a dining room, an activities building for crafts and small gatherings, a bookstore, a heated swimming pool, tennis courts, and a few guest houses. It was in a beautiful setting with nicely manicured grounds and the lodge overlooking a small lake. It also adjoined Keswick Christian School—where our son taught upper level math courses—with its approximate 700 Pre-K through high school students. In the "off" season (May–December), the conference center campus was available for retreat activities by churches or other groups. There was a small full-time staff which blossomed with many volunteers for the thirteen-week Bible conference season and for retreat weekends through the year.

WERE WE JUST VOLUNTEERED?

The lady (to whose house we returned the chain saw) took us to the conference center's office, introduced us to a couple of people, and told the secretary: "These two people want to work here. Get them signed up!" Had we unknowingly volunteered? I guess so! The secretary pulled out a couple of applications and handed them to us. She told us that all positions were full for the upcoming conference season but that sometimes they need substitutes, so please fill out the forms.

We completed the forms that night and took them back to her the next day (Thursday) just to get them out of the house so they wouldn't be lost among all our things while we were still getting settled after our move from Virginia. The secretary then told us about a banquet that evening for all the staff and volunteers and that we should come to meet other people. We were to get on a bus at a certain time and be taken with others to a beach hotel for the dinner—and that there was no cost! Being a missionary kid, I always liked to hear "no cost" or "free," so we agreed to go!

MEETING THE BANQUET SPEAKER

Arriving at the banquet room, Betty initially went to the ladies' room and I went into the dining area where people were gathering. I saw a man standing by himself over to one side and since I didn't know anyone else, I started talking with him. He said he was T from Moody Bible Institute in Chicago but didn't mention his duties there. Betty and T's wife soon joined us. We chit-chatted a little while as others began to sit at the round tables with their friends. It appeared that everyone knew everyone else!

As it came time to be seated, Betty and I went to the secretary and asked where we should sit. She said to sit at the table with her. Pretty soon, the conference center director and his wife sat there, and then this gentleman and his wife from Chicago also joined us at the table. We suddenly realized we were at the head table! As the dinner and program progressed, the director stood up to introduce the speaker—a vice president and assistant to the president at Moody Bible Institute! Needless to say, we were shocked to see this man at our table take his place at the podium. We had been visiting with a VIP and didn't know it. We later came to know T very well as he was in the leadership chain over the conference ministry.

At the banquet, the conference director told everyone to come in the next morning (Friday) for orientation, and the secretary motioned to us that we should come to see what we might possibly be doing if she called us to work as substitutes for someone who couldn't work that day or shift.

VOLUNTEER ASSIGNMENTS

The next morning, all the volunteers and staff gathered for orientation and duty assignments. Most of them knew where they would work because they had been there in previous years. We went merely as potential substitutes for positions as needed with no intentions or thoughts of regular duties. However, as a "substitute," Betty was assigned to the dining room waitress staff and was given a schedule for all those workers. While looking down the list, she realized that her name was in certain blocks which meant that she would be working regularly for thirteen more weeks! Also, Betty, being a nurse, was soon taking blood pressures and giving medical shots to some of the guests and workers each week.

I found myself assigned to the maintenance department and was paired up with one of the other men on the grounds crew. Our maintenance team started work right away on that Friday and didn't finish until five o'clock! Then we were told to be back to work Saturday morning at 7:30 a.m. because the conference guests would be arriving that afternoon. And, we men would work every day through the conference season. Really? We hadn't known anything about the conference ministry on Tuesday, and now on Friday both Betty and I were volunteers on the working schedules!

Betty and I hadn't even said we *wanted* to volunteer, let alone work on a pre-assigned schedule! But the Lord knew our future there. We really enjoyed the work and became very involved in as much of the conference program as we could—seven days a week! Only the Lord could have planned this unbelievable

been there, done that!

turn of events for us. We had expected change when the Lord led us to move to Florida, but we had no concept of the nature of this alteration of our lives!

GETTING TO KNOW EVERYONE

Desert Storm (the war in Iraq) had just begun in January 1991 during that first week of Bible conference and having retired recently from the Pentagon, I was asked to give conference attendees information about our military forces and equipment in the war. We came to know guests and staff quite well because of these "briefings," which were then requested in subsequent weeks. Betty and I also became deeply involved in almost everything going on at the conference—meals, services, evening afterglows, guest and staff activities, shuffleboard, and trips to local attractions. We enjoyed every aspect of the Bible conference weeks! However, we had previously told the conference secretary that we would be going north for a few weeks in February when our first grandson was to be born to our daughter just west of Chicago.

MEETING AT MOODY IN CHICAGO

One morning while lying in bed at our daughter's house, I received a call from the Moody vice president whom we had met at the volunteer banquet in Florida. He asked if we could meet him at a place and time of our choosing. He and the president had just returned from a conference week in Florida and wanted to meet us since apparently our names had been mentioned to him as volunteers who had helped a few weeks and had given those military briefings.

I said that we had not been on the Moody Bible Institute campus for years, so we would like to meet him there. He mentioned that he would have some orange cones in front of a "No Parking" spot by the dispensary and that we should park there and give him a call so he could come meet us. When we arrived on the Moody campus, he was already waiting at that spot for us. I told Betty that this must be something serious. T graciously greeted us and said that we would first go to the president's office (Dr. Joe Stowell) to meet him. Now, some curious thoughts began swimming through my mind! What was this all about?

We spent about twenty minutes in the president's office, just conversing about our backgrounds and families. (We discovered that our fathers knew each other!) Then T escorted us to his office and told us that while in Florida the previous week, he and the president had sensed some serious discord among the staff and volunteers. In fact, he said that a number of them indicated that they would not come back another year if management issues were not addressed. A few on the staff had recommended that he get hold of me and see what my views were—although Betty and I had only been on the volunteer staff for about five weeks.

T wanted to know what I had sensed in my few weeks there. Not wanting to criticize others, I started off by telling of all the good things about Moody Keswick Conference Center (MKCC). Then he asked me about things I had seen that might need the attention of administrators in Chicago. So, I cautiously mentioned some of my observations, and he said those were some of the same issues brought up to him by the staff and volunteers who had been at MKCC for several years. He asked me for some recommendations to improve the situation and staff morale. All the while, he was taking notes and indicated that my comments would be considered. He thanked me, we had prayer together, and he said he would be back in touch about what some of Moody's actions may be. Whoa—I would have never guessed all of that would be part of our getting together! Betty and I soon returned to our duties at the Bible conference and didn't tell others of our meeting at Moody. However, we did keep our eyes open for verification of its management struggles.

SERVING AS INTERIM DIRECTOR

We thoroughly enjoyed our volunteer work and spent much of our time on the Florida campus. T came to Florida for the last week of the Bible conference season. On Monday of that week, while I was working on the maintenance staff with a ditch-digging machine to install a sprinkler line, he came over and called me aside. He said the conference director had resigned and would I consider acting as the interim director for about six weeks until they could find someone to fill the position. I was rather surprised!

I could think of no reason not to assume the responsibilities, and after praying with my wife, I agreed to be the interim director of the conference center. But I said that I did not want the platform duties in that last week. T said he would do that so it wouldn't appear as though I was part of a previously planned "takeover". I then told the volunteer and paid staff that I would like input from them if any wanted to meet with me privately to give me their ideas about improvements in conditions at the center. I said that I would not listen to any criticisms of the previous director but that I wanted a positive approach to move forward. I received a lot of good input.

As part of the transition process, I asked Moody for complete access to all records and information of the conference center so that I could scrutinize and analyze areas which would need attention or enhancement. I had learned principles for evaluation and analysis of organizations while I was in the Army, and now those previous experiences were becoming useful in my retirement life.

After a couple of weeks as the interim director, I sent to T my findings and recommendations for issues that needed the attention of key individuals at Moody Bible Institute in Chicago. I categorized the issues according to Moody's departments: Facilities, Maintenance, Personnel, Food Service, Finance, Administration, Technology, and Public Relations. Based on those findings and recommendations, I was called to the Chicago campus for discussions. I said I would come only if I could meet with department heads who had authority to make decisions that would be needed in the future to aid a new conference center director. We did have these important meetings.

MY HAT IS IN THE RING

A couple weeks after that Chicago visit, I was on an informal telephone call with the pastor of our former church in Virginia just to follow up on the ministry of the new church we had helped to start and build. Casually, he happened to mention that the director of personnel at Moody had called him and had asked all sorts of questions about me. Instantly, I thought: "Oh, Oh, My hat is in the ring for the leadership at Moody Keswick Conference Center—and I hadn't even considered putting it in!"

Within just a few days, I received a call from Moody, asking Betty and me to come back to Chicago for further discussions about the issues I had raised previously. Moody's president then asked me to be the permanent director of the Moody Keswick Conference Center! He hosted a nice luncheon with all his key personnel to introduce me as a new member of the leadership team at Moody! Only one problem now—I had to work to implement all the recommendations I had made for whoever the new director would be! But it would be worth the try. God had now made another significant change in my life that I had certainly not anticipated! But He knew His plan in advance and led me down a new path in

His way. My military background and training would be of great advantage to me in this new responsibility.

I told the Moody administration that I would do my best to help return the conference center ministry to efficiency and to be a real asset to Moody Bible Institute. I wanted it to have a greater impact in the lives of conference guests than ever before. However, I needed Moody's leaders' full trust, and I would give them mine. I said that this position as the director would be a real privilege and that I would make every effort to lead in a biblical, godly, and professional manner.

Our conference center's full-time staff members and our volunteers were fantastic, dedicated, highly-motivated, and capable people who bonded tightly with each other and the guests each year. Many remain best friends to this day. Our regular staff consisted of about ten people who were supplemented by approximately eighty volunteers, some who were local and worked occasionally throughout the year and others who came just for the winter Bible conference season. Our volunteers came from many different states and several Canadian provinces to join us in making Moody Keswick Conference Center an excellent, professional, beautiful, and spiritually uplifting place for worldwide guests. I was so thankful for the wonderful paid and volunteer staff with whom the Lord let me serve. Although many have passed on to glory, we still keep contact with others who remain.

BIBLE CONFERENCE EXPERIENCES

The Lord gave me the unique and unusual opportunity to serve as director of the Moody Keswick Conference Center (MKCC) for more than five years. This was a time of real spiritual enrichment in my life. Each winter season, we held a thirteen-week Bible conference beginning in early January with each week starting on Saturday afternoon with a concert by a well-known, Christian musical artist. That was followed by a nice welcome reception for all the guests who stayed for the week in our forty-eight-room lodge. After a delicious dinner in our excellent dining room, we held another concert by the same afternoon concert artist. Community personnel enjoyed the concerts along with our lodge guests.

During the Bible conference season, beginning on Sunday morning, a highly-respected and renowned Bible teacher preached each morning and evening through Friday. I was privileged to select the conference speakers and musical artists and got to know them quite well as we interacted on and off the chapel platform. I invited the speakers and concert artists well over a year in advance

been there, done that!

so that the following year's schedule could be published and guests could sign up early for the week (or weeks) they preferred for the next year's conference. Almost every night after the evening service, our guests gathered in the dining room for delicious snacks and some kind of fun program.

Betty and I made special efforts to learn the names of our Bible conference guests. Upon arriving on Saturdays, each guest was given a name tag—not only for our benefit but also for recognition by other guests and staff. We determined to be able to call each person by their name before Tuesday's dinner as we welcomed them into our dining room. Often guests would try to trick us by wearing another person's nametag or by covering their nametag as we greeted them. This would become a fun game throughout the week, but we were pleased that God gave us the ability to remember names and we were rarely fooled. Learning and remembering names has been a characteristic of mine, and people have often commented on how much they appreciated the personal greetings.

I had some very interesting experiences at the Bible conference. One Saturday, I had to tell a vocal soloist that the next time she came that she needed to dress more appropriately for our fairly conservative audience. That did not sit well with her and the next year she came, she conveniently left her dress across town and said she had to wear something "less appealing" for the type of formal concert she was doing. That was fine with me as I desired a musical ministry and not a fashion show! Because I wanted variety from year-to-year in our concerts, I had not invited her back for the following year. She knew that, and when she first stepped on stage for both the afternoon and evening concerts, she proceeded to tell the audience that they needed to talk to this inexperienced director (me!) and make sure she would get an invitation for each year! Obviously, she didn't get her wish!

For another concert, Moody had encouraged me to invite a young, talented couple for the concerts. She had been a Miss Illinois (a soprano soloist) and he was an outstanding trumpeter. Their CD sounded great, so I invited them. For our concerts in the chapel, we had our own sound system and a practice sound check was always conducted a couple of hours before concert time. This couple brought and insisted on using their own sound system up on the platform. The practice went well, and the sound through both their system and ours was carefully balanced.

At the concerts, I always welcomed the crowd and did the introductions of the artist(s) and then sat on the front row with my wife and a guest or two from the community. At this concert, the concert artist couple tuned their sound system up beyond what it had been in the rehearsal, and the first number was horribly loud. From the front row, I motioned to him to turn it down. He went over to his machine and touched the controls. The second number was equally loud.

That day, my wife had been in the back, taking pictures for publicity of these very photogenic artists but came up to me in the front row after the second song and whispered that people were leaving the chapel complaining about the volume. I then called the husband to the front of the platform and kindly asked him to reduce the volume. He told me that it was coming from my control system in the back, which I really didn't believe, but I sent word to my sound man to shut our system off.

Since I was on the front row and really couldn't tell what the sound was like in the back, during the intermission I asked the audience about the sound levels. All of a sudden in unison, a number of people put their hands over their ears and shouted: "IT'S TOO LOUD!" While the people were milling around during the break, I pulled the artists aside and again told them to turn their sound system down and that our house sound system was completely off. The second half was better but still not satisfactory, so I said I would meet with the artists and my sound man before the evening concert to resolve the problem.

Immediately after each Saturday afternoon concert and before dinner in our dining room, we had a very nice, dressy reception for our lodge guests, the musical artists, our conference speaker for the week, and other special guests. This musical couple had been personally invited to the reception but without telling me, they did not show up. Neither did they come to dinner, but I hoped they would show up to work out the sound issue before the evening concert.

They did come early to the chapel and emphatically told me that they were the professional musicians and they knew what was best for our audience. I said to them that they get to leave after the concert but I have to deal with my audience who come back week after week and year after year—and I know what our people like! I also said that I had been music major in college for a year and that I thoroughly understood the value of quality music, which is what we wanted and expected at our Bible conference. I think they were a little shocked to hear what I was firmly saying to them.

The couple continued to complain, so I asked them to join me in my office where I told them that if they would not meet our standards, we would call off the evening concert. It was their choice. I prayed with and for them and left the

been there, done that!

office, saying I'd be back in five minutes to hear from them about whether they wanted to play and sing at the evening concert or not. When I came back, they said they would hold the volume levels to our standard—but that it would not be a good concert. I said I didn't like that attitude but would trust their word. In actuality, the evening concert was quite good! Confrontation is never fun but at times is very necessary. As a leader, I had similar difficult situations to deal with before, and I was sure this time would not be the last.

There were many other interesting things and sometimes surprises during the conference season. Brief examples include: a concert artist who didn't show up on the date he was scheduled, strange people on our conference grounds, a couple of tremendous speakers but with boring personalities, nearly losing an elderly guest on one of our afternoon tours, piano strings breaking in the middle of a piano concert, health issues of our guests, and icicles (yes in Florida!) hanging from our trees and yard swings. But I learned that in all circumstances, I must demonstrate leadership, move on, remember to be flexible, and always trust the Lord for His guidance!

RADIO AND TV INTERVIEWS

My public relations experience in the Army proved to be very valuable during my tenure as director at Moody Keswick Conference Center. We upgraded our campus and our literature and re-branded the ministry. In addition to providing displays at some large Christian organizations' annual conventions, I was often invited to radio programs and TV stations to talk about our conference center and ministry. Moody Bible Institute had its own group of radio stations and affiliates in many states, and I would be on call-in interviews by several of their station managers. However, as I traveled, I would actually go in to a Moody station for on-site programs—locally in St. Petersburg and Boynton Beach in Florida, Tennessee, Indiana, Michigan, Chicago, the Quad City area in western Illinois, Alabama, and Washington state to name a few.

The radio interview in Spokane, Washington, was during the morning drive time. When we concluded the 7:30 a.m. program, a call came to the station, and the person asked to speak to me. Who did I know that lived out there in eastern Washington? I was really surprised to learn that the caller was my former high school basketball coach at Wheaton Academy in Illinois! I had not seen or heard of him in thirty-seven years! He just happened to be listening to Moody's Spokane station that day when I was sharing. It's a small world!

Because of my Moody connection, I was occasionally on Christian TV or other radio stations not in the Moody family network. Sometimes I would have to write radio script for others to use on their programs or stations. I was very thankful for all my public relations training provided through the courtesy of Uncle Sam and the Defense Department!

"YOU NO LIKE DUCKS?"

In the off season (basically May through December) we rented our conference center to diverse retreat groups. We had nice lodge facilities and a wonderful dining room, which had a great reputation for its excellent variety and food quality. For my first few years at Keswick, our primary cook was a lady from Pennsylvania who made all our baked goods from scratch—including breakfast rolls, pies, and cakes, as well as the occasional hamburger and hot dog buns! From 1991 to 1996, the number of retreat groups increased from twenty-six in my first year to eighty-nine in my last full year, thus demonstrating the value of the facility to many organizations. Of course, with that level of occupancy in addition to the Bible conference season, we had to maintain housekeeping, food service, bookstore, administrative, grounds keeping, and general maintenance personnel throughout the year. Again, it all made me thankful for the training and administrative experience the Army had given me. It was sort of like being the commander of a mini military base—yet without all the white-glove inspections which some had feared when I was asked to be the director!

One year, we hosted a group from an ethnic church. And as I did for all retreat groups, I gave an orientation to the people at the beginning of their time with us. I always warned them about the large Muscovy ducks which would come from the little lake on our center's west side.

The ducks liked to hang around on the walkways in front of our lodge doors. We had reflective film on the floor-to-ceiling, glass, sliding doors to keep the heat of the sun out of the rooms, and the ducks liked to look at their own reflections—at least I presume that's why they were there! Sometimes, the ducks' "poop" would be slippery where our guests would walk, and we constantly had to be cleaning the walks and inside carpets. The retreat group leader came to me after my initial briefing and said: "You no like ducks?" I said the ducks are OK except

been there, done that!

for the mess they leave and the extra work they cause us, so I didn't like the ducks there on our walkways.

The next morning, I noticed that there were no ducks around! The leader came to me just to tell about their evening program and then he asked if I noticed that the ducks weren't around. When I replied, he said: "You said you no like ducks. See, no more ducks!" I didn't ask any questions at that point but I imagine some folks from an Asian nation had some unusual (for us!) eating at home the next night! It would be interesting to know how they caught the ducks.

TRAVELS FOR THE CONFERENCE CENTER

Because we were a winter Bible conference, we were free to travel in the summer times for recruiting new guests and staff. One of my goals on these summer trips was to meet with directors of other Christian conference centers and camps. Some of them had been in that type of ministry for many years and had "been there, done that". I wanted to learn from them about issues they had previously faced, were addressing now, or anticipated for the future of conferencing. In our more than five years at MKCC, we visited thirty-five other conference ministries (in addition to numerous churches throughout the United States and Canada). Most of their Bible conferences were in the summer, and ours was in the winter, so it was a good opportunity for me to see their ministries in action.

Often, we were gone from home for four to six weeks with very full meeting schedules. During one of our six-week trips, we conducted fifty Bible conference-oriented presentations of one type or another—some were breakfast gatherings or lunch and dinner meetings in restaurants, others were in churches, and some were group meetings in private homes. The majority of our winter conference guests were from the Midwest and Northeast, and they regularly invited me to share MKCC ministries with their friends and churches. It was wonderful to meet many new people. We traveled many thousands of miles within the US and Canada, and our conference ministry grew from all of these contacts. While in an area for meetings, we also made special efforts to see or do "touristy" things when we did not have meetings or were traveling between geographical regions.

CANADIAN ATLANTIC PROVINCES

Because we had several volunteers and guests from the Atlantic Provinces in eastern Canada, we went to that region a couple of times. One of the couples lived in Dawson Settlement, New Brunswick, just south of Moncton. They lived in an old house, sitting on property, which had been deeded to their ancestors in the 1600s. Of course, it had been upgraded a few times and was a very comfortable home. B and S also had a small trailer on a bay off the Gulf of St. Lawrence at a camping resort.

B and S took us all over the area from the Acadia section in the north of New Brunswick, to the southeast with its Fundy Rocks, to the south with its wonderful, rounded-rocks "beach" (as she called it!) at Cape Enrage, the reversing falls in St. John, and to the far west of the province to the world's longest covered bridge in Hartland. We also visited the New Brunswick Bible Institute and the Atlantic Baptist College.

On one of our excursions, we tried to find some remote waterfalls. As we headed down this narrow, one-way "jungled" road, we could hear the falls but found no place where we could stop and actually see them. At the bottom of the ravine was an opening and, much to our surprise, we saw another car, which had come down a dirt road into the area from the other end. We met a couple there with their mother and a dog and wondered what they were doing in this isolated place. The ninety-two-year-old mother told us that she grew up and went to school in that county. As she sat on a rock, she sang her school's fight song for us! She said that she now lived in Maine but that her kids from Florida wanted to bring her back to her original stomping grounds for a last visit. Oh, from Florida? Where? Come to find out, they were from St. Petersburg area (same as us) and owned a dog kennel in our town! What a small world it was for us to have met a couple from our area who were just visiting at the same time in a remote dense forest area of New Brunswick, Canada!

ATVs TO THE RESCUE

Along this same line of unexpected events regarding our friends in New Brunswick, we had an unusual incident a few years later in 2016. We were going to visit B and S at their home in Dawson Settlement. We had been there a couple of times in the past, so we basically knew the area and the roads. However, this

been there, done that!

time our GPS directed us on a different route. Betty was driving and before long the GPS took us on a wide gravel road, which soon turned into a narrow dirt road. It seemed a little strange to us. Betty said if we were to go any farther on this deteriorating road that I was going to drive! So we switched seats and onward we went. The little road became a rutted, washed out, dirt and dried mud trail—yet the GPS showed that up ahead was an intersection, which seemed to then lead toward our destination.

I was carefully riding the high spots in between the rain-washed gullies in the road when the left front tire slid down into one of the ditches crossing the road. We could not move forward or backward. Yes, we were stuck—not in mud but in a small rain-washed rut. I got out and began to gather rocks and branches to put where the wheel could pull out, but it was to no avail without jacking the car up. The mosquitoes were vicious and swarming and seemed to increase after I applied repellant which Betty had gotten out of a suitcase. I tried calling B & S but found that we had no cell service in that spot. But the Lord did hear our emergency prayers from there!

I thought I heard some vehicles back down the road where we had been—but then the sound stopped. I hollered as loud as I could at off-and-on intervals but received no response. Finally, we decided to walk up the hill in front of us to what the GPS showed to be an intersection with the road we were on. Also, we thought that the height there plus the better opening in the overhead trees would give us the ability to make a phone call to B. It worked! But B said he had no idea where we were.

Just as we hung up with him, we heard the motors again and were pleasantly surprised to see six or seven heavily-tattooed people on four ATVs coming up the hill toward us! In looking toward them, we noticed a small, weather-beaten sign on a nearby tree which read "ATV Trail 4". What? The GPS had taken us on an ATV trail. My faith in our electronic GPS suddenly disappeared!

The ATV folks told us they had heard my hollering when they stopped for a brief break at a spot down the trail from where our van was stuck. (Thanks, Lord, for the Army's training to have a strong command voice!) They headed toward my call and saw our van stuck and decided to follow our footsteps up the hill to where we were. After we explained how we got there, they offered to go to the van with us and using some of their towing straps they carried on their ATVs, they felt they could get the van unstuck.

They fastened a couple of straps to my van and to two of their ATVs, and the van came right out. They pulled it backwards down to a spot in the road where we could turn it around. I profusely thanked them and said they were an answer to our prayers. I think they were a little surprised as it appeared they had not heard of God answering prayer like that! I shared a very brief testimony with them and asked if I could thank the Lord for bringing them to us. Looking at each other, they agreed. After the prayer, they said they wanted to follow us to make sure we made it out to the main road. Why should I question that? I'd sure like to know what their conversation was about after we went our separate ways.

We got to B and S's house a couple of hours late for lunch and had quite the story to tell. This was a great reminder of how wonderful our Lord is and that He is watching over us in all of our circumstances. He is still in the business of answering prayer!

EASTERN CANADA MEETINGS

B set up our MKCC meetings for that eastern Canadian region. We had several in New Brunswick, but others were held in Nova Scotia, Newfoundland, and the very pristine Prince Edward Island (PEI). To get to PEI on our first trip there, we had to go by ferry to and from the island—although in later years, a long bridge was built to connect it to the mainland. Everywhere we went for these meetings, we tried to take in all of the interesting sites in the area. One meeting in PEI was near the eastern end.

The missionaries with whom we stayed had a home just a short distance from a huge, stone, Catholic church which really looked out of place for the sparse population in that area. It was an historic building, and we wanted to take a look inside. The missionaries said it was probably open, although no one would be around, so we went for a visit. It was marvelous architecture, and with the sun radiating through its stained glass windows, it was beautiful. Towards the back of the church, we saw a large chair with a sign saying it was the "Pope's Seat". We read a little informative sign nearby which said that at some point in a previous year, a pope had visited this church and sat in that chair. Seeing that it had no restrictions except a little velvet rope, I went up the couple of steps and sat in the "Pope's Seat". Having "been there, done that", I can't say that I felt any more religious there than anywhere else, but I do regret that I didn't have the pope's pointed hat to wear!

been there, done that!

Prince Edward Island was spectacular and remarkably clean. We never saw any trash anywhere! As we encircled the island, we loved seeing the steeples of churches in nearly every community on prominent places as we traveled the rolling roads. We visited the Anne of Green Gables homestead, learned a great deal at the Potato Museum, watched horses harvest seaweed, and spent time at a complex constructed of glass bottles and cement.

The full-sized structures there used many multi-colored bottles held together by cement for the walls and interior furnishings in a house, a chapel, a bar, and a community room. The necks of the bottles faced inside and the walls clearly showed the brilliant reds, greens, browns, yellows, blues, and other colors as the sun shone from the outside through the glass on the bottles' bottoms. These buildings were unique, fascinating, and very captivating as we sat on the bottle pews—thankfully their bottoms were up when ours were down!—in the chapel and as I pretended to speak from the pulpit also made of bottles! No one had to worry about a place to hang their purses or coats with the myriad of bottle necks sticking out on the inside of the walls and on the backs of the bottle pews.

We were welcomed into Nova Scotia from New Brunswick by bagpipers. At the welcome center, we were told of several designated car trails to give us a good feel for the province. Going to and from some of our meetings, we did travel these all the way from the northeastern John Cabot Trail to those along the south and west coasts, visiting many historic places which we had not known about previously.

Everywhere we went, I was interested in the many little side roads and the unusual places where they led. Therefore, each trip took us longer than it would for any "normal" tourist. I like variety, and we visited many out-of-the-way places to take in cultural vignettes of the region. We also visited historic military forts in Halifax and Lunenburg. In the far west, we went to Digby Neck where we dug for the famous Digby clams. Speaking of that, one place where we were digging clams had big warning signs to be aware of the times that the tides came in. It would be very tough to rescue you if you were caught out there during those times. Our friend did get stuck in the muck remaining from a receding tide once when she was bending over to dig up a clam. She had on white Bermuda shorts and from behind it was quite the contrast to see against the dark muck background! We did get her out!

We were in the Atlantic Provinces during blueberry season. Their blueberries grow in short, ground bushes rather than the taller bushes we are used to seeing in the US. The berries were being picked by mostly women who wore their everyday multi-colored skirts. At first, I had no idea what these folks were doing out on the hillsides along the roads because all you could see were these beautiful, round, multi-colored spots all over the area. Come to find out, it was only the skirted bottoms of the ladies bending over to pick the berries! We ended up calling them "bottoms-up pickers".

While in Nova Scotia, we had a wonderful meeting at a home in the middle of the province, of a doctor who came yearly to our Bible conference in Florida. He invited friends from his church, clients in his medical practice, and community leaders to learn about the ministry he went to for a few weeks in the winter. We were pleased to see some of those folks at the next year's conference and enjoyed getting to know the doctor and his family on his home turf.

Little did we realize how far the Newfoundland province was from the mainland and eastern port in Nova Scotia. One day as planned, we boarded a ferry with our car, and after fourteen hours on the water, we arrived at 10 p.m. on the west coast of Newfoundland. We told some people that we were going to drive across the island to the capital city of St. John's that night, and they all warned us about the moose we would likely encounter on the way. We were a little disappointed that we didn't see one moose that night. In fact, in traveling later for several days around the island, we only saw one moose cow with her calf—and fortunately she was not on the hood of our car! Moose strikes are so common that their numbers are recorded on signs along the highway.

We certainly didn't think about how cold it could be in Newfoundland in the summer and being scheduled to go on a boat trip to see puffins (cute little colorful birds) on an island, I asked our B&B hostess if she had some headgear and scarves we could use. She said she would go upstairs and get a "tuque" for me. What? A tuque? To me, being from Africa, a tuque was a fifty-five-gallon gasoline drum! How was I going to see anything with a tuque over my head? Soon she came down with a knit cap and said I could use that "tuque" to keep my head warm on our boat trip. Was I ever relieved! Other words we had to get used to in Canada were: chesterfield for a couch—being from America, a chesterfield was a cigarette, and you didn't want to sit on that—serviette for a napkin; bonnet for the hood of a car; what sounded like shool for school or shedule for schedule; and project (with a long o) for a project (soft o). But we got used to these language variations! Eh!

We had some good meetings in Newfoundland with a couple of them being in the very heart of the island at a small church attended by some of our Moody Keswick Conference Center guests. Betty and I always like to mingle with the church family before our meetings, but here the folks spoke a mixture of Irish, English, Scottish, and whatever else. We never could understand a couple of gentlemen who tried to give us their names several times! In that area, the people also would leave the "h" off the beginning of a word and add it on to some words that began with a vowel—such as "I urt my heye". Also, they replaced the long "i" with an "oi" in words like "light" and "right" so they may say, "Go down and take a roight at the loight." It made some tough listening until we could catch on to the dialect they used.

In one little church in the heart of that big island of Newfoundland, we thoroughly enjoyed the hearty singing and then I was introduced to speak by a ninety-two-year-old man. With tears in his eyes and a broken voice, he said that he had studied the writings and sermons of Dwight L. Moody for many years and sometimes used Moody's messages (with appropriate credit) as his own when he preached. He continued to say that in all his years, he had never met anyone affiliated with Moody's school, and finally someone from Moody had come to him.

I felt quite humble (but very inadequate) to be representing Dwight L. Moody to this man!

Being military, I wanted to go to the site where one of our US military planes had mysteriously crashed immediately after takeoff in Gander, Newfoundland. The plane was loaded with troops returning from a peace-keeping mission in the Sinai. Our men had expected to be home for Christmas, but all 258 on the plane died on the hillside that day in December 1985. I was in the Pentagon at the time of the crash and remember the great sorrow among all our military forces and the agony of families of the men as reported in the media. There in Gander, it was rather an eerie feeling for me but also was one of great respect and honor to stand in that hallowed, crash-site spot with its memorial to our soldiers and airmen.

In Newfoundland, we were on many kilometers of gravel roads as we went from the capital city of St. John's in the east all the way to the northern tip and back down the northwestern side of the island. Many of the roads had signs saying: "Travel at your own risk" or "Warning, Moose Strike Area". We went anyway!

At one spot we had seen an iceberg—this was August!—floating in the sea, and we wanted to get closer to get a better picture. We followed in our car a little trail which led us up a hill for a better view. As I was getting out to take a picture of the iceberg, our big Lincoln Town Car began to sink, and looking around, I realized we were in a mucky sheep pasture! Believe me, there were some quick prayers as I jumped back in the car and fortunately was able to back down the hill before we got stuck! If we had become stuck, it was a lo-o-ong ways to walk to get any help.

Before leaving Newfoundland, we stopped at Gross Morne National Park on the west side. The park is famous for its fjords, and we wanted to see these unusual, beautiful evidences of God's creation. Over the years, much of the land there had filled in by nature between the fjords and the current coastline. We had to walk about a half hour over a board walkway to get to the fjord area.

Upon arriving, we saw a medium-sized passenger ship which we boarded and immediately wondered how the ship got to the lake—so far from the sea and with all that land in between! Later we were told that it was brought in during the winter season over the tundra on sleds and huge log rollers when the ground was solid. The views of the fjords were absolutely stunning as we looked high up from the water's surface to the top of the cliffs and then watched as glistening wide or slender waterfalls splashed down to our level. From that part of Newfoundland, it was only an eight-hour ferry ride back to Nova Scotia instead of the fourteen hours it took us to get to the island. What wonderful memories we have of that

been there, done that!

unusual Canadian province! Some of our friends from Newfoundland still come to Florida in the winters and we always enjoy seeing them again and discussing our special days in their province.

ONTARIO

The majority of our Canadian friends live in Ontario and as a result, we have been there numerous times. While visiting, we have covered most of the province, from the nation's capital in Ottawa in the east to Hudson Bay in the west, and from the huge nickel mines in Sudbury in the northern part to Niagara Falls in the south. We were impressed with the variety of small and large locks on the rivers and canals to the gem stones in Bancroft and the unspoiled beauty of Algonquin National Park.

In Ontario, we interacted with the directors and guests at Bible conference centers such as Elim Lodge, Muskoka Baptist Conference, Guelph Bible Conference, JOY Bible Camp, and Fair Havens Conference. I have been the speaker, representing our Moody Keswick Conference Center in all of these and many churches throughout the province. A friend from college was an associate pastor at the great People's Church in Toronto. He invited me to speak there, but I also spoke in numerous small churches which our friends attended. We enjoyed socializing with groups of varying sizes in wonderful homes. Everywhere, the people were so welcoming!

One of the very special events for me in Ontario was visiting a monument at the burial site of Joseph M. Scriven, an Irish man who had lived in Canada. I love Christian hymnody, and one of my favorite hymns is *What a Friend We Have in Jesus* that Mr. Scriven wrote in 1855. Because of tragedies in his own life and a resulting commitment to serve underprivileged individuals, Scriven had no money to return to Ireland to help his own ailing mother. Instead, he wrote the text of this hymn as a poem to comfort her. Dwight L. Moody found the poem that had by then been put to music, and he used it extensively in his ministries. Scriven died at age sixty-six in 1886. His memorial is a small obelisk behind a home in a rural environment near Rice Lake, Ontario. On each of three sides are engraved the words of a verse of his famous hymn and on the fourth side is an inscription regarding the author. Thank you, Mr. Scriven, for penning those words which have meant so much to me and to so many people around the world. Truly, we do have a wonderful Friend in Jesus!

UPPER MIDWEST USA

One of the MKCC trips in 1994 took us through Wisconsin, Minnesota, and North Dakota, to Manitoba, Saskatchewan, Alberta, British Columbia, and then south to Washington, Oregon, California, Arizona, Texas, Arkansas, Alabama, and back to Florida. We were gone fifty-three days, had more than fifty meetings in that time, clocked over 10,000 miles on the car, and stayed in numerous wonderful homes of our friends!

On that lengthy trip, we were in Minnesota when Betty got word that her father had died in Chicago. We were so glad that we had just seen him three days before on our way north. She booked a quick plane trip to Chicago while I continued to hold my meetings, but I did fly to Chicago for the funeral service. Late that same night, I flew back to the airport in Minneapolis so I could start driving to Fargo, North Dakota, for a meeting and from there to Winnipeg, Manitoba, for the next night's meeting. Betty would meet me in a few days in Regina, Saskatchewan, after spending some time with her family. I knew the value of being with family in sorrowful times like this since my own dad had died about three months before the passing of Betty's father.

MANITOBA TO BRITISH COLUMBIA

Things went fine for me, driving by myself the long distances, and I had carefully planned to ensure that I would arrive at each meeting on time. Going north from Fargo, I arrived at the Canadian border just before noon. The border agent asked me all the normal questions, including for whom I worked and if I was going to leave anything in Canada. I said I worked for Moody Bible Institute and that I had some coffee mugs which I would leave as a gift for different individuals who would provide accommodations for me during my visit. The agent said to pull over and go inside to see the immigration officer. I tried to figure out what I had said different than other times at Canadian borders but couldn't come up with an answer.

As I came near the officer's desk, she said that she was headed out to lunch and would be right back and that I should wait for her. She returned an hour later! By now, I had lost more than an hour out of my detailed, schedule. The grilling then started and went on for over a half hour. At the end of the conversation and since I had crossed the border several times before without any problems, I curiously

been there, done that!

asked what it was that caused me to be stopped and interrogated. Hesitatingly, she told me that the window agent at the border crossing thought that I said I was with the "Mooneys"—as in the Korean religious sect. She said that those folks were all over Canada, selling roses beside the road and in shopping centers to make some illegal money. I was more than a little disturbed due to this delay in my travel because now I had to call the church in Winnipeg and say that I would be late to my meeting. I got there about ten minutes late, quickly set up my display and projector, and ended up having a great time with the folks.

> [Out of all my meetings over the years, I was only late to one other meeting in a different summer. On a Sunday afternoon, we were coming out of Ontario into Michigan for an evening meeting and got into a terrible traffic jam at the Bluewater Bridge at Sarnia. Adding to my frustration at that time was the fact that I was running low on gas while sitting in the traffic and wondered if I could make it across the bridge or if I would be stuck on the bridge. I think we made it to a gas station only on fumes and prayer!
>
> For that Sunday evening meeting, I had to call the church, which was gathering by this time, and said I would be at least a half hour late. I asked if they still wanted me to come. They said they would wait for me. A couple of our Bible conference volunteers had set up the meeting and really wanted us to share with their friends in the church what they did in Florida each winter. Fortunately, on this Sunday afternoon, the highways were fairly open. (Admittedly, I did not hold to the speed limit that day.) The church graciously accepted us with a warm welcome when we arrived, demonstrating their understanding and Christian love!]

We did enjoy seeing many "touristy" things in these travels in the western parts of Canada. Some of these included the gorgeous and massive fields of golden canola, blue-flowering flax fields, and green wheat fields in great patchwork quilts as we came over the hills of Manitoba and Saskatchewan. At one place, our friends took us to a farm and showed us the mammoth tractors in Saskatchewan that could plow, disc, plant, and harvest sixty-four rows at a time. Unbelievable! In that province, we also visited a couple of Bible colleges and shared our ministry several times with different groups of people.

In Edmonton, Alberta, our friends wanted us to see the world's largest mall (at that time). It was huge! While there, we wanted to pick up a souvenir of a Ukrainian painted egg which we had heard about. No one had one for sale. Disappointed, we went with our hosts back to their home. In the short time we were with them, our host was talking with a neighbor, telling them about our visit and that they knew us from spending time in the winter with us at a Bible conference in Florida. Casually, it was mentioned that we tried to find a Ukrainian painted egg but didn't locate any in the mall. The neighbor went into her house, took a framed egg off her wall and said to give it to us! We were so very thankful. Today it hangs on our wall with many other souvenirs!

The Canadian Rockies, Lake Louise, and the Columbia Icefields in Alberta were amazing. Our travels were in the summer and we were rather surprised that we could still read by our hotel window even though it was after 11 p.m. The late daylight was new to us. As we progressed on our trip into British Columbia, we visited missionary friends in Abbotsford, saw the iconic Lion's Head Bridge in Vancouver, walked across a deep ravine on the swinging Capilano Suspension Rope Bridge, and strolled through the beautiful Butchart Gardens on Vancouver Island where some of our conference center guests lived. In all these provinces, we were privileged to share God's Word and our Moody Keswick Bible Conference ministry through the gracious hospitality of many of our winter guests.

WEST AND SOUTHWEST USA

Heading south, we stopped at the Mt. St. Helens' volcano and met with several conference center directors in Oregon, California, Arizona, and Texas before heading back to Florida. All of these fit nicely into our itinerary, and at the same time, we visited people with whom we had become friends at MKCC. We promoted our Bible conference ministry every opportunity we could. This trip did bring several first-time guests to our center in coming years. We also were privileged to connect with some of our MKCC speakers while out west and when in Texas.

At one of the California conference centers, we had gone to their evening meeting and while waiting for it to start, Betty was talking with some people next to her. Suddenly, a lady nearby heard something she said and turned around and recognized her. She and her husband had been missionaries in the Central African Republic where my parents had served! We didn't know they lived in California, and they didn't know we would be at that conference center, but the Lord put us

been there, done that!

each in a place where we would meet. What a great reunion that was! It sure is a small world!

Some of our Bible conference speakers were from Great Britain. Betty and I were invited to go to Scotland and Ireland in the summer of 1996, but Moody closed the conference center that spring, which forced us to cancel those meetings. We were disappointed that we couldn't go to the British Isles because some of our conference guests and speakers wanted us to come and encourage more people to vacation in Florida and enjoy the abundant life ministry we desired for all.

MOODY CLOSES CONFERENCE CENTER

When Moody Bible Institute announced in November 1995 that MKCC would be closed after the Bible conference ended in the spring of 1996, I immediately began receiving some very interesting and potentially exciting job offers from a number of varied ministries around the US, in Canada, and even overseas. I said to the principals in each situation that I would not make a decision until I had formally closed the conference center for Moody. I wanted the closure to be professional and the property in excellent condition for the future owners.

Because the leadership at Moody anticipated that there could be many questions about their closure decision, they told me to make the announcement each week to the conference guests in 1996. This was a very emotional time for conferees who had come to Moody's Florida site for many years. They had established lasting friendships by coming when their favorite speakers or musicians were on the schedule, and they had connected with guests whom they would see year after year.

Oftentimes, questions to me about the upcoming closure were harsh—especially when I could not give them satisfactory answers as to why Moody's leadership made such a decision. A number of them felt betrayed by the institute which they had loved and supported for many years. Some people said that they would help buy the MKCC property if I would continue as the director, but I did not feel led to pursue that as much as I loved the conference center ministry. I did not want the continuation of the ministry to be based on my presence, personality, or leadership. Moody later sold the facilities to the Keswick Christian School which was co-located on the St. Petersburg campus. An era ended in 1996 with the closing of one of the well-known Bible conference ministries in the nation!

Too often in my travels and former assignments in the military, I have seen or visited secular industries, organizations, ministries, boards, and churches—or even departments within these—which chose key people who were not trained or experienced in leadership and administration. Often, they had chosen a new leader merely based on his/her availability—and not their capabilities—to direct that type of organization or ministry. In some cases, job descriptions were non-existent, there was little accountability from the leader to a higher authority, leadership evaluations were not completed, and there were no strategic plans for the leader to pursue. I knew that when I accepted the leadership responsibility at MKCC, I would have to address some of these past weaknesses or failures. This was a promise I made to myself and to those on Moody's Chicago campus who oversaw the ministry.

In my military experience, accountability was a big thing, and how I performed was reflected on regular, personal efficiency reports. That enabled me to work on improving my own leadership and administrative skills, and I always wanted to continue to grow in my professionalism into whatever field God was leading me. I was a results-oriented guy and was really serious about making modifications where *needed*. Sometimes I had to expect change in my own thinking as well as how change may be perceived by the outside world.

Two weeks before the MKCC closure in June 1996, I was asked to become the president of D&D Missionary Homes in the St. Petersburg area where I already lived. Although some other positions of leadership in other organizations were enticing—and would have been much more financially rewarding!—I was thankful for the Lord's leading to a ministry where I would not have to move, even though we were willing if that was what the Lord planned. Missions were a passion of my heart, and perhaps my leadership at D&D would have an impact for the gospel around the world. Betty and I were comfortable in our home, with our church, and the many friends we had made in Florida for this next phase of our lives.

D&D MISSIONARY HOMES, INC,

D&D Missionary Homes was a ministry founded in 1949 by two ladies whose last names began with D—Miss Alma Doering and Miss Stella Dunkelberger. Its purpose was to provide fully-furnished housing and other support services for active evangelical missionaries in their transitional times, such as deputation/pre-field ministries, furloughs, educational periods, medical care, getting their kids into college, or even for needed vacation breaks. They could stay for a very few days or up to a year on the D&D campus. This was not a facility to meet the

been there, done that!

housing requirements of retired missionaries. Other places provided retiree care, but D&D was for active missionaries.

Some of D&D's services included a library, clothing center,—which some ladies called their boutique!—food pantry, playground, fitness center, laundry, spiritual counsel, and weekly times for mutual enrichment. The ministry started with one small home in 1949 and grew during my time as president from fewer than forty-five homes to fifty-two fully furnished homes varying in size from one to five bedrooms. These were all located within a four city-block area on the north side of St. Petersburg, Florida. D&D was certainly the largest of transitional missionary housing organizations and was also one of the oldest. Schools, churches, and shopping venues were abundant in the immediate urban area, and commercial transportation was very convenient for missionaries. My parents, brother, and sister had all stayed there several times during their missionary ministries and had been blessed by the services it had offered.

BOARD MEMBERSHIP

I was invited to be a board member for D&D Missionary Homes in 1992 and became quite involved because of my passion for meeting missionaries' needs. I noted that the board was mostly a bunch of men who had been on the board for years and years. It was an administrative board that oversaw all of the little intricacies of the organization. It seemed to me that the administrator/executive director had few direct responsibilities and little decision-making authority. The finances were tightly controlled by the board treasurer and included a fairly large reserve in comparison to the budget. There were very few significant fund-raising events, and only occasionally the director would go out to churches to encourage support.

In board meetings, there were few in-depth questions asked as to *why* things were being done—or not being done. I felt that the content of board meetings and composition of the board needed to change. It should be a policy board rather than an administrative board. I began to ask questions, and sometimes other board members would glare at me as though they were thinking: "Why did we bring this guy on the board?"

After a few board meetings, however, things began to change. A couple of the older board members resigned—seeing they were not having much impact—and we added some new, visionary, and more enthusiastic board members who were from diverse missionary, ministry, or business backgrounds. They were interested in seeing the ministry break out of its routines of the past. Those were exciting days to see an important, vital service to missionaries move forward out of its relatively stagnated and weakly-led recent past.

Again, as at Moody Keswick Conference Center (MKCC), I felt that some of the previous leadership had not been fully vetted, were not trained in administration, and were not experienced in such a ministry even though they were very willing and capable workers. I knew the board had to be responsible for properly selecting a leader. When Moody Bible Institute announced the closing of the MKCC campus in St. Petersburg, my D&D board term was coming to a conclusion, and rather than stay on for another term, I left D&D's board so I could focus on closing MKCC.

Right around that time, the then-current director of D&D came to my office and suggested that I should consider being his future replacement. I am not sure that anyone foresaw that he may be leaving. I thought nothing of it at the time, but two weeks before I closed the MKCC campus, a member of the D&D board approached me and asked me to pray about becoming the new executive director of D&D. I knew the organization and its needs and had a passion for that kind of ministry, so after consultation with my wife and intense prayer, I accepted the leadership position.

been there, done that!

EFFECTS OF CHANGE

When I became the executive director of D&D, I felt that an excessive amount of money was being held in its reserves. I immediately challenged the board to use some of that reserve money for a rapid upgrading of the buildings and grounds. The campus had not been adequately maintained in recent years, and it was not a good testimony in the community or to our missionary guests. Several volunteers and staff who had been with me at the Bible conference came to serve at D&D and the campus got a speedy renovation. This increased the morale of missionary residents and the attitude of the community around us as they saw my strong desire for quality care of missionaries and God's property.

Our missionary occupation rate increased, we tore down some older buildings and built new ones, the clothing center was enhanced, furnishings in the homes were upgraded, and our staff grew to better meet the needs of our missionary guests. D&D truly became a real home to missionaries, rather than just a place to stay. A missionary family, who had stayed with us previously, came back for another furlough and was placed in the same house they had lived in before. Upon entering the house, one of their young daughters joyfully exclaimed: "Mom, we are home again!" That meant so much to me to hear of that love for our ministry.

One year, we accommodated more than 800 missionaries who served in sixty-two nations. Our occupancy rate grew to and was sustained at over 90 percent, which would be the envy of most commercial hospitality organizations. The missionaries paid a small maintenance fee—in comparison to rental rates in the area—and provided five hours of work per family per week to help keep the ministry's costs low.

After a couple of years in dealing with large mission agencies, churches, and businesses, I realized that my title as executive director was actually a detriment to having effective and meaningful dialogue with the leaders of mission agencies, other organizations, and even some businesses. I prepared rationale and presented a proposal to the board to change the leadership title to president to put me on more of an equal footing when dealing with other leaders. This required modifications in the bylaws, which also opened up the opportunity to make other changes to increase the efficiency of the ministry. These changes proved to be a strong benefit to D&D.

D&D was special to me because of my own background in missions. I had seen the need for spiritual and emotional support of missionaries and their children who had been traumatized by war and hastily evacuated with no place to live and with very few of their personal belongings. Others were struggling in their marriages or with wayward kids who had been separated from the family because of schooling needs. Some just needed to vent about their relational frustrations with field personnel or their own mission agencies. Since we were an independent ministry, they felt comfortable opening up to me, knowing I would maintain their confidence and hopefully provide increased understanding and guidance. For some of them, I was able to encourage them in making their presentations more exciting and acceptable.

Many missionaries expressed their deep appreciation for D&D being physically, economically, and spiritually available for them in their times of need. I was so glad that we were there to support them. Where else could they find such a nicely and fully-furnished home for whatever time period they needed it—all for such a minimum cost and in such a helpful environment?

"PREACH IT, BROTHER!"

While on the road representing the Lord's work at D&D, I had some interesting experiences raising prayer and financial support for D&D. I received a call from a pastor who knew about D&D and wanted his church to consider supporting our ministry. I went to the church at his invitation on the appointed date and got there early on Sunday morning in order to set up our display. No one was yet at the church, so we patiently waited in the parking lot for the church to be opened.

Before long, a man drove up in his pickup truck and came over to greet us. He asked if he could help, and I told him that Pastor D had invited us as the missionary speaker that morning. He quizzically asked, "Are you sure?" "Yes," I replied. Again he asked: "Is this really the church you are supposed to be at or did you want to be at that other Baptist church a couple of miles down the street?" I verified with him that Pastor D was at this church and finally he welcomed me into the building, but I think he still had big questions in his mind.

We went to an adult Sunday School class and really enjoyed it, although by now we realized this was a church of African Americans! This didn't matter to me, but I had no clue before arriving there about the congregation. I had not previously met the pastor in person but loved his heart for missions when he first called me.

When it was time for the morning service, the pastor and I had prayer together, and he told me where to sit on the side of the platform. He then went back to his office for something. The choir came into the back of the sanctuary, lined up in the center aisle of the church, and began to sing antiphonally with the organist as they swayed in their tradition while moving forward into the choir loft where they continued to sing while facing me. I didn't know if I was supposed to respond in some manner, and the pastor wasn't there to give me any guidance, so I just sat and smiled at the choir. Soon on some signal, they all turned to their left and continued singing toward the congregation. I felt somewhat relieved!

I had preached in many, varied churches both stateside and overseas but nowhere like in this church. As I preached, the congregants were constantly interacting with me: "Say that again, brother." "Amen, Amen." "Keep on preaching." "Yes, Yes." "You said it." "Come on, keep it going." "Preach it, brother." All of that feedback was almost interrupting my thoughts, and I sent a quick prayer to the Lord to help me stay on my message. My preaching went on for about a half hour, and actually I was beginning to enjoy this ministry because the people were listening and they were responding—much in contrast to many white churches where the people sit there with frowns on their faces, waiting to get through their weekly habit of going to church on Sunday mornings—and probably anxious to get to their favorite eating place.

At the end of the service, many people seemed genuinely interested in the missionary message I had preached and spent quite a bit of time with Betty and me at our display for D&D Missionary Homes. The pastor seemed very encouraged with the response of his people to the mission challenge. However, a couple of months later, the pastor called me and sounded very discouraged. He told me that the people wanted to build a bigger building and now they were not interested in missions. It wasn't too long after that that the pastor called again and said he was resigning from the church since he couldn't help his people turn their hearts toward missions. He said they seemed only interested in making things better for themselves. I had a season of prayer with him that God would honor the desires of his missions-oriented heart. He was refreshing and encouraging to me, even as I tried to encourage him.

OTHER UNUSUAL CHURCH OPPORTUNITIES

A church in northern Ohio near the lake was a very old church that had not been modernized and had no air conditioning. We set up our D&D display and were about ready to begin the service when the pastor said we should move downstairs where it was much cooler. I was really thankful for his last-minute decision.

In another very conservative church, we were not allowed to have our little automatic slide projector box working on our display table because no "moving pictures" were permitted on the main floor of the sanctuary. They showed me a place where we could put our display down in the basement. However, I knew it would not be seen by the church people down there, so I just removed the projector box from our presentation table.

We arrived at a church in Pittsburgh in mid-afternoon and, as planned, met a person there who would open the church for us to set up our display for the evening service. It was 96°F outside, and there was no air conditioning in the church. I took off my suitcoat as the sweat began to roll while Betty and I set up our display. I saw a couple of floor fans near windows, so I turned the fans toward where we were working to get some moving air. That really helped! About fifteen minutes before the service, a man came in to the auditorium and noticed the fans blowing toward us and loudly asked: "Who moved my fans?" I said that I had done it and had planned to put them back soon. He further proclaimed so all who were there could hear: "I am the deacon in charge of fans here, and no one touches them except me!" as he stomped toward the two fans I had turned and rearranged them. I apologized, but I am not sure that his rage died down enough for him to hear what I was saying. I had never before—nor ever since!—heard of a deacon in charge of fans—even though it was a logistical decision. That church must have had a real problem in the past!

A sequel to this incident is that I had my suitcoat lying on a chair while waiting for the service to start. My shirt was already soaked with sweat when the pastor came over and diplomatically and kindly told me to put my coat on so the service could begin. Reluctantly, but in compliance, I put it on and during my presentation, I think my shoes almost filled up from the water running down my torso. Needless to say, my coat and pants needed a good dry cleaning after that evening! In spite of the "hot" situation, I was delighted to share our heart for missionaries, and the church did provide some new support for D&D.

FUNDING OF THE MINISTRY

In great contrast to the MKCC ministry where I was not fully responsible for its funding, as D&D's president, I had to generate all the resources to sustain this mission organization. We received minimal income from missionary maintenance fees, but we relied heavily on the Lord's people outside of D&D

been there, done that!

to provide sufficient donations to meet the financial needs. We were a growing ministry, which was having a greater impact in the larger world of missions than it had before. Good and regular publicity was an absolute necessity. Therefore, I was constantly visiting local churches and groups to make them aware of our efforts to aid them in their support of their missionaries. I also would travel into northern states and Canadian provinces to generate interest in this unique ministry. The Lord gave many opportunities in churches, large annual meetings of mission groups, denominational conventions, and a variety of other venues for our presentations. I was so thankful for the public relations training I had received in the military.

Another contrast with my travels for Moody Keswick Conference Center, was that now my D&D effort was not so much to recruit guests and volunteers. My challenge was to spread information about how we assist churches and pastors in providing quality care for their missionaries, and in turn, they could help us provide for their missionaries. Our reason for seeking financial support was to keep the costs to missionaries down to a more manageable figure so they could have more of their funds available for spreading the gospel in their ministries. Churches are not as open to supporting a mission agency or US-based ministries as they are to taking on the support for an individual who is planting churches overseas or for funding a project.

We were blessed in that D&D operated in the black each year and never needed a loan to cover expenses for operations, construction, or acquisition. One year, we filed a request for a grant to refurbish our library. The grant was awarded to us and we put in all matching shelving, new furniture for a children's area, computer study desks, and new furniture for the library office area. The renovation made a great difference for our missionary residents.

Each year, we planned an annual fund-raising banquet for the community to learn even more about the D&D hospitality ministry for missionaries. At one of our banquets, more than 600 people attended! Of course, many people from outside the St. Petersburg, Florida, area also supported D&D. We maintained contact with them through monthly newsletters, phone calls, personal letters, and occasional visits. To them, we regularly communicated our needs as well as our deep appreciation for the support of the ministry. Additionally, the Lord provided future funding through annuities, wills, trusts, and other estate gifts. How thankful we were for all these wonderful friends.

BENEFIT SALES

One other revenue stream for D&D was our benefit/yard sales. Almost everything in our 52 homes and campus came through donations of goods—furniture, kitchenware, linens, sports and fitness equipment, home decorations, toys, books, large and small appliances, and maintenance equipment. Additionally, vehicles, mobile homes, boats, cemetery lots, properties, and such large items were occasionally given to D&D. The clothing center always received an abundance of clothing. We always kept the best of everything with the remainder being made available for purchase by our community. D&D often received excess items from local personnel and businesses. What we did not need for the homes or for the missionaries' benefit, was then sold in weekly benefit/yard sales to aid in the funding of the ministry. The sales process was a lot of work but generated from $50,000 to $80,000 each year.

Some of the goods were sold on eBay, and we had some great successes. Here are some examples of eBay blessings: a drinking tumbler garnered $80, a knight's breastplate and helmet sold for $700, and a pewter set of fireplace sconces and chandelier provided $1,200. A lady did almost all of our eBay sales by preparing and marketing the goods for us. She was a tremendous asset for D&D.

Many other items provided excellent income and/or surprises each year. A high-quality saxophone was sold for $4,000 to a lady whose son was going to college on a musical scholarship. The young man was thrilled with the saxophone, its manufacturer, its age, and the excellent quality of this special instrument.

One day, one of our volunteers was polishing shoes and felt a lump in the toe of a man's shoe which had recently been donated. Pulling the unknown lump out, it was a wad of money totaling $900. The clothing center staff knew that they would recognize the anonymous donor if he came back to our office. We contacted a local TV station and said we wanted to return the money to the rightful owner. The station sent a reporter out, and we re-enacted the money discovery for them, and they aired the segment that evening. The following day, the shoes' donor came back and we gave him the money. In turn, he gave D&D $100. He had not known about grandpa's "secure" storage spot! Honesty and integrity paid off.

On another occasion, our staff discovered $200 taped in an envelope to the bottom of donated dresser's drawer. Another great find was a diamond ring in a decorative vase under the green floral foam used to hold flowers in place. One of our staff was going to change the artificial flowers in the vase and saw the

been there, done that!

sparkling ring in the vase's base. The vase had been in one of our homes for a couple of years, and we had no way of knowing who the donor might be. We did announce the find in our newsletter and asked a possible owner to contact us if they could give us the ring size and the diamond size and style. It is amazing how many people were sure it was their grandma's ring and guessed at sizes and style. No one ever came close to the ring's characteristics! We did finally sell the ring. A jeweler had appraised it at $1,200, but I know we didn't get that much when we sold it. All of this makes me wonder how much "stuff" went out through our benefit sales when we had no clue of its total value. We didn't cut apart mattresses but perhaps there was money hidden away in some of them!

We rarely bought anything for the homes, yet they had some really nice, expensive items in them. I can think about a donated new, solid wood bedroom set that cost well over $5,000 (by the estate attorney's own words!). Often missionaries would comment that they couldn't believe they were living in such great wealth. Praise the Lord for the generosity of His people for the benefit of missionaries!

D&D's GREAT STAFF

D&D was blessed with a great staff which had amazing skills and servants' hearts. Many staff members became personal and supporting friends of the missionary guests who lived in D&D's homes. The year-round staff was complemented by snowbird volunteers who came to Florida in the winter months. Skills in maintenance, library, clothing care, housekeeping, benefit sales, and office assistance helped D&D provide a quality living and support environment for missionaries in their transitional periods. We got to know our staff very well and learned of some of their unique characteristics.

One volunteer lady did not like chickens. Of course, that enticed others to joke with her and give her items of clothing with chickens on them, pictures of chickens for her walls, and even a regular sized chicken made out of rubber! We could sometimes hear a loud squeal when she saw or found one of these in an unexpected place—such as when the chicken's head plopped out of her mailbox when she opened the door! The lady took it all with a good heart and could laugh at herself when a chicken showed up at unusual times!

Another lady had a dislike for cats. As with the "chicken" lady, cats (pictures, clothes, ceramic cats, salt and pepper shakers) kept showing up in her house (both in Florida and in Pennsylvania). We had a lot of fun with her and her "favorite" animals. But she had her little ways of "getting back" as one time when she placed a uniquely sounding alarm clock under our bed in her house. It went off shortly after midnight. Initially we couldn't find the alarm and I ended up on my hands and knees to grab it from under the bed and shut it off! Life is full of joys and surprises. The next morning, she discovered the clock behind some dishes in the back of an upper shelf in her kitchen—when the alarm went off again! I wonder who might have put the clock up there in the middle of the night.

A couple of ladies who worked in our clothing center (some missionaries called it their boutique because of the wonderful quality of the goods they could take for free) would sometimes find unusual donated things and dress up in them. An example was some very large clothes that were donated. These two ladies both got into the one set of clothes and paraded around a little. What a hoot! Annually, our staff would hold a fashion show to highlight many of the wonderful (and sometimes unique) items that were donated to D&D.

One of our maintenance men remembered me from 1949 when we were in the same junior church together in Indiana. We had not seen each other in close to fifty years and now we were serving the Lord together!

It was always a joy to see the willing hearts of all of our paid and volunteer staff who came from many states and Canadian provinces. I thank the Lord for the privilege I had to get to know these wonderful people and to see how they were willing to serve in whatever capacity help was needed. The staff loved the Lord and showed their love in their service.

BEGINNING OF A DOWNWARD SPIRAL

Having been in the military and working at the Pentagon, I understood the need for an organization to operate off a plan which provided direction for the organization's future. In 2000, we developed a strategic pathway for D&D, following a major consultation, which brought people together from a wide variety of disciplines and ministries. That plan's goals were nearing completion, and we needed a new strategic plan. Under the chairman in 2007, the board began the process and a committee had a major planning weekend out of the state.

One aspect of that potential new document was to develop a succession plan—which I requested—to replace me when I would turn seventy years old. I proposed that we begin looking for someone who would work with me for a period of time and whom I would introduce to mission agencies, churches, businesses, and our individual donor base. I felt the board should take the lead in this search. I was not a member of the board but was a participant in many of its discussions and decisions.

We had a change in the chairmanship of the board in the next year, and the new chairman did not seem interested in a new strategic plan nor did the board pursue the search for a future president on their own initiative. Knowing I was going to retire in a couple of years, I wanted the ministry to continue to make progress, but I became somewhat discouraged by a lack of forward thinking from the leadership of the board. However, I kept pushing for a new long-range plan which would include a section to find my successor. Without a vision for D&D's future, where would it be in a few years?

In 2008, there was a radical change in the thinking of some of the D&D board members. It appeared to me and to a few on the board that the previous passion for missionaries and their transitional accommodations and needs became diminished by influential board members in favor of getting, preserving, and growing our financial base.

Although there was never a lack of sufficient resources to fulfill our mission, some board members wanted increased monies in reserve accounts. It had been my understanding that a reserve is always valuable for future needs. But most donors give to small, nonprofit organizations with the understanding that they are helping to meet a current budget need and that their gift will be used for that necessity and not just to build up a larger reserve. I knew that the Lord would continue to be faithful as He always had been to provide for D&D if a "rainy day" should occur. For the long-term future of the ministry, we developed an annuity program and provided help to those who wanted to include D&D in their estate plans. These were very successful programs.

DIVISIVENESS BRINGS ON DEMISE

The board's executive committee began to assume authority to make decisions without informing the other board members, and this caused some consternation and division within the board. Seeing this and without an effort to reestablish unity, I resigned from D&D in late August 2008, and I was told by the chairman that I was to inform the other board members of my resignation. I included factual information about the executive committee's actions. The executive committee's decisions concerned some other board members who called a special meeting in which they urged me to reconsider my resignation and remain in my leadership position. I agreed only on the basis that the board work to reunify itself by the next board meeting in October. That effort was not there.

One of the board members in that October meeting took over proceedings from the chairman (with his concurrence) and offered some twenty motions for the board to consider. Some pertained to increased fund-raising efforts, but others dictated some changes which to me were not missionary friendly. For example: motions were submitted to close the clothing center and the library—which were of such value to missionaries over the years. Yet another motion said that volunteers were a liability to D&D, and their use should be stopped. How could a non-profit ministry like D&D continue without the passionate, hard work of volunteers? Other motions would have been impossible to fulfill.

My heart was for the care of the missionaries and not for focusing primarily on finances, which God was continually and sufficiently providing. If the organization had been in fiscal difficulty, perhaps I would have had different feelings, but as evidence of the Lord's goodness, D&D had received special gifts amounting to $430,000 just prior to the October board meeting. Those were significant and loving gifts—and were from one person!

Divisiveness is often the devil's tool for accomplishing its purposes, and wedges were being further driven between some board members and the executive committee. The last motion presented to the board was that I give my "enthusiastic support" to all of the motions—which I could not do. As a result of board decisions at that meeting and my feeling that I should not fight the majority of the divided board in its overall proposed direction, I resigned again after twelve and a half very successful ministry years. This time, my resignation would stick!

My resignation was one of the most difficult decisions I have made in my life. I loved D&D and its valuable service for missionaries. I believe that conscience built on moral principles often dictates a leader's actions, and it certainly did mine in this decision. I was extremely disappointed in the board because of the adverse impact their rulings would have on so many people—but especially missionaries. Some of the board members also submitted their resignations within the next few months because of the new direction that the ministry was headed.

Betty and I both felt at the time that since most of the remaining board members' passion for missionaries seemed to be gone, the entire ministry was destined for demise. Sure enough, within the next couple of years, donations were significantly reduced, some governance policies were changed, some missionary services were halted, long-time staff was released in an unprofessional manner, and accountability and transparency were minimized by the new leadership. About eight years later, the D&D campus in St. Petersburg was sold. There was a failed attempt to re-open the ministry in the middle of the state on some property that I personally did not feel was suited to missionary housing. After four more years, the ministry, which had been so valued by missionaries for almost seventy years, was shut down. What a disappointing, discouraging, and disheartening end this was for missionaries. The closure was difficult for staff and volunteers who had worked so hard to provide a quality housing environment for transitioning missionaries, and for the vast number of churches and individuals who had financially supported God's work at D&D in St. Petersburg for all those years. The two D&D lady founders must have rolled over in their graves.

I must tell you that working at D&D Missionary Homes with God's selected servants from around the globe was a very rewarding time of my life! That position ended for me in November 2008. This gave me more time to pursue other opportunities in Christian ministry, enjoy some overseas teaching and preaching, do some long-desired travel, and spend more time with my wife. I never regretted the opportunity the Lord gave me to serve Him and His servants at D&D Missionary Homes. I was blessed over and over!

BAPTIST MID-MISSIONS ELECTED COUNCIL

My parents began their ministry with Baptist Mid-Missions (BMM) in 1937, and I was born into this great family of world-wide missionaries in 1941. I have enjoyed meeting and being with BMM personnel in one capacity or another all my life. In the 1990s, I was a presenter in the BMM candidate classes for several years, teaching on the subject of "Parenting an MK"—not from the perspective of a missionary kid's parent, but as an MK, having observed MK parenting from many different aspects and for many ages—from a young missionary kid to now a much more mature missionary kid.

I was asked to join the governing council of the mission and willingly accepted. Knowing some of my military background, the president of the mission approached me about what a strategic planning process could look like. He came to Florida and spent three days with me—listening intently about the development of a long-range plan. He then informed the mission family that he was initiating a strategic planning process and asked me to be the facilitator. He put together a great planning team which, over a period of eighteen months, cast a forward vision and plan, which would be implemented in the organization from top to bottom.

As a result of the positive impact of this plan, a second strategic planning committee was established ten years later to keep the forward momentum going since-many of the goals and objectives of the first plan had been accomplished. I was also delighted to be part of that group. In addition to that BMM committee, I was also placed on the Finance Committee, the Administrative Committee, and the Search Committee for key personnel in the mission's leadership. In 2019, I was given emeritus status on the Elected Council but I continue to attend meetings as much as possible. I love BMM and have found it difficult to "break away" from its myriad ministries and activities of supporting the worldwide spread of the gospel through church planting and discipleship programs. I have also served as an advisor to, or as a board member of other mission organizations and have facilitated strategic planning processes for additional non-profit ministries.

CHAPTER XVI
OVERSEAS MINISTRIES

MISSIONARY ENCOURAGEMENT IN GERMANY

In my twenty-six years of military service, I had never set foot in Germany, although the Army had thousands of troops stationed there. However, the Lord gave me the privilege to go there after my military retirement.

Baptist Mid-Missions was beginning a program where the home office planned a time for missionaries from a geographical region to get together for encouragement and to get to know other missionaries better. I was invited to be one of the conference speakers for the missionaries from Germany, Italy, France, Spain, and Great Britain. This initial conference was just for men, but it kicked off a continuing plan that in later years would include missionary women and children, as they were an important and integral part of the ministry on any field.

This was an exciting trip for me to be in another country with a ministry—rather than military—purpose. Being a missionary kid who was born into a Baptist Mid-Missions family and now on the mission's Elected Council, I was especially delighted to connect with other missionaries whom I had not yet met and to reach into their lives to encourage them from my own experiences and background. This was a fairly fast trip, going in and coming out of Germany, but it opened my eyes to the value of meeting with US and national missionary leaders in their ministry environments. Since that time, I have been privileged to teach and preach in many different venues in many different countries. Years later, Betty and I were back in Germany to see other places of tourist interest.

been there, done that!

PEP MINISTRY TRIPS

After many years as a missionary with Baptist Mid-Missions (BMM), having had ministries in the Central African Republic, Zambia, and Bibles International (Bible translation), my brother, Larry, was challenged to begin a new ministry with BMM. He called it PEP (Pastoral Enrichment Program). It was to be a teaching and preaching ministry to national leaders in countries where solid biblical education and training may not be routinely available. Larry usually took another person overseas with him to help carry the ministry load, which involved teaching about thirty hours a week, plus preaching on weekends or evenings in different local national churches. (Most of this was done through translators.) In the early years of PEP, before augmenting his efforts with additional full-time team members or adjunct teachers, Larry asked me to accompany him a few times—and especially to some remote, rural areas. He knew I could handle the village life, accommodations, and foods!

INDIA AND NEPAL

Larry is an excellent teacher and preacher and can be very animated as he illustrates some of his points. I knew I was not trained as a preacher, but the US Defense Department had given me many public-speaking experiences, and I felt I had sufficient platform presence to handle any assignments Larry offered. I was first asked to team-teach the subject of Biblical Stewardship. He had a great syllabus to work from, and for my teaching portions, I added my own touch and research and really enjoyed the preparation. My first ministry with PEP was in northeastern India and then into Nepal. We provided weeklong stewardship seminars in three locations in India and preached two to three times a week in the evenings in different churches. We each also preached in separate churches on Sundays.

In those weeks, I got used to Larry's intensity and strong adherence to his schedule of progressing through the material. Separately, I also provided several hours of teaching on Christian Leadership. Together, Larry and I had a good question-and-answer time with the students in the Bible Institute in northeast India and another period with pastors and ministry workers. I felt our time in that section of India was very profitable. We held three seminars in three different places in Northeast India.

MY TICKETED FLIGHT IS INVALID

Before we left on this five-week trip, I had asked Larry if I could break away for a few days to go to North India and serve with and support a missionary friend from my days at D&D Missionary Homes. Larry said this would work well since an additional teacher from the US was coming to help when we would be in Nepal. I flew from Northeast India to Delhi without incident.

When I went to the airport early the next morning to continue on my trip, I was told by the agent that my flight to Shimla in northern India was not flying anymore and that it hadn't flown for three months. Yet I had been issued tickets through my travel agent in the US. What were my options at this point? The airline agent said I could get a train, which would take almost a full day to get to my destination in Shimla, or I could fly to the town of Chandigarh (farther west) and get a taxi from there for an approximate four-hour ride to Shimla. When you're traveling overseas, you have to be flexible!

I called my missionary friend in Shimla to get his input. He said to go ahead and fly to Chandigarh and he would send a driver to meet me at the airport. That was a good solution for me, so I got on the plane with not much inner assurance about meeting a driver on the other end. Thankfully, as I exited the airport in Chandigarh with great trepidation, a man was waiting there with my name scribbled on a cardboard sign. Well, guess what! He didn't speak English, and I don't speak Hindi. Now my life was in his hands. He guided me to a pickup truck, and off we went, trying to use sign language to communicate when possible. This was one of those "been there, done that" experiences which could have been a disaster but actually turned out very well!

MOUNTAIN ROAD IN NORTH INDIA

Most of the road to Shimla followed the edge of the mountains. Often I was sure we were going over the side, but thankfully, my driver kept his vehicles' wheels on the road. Occasionally, we would face an oncoming transport truck driver who would honk his air horns vigorously for us to move closer to the side. His truck was bigger—so my driver complied! At some places, my driver and the transport driver had to fold in the side mirrors to get by. I learned later that our road had been one featured on the *Ice Road Truckers* TV show where truckers would race on dangerous roads to deliver their cargo to certain destinations.

been there, done that!

Thankfully, the road was not icy when we were on it! I had no clue where the road was going and just had to trust that my driver knew how to get to our destination. After about four hours on the road, we safely came to the outskirts of the crowded city of Shimla. Many of the city's businesses and homes were cut into the steep mountainside and most of the roads seemed to be very narrow one-way streets. In looking at the city from afar, it appeared that the houses were built one on top of the other because of the steepness of the terrain! I was very happy when we finally arrived at my national Indian missionary friend's house and am not sure how long it took for the color to come back into my knuckles from hanging on so tightly to my seat!

HIKE UP TO THE SHIMLA CHURCH

I did a few hours of teaching and a question and answer time with some of the national leaders from that region. On Sunday, I was the preacher in the church the missionary pastored. His church was near the top of the city. To get there, we drove up the mountainside quite a way and ended up parking his vehicle in the parking lot of a Catholic church where he had made previous arrangements. Then we had to hike upward over many steps zig-zagging up the edge of the cliff.

I thought I was in good shape, but with Shimla's elevation of 7,500 feet and constant climbing for about twenty minutes, I was really beat by the time we arrived at the mountaintop church. A brief pause before the service renewed my strength I needed before preaching my message.

The people there are used to the hills and thinner air, and I saw many individuals carrying big loads on their backs as they made their way to various places where vehicles could not go in town. I learned that carrying the heavy loads seemed to be easier for the people than pushing a cart or riding a bicycle up the steep streets. There is no way I could have done what they were doing!

As in all of India, the music was very different from our traditional Western culture but was done in a sincere and worshipful manner. I was blessed by the people even though almost all my communication was through a translator. At 4 a.m. on Monday, the driver came to take me back to the airport in Chandigarh. I think I was a little relieved that it was still dark once we got outside of the city so that I didn't have to look down the mountainside. When daylight finally came, I almost wished that it was still dark!

EXTRA TEACHING IN NEPAL

From Chandigarh, I flew through Delhi again but then went straight to Kathmandu, Nepal (instead of where I had been in Northeast India), where our next PEP seminar would be held. There I learned at the airport that Larry had gotten sick in India. His deep cough, sore throat, and laryngitis would not allow him to teach more than a handful of his class hours, so I was asked to teach much of his material, plus mine. Another American teacher would cover his own previously-assigned portion, and a national missionary would also take responsibility for a small amount of Larry's material. Thankfully, I had already heard Larry teach his material three times, so with extra time in preparation, it was not that difficult to add his teaching material to my own.

I had arrived at the Kathmandu airport by myself but soon received a phone call from the national missionary as to where I should go to get my passport stamped and then where to meet him. A lot of my concern was eliminated when we finally got together! Because of a cancelled flight, Larry and the American pastor scheduled to team-teach with us arrived in Nepal a day or so after we had started the seminar. Although Larry stayed on a bed in a back room of the church where he could hear us teaching, he continually monitored our progress to ensure we remained on schedule. In the last day of the week-long seminar, he had gained enough strength to help finish his teaching for the week and challenge the people to apply what they had learned through the week.

In Nepal, the people all sit on a thinly carpeted floor and usually sit cross-legged. The only chairs in the room were for the teachers and was I ever thankful for their thoughtfulness! I am not a floor-sitter and would have been very miserable if I had to do that during the long hours of the seminars. The people all take off their shoes before entering the building. They put their Bibles and notebooks on the floor and lean over to write on them. Their music was accompanied by men beating on several varying-sized drums. In a couple of churches a small electronic keyboard was played. It was powered by a small portable generator outside the church.

I was pleasantly surprised at how attentive and responsive the people were in spite of what I thought was very uncomfortable seating, but that was the norm for them. Larry and I routinely taught for a couple hours at a time while rotating platform work throughout the day. There was usually a tea break each morning and afternoon with a community lunch served at noon. Most of the "students" went to homes for the evening, although a few brought mats with them and laid them out on the church floor to sleep at night.

While in Nepal, I was given the privilege of preaching at a new church planting site held in an orphanage sponsored by the mother church where we held our seminar. Interestingly, as soon as the orphanage was built and services began there, the other dominant religion in the area bought the property between the main road and the orphanage with plans to build a temple there. For practical purposes, this would cut off the path used to go to and from the orphanage. I am not sure how that issue was finally resolved.

We heard some wonderful testimonies of how some of these people had persevered through difficult times. One eighty-year-old man had been accused of converting to Christianity and was put in jail for eight years. The father, of a young lady attending our Biblical Stewardship seminar, was a prominent Hindu priest in his area. The young lady would sneak out of the house early in the morning and be at the seminar all day. Upon returning home and being quizzed about her whereabouts, she truthfully responded that she was away studying. At one point in the past, she had been beaten because she had gone to a Christian church. (I heard later that within seven years of our trip, the young lady's mother, brother, and eventually the father [former Hindu priest] had all become baptized believers in Christ and that they were all growing in the Lord! Praise the Lord!)

Other attendees' homes had been burned down, and they had been abused or persecuted in various ways because of their biblical faith. In America, we really have no concept of the genuine, sustaining faith of believers in other lands and the persecution it may bring into a person's life. If only we could demonstrate such faith, our nation and our churches would be very different.

TREK TO SUNKHANI CHURCH

One of the local believers attending our seminar pastored a church deep in the mountains. He would go to his church in Sunkhani late on Friday and stay there until Sunday afternoon when he returned to Kathmandu. Usually he rode his motorcycle up some back trails over the mountain. He wanted us to go and preach to his small congregation, but how would we get there?

We had to take the long route and rode in the back of a pickup truck through a Nepalese Army checkpoint and garrison and over some very crude and rough roads until we got to a place where the truck could go no further. We got out, carried our backpacks and followed a footpath over and down the mountain for another forty-five minutes.

Because of the difficult roads, we arrived at the little church almost two hours late for the scheduled service time, but the people from the scattered homes on the mountain's side had come to hear the Word of God and patiently waited for us. As we were coming down the final section of the mountain footpath toward the church, the people started clapping and cheering. How many people in an American church would patiently wait two hours for their preacher to arrive?

Arriving at the church, the women had all made wreaths/leis from local flowers and with great respect hung them around our necks. I must have been given ten or fifteen leis, and our other PEP teacher probably had the same. What a reception! We all crowded into the small church for the service. To help keep the singing together, rhythmic hands and small foot-held drums provided the accompaniment. I shared a testimony there, and the other PEP teacher gave the message that day.

After sharing a meal with the people, we returned to Kathmandu. The trek up the mountain was much tougher than going down to the church, and it took us about an hour and a half to get back to the truck. The rough ride back made us really appreciate our beds that night!

I have remained in touch with the pastor of the little congregation in Sunkhani in the mountains. It has continued to grow, and a new building has been constructed. People carried all of the building material on their backs to the new church site on the mountain side. This included a pre-constructed pulpit, cement, lengthy rafters, and roofing materials. The people have really stepped up to provide for their own church facility. As we stood at the earlier church site, the pastor shared with me his vision to be in every home, which could be seen in and around the valley. Some of the houses would be very difficult to get to from the church but as the Scriptures tell us: "Without a vision the people perish." I thank the Lord for people like the pastors in some of these remote places, who work in some very difficult environments.

MYANMAR

Larry, my brother, and I were scheduled to go into Myanmar (formerly Burma) when it was not yet firmly supportive of our United States' methods of governing and respecting human rights. We arrived by plane in the major city of Yangon the

been there, done that!

day after our US Secretary of State departed, having just opened some significant doors of cooperation between our nations.

On a trip in an earlier year, Larry had observed that soldiers were all over the streets and that foreigners entering the country were carefully monitored. Even when we arrived in 2011, foreigners were still not permitted to stay in private homes and could only stay in certain government-approved housing. But when I was there, the military presence was not as visible. It was obvious, however, that tensions were still fairly high as we were picked up and whisked away to our destination.

A COUNTRY OPENING UP

The next day we flew northwest for a church leaders' conference in a location where our North American missionaries previously had not been permitted to go. Upon arriving there, I was surprised at the gathering of about 120 believers who were eager to receive more biblical training. Many of these folks had come in from the state to the west, which was primarily comprised of tribal folks rather than the national Burmese.

Because the Myanmar government considered these tribal individuals to be rebels, for years no Western foreigners had been permitted to enter their state for fear of their potential support of an uprising. So these believers came out of their home territories to where we were teaching. In reality, this identity as a "rebel" group in the country probably had some truth since the tribes in that state had been somewhat Christianized through the ministries of missionary Adoniram Judson more than 150 years before. The Buddhist leadership and culture of Myanmar interpreted this as being anti-government and were almost constantly in conflict with the tribes of that state. In spite of the religious wars, Christianity grew rapidly, and now those tribes' members were sending out their own missionaries to their own people groups!

These missionaries, pastors, evangelists, and other ministry leaders were now gathered to learn more about reaching out to others with increased biblical understanding and knowledge they would receive from the Lord through us. They were very enthusiastic and told stories of how God had provided for them in so many different ways, even in times of extreme hardship, government pressure, and persecution.

A number of these people had attended or taught at a secret Bible school within Myanmar in earlier years, but when the government learned about the location of the school, it was immediately closed. With persistence to teach and learn from the Bible, the school moved to another secret area. It was closed down again, but this time a "friendly" government soldier told them that if they would move into Yangon—right under the nose of the officials—the believers probably would be ignored. Why there?

The soldier said the police in Yangon had too much to do and therefore might overlook the Bible school. That did happen, and what the soldier said turned out to be true. A thriving Bible school with its dormitories and classrooms is operating there today. But also, the government's hostile attitude toward these particular tribal groups was considerably lessened then from what it had been in earlier years. To demonstrate some of Myanmar's openness now, Baptist Mid-Missions has a Bible translation center in Yangon. Several teams are translating the Scriptures into the heart languages of the people. However, the latest civil war in the country has recently hindered missionaries from physically serving with the translators. When the internet is available, the missionary consultants can work virtually with the tribal teams to keep Bible translation projects moving.

We had a wonderful conference with the people. They were very attentive and took extensive notes on the translated outlines which Larry had provided for them. Not only did we teach all day, but each evening we had a worship service in which Larry and I alternated preaching and also sang duets together several times.

FIRST WHITE MAN IN CHURCH

As normal on these PEP trips, we each preached in different churches on Sunday mornings and evenings. One evening service was very special to me. A driver took me out to a small bamboo, mat-walled church right on the border with that "rebellious" western Myanmar state and said that this was as close as we could get without violating the government law. It was dark as we pulled into the village, and my driver turned off the vehicle lights so as not to draw attention to our arrival. We drove into the church yard, and suddenly people started coming from everywhere with very dim flashlights to see this foreigner coming to their church. They would shine their light in my face, giggle a little, and reach out to touch me. I was told that I was the first white man to be there (although I cannot verify that), and they were especially happy that I had come to share more about

been there, done that!

Jesus with them. (This reminded me of my dad who had been the first white man to go to some of the villages in the Chad when he was a missionary there in the 1940s into the 1960s.)

The lights in the little church (maybe sixty people) were very dim and occasionally I could see a light reflect off decorations wafting in the slight breeze blowing through the mat-walls, grass-roofed building. The people had gone all out for this special occasion of the white missionary's visit and had hung a variety of "almost Christmasy" types of things from the bamboo rafters. The people were very attentive and interactive as I preached. I think most of the individuals had heard the gospel before but not from a white man through an interpreter who translated into the tribal language rather than into the Burmese national language. It was a real privilege for me to share God's Good News with them! This was a very humbling experience for me to be with those people who had been persecuted in various ways over the years. I sensed their sincere love for the Lord and deep gratitude and respect for God's Word.

BIBLE COLLEGE IN YANGON

From our seminar and preaching in the area up north, we flew back to Yangon in the south part of Myanmar. As I looked down from the airplane, I was impressed with the vast number of Buddhist temples I could see. They were very visible with their gold-colored domes and spires sticking up through the trees out in the countryside as well as in the towns. My heart cried out to the Lord that someday there would be as many church steeples visible as there were gold domes.

We were in Yangon for another week-long seminar—only this time we were teaching upper-level Bible college students. The students were supposed to know English, so our instruction did not need translation. Larry and I could cover more material and go through it faster, thus allowing time for the school's required tests and quizzes, which were also in English. However, based on their written answers, it was clear to us that some of the students had limited comprehension of the English test questions.

Larry and I had some long evenings trying to decipher and grade their test answers and to give them as much grace and leniency as possible. Frankly, the grading curve was quite low for the class as a whole, even though some of the students really did excel in their work. Some of the professors in the school have graduate degrees, and a couple even have doctoral degrees from seminaries in

India. I believe that when a student graduates from this Bible college, they are well prepared to enter ministry.

CHURCH IN MIDDLE OF A RICE PADDY

On Sunday we spoke in different churches, and again my evening service was unusual and special. I got in the vehicle, and within about forty-five minutes, we were driving in the dark in a rice paddy with all its lumps and grinding up and over the little dikes in the field. Thankfully, it was the dry season, so we didn't have to worry about getting stuck! We arrived at a small house in the middle of the large paddy and heard a small generator going, so I assumed we would have lights for me to efficiently use my message notes. The windows were shuttered, and I could not see the interior of the building.

The people gave me a very warm reception as we entered the house church and got set up for the service. There were a few chairs but not nearly enough for the twenty-five to thirty people, so the majority had to sit on the floor. I am not sure where all the people came from, but they were really packed in, which made the room quite warm. Kids were all over the place sniffling and crying.

When the group leader—I don't think he was a trained pastor—started them singing, the extraneous noises stopped. The singing was soft and somewhat muffled to keep the sound from carrying across the field. The hushed but worshipful singing in that crowded room was almost surreal.

It was not planned, but as soon as I was introduced to speak and stood up next to my translator, the generator stopped running. The room turned absolutely black until a few flashlights were turned on. I began to wonder if the batteries in my flashlight would last through the duration of my message. All sorts of ideas were running through my head: Would I ask someone for lighting help? Would I cut my message short? If so, where would be the best place to stop? Would the generator come back on? Was there a threat as the reason for the generator stopping? They had asked me to speak about an hour and thankfully all of those issues were put to rest when someone brought a big candle and put it on the table near my notes! I should not have been concerned—the Lord had it all under control! I will say, however, that I struggled to read my notes under the dim and flickering candle's flame. Again, I was so happy to be sharing God's Word even under such rudimentary conditions. The ministry in Myanmar was unique and very special to me. I look forward to seeing those believers when we get to heaven!

been there, done that!

BAHAMA ISLANDS

Our PEP ministry in the Bahama Islands came about through one of my high school classmates, D, who has been a missionary pilot and counsellor for many years to the men and women there. D worked with the Christian leaders of many different churches on several of the islands. The culture there was quite diverse as people from many of the Caribbean Islands had come to the Bahama Islands and intermixed over the centuries. The Bahamas Islands have sometimes been called the "Deathbed of Missions" because of the many missionary efforts from many denominations and cults, which had been started in the islands over the years. But rarely have missionaries completed their career in these islands due to sickness, discouragement, lack of local people's interest and support, and lack of unity of doctrine between groups.

I must give you a little background on D. His folks were also missionaries under a different mission agency in Chad. But D had never been on that field since when his parents first went there, D was going into high school and ended up as a boarding student at Wheaton Academy where we first met. We both were on the football and track teams. He was in the Ham Radio Club and enjoyed communicating with missionaries around the world. He later enlisted in the Army. After leaving the military, he had his own taxidermy shop when the Lord called him and S to use his airplane for missions in the Bahamas. In the last couple of decades, the small airplane has been the primary enablement for D and S's missionary work on the numerous islands in the Bahamas and the distances between them.

START OF A BIBLE INSTITUTE

For years, D had a vision to begin a Bible institute in the Bahamas. He was struggling as to how to accomplish that because of the low income of the island folk and what he perceived to be the necessity for modular teaching. Potential students could not afford to take some years away from work to complete a defined residential training program.

The PEP ministry offered a model that D wanted to look at, so we were invited to go and teach a two-week module for him at one of the larger churches on Andros Island. That module got their church leaders excited about learning and set the pattern for what followed. Since our ministry there in 2011, D has been able to establish a Bible institute, which is recognized by the Bahama's education system.

I preached in three other churches in the islands. It was a blessed time with the people there—not only in our seminar's host church but in the churches whose people came to the seminar. In the islands, when people come to church on Sunday, they get dressed to the ultimate limit. Ladies wear high heels, bright colors or solid whites, wide-brimmed hats, and gloves while the men are in their best suits (black or white) and often white shoes. They all are extremely courteous, gracious, and super friendly.

TOURING BLACKBEARD'S CAVE

Since we only taught the seminar in the mornings and evenings in order to give the people some time each day to go to work, we did a little touring on Andros Island (the largest island) as well as on Eleuthra Island—where D and S's house was. We also picked grapefruit for the church people at a huge orchard grove established by the Dole Company years ago. It has now been abandoned because they can't get sufficient workers to care for it. Individuals may still go and pick the fruit from trees that are still producing. It is some of the best grapefruit I have ever eaten!

On Andros Island, we went to one of the hideout caves where Blackbeard, the pirate, and his mates would stay when being hunted down to avenge their illicit activities in the late-seventeenth and early-eighteenth centuries. I almost felt like I needed a patch over one eye for me to be in the cave! While at the cave, Betty slipped and broke her wrist. Thankfully, the US Navy had a base on Andros Island, and we went there to have her wrist cared for. After the seminar concluded, we went to Eleuthra Island, where we ate some great local food, saw the pink sand beaches on the east side of the island, and I spoke in their small local church.

BAD FISHING—AGAIN!

On a gorgeous day, D, Larry, and I went fishing off of Eleuthra Island with one of the church members. In that area, they use broken conch shells shining in the shallow waters to attract fish. The day before, the local fisherman had caught more than 200 fish by himself, but on this particular day, the four of us caught a grand total of thirty-two fish! Bad! However, that is the regular story of my

been there, done that!

fishing life, so why would this fishing trip be any different? At least we enjoyed each other's fellowship.

> [I have not had a successful fishing life. We were on a charter fishing boat off the east coast of Florida and the captain told of taking people to special spots to fish. We arrived at one area and the captain said he could see a lot of fish below so bait your hooks and enjoy fishing. Of about forty people on the boat, I think only a couple fish were caught so the captain said he would move to another spot. Again, he said his fish finder saw many fish below. Still only a couple of fish were hooked—and they were from up front of the boat and we were at the back. We moved again. While fishing for four hours, less than fifteen fish were caught by the forty people! The captain could not understand why. I think it was because I was on the boat!
>
> I was part of a mission conference at a church in Fort Myers, Florida. On Saturday, the church's fishing club took all the missionary men out fishing in several small boats in the Gulf of Mexico. The captain of my boat took us to his favorite fishing spots. Again, he could not believe that we came back to shore with no fish. Fogle was on the boat!
>
> Betty and I went fishing with our friends in New Brunswick, Canada. The two ladies sat at the back of the boat with their fishing rods and we men fished off the sides of the small boat. The ladies reeled in several mackerel but we men went "fish-less" for the day. The boat captain said he had never had such a fishing experience. I guess fish do not like my fishing lines! Fishing must not be my kind of sport as the same story happens time after time!]

CENTRAL AFRICAN REPUBLIC

One other PEP trip stands out to me. That is when Larry and I went to the Central African Republic (CAR) and Chad in the spring of 2012. The CAR is where Baptist Mid-Missions began its ministry in 1920. In the mid-twentieth century, the CAR/Chad (these nations were formerly part of French Equatorial Africa) had BMM's greatest number of resident missionaries. (Currently, Baptist

Mid-Missions has only two American missionary couples in the CAR, and they are primarily ministering in the capital of Bangui. One couple and a single lady serve full time in the Chad.) Over the years in the CAR, more than 400 churches had been planted with many additional Bible study groups meeting in other villages. It was a fruitful ministry with other supporting programs such as Bible schools and a seminary, medical clinics and a hospital, a school for missionary kids, printing facilities, and so on. Now, the church and ministry programs have been nationalized (as was the original goal).

> [On a side note, in December 2012 after our trip, a civil war broke out in the CAR and has continued through this date in 2022. The resulting persecution of many believers and pastors is a sad story. Churches, Bible schools, homes, and medical facilities have been destroyed or disrupted, hundreds of thousands of the nationals have been displaced, and many have been forced into refugee status in other countries.]

We flew into Bangui, the capital of the CAR, and within a day or so, a missionary drove us farther to the east for our first week's seminar. I had never been in that section of the CAR because when I was in Africa as a boy, my family was only on mission stations in Chad and the CAR station where the boarding school was.

This PEP ministry trip was approximately four weeks long. Three were in the CAR and one in Chad. In a way, this was a marvelous opportunity to go back home—while sharing with Larry in a PEP ministry. I had not been to those countries since 1954.

I still remembered some of the national trade language, Sango, but certainly did not know enough to be able to teach in the seminar or preach in the churches in that language, so I regularly used people to translate for me. Larry had spent more years there growing up and had later returned to the CAR as a missionary. He was extremely fluent in Sango and could almost be identified as a native speaker. After a few days into our first week's seminar (and after almost fifty-eight years of absence from the country!), I realized that I could speak the common village language fairly fluently with the attendees during break times. That was amazing to me and probably to the African people as well! I was so thankful for the blessing of recall!

been there, done that!

CELL PHONE WORKS!

In 1967, when Chad was closed to missionaries due to nationalism, my parents moved into the CAR to minister at the Bangassou mission station. My younger sister Maribeth, with her first husband, Don, and Larry and his wife, Sallie, also served the Lord as missionaries in that general area, but this region was all new to me. National believers and church leaders now reside in the homes on the numerous former mission stations and sometimes keep a house or a room for visiting missionaries or other guests.

It took a couple of days for us to drive from the capital to Bangassou (See map in Appendix D) with an overnight stay on another station in Bambari. I had heard a lot about Bangassou, and we actually stayed in the house where my folks had lived! I knew other missionaries who had been at the station in earlier years, and one of them had a son who became one of my best friends from second grade through college, and now into these later years of life. It was a real privilege for me to finally be at the very place where my parents had such a wonderful ministry and impact in African lives after I left the dark continent.

And something else was unique and special for me at Bangassou. Out of curiosity, I pulled out my cell phone and punched in Betty's phone number at our home in Florida. She answered! Here I was in the center of Africa talking very clearly with my wife thousands of miles away and across a big ocean! What a change from my days as a young boy in Africa! UNBELIEVABLE!

THREE GREAT CONFERENCES

We drove from Bangassou to our conference site at Kembe where the people packed the church. While most of the individuals sat in the church for our seminar, some ladies fixed the meals out in the church yard. Water was somewhat rationed from the one covered and clean-water well in town. Each morning about ten of the ladies went to the well, filled a plastic five-gallon, yellow container (like our red gasoline containers), put it on their head, and carried it back to the church on the edge of town. They also had to carry in wood for the cooking fires—which were almost extinguished by the heavy rains that came through the area. On one occasion, we had to temporarily halt our teaching because the rain was pounding so hard on the aluminum roof of the church!

We ate a lot of rice, manioc/yucca/cassava, greens, and a little meat from a cow purchased and butchered just to feed the conferees. A temporary palm-thatched shelter was set up to give a little shade when we ate together.

As undeveloped and rural as the environment was, I was shocked to see that some of the men had cell phones. A few men even came early to the church so they could be near a window. That wasn't for them to get air, but rather so that they could hang their portable, flexible, solar panels out in the sun to charge their phones. This was uniquely different—in the heart of Africa!—from what I remembered! My mind could hardly grasp the idea that the Africa, which I knew growing up, was now able to support modern technology—out in the villages, nonetheless, and not just in the cities. But over sixty years had passed since my initial days in Africa!

After that conference week and the weekend when we preached in the local churches, we moved on to our next seminar and church ministries in Sibut. This was one of the very early mission stations established in the early 1920s by a Baptist Mid-Missions' missionary. His house was built on the highest hill in the area. Down the hill, other missionary houses, a church, a Bible school building, a print shop, housing for Bible school students, and other supporting structures had been built over the years. Again, the large church in town for our seminar was filled for each teaching session, and our eating arrangements were similar to our earlier conference in Kembe.

The open-windowed church was very warm. Even with the slight breeze blowing through the church, my shirt was constantly soaked with sweat. On the Sunday following the conference in Sibut, I spoke in that same large church for their morning service. Afterward, I was invited by the pastor to his house for lunch with his deacons. It was more comfortable at his house, sitting in the dense shade of the mango trees.

I looked at my watch and saw that it was about an hour before our adult Sunday school class was to start at my home church in Largo, Florida. Pastor M was our teacher, and I worked closely with him. I decided to call him—since my phone had worked in Bangassou—to ask him to pass my greetings and thanks to the class for their prayers. He answered and after we briefly talked, I passed the phone around to the African pastor and deacons for them to give him a short greeting—in Sango! "Balao [Hello]." "Ani mou merci na mo [We give thanks to you]." "Ani yeke na ngia mingui teti Pastor Fogle a ga na ani [We are very happy that Pastor Fogle has come to us]." "Merci na Nzapa [Thanks to God]." Pastor

been there, done that!

M got the general idea of these congenial greetings from the people in Africa to the people in America. Cell phones are such marvelous inventions!

Passing back through Bangui for a short rest and restocking, we headed to the western part of CAR on a Sunday to be prepared to start the seminar on Monday in Bossangoa. On the way, we stopped at a little church and on the spur of a moment, I shared a brief testimony, and Larry ended up giving the morning message.

By mid-afternoon, we had arrived at our next conference site and were offered an invigorating treat of fresh mangoes. Oh, were they ever good! Our accommodation there was a two-bedroom, mud-block house which had no screens on the windows, but thankfully it did have wooden shutters to keep many of the mosquitoes and other critters away. Our mosquito nets were quite effective once we killed all those bugs that had become trapped inside them during the day! The latrine was a hole in the ground with a woven mat around it, and our "shower"—really just a bucket bath—was outside in another storage-like building. Although it was not really necessary, the folks did warm up some water for our baths. A curtain at the doorway offered a little privacy. I felt that our facilities were reasonably comfortable for the week in the village.

I think I kept a little cool during the teaching day by the trickle of sweat that was constantly running from my head down my front, back, and sides all the way into my shoes! Many of the conferees had brought their own sleeping mats. During nights when it wasn't raining, they just slept out in the open on a cement slab. I never heard one complaint.

After the conference, we were asked to deliver some chickens to a pastor who couldn't get to the conference. He lived in a distant village, which necessitated that we take a longer route to get back to Bangui. Did you ever ride with five adults squashed into a small Toyota RAV4? Now throw in three chickens flopping around on the floor behind the driver's seat since the back of the vehicle was full of luggage. Add to this the bouncing through or swerving around the deep potholes in the road! Travel can be interesting! Thankfully, we dropped off the chickens, a passenger, and some luggage after riding like that for a couple more hours!

You may wonder where the chickens came from. In each of the three conferences in the CAR, an offering was taken in one of the services to provide for some of the needy pastors and their families. Not having much currency, the people brought to the Lord some of what the Lord had entrusted to them. In a wonderful worshipful and thankful spirit, they carried to the front of the church pineapples, mangos (fruit, not vegetables), peanuts, gozo (manioc), honey, eggs, rice, coconuts—and flapping chickens! My heart was blessed to see the people sacrifice from what little they had for the benefit of others in need.

The route took us over the main freight truckers' road, which obviously hadn't been maintained in years. The trucks were the only way of getting bulk cargo into Bangui through the Atlantic Ocean port in the country of Cameroon. The road was in terrible shape! It seemed that we were either going up or down or swerving side to side to try and avoid the many potholes. We had to travel very slowly to prevent damage to the springs of our vehicle until we got closer to the capital where the road allowed us to travel at regular speeds.

In the three weeks in the CAR, I saw only one wild animal, a small lekpa antelope, which crossed in front of us that evening while we were going so slowly. I was a little surprised that I didn't see more wild animals like I did when I lived out there as a child.

CHAD

From Bangui in the CAR, we flew to one of the very few commercial airports in southern Chad at the time. That airport was in N'Djamena, Chad's capital, which is in the approximate middle (from north to south) of the country and on the very west side. The only problem was that N'Djamena wasn't our final destination. Our commercial flight had forced us to fly farther north than we wanted to go so we needed other transportation to get us back into the southern part of Chad.

MAF FLIGHT TO KOUMRA

Larry had pre-arranged for a Missionary Aviation Fellowship (MAF) plane based in N'Djamena to fly us to Koumra. This town had been the location of BMM's major Chadian medical ministry with its sprawling teaching hospital, a church, and a Bible school. Each portion of the ministry there had been nationalized under the church's leadership. I was grateful for the opportunity to briefly share my testimony at the devotional time for the hospital staff.

> [As a kid, my main memory of Koumra was shortly after a new missionary had arrived in 1950 in Fort Archambault (now called Sarh) where we lived. My dad loaded up that missionary's goods on our two and a half ton truck and took him and various

been there, done that!

hospital materials to the mission station in Koumra. The truck was piled high, and we kids sat in the back on top of the load. It was dry season, and the road was mostly deep, soft sand demanding that Dad drive in second gear much of the way to plow through it.

Each time we came to a small creek—which was rare—we stopped to get water to refill our water cans and the radiator because the engine was so hot! For the whole trip, we were sitting up there, fully exposed to the blazing sun. With my fair skin and wearing only shorts and a T-shirt, I got a very bad sunburn. Thankfully, my pith helmet protected my head and face. I was miserable for days from that burn.]

Larry and I were in Chad now to encourage our missionaries and to visit our old stomping grounds where we had grown up—especially in Kyabe. After spending a couple of nights with the missionaries in Koumra, a missionary single lady and her driver took us approximately fifty miles to the Fort Archambault (now called Sarh) and Balimba mission stations. I had lived in Fort Archambault for a few months following a couple of school terms in the Central African Republic and was very familiar with Balimba where BMM had a Bible school, school for African kids, dispensary, Bible translation center, and a couple of missionary houses. These ministries also were nationalized although we still had a couple of single missionary ladies there in 2012.

MEETING FRIENDS IN SARH

I asked around to see if any Chadians, whom I had known in the early 1950s, might still be living. Mouajide had been a helper, mechanic, and driver for my parents when they went to Africa in 1937. He was still in town! I went to his home and found this elderly man lying on his bed. I talked to him in Sango and told him who I was. He slowly sat up, and his eyes lit up as he reached out his trembling hand to greet me. He immediately began to talk about my parents and how much Dad had helped him.

I asked him how old he was. He didn't know for sure but remembered my father hiring him as a young man. So if he was about in his twenties then, now seventy-five years later, he would be nearing 95–100 years old! He had such positive memories of my parents and expressed how much they loved his Sara Madjingay tribal people. Mouajide still had his heavy tribal scar markings which had been cut into his face during initiation rites as a young boy and spoke in proud terms of the many of his tribe who had come to faith in Christ because of the Fogles and other missionaries coming to his area.

Another man that I found was Samuel Beredita. Samuel and I used to play together on the mission station in Sarh. His father was the pastor of the big church in town that Dad finished building in 1950. It could seat 2,000, not counting the children and other adults who often occupied the open window sills! Samuel and I used to play tag and other games during the week in the big church, and he remembered those times. For the fun of it, now as seventy-one-year-old "kids," we re-enacted chasing each other around and took some videos! Great memories!

MARTYRDOM OF FORMER PASTOR

The following was told to me by Samuel in 2012. In the early 1970s, his dad, several other local pastors, and a Bible school student took a stand against the devilish tribal initiation requirements which were now being enforced by the government. The Christian men's resistance to this evil custom led to their arrest.

The church leaders were told to renounce their faith and submit themselves to the president's initiation decrees, but they refused. They were called before the authorities a couple of times until they were finally given one more opportunity to give obeisance to the president rather than Jesus Christ. Rejecting that, the fourteen men were taken out into a field, forced to dig their own large grave, and lined up and shot. Samuel said that the government refuses to tell him the exact location of the mass grave, but he had learned that the men were singing a hymn as they were executed. Samuel took Larry and me to the big field (now planted in sugar cane) where the martyrdom of these fourteen believers occurred. That was a sobering and humiliating experience for me as we thanked the Lord for the commitment of faithful men who followed Christ in spite of their known and upcoming death.

I personally only knew this one person who has been martyred for the cause of Christ. It often makes me wonder and deliberate about my own commitment and dedication to my Lord if I were knowingly aware that I could be killed for publicly standing up for Jesus Christ and my Christian beliefs. In America, we don't face these types of spiritual battles as many of our fellow believers do in

been there, done that!

other parts of the world. We need to pray for deeper steadfastness in our own lives as well as for our brothers and sisters around the globe.

Samuel's career was as a photojournalist in France at the time, and he learned of his father's martyrdom through his sister, who had very little information. After he retired, Samuel and his wife returned to Chad to live in his home town with his tribal people. He has continued to investigate all of the circumstances of the martyrdom of his dad and the other thirteen men, but for some reason, he said, the records are sealed and are not to be released. He cannot locate the exact location of the gravesite of his father and the other men.

WELCOME HOME TO KYABE, CHAD

From Sarh, Larry and I went to Kyabe, which was about fifty miles further to the east. That was our primary boyhood home, and what a return it was! Where there had been a very crude bac (ferry) to get across the river, a big bridge was now being constructed. What I remembered as lightly forested savannah land was now just a few scrub trees and lots of sand, which had been blown in from the great Sahara Desert to the north.

When we arrived at the edge of Kyabe—then just a village but now the provincial government seat—we noted a fairly new and large sign arching over the road welcoming people to Kyabe.

I was very proud of the progress in my little home village, especially since I had not seen any such signs at all the other villages we had been through. Unknowingly to us, the town had been apparently been notified that we were coming, and we were told that the mayor wanted us to visit with him. Larry and I met him under a thatched-roof structure where he served refreshments to us. He told us that he was a Christian and said that he never met our parents although he had heard about them. In fact, he said that when he was born, one of the names given to him was "Fogle"—obviously in honor of our parents. I hadn't known before this time that I still had kinfolk in Kyabe! I had to get a picture of the Fogle brothers.

Driving a very short distance further into the village, a man stopped our vehicle and said the province governor wanted to meet us. He was an Arab man. We went into his small office, consisting of his straight chair and a wooden table piled with papers. Behind him was a fabric map with hand-drawn lines of the province and its districts—and that was about it! This was the governor's office! Seats were provided for Larry and me and our missionary escort. We talked for some time about our memories and our purpose of coming back to our former home. He seemed quite interested to know of our desire to return to his province's capital.

been there, done that!

BIG CONTRASTS TO THE PAST

We then drove out to the mission station and what an emotional time that was for me! Out at the long driveway entrance from the road was an old rusty sign, pointing to the church and dispensary. It probably was the same one my dad had put there as a new sign back in the early 1950s. I didn't feel that it was a good example to others of the ministry, so later I sent money to have a new sign made.

The entire area seemed so barren compared to the past. Before, we could not see far because of all the trees, but now the desert was taking over, and you could see a long way even to where the village huts were outside the former mission compound. The driveway to the main house was approximately seventy-five yards long and had been lined with thick mulberry bushes and some other fruit trees, giving the area back then a tropical look. Now there was very little green vegetation. Continuing down the driveway, we passed the location—and what were now merely remnants—of the well-structure where we had gotten our water. Formerly, we had a big lush garden near the well, but only barren dirt was evident now. Straight ahead was our big house, and off to the right was another house where other missionaries had lived.

We saw a group of people over there, so we headed that way. Upon stopping the vehicle, a group of ladies stood up from their mats and started singing some Christian hymns. A row of several men and women were standing nearby to greet us. They were individuals who had personal contact previously with my parents some forty-five years or so in the past. Other men were seated on the house veranda.

As I got out of the vehicle, tears of joy swelled up in my eyes, and to hide them I pulled my camera out of my pocket, put it in front of my face, and started taking pictures until I could regain my composure. Was I in a real world? Was I having a genuine experience? I could hardly believe that I was back in Kyabe—my boyhood home in Africa! We were quickly introduced to those who were standing nearby: a woman who had been in Mother's sewing class, another in Mother's Bible study, a son of our maintenance supervisor, a son of our gardener, some former Bible school students whom my dad had taught, a cook, and a pastor. Wow!

"YOO HOO, LESTA"

We were invited to listen to the ladies sing and then Larry and I greeted each of them before being escorted to the front porch of the building where a good-sized group of men had gathered. Again, we were given some food and beverage, and then the men introduced themselves. Most of them were pastors from the province who had been told of our coming. Some of them came from far away in the outlying districts of the province. They had come on bicycles, motorcycles, bus, truck, and foot. Some had traveled for many hours just to meet us.

As they talked to us, one said: "Many missionaries have been here with us but Monsieur Fogle (my dad) is the one that really loved us." Again, it was hard to contain the emotional tears of gratefulness for how God had used my parents to reach this Sara Kaba tribal group. The cook said that he remembered Mother standing on the back porch calling out: "Yoo Hoo, Lesta" (Lester, my dad) and "Timmy, Tommy, Laddy (Larry), Deo (Dale)". The cook's accurate imitation that day made me recall Mother saying those exact words and in the same tones when she wanted Dad's and my brothers' attention! We had a good laugh!

The church's pastor and Bible school leader, who now lived in our old house, introduced us by saying something like this: "All the missionaries left us many years ago, but these Fogle boys remembered us and have returned to be with us in their real home!" We then shared how the Lord had been with us and led in our lives. Many of the men leaned forward on their chairs and benches, demonstrating great interest as they tried to capture every word we were saying. How precious those unique and special moments were for me! I could hardly believe that I was experiencing this wonderful time with the extended fruit of my parents' ministry.

We then toured the station property and constantly commented on how much things had changed but in other ways remained the same in my mind. The big old fig tree was gone from in front of our house. The arbor at the walkway was still there, but the beautiful desert roses on its sides were missing. The big half-circle veranda where we took our family picture in 1953 was still there and basically looked the same.

Going through the house, some of the furniture Dad had made was piled unused in the living room. It was constructed out of mahogany, which was also used for the rafters in the house since it was plentiful in the woods and was somewhat termite resistant. The little footprints of my younger brothers were still visible in the cement in their bedroom floor. My little 6x10-foot bedroom off the back porch was now just a storage room jammed full with an old bike frame, other unusable things, and some full sacks of unknown items.

Out back, where different structures had been, the kitchen building was gone as was the chicken coop and sawmill shed. I had wanted to get a picture of Dad's little prayer building, but it also was missing. The stump where people sat when Dad pulled their teeth was all rotted, but I am sure that the many teeth he had pulled were now deeply buried in the sand. (What would an archaeologist think about if he were to dig up that area and find all those teeth?) The tree where we hung freshly shot animals before butchering was no longer there. The tour of the station brought back vivid memories from long ago!

FINDING MY SISTER'S FOOTPRINT

In a corner of the big workshop and garage building, I had hoped to find the long, grand eland antelope's spiraled horns (probably about three feet long) that I remembered being there. If possible, I was going to try and bring one home. But alas, the whole building was gone! Only the cement floor and car pit in the floor were still there to identify the shop's exact location.

Before Larry and I went to Chad in 2012, my younger sister, Maribeth, had asked me to try and find her footprint which she had put in the cement in 1948 near a corner of the car pit. She remembered specifically where it was, so I went to that spot and saw that the old cement floor was all covered with dirt. I asked for someone to bring a little ngapo (hoe) so I could scrape the dirt away to find her print—but also thinking that it might not be there at all.

As I kept pulling dirt back, I saw a semblance of a print. I asked a person to get some water and I carefully began washing the area. By now an excited crowd had gathered around wondering what this was all about. But—the footprint (with his name) was from another missionary kid who had been on the station at the time. I didn't want to give up on finding Maribeth's footprint since she had such a clear memory of it and its exact location. Sure enough, persistence paid off, and everyone cheered and clamored in close to see a second footprint with her name as I washed the dirt away. My sister was so happy when I sent her a picture.

EFFECT OF PEP MINISTRY

Of the four trips and six countries in which I was with Larry on these PEP trips, I was always impressed with the eagerness and heart desire of the people to learn more from the Lord through our teaching and preaching. They wanted the Word of God to make a difference in their own lives as well as in the lives of those to whom they ministered. True biblical stewardship had not been taught previously, nor had they heard much about Christian leadership. I also learned a lot while preparing for my teaching and preaching in those nations. But I probably got the most out of this trip to the CAR and Chad because of my personal connection with the countries and the people. I thank the Lord for the privilege of serving with PEP and Larry in these places.

The PEP ministry trips for me were always a challenge—but each time, I excitedly anticipated, not only the country we were going to, but also the personal challenge of teaching and preaching God's Word more effectively each time. I loved the travel, the new things I would see and probably eat, and the daily interaction with people of different cultures.

Each trip also opened my eyes to new ways to pray for the peoples of the world, who did not have the privilege of these kinds of in-depth Bible ministries which are available to us in the United States. Many of the national leaders in our seminars made decisions to intentionally apply what they had recently heard. It is so gratifying to see the nationals step in and assume leadership responsibilities and to watch our American missionaries transition to serve as co-workers and helpers to those local leaders. These are exciting days for the national church in so many countries.

CHAPTER XVII
SHORT-TERM MISSION TRIPS

In addition to the teaching and preaching trips I took with Larry in the PEP ministry, Betty and I have been on other short-term mission trips. Our first was to Colombia, second to Cambodia, third to Argentina, and the last to Romania. Each was unique and special in its own way. Two of them were construction trips and two were medical ministry trips. Betty is the nurse, not me!

COLOMBIA

In 1973 we were living in Virginia, and I was one of the deacons at our church. At a deacons' meeting, the pastor said that he would like the church to consider a mission trip to Colombia, South America, to help build a home for a missionary opening up a new work in the jungle. He said the missionary, D, was a pilot and would have to fly us to our workplace in his plane. Most of the construction materials were supposed to be there already because they would be brought up river in a boat.

One work site was La Pedrera, which had been a small, remote outpost of the Colombian army. It was built there to prevent people from neighboring Brazil coming up the river to steal raw rubber from Colombia's interior regions. This place was chosen for that military base because there were some river rapids, which could keep larger boats from moving farther west into the Colombian jungles.

Most of the outpost was now abandoned by the government, although there was still a short row of three or four mostly empty structures; a Catholic church across the river; a small, old barracks complex; and an unused dirt airstrip. National Indians rather than Spanish Colombians lived in the region. Leaving the deacons' meeting at church that night, I told the pastor that I would like to go on that mission trip.

At home, when I mentioned the trip to Betty, she said she immediately knew that I would be involved. Almost instantly, Betty said, "But I am not going!" When the trip was confirmed, the pastor put me in charge of getting the team of fifteen to twenty together and organizing the trip. It ended up that we had fifteen men who were eager to go. One of them had been in construction, and he wanted his teenage son to go with him. Another was an architect who could help in finalizing the house plans, and the rest of us were common laborers who would dig, carry materials, help build, and follow orders. As the trip developed, five of our team would go to an established mission location workplace within Brazil where one pilot was already based, and the other ten of us men would go to the new work in Colombia. In the very southern tip of Colombia was the town of Leticia. Across from it in Brazil was another mission station where other missionary pilots and their planes were based on the Amazon River. Leticia would be our team's entry point to our two projects.

Betty had said initially that she was not going. However, the Lord works in mysterious ways! Within about two weeks of the announcement of the trip to the church, a young, newly married couple came to her and said they would watch our three kids if Betty would go on the trip. Betty hadn't even thought of going, let alone leaving our eight, six, and four-year-old kids with a newly married couple who didn't even have any kids of their own. She basically said she wasn't going so wouldn't need someone to care for our children.

Shortly after that, another woman from the church came to Betty and said her husband was going on the trip and that she was going to take care of our kids while Betty went. I think she knew Betty was a nurse (in case of a physical need) and that the missionary wife on the field would need some help in caring for the meals for the team that was going. She was rather insistent that Betty was going to Colombia! At that point, things started happening. Soon Betty was preparing subconsciously to go with the fifteen men—although still saying she wasn't going! That took a lot of courage because Betty was pretty much a city girl, had never been out of the United States, had never been on a small plane as would be necessary to get to this new mission work in the jungles of Colombia, and had never left the kids for such an extended period of time. But she decided to go anyway—with the fifteen men! The Lord has ways of making things happen even when we don't expect them.

BLACKMAILED?

I did some looking into flights from Washington, DC, that could get us down to Leticia, our commercial destination, at the southern tip of Colombia in South America. I talked with several airlines, including the Colombian airline, Avianca, which could take us all the way, but I found that a US-based airline could at least get us to Bogota in Colombia at much less cost. So I booked with the US airline to Bogota. Since Avianca was the only airline that flew to Leticia, I made round-trip reservations for that part of the trip with them. A good group from our church was at the airport to pray for our team of sixteen and bid us farewell.

All went fine as we arrived in Bogota as planned. But when I went to the Avianca airline counter to check in for our flight to Leticia the next morning, the agent said we were not scheduled on that flight. What? I showed her our tickets but she said the flight was full, and we weren't on it. We needed to be on that flight since the airline did not have another flight to Leticia for several more days, and we could not afford to sit around Bogota, wasting good construction time for our project. Thankfully, the missionary, D, whose house we were going to build, had met us in Bogota. Because he spoke Spanish, I got him involved with the agent at the airport, who finally said that we would have to talk to some higher authority when we got to our hotel in town.

At the hotel in mid-afternoon, we learned that there was an Avianca airlines ticket office right there! The missionary and three of us left the rest of our team in the hotel lobby while we went to the Avianca office. The regular ticket agent was away that day, and someone from the main airline administration headquarters was filling in. (That was a special blessing from the Lord because she could make decisions.) We explained our situation and showed her our reserved tickets, but she quickly shook her head and said that just in the last couple of days, all of the seats to Leticia had been filled. But, we emphasized, our tickets were reserved weeks ago.

She replied that she didn't understand how our sixteen seats happened to be filled in recent days. After a couple of phone calls, she told us that Avianca didn't have any more planes they could use to get us out the next day as originally scheduled. One of their planes had crashed within the last few weeks, and that would have been their only reserve. That really gave us a sense of confidence! Ha, Ha!

We asked if she could possibly get a military plane to take us since she was an authority from the airline administration. She made some phone calls but said that was not a possibility. Every now and then, one of us from our "negotiating team" would go out and report to our other team members about our lack of progress and tell them that, if they wanted, they could go to get something to eat, and we would keep them all informed through the evening hours.

Our discussions dragged on and on. Although this idea was not my preference, I suggested that since our tickets were all dated before the last sixteen booked on the morning flight, that perhaps the airline should contact those individuals and cancel their tickets—as apparently ours had been deleted by the airline without our knowledge.

I was beginning to feel that we had been blackmailed because of my original investigations about flying round trip on Avianca all the way from DC to Leticia and back again. That flight possibility was only talked about at that point months ago, and no commitments were ever made. Avianca must have thought they had a lock on some good income. However, since I had found a cheaper flight to Bogota, we were only going to fly with Avianca within the country of Colombia and only those tickets were purchased.

Finally, after about five hours, the lady agreed that calling and cancelling those later tickets would be the fair thing to do. We left the office feeling that she would carry out that plan and that we would be on our scheduled flight in the morning. We then had to contact our teammates—some of whom were already asleep in their rooms—but most were still anxiously waiting and praying in the lobby.

Several of us then went out about 9 p.m. to eat at a small restaurant a few blocks away from the hotel. The missionary who was familiar with the city and our pastor were both quite tall and led the small group of us—walking at a very fast pace for Betty. In a rather dark area, we had to walk around lady beggars with their children reaching out and trying to grab us to get us to stop and give them something. At the restaurant, we asked D why he walked so fast. He said that he didn't want to tell us ahead of time that this was a very tough neighborhood to walk in after dark. Thankfully, he was more cognizant of Betty's short legs on the way back to the hotel. We did get on our originally scheduled flight the next morning!

FLYING OFF THE AMAZON RIVER

In Leticia, we divided our team so that five men (including our pastor) would go to a mission station on the Amazon River in Brazil and the other eleven of us would fly with D to the new work in La Pedrera. It would take several trips since the small plane could only hold four of us (counting the pilot) and our luggage. Betty and I and our construction supervisor would be on the first two-hour trip with the missionary pilot.

At the time, I guess I sort of assumed that our flight would be on a wheeled plane at the airport. But—surprise! It was a float plane on pontoons anchored on a little raft on the Amazon River! To get to it, we had to carefully carry our luggage through (lengthwise—not crosswise!) some very "tippy" dugout canoes! That was a little scary—especially since we had heard about the piranhas in the river! But we made it.

I had been in a number of single-engine planes before—but Betty had not had the experience—and this was my first float plane flight. We built up speed as we headed up the river, and then the pilot started pulling back and pushing forward on the yoke (control wheel) which sort of bounced the plane up and down. He had to do this to break the suction on the pontoons, and we finally lifted off the water. Looking back at Betty from my co-pilot seat, I noticed she was a little pale, but once in the air, most of that anxiety dissipated.

The flight was smooth and beautiful as we looked down on the tops of the dark green jungle. Winding rivers glistened up at us as they snaked through the carpet of trees. There was no radio in the plane, and I didn't see a compass anywhere. D seemed to be piloting the plane by the seat of his pants, but obviously, he was following various landmarks along the way. His primary target would be a big rock—thus the name, La Pedrera—outcropping across the river from the new mission station.

Being near the equator, when the sun went down, it got dark—very fast! Shortly we saw the big rock hill, and D headed for the river landing as the sun was quickly descending below the horizon. Knowing that D had said he had to land before dark because of some rapids on the river, Betty nervously asked him what the latest time was that he had ever landed on the river there. He emphatically replied: "This is it!" This was a good time to build confidence in our heavenly Pilot and in our human pilot!

He turned on the plane's headlight and suddenly we felt a bump as the pontoons hit the water. We were down safely but the reversing of the props told me that he wanted to stop fast. Then I saw why as a short series of rapids churning ahead sparkled in the headlight! No wonder he wanted to get the plane stopped! We made the U-turn and headed back up the river to the anchor spot.

been there, done that!

ARRIVAL AT OUR JUNGLE SITE

By now it was really dark as the missionary pilot got out of his plane and asked an Indian to help tie it up before we got out onto this little wobbly platform floating in the tall, river grass. I felt Betty grab me to hang on. A couple of local Indians picked up our luggage, and we followed up the shallow bank on a narrow path where the long grasses were bending over, tickling our legs and arms. This was all new to my wife from the big city of Chicago! Betty was hanging on tightly to my shoulders from behind, and I thought sure that I would have deep fingernail marks by the time we got up into a clear area away from the river.

In earlier correspondence about the trip, we understood that we would be sleeping on air mattresses or hammocks that we brought—perhaps out on the airstrip next to their little hut which D's family had been living in for about three weeks. Their place would not have been big enough for the eleven of our team and his family of five!

Much to our surprise, D led us to the only two-story house—and really the only building you could call a house!—in that little village. It had been built by a government engineer who had been sent there to oversee the small military cantonment next to the rapids. The engineer was going to be gone for six weeks and said that the missionary could use the house for the group that was coming to help construct his new home. We wouldn't have to sleep outdoors on the airstrip after all! But, the house wasn't ready for us that first night.

D said that our builder and Betty and I would initially stay in the military barracks which consisted of six or eight rooms. If we were going to go anywhere that night, Betty insisted on getting our flashlights out of our luggage to see where she was stepping. We headed on a short walk along the river with the noise of the rapids drowning out other night sounds and soon arrived at our room where there was no electricity.

Once we finally got settled in, we got a little sleep. In the morning we woke up to hear our builder shouting from the cold-water shower room. I called over to see what the problem was and he said that a bat was flying around in there with him and could I open the door to let it out. No problem! Even when we moved up to the big house the next day, we used a shower, which was in a little enclosure outside the main building near our cooking area. The water was never as warm as we would normally like it but at least it wasn't just a bucket bath.

D made more trips the next day to pick up the other eight men from our Virginia church, who would be working with us to build his house. In the meantime, the builder and I began to get things organized for the team to get to work as they arrived. Betty got with the missionary's wife to figure out sleeping arrangements and how they would feed our eleven-person group and her family of five. Her family would be in one bedroom and Betty and I had another bedroom upstairs. The other nine men blew up their air mattresses and all slept on the floor in yet a different room. I think some of the men could have gotten jealous of Betty and me having a private room and bed. Maybe they were thinking that their wives should have come along! At least they were not sleeping in hammocks or on air mattresses out in the open along the gravel runway.

The missionary wanted to provide something extra for each of us on the team. He offered a trip to hunt crocodiles on the river, a flight search for an Indian group he wanted to evangelize, a canoe trip for Betty to accompany his wife to an Indian village where there was a mud brick oven to bake some brownies, and a couple of other such activities. Because I had done flight searching in Vietnam, I felt I could be most valuable to do that with the missionary pilot. Two of our team wanted to do the crocodile hunt and others didn't want to take any of the extra events.

ANSWERED PRAYER FOR DRINKING WATER

What would we do for drinking water to keep everyone from getting dehydrated while working out in the sun? The river water was not safe for us Americans to drink, and it would be difficult to boil enough water and cool it to satisfy the need. The missionary wife told us that they had prayed about this problem and she told us the story of how God provided. A young boy was out in the jungle two days before our arrival and had found a fresh spring about a half mile away! Knowing that, D asked some Indians to cut a new direct path to the spring so that our men could get water each day. We had brought collapsible five-gallon containers with us to carry water if needed—and yes, they were needed. The Lord had answered prayer in a timely way.

Construction of the house went very well under our builder's skilled supervision. Everyone worked very hard, digging for the footers and foundation, keeping the wall's brick stories straight and level, cutting the window framing and door lintels, and building the trusses which our architect designed. It all went well—that is until we began to run out of cement. More cement was supposed to have

been there, done that!

come up the river on a launch from Brazil, but the boat had not come thirteen days before, as it had been scheduled. So D decided to fly to Leticia and get more cement so we could continue working.

PLANE CRASH THROUGH TRIPLE-CANOPY JUNGLE

Because the plane had no radio, and there was only daily morning contact with missionaries at other locations, we could not track D's return which was expected around noon. Late in the afternoon, he came <u>walking</u> into the village. The plane had crashed, nose down, in the jungle on his way back. Apparently, he had gotten some bad gas down in Leticia, and the engine quit running.

He gathered the Indians around and told about his crash and how he had not been seriously injured as the plane plummeted through the triple-canopy jungle with its wings catching on branches to slow its descent before the nose touched the ground. He told of having seen the big rock at La Pedrera, so he knew he was headed in the right direction. Tromping through the jungle, D remembered crossing a creek where there was a large swarm of electric eels. The Indians knew where that was! In another spot, he passed a partially eaten antelope, and the Indians knew where that was! Because of those clues, they would be able to find the crashed plane.

His bags of cement cargo had been put in a fifty-five-gallon empty gasoline drum and strapped in behind his pilot's seat. Fortunately, the straps held solidly and only allowed the metal barrel to bend at the strap line when the plane crashed. If the barrel had come loose, D could have been severely hurt, but he only had bruises from his own shoulder straps and a bruised knee. Praise the Lord for protecting him because if he had not survived and walked in, no one would ever have known what happened to him.

D asked the Indians if they could try and find the plane because we needed the cement. And, he had left his passport in the plane! The next day, they used their tracking skills and found the plane, made some backpacks out of palm branches and vines and brought most of the contents from the plane back to the village. The work on the house could be continued since the Indians carried the heavy bags of cement through the jungle to us. We serve a God who protects us with His guardian angels and who continually provides all we need!

As a follow-on to this plane crash story, the missionary helped the Indians take apart the plane in the jungle and bring it piece-by-piece to the mission station where D repaired the crash damages, put the plane back together, and re-installed the original wheels. Months later after the crash, D continued to use the plane in the ministry!

THE HOLE IN THE CLOUDS

When we left to fly back to Virginia almost two weeks after arriving in Colombia, the basic house structure was almost completed with about half of the roof put on. We were all scheduled to depart Leticia in a couple of days, but first we all had to get there. The problem was that we had no plane to ferry us out of the jungle! Would it be possible for us to extend our time there? Not really! One of our team was supposed to give his daughter in marriage two days after we were to arrive home. Another of our men's wife was expecting to deliver their first baby that same weekend. And finally, the airport in Leticia was to be shut down for two months for runway repair, and our flight was to be the last one out before that closure! How would the Lord work this out?

Once a day, the mission stations did have shortwave radio contact, and D told the other missionaries about the predicament we were in. He asked that one of them contact a zookeeper who was a pilot with his own plane in Leticia, and ask him to come and get D, who would then try and get another missionary plane to fly us all out of La Pedrera.

Successful contact was made with the zookeeper and D got a second missionary plane and flew it to the site in Brazil where our other team members were at a missionary's house along the river. However, a plug in one of the plane's pontoons was accidently left off and that night, the winds blew water up over the pontoon and filled it up. The plane tilted to one side and in the morning, the tail of the plane, a wing, and one pontoon were under the water. Thankfully, the engine was sticking up in the air! With some ingenuity, by floating a log under the sunken wing, the plane was resurfaced and water pumped from the pontoon. But in the process, a wing strut was bent and D knew he could not fly that plane over the jungle to pick us up from La Pedrera.

D flew the damaged plane just over the Amazon River back to Leticia to pick up the last available missionary plane. It was in need of some significant repairs but with D's training, he cannibalized a variety of parts from around the area, used some baling wire and lots of prayer and got the plane air worthy. That was a successful effort, and with skilled jungle flying, he came to our work site to get us all out from La Pedrera and down to Leticia to catch our flight back toward America.

been there, done that!

Betty and I were on the last flight out from La Pedrera. The clouds were extremely low and dense that day, and when we got into the air, D was forced to fly just by his gut feeling and timing because he had no visual landmarks or aircraft instruments to go by. At a certain time, he said we needed to pray for an opening in the clouds since we should then be about the right time and distance to be over Leticia. All of a sudden, D spotted a hole in the clouds so he flew down through it. We were right where we needed to be! God had again answered our emergency prayers and used the skills of a jungle pilot to get us where we needed to be.

RACING FOR THE LAST FLIGHT

At the moment when we landed on the Amazon River, we were about a half hour away from the time when our Avianca flight was to leave the airport. D quickly parked the plane on his raft in the river. He then ran up the hill from the river and commandeered a jeep, while we unloaded the plane and cautiously walked through the tippy canoes again. We sure didn't want to feed the piranhas at this point! D basically told the jeep driver that he was taking the jeep and would bring it back later, but that he had to get us to the commercial airport for our flight.

As we sped toward the airport, we saw another member, F, of our team on the back of a motorcycle headed the opposite direction. Seeing us in the jeep and knowing we were the last to arrive, F told the motorcycle driver to turn around and head back to the airport. He was not going to be the only one left behind! When we got to the airport, we learned that F had fallen into some barbed wire and the authorities were taking him for medical attention.

Betty had left most of her medical supplies back at the mission station in La Pedrera but, for reasons known only to God, had kept in her backpack a roll of adhesive tape and a bottle of iodine. Long story short: the plane took off on time with all of us on board! Thankfully, Betty's nursing skills—with that stinging iodine and homemade butterfly band-aids made from the adhesive tape she had "mysteriously" retained—prevented any infection, and only some pretty big scars remained as evidence of God's healing power of F's arm.

JUNGLE UNDERWEAR FOUND!

A little side story provided some humor for all of us who went on this mission trip. In his messages preceding our trip to Colombia, our pastor would occasionally mention different things he anticipated while we were gone. He had told everyone that he was taking old clothes—including what he called his "jungle underwear"—which he could just leave there with the local people.

After the long day of travel and negotiations with the airline when we were traveling to our mission project, he slept very well in the Bogota hotel in Colombia. Just for fun, his roommate quietly went to the pastor's suitcase and pulled out all—except for two sets—of the "jungle underwear" that our pastor had talked about in church. He wanted to keep them—as a joke—for the pastor later so that he wouldn't have to buy new ones when he came home!

For the next two weeks, pastor couldn't understand how he had left those important items of clothing at his home. So each day while on the trip, pastor would give underwear he used the previous day to an Indian lady to wash and dry while wearing his one extra set. He alternated between his underwear each day for the two weeks we were in the jungle.

Now, here is the good and fun part and reason for this story. Arriving back in the airport in America at 2 a.m., a crowd from our church joyously welcomed our mission team home. We gathered in a big circle and sang the *Doxology,* and pastor said a few words and closed in prayer.

But before we broke up, I asked to speak briefly. I talked about the great vision our pastor had for this trip and for his spiritual leadership and that we had a small gift for him. I gave him a package wrapped in very colorful Colombian paper.

With glee and a prideful, huge smile with his wife at his side, he gladly accepted our gift and tore open the package only to have a bunch of his old "jungle underwear" fall out. He immediately knew where it had come from and picked up some of it and threw it at his roommate from the hotel in Bogota. Life is full of fun, and Betty was now an experienced participant in overseas missions even though she was "not going!"

CAMBODIA

Betty and I have assumed an attitude of serving the Lord whenever He gives us opportunities. We agreed that if we don't accept the prospects He lays before us, He may not give us others. Our feeling was to accept an opportunity unless God closes the door for it. In 2010, Baptist Mid-Missions through its medical director, Dr. J, was planning a medical mission trip to Cambodia to support the ministries of missionaries there. Betty, being a nurse, volunteered to be a part of the medical team of doctors and nurses. I would tag along as a "go-fer" to help in whatever capacity Dr. J could use me—perhaps as a driver, as someone to help in crowd control, or serve in other administrative functions. I could also teach or preach in the community or outlying villages.

BACK OF PICKUP TRUCK TRIP TO BORDER

Getting there was a unique trip. Betty and I met the mission's medical team of three doctors and three other nurses in Detroit, Michigan, and then we had the long flight over to Bangkok, Thailand. We spent some time with missionaries there, and I preached in the little church they had started. To move on from Bangkok to Cambodia, we left early in the morning on a small local bus to reach an end-of-the-line village "bus depot".

Then we transferred into the back of a pickup truck. For a couple of hours, we bounced along on wood bench seats to reach the Cambodian border. Our vehicle was not permitted to go into Cambodia, so a missionary had come to pick us up at the border control point to take us on to his ministry location in the coastal town of Koh Kong. Our missionary doctor who, was serving there, worked in a small community hospital and made numerous contacts for the medical ministry through her service. Through her, arrangements were made to do medical mobile clinics in some of the more remote villages.

MEDICAL MISSIONS IN THE VILLAGE

We had carried a lot of bulk medicines with us, and other medical supplies were obtained in country through the help of help of the missionary doctor. Our first day was spent sorting out medicines, bagging them into prescription sizes, and organizing them for easy access by our nurses for distribution as the doctors ordered.

A clinic day started with sharing a devotional time with the people who had come for medical care. That was followed by a minimal triage system where I would briefly evaluate through a translator the reason for someone needing to see a doctor. I would then hand out large, brightly-colored, numbered cards to give some semblance of order and control for the clinic. If I didn't give them a card, they could not see any of our doctors. That was quite the ordeal as this crowd around me was grabbing for the cards and trying to get my attention by hollering and waving and jumping. I had to carefully secure anything in my pockets so that things were not taken from me.

Our team had four doctors, and we knew approximately how many cards we could give out in the mornings and how many in the afternoons when we would start the clinic over again. Once the cards were distributed, I continued to do crowd management to move sequentially numbered patients into a waiting area and then after they saw the doctor to get them to the pharmacy area where my wife and other nurses distributed medicines and gave instructions in their proper use. Occasionally, the nurses were called on to treat wounds. I think we did four or five clinics out in villages on different days. Translators were available to each doctor, to me, and to our team's nurses in the pharmacy area.

One of the really fun responsibilities given to me was to find places for our team to eat in the villages where we held the clinics. I would ride on the back of a motorcycle driven by one of our interpreters and go around the village to find a place that was big enough to feed our group of sixteen people (doctors, nurses, interpreters) at tables and to ensure that the food would be prepared in a "clean" environment. Most of the cooking was on outdoor fires in well "seasoned/blackened" pots and pans. In each village, I talked with several ladies about their menu potential for us and whether they could have it ready in time for our team's noon break. We never went hungry! I'll discuss more about the menu in a later chapter.

been there, done that!

TEETH FOR SALE

While walking along the littered street—plastic grocery sacks, paper, junk metal, and so forth—in the town, I saw a glass display case outside one of the small shops. The case was about four feet tall and maybe two feet square with four shelves. What was in it? Teeth for sale! Some were full sets of false teeth while others were bridges with varying numbers of teeth. They were all different sizes. My first assumption was that they were from deceased individuals but some could have been from people who had outgrown the teeth or needed more teeth added to a bridge. I didn't see any dentist signs at the shop, which appeared to be a hardware store. Maybe these teeth were considered "hardware"! They were hard, and people could wear them! I had to guess that if you needed some "new" teeth, you would just reach in the case and try one on that may fill a gap in your mouth! Yuk! How many others had tried that bridge in their mouth, and had it been washed after they decided it didn't fit?

GOSPEL OUTREACH OPPORTUNITIES

Part of my role in Cambodia was to counsel, through an interpreter, individuals regarding their spiritual understanding of the devotions, which had been given each morning and afternoon. I was thankful to help lead a few people to believe in Christ after counseling with them. I also helped one of the church leaders with opening and explaining the EvangeCube as a gospel presentation tool. The EvangeCube looks like a box but can be opened in a variety of ways to pictorially present the biblical story. We also had some comic book–like Christian tracts we used. Many of the local people could not read, so picture stories and tracts were things they could take with them to share with others.

After one person got a tract, I saw him go out away from others to sit down and page through it. As I watched, people gathered around him as he would explain the tract's pictures to others who perhaps had not been at the devotions time—even though he himself had not accepted Christ. He may not have been able to read the words on the tract but through the pictures, he was presenting the gospel! Hopefully, he would accept Christ into his life as he reviewed the tract at other times.

In addition to the counselling and devotional opportunities I was given, I did preach in the little church. Also, one evening, I went with the missionary in a small boat out to a village on an island off the coast. The missionary had a small battery-powered projector with speakers to show a video about the life of Christ. It was made in the Khmer language so the people could understand the film's message. We hung a white sheet off a building and played games with the kids while waiting for darkness to settle in.

When we finally started the video, more and more people gathered and sat on the ground to watch and listen. As the film progressed and people saw the goodness of Christ in His actions and words, they became quite emotional and would clap for Him. Then when the video showed accusations and slander against the Lord, the villagers became angry with the Jewish people in the movie and would stand up and shout against them. The beatings and crucifixion scenes had the villagers standing and crying and hugging each other and complaining about the treatment of Jesus. At the end, the missionary further explained that Christ had endured His sufferings for all of them because He loved them so much. I do not remember what the direct response of the villagers at that time was to the invitation, but the missionary said he would be back to further talk with them about this Jesus. That was quite an experience for me to be with those villagers and to see the impact of the film for those who did not know our Savior.

A very special privilege for our medical team was to witness the baptism of some new Cambodian believers in Jesus Christ. The service was to be out in the bay at a sandbar. To get there, we had to go down a steep embankment and get

been there, done that!

in a borrowed fishing boat big enough to handle about fifteen of us, including those to be baptized. At the baptismal site, we sang a couple of songs and then the people were baptized by the missionary. God's church grows through committed men and women, such as these precious believers. This is the continuing fulfillment of the Great Commission in Matthew 28. Praise the Lord!

ARGENTINA

The mission trips I had been on were generally comprised of ten or fifteen people. I had not been on a large team, such as our church's missions pastor was proposing for a construction project in Argentina. I wanted to see how a large team worked together and how all the details were managed, so Betty and I signed up to go with our church's mission team in 2012.

I had no special skills in the construction trades like many of the team's other people, but I knew I could be of help in hauling materials, cleaning up, demolition where needed, and in preaching opportunities. Betty helped the missionary's wife with the cooking and cleaning up the kitchen, as we all ate our meals together. The noon meals were fantastic as huge steaks and chicken pieces were grilled in the church's backyard for us each day. I don't think that I have had such delicious steaks as we had in Argentina! They were huge, tender, and absolutely great!

[Just prior to our departure for this Argentina mission trip, my nearly ninety-six-year-old mother had fallen and broken her hip. She had an operation and the hip was reset, but being her oldest son and being reasonably close by, I felt a heavy responsibility for her welfare. I asked her if she wanted me to stay and help with her care, but she emphatically said Betty and I should go on this planned mission trip. By our going, we had many more people praying for her as she recovered in the US.

We went to Argentina and arrived back home on a Sunday. I called and told Mother that we would be over on Monday to see her. She seemed in good spirits and said she looked forward to our coming. We had a great visit with her, and we came on home the same day. The next morning she entered her heavenly home. It was as if she wanted to wait to go to glory until she knew that God had answered her prayer for our safe return from the mission trip. We are glad that nothing happened to her while we were in Argentina. That would have been very tough for us. But we got to see her wonderful smile and sense her enduring love again and were so thankful for that last day with her.]

CONSTRUCTION PROJECT

The construction project in Argentina was to modify a solid two-story house into a facility that could be used for church services. It would also become the home for one of our church-supported missionary families. As in most missionary building projects, flexibility is extremely important. In contrast to America, building codes are not the same and usually not as strict, certain tools used here may not be used (or even available) there, and sometimes labor is managed differently. When we go to a foreign area to help, we have to make adjustments to accomplish things in the manner the missionary and local people desire, rather than adhere to the way we do things in America.

For this project, the interior's first floor had to be reconfigured to accommodate a large meeting space, classrooms, and bathrooms. The upstairs needed to be remodeled for the missionary family's living space. I got to enjoy some demolition activity, as well as the necessary cleanup afterward! Additionally, I helped with some of the electrical rewiring and some plumbing installation. It was hard work, and the building definitely showed real progress by the time our team left. We did take part of one day to take a quick tour around the crowded city of Buenos Aires and stopped in a very large, multi-building market for some souvenirs.

CHURCH MINISTRIES

On our last day in Argentina, we held a praise and worship service in the building we had been working on. And as in other countries, I was privileged to share God's Word in several established Argentine church services throughout this mission trip. Unlike in America, the primary church service on Sundays is in the evening rather than the morning to accommodate work and transportation schedules of the people.

One of the church members is a world-renowned pediatric surgeon who has written a highly respected volume on his subject. He does extensive travel to address medical conferences. He and his wife took time to share their exciting testimonies of the work of God in their lives, which strongly encouraged each of us on the construction team. I was also glad to see how efficient and organized our mission pastor was in coordinating the work of a large construction team. He has done several of those now and really makes a project go very smoothly.

ROMANIA

Betty and I had enjoyed the medical mission trip we took to Cambodia with the medical director of Baptist Mid-Missions. We had told her that if she was directing another such ministry that we would be interested in joining another medical team and go with her. We learned of a team going to Romania and felt that our schedule would allow us to be part of that group. Again, Betty would help from the nursing end of the visit and I would help where needed. The team had two doctors and five nurses—plus me.

THE ROMA PEOPLE

The Romani (different from Romanian) people, or Roma for short, are an Indo-Aryan ethnic group originating from the northern Indian subcontinent. They are traditionally an itinerant people group, living mostly in Europe and the Americas and have been commonly and derisively called gypsies because of their nomadic nature, most of the time without work. The Roma had often brought disrespect on their own people group by illegal activities to provide for themselves. There are large groups of them in Romania. They are separated and despised by the Romanian people and government—just as they are in several other nations.

In most situations, the Roma people live in their own communities away from the traditional Romanian culture. They have been provided some healthcare but typically are the last to receive it. Generally, the kids have not been treated well in the schools, and many drop out after just a couple of years in the education system. Life in the village seemed to be very tough. We saw and heard about lots of abuse with men beating on women, women taking advantage of other women, adults hitting kids, and kids hitting and throwing stones at other kids. Because of the big divide between the Romanians and the Roma people, very little work outside the village was available to provide income. Basically, the Roma people are a rejected group.

Sometimes a Roma husband would actually leave his village in Romania and go out of the country for six months or so to find work and get money to bring back home to the village. They would use it all up, and he would leave again. This made it challenging for the missionaries to have sustained ministry and discipleship programs on a long-term basis with some of the people.

MEDICAL CLINICS IN CHURCH BUILDINGS

Dr. J, the medical director of Baptist Mid-Missions, arranged for a medical missions trip to aid the missionaries in their outreach by providing mobile clinics in a couple of Roma villages where churches had been started. Our missionaries in Romania provided gracious hospitality in their large home, which could adequately accommodate our mission team during our time in the country.

The clinics were conducted much the same as we had done in Cambodia. Through a translator, Betty was helping in the temporary mobile pharmacy and I was doing some of the crowd control and patient management. At times, I would walk through the village with the missionary to tell the people about the clinic and to use that as an opening to share the gospel. The missionary was really good at that!

Our clinics were held in the church buildings under construction in the villages. Since the roofs were not yet completed, we hung tarps and sheets up for ceilings to keep the sun from blazing into the rooms where our doctors were doing their patient evaluations. People did not hesitate to come to the church (as a community building) since it was not the home of one of the villagers.

Kids are curious in any culture, and at our clinics, they constantly were trying to see what was going on by hanging out around the windows' openings, thus disrupting the doctors, nurses in the pharmacy section, and the patients. They were nosy and noisy! At one of our clinics, a fence surrounded the church compound, but the kids were constantly finding ways to get through, crawl under, or climb over the fence. With kindness, I had to try and keep them away and outside the fence by sometimes playing little games with them. It was basically a hopeless cause, and I finally had to get help from a Roma authority. We were never fully successful, but we did manage the kids' disruption most of the time.

been there, done that!

MINISTRY IN THE ROMA COMMUNITIES

The missionaries had learned over time that there is such disdain between some of the Roma families in the village that they hesitated to enter each other's homes. To hold a Bible study, any kind of small group, or clinic in an individual's home where others could be invited would generally not be an acceptable practice in the village—although we did hold one house meeting. So a separate community church building had to be erected and used in most cases for anything having to do with the gospel.

The real challenge is trying to help the Roma people within their own culture and their lack of working opportunities in the immediate vicinity of the Roma villages. All of this has made the ministry difficult for our missionaries. Yet God has blessed as the missionaries have worked to teach the people about God's love that can make such a difference in their lives. A few small churches have been established and Roma pastors are being trained.

Again, I had the opportunity to preach in the churches—the very places where we had held the clinics. I am not a trained or polished preacher, but I do enjoy sharing with others some of the things that the Lord has taught me. We really enjoyed meeting and fellowshipping with the missionary families and the Roma people. One of our medical team members committed her life to continue to serve the Roma people and is presently serving the Lord among them today.

UKRAINE

A couple from North Carolina attends our Florida church in the winter seasons. They have been on many mission trips in the southern part of Ukraine, helping with some major building projects. In 2018, they invited me to join them and a small team for a couple of weeks. Part of the trip was to evaluate the continuing growth of a couple of churches and help plan for future facilities. I was pleased to accept the invitation. My role would primarily be in some preaching, sharing my testimony, and individual counsel. Others on the team were experts in church planning and construction, and another was a pastor. Betty did not go with me on this trip, as there was not much she could be involved in each day.

MINISTRY IN YUZHNY

We first went to the city of Yuzhny on the Black Sea near the Crimean Peninsula which the Russians had recently annexed. In 2018 when I was there, the Ukrainians and Russia were still fighting for control of the eastern portion of the Ukraine. Where we were in the south, the local people demonstrated a lot of anxiety about the Russians possibly trying to take other port cities along the Black Sea. Some of the believers in the churches where we ministered were recent refugees from the continuing battle regions in the eastern part of the independent nation. (We were in the Ukraine prior to the Russian invasion of the country in 2022.)

A very nice church building had been built with the help of this North Carolina team in the past, and the church was considering construction of a new building to accommodate increasing needs for after-school children's ministries. We thought we would be involved in beginning its construction, but they were not ready for that.

The Ukrainian pastor's wife was a teacher of ethics and morality in the public high school and gave us access to her classes. Our team shared testimonies and responded to questions from the students. Some of the students seemed to focus on my military career and how the Lord had sustained me through my tours of combat in Vietnam.

I also preached on Wednesday evening to a large group in the church. The pastor said that their Wednesday evening prayer services were just about as well attended as their Sunday services. (We need that same kind of zeal in our American churches!) Their prayers demonstrated great faith and earnestness as they talked with the Lord. After the service, I spent about a half hour with one young man who said he was a believer but had no direction in his life. He said that now he was going to be more intentional in his Bible study and seek God's will for his future.

I went to a little house church in an outlying village on Sunday evening to encourage them as they reached out with the Gospel in their community. I was supposed to speak there, but that evening they had some unexpected visitors from Belarus and Russia, and the group leader asked them to share God's work in their nations. The visitors were in the area for vacation and wanted to worship somewhere, so they asked around until they found out about this little Christian group. It was a blessing for me to listen to the testimony and reports of these dedicated believers. After the visitors concluded that evening, we realized there

been there, done that!

was no more time for my message, so I just shared a short testimony, and the service ended.

WORK AT COUNTRY CHURCHES

On our way west a few days later to another major port city, Odessa, we stopped at a couple of small country churches. One seemed to be quite developed in its reaching out to the youth of its area, and they asked me to share my testimony. The youth were very interested and alert to their responsibility to reach further with the truths of the Gospel into the lives of young folk in their community. At that village, we were supposed to have helped reconstruct and paint playground equipment, but when we arrived, we found the work had already been done. Interestingly, a lady missionary served at that church and I learned that she was from the church in Florida where our son and daughter-in-law had attended in the past. It is a small world!

At yet another country church, they needed a room in the basement refurbished so that they could meet there in the winter. When we arrived, the room was just unfinished stone walls, and we were to put drywall up and install the electricity. We were fed a delicious lunch while working on that room. The pastor of this village church had been there for years, and his daughter, who was blind, faithfully helped him in the ministry. In fact, she was my primary interpreter—and did a great job!—while I was in the Ukraine. She and her dad would get on a train in Odessa and ride to this village area where there was no train station. However, when the pastor was on board, the train would always stop to drop him off, and engineers knew to pick him up again if he was out waiting by the tracks to get back to his home in Odessa.

CHURCH REPLACES RADIO JAMMING TOWER

Part of our ministry in Ukraine was in the Black Sea port city of Odessa where the people also seemed to be quite skeptical about the Russians' plan for it in the future. (The Russians invaded Ukraine with one of their attack avenues through Odessa with their massive and destructive forces in 2022.) The Lord has done a major work in this city since the Ukraine gained its independence from the USSR in 1991. The main church there was helped to be built by our friends' teams over the years, and it had spawned several other daughter churches in and around the city. There is also a blossoming seminary in the city. The church has its own apartments right behind it, and we stayed in them and ate there most of the time.

The uniqueness of this church is that it is built on the property, which formerly—under the Soviet Union—had been the location of a primary radio jamming tower to block Voice of America and other Western broadcasting from reaching into the communist nation. When Ukraine became independent, the property was eventually donated to the church and immediately the church began its construction with our friends' help. In fact, the church was built up on three sides around the tall broadcast-jamming tower before permission was given to take the tower down and complete the church. The image is taken from a display case in the church.

It now seats 3,000 people on its main floor and in the two balconies above it! Our amazing God arranged for the property to be given to the church, for permission to initially build around the tower, and then to allow a large church to proclaim the gospel to thousands of people in a major Ukrainian city. Thus, instead of blocking the proclamation of the gospel via radio broadcasting, now the site is reaching out to the world through this church and its daughter ministries! What an amazing God we have and serve!

I preached in that church on a Sunday morning and I think if I had known it was that big, I would have had second thoughts about it. But it was a special blessing for me to worship with all those folks and minister to them. After the service, a young lady in the seminary came to me and asked me to pray with her about doing missionary service in Africa. I told her about our granddaughter who was with Word of Life International in Uganda and gave her contact information. I regret that I have not been able to follow up with her to see how the Lord has led in her life. Also, a man came forward and told me that the message challenged him to be more intentional in his walk and witness for the Lord and not let his life's adversity hinder his spiritual growth.

That Sunday evening, our team planned to worship at a daughter church facility that our friends had also helped to build. It probably held around 500 people. The pastor gave us a tour around the building and then said he would like for one of us to preach that night. One of our team was the pastor of the church in North Carolina, and I expected him to offer but he said that he had not brought any notes with him that evening. Then he asked if I had notes with me, and if so, would I speak? I couldn't deny that I had notes with me in my Bible so on the spur of a moment, I was the speaker that evening. Again, I was challenged to always be ready to serve the Lord in all situations.

Following the service, our team had a wonderful time around locally-made, delicious snacks with the Ukrainian church family. I never dreamed that this missionary kid from Africa would ever have the opportunity to preach in the former Soviet Union, but God had a way of giving me another unique story! Now it is easy for me to say that I've "been there, done, that" in that former communist nation.

CAYMAN ISLANDS

SERVING WITH FORMER D&D GUESTS

While at D&D Missionary Homes, the Lord gave Betty and me a special opportunity to minister with some of our missionary guests who were serving the Lord in the Cayman Islands in the Caribbean Sea. This couple had a long history with D&D, as their missionary parents had been there many years before. In fact, the man and woman had met at D&D, had their first date while at D&D, had been married and first gone as missionaries while living at D&D, and gave birth to some of their children while on furloughs at D&D! Because of this long-term connection, they wanted their church in the Cayman Islands to learn more about our ministry to missionaries. We were invited to be speakers at their church's week-long mission conference.

We had wonderful meetings with that very diverse and multi-national congregation. Some had come from eighteen countries—mostly Caribbean islands—but some were from Central and South America. The conference schedule was such that we had free time during most of the days, giving us time to tour the island in a car provided to us. These islands had been British in the past, and the driver is on the right hand side of the car. For us, driving was on the "wrong" side of the road. That took some getting used to as we drove more than 300 miles on that little island that is only about ten miles wide and twenty miles long! Betty kept reminding me to "Stay left," and we did negotiate the roads without incident.

The beaches there were a very powdery white sand, and lengthy! From one beach dock, we got into a two-person submarine to view the coral reefs. This vehicle was unique in that we were inside a big bubble and the "driver" was in scuba gear on the outside piloting the bubble around. We could talk with him through an intercom system. One time he alarmed us by suddenly appearing in front of us with a big loud "Boo" and made us wonder who was steering this thing! We had a great time in that little submarine!

SWIMMING WITH STINGRAYS

We went swimming with stingrays which hang out in this one large bay. A boat took us out to the middle of the bay, which was actually very shallow. The captain let us get out of the boat to be with the stingrays. We were given some bait and instructed how to hold it in a special way so that the rays would not take our thumbs as part of their snack! The skin of the sting rays is very soft and silky as they swam between our legs and brushed against us. This is one of those unique experiences where I can say that I have "been there, done that!" I don't have any idea why tourists are not stung by these creatures, but we were told that a sting is very rare down there—quite a difference from what we have heard about in Florida.

been there, done that!

One of the prime meats for the island's people is sea turtle which they raise in huge vats on the island. It appeared to me that there were hundreds of turtles in each vat container. We learned that turtle meat as a staple part of the diet was very healthy. Some of the turtle shells were really big and beautiful when they were polished up after the turtle meat was eaten. Almost everywhere you looked around the island, these shells were displayed, but none were allowed to be removed or sold from the island.

One of the things I especially enjoyed on the island was the many little roadside stands selling coconuts. I would walk up and ask for a coconut, and they would cut the end off and insert a straw for me to drink the refreshing coconut milk. After that, it didn't take long for me to consume that white, delicious coconut meat they would extract for me. That sweet snack added to the sweet fellowship with our missionary friends and the warm welcome of the Cayman Island people. I was so thrilled to hear after we returned home that the church in the Cayman Islands chose to financially support our D&D ministry. It was our only overseas supporting church! Memories from the Cayman Islands just add another wonderful story to my life. Along with the other mission trips, my life has been encouraged and tremendously blessed!

PART IV — TRAVELS

CHAPTER XVIII
PERSONALLY PLANNED TRIPS

It is hard to give a priority to any of the wonderful pleasures I have had over the years in my extensive travels for sheer enjoyment or for ministry purposes. (The US government planned many other trips when I was in the US Army.) I have been in all fifty US states and all but two of the Canadian provinces. My travels have carried me into approximately eighty-five nations of the world, and I could write of excitement I have felt in each of them. Some visits were obviously shorter than others, and some of these trips have included a brief layover at a foreign airport. My time in Vietnam is discussed in a different section of these memoirs since it did consume almost two years of my life as a US Army officer. Most of the countries and states shared below were primarily visited for pleasure as tourists. However, while in several others menitoned previously, I accepted opportunities to preach or share a devotional when invited.

ALASKA

Betty and I wanted to do something special for our forty-fifth anniversary in 2009 and decided to go to Alaska. We looked into several potential cruises but soon realized that we had too many friends—military, missionary, and family—in Alaska whom we wouldn't get to visit if we were on a scheduled cruise and land tour. So, we wrote to the chambers of commerce in a number of the Alaskan cities, contacted several of our friends, and began to pour through various magazines, internet sites, and cruise brochures to get ideas of things to plan and do on our own.

Without a commercial agent, we set up our tour but then realized that we still couldn't get everything we wanted to do within a couple of weeks. Our

been there, done that!

self-established itinerary expanded to three weeks on the ground in Alaska. After that, we would take a cruise from Anchorage down to Vancouver, British Columbia, before our flight home. We planned it for August 2009, and everything fell in place nicely, except for the car rental aspect. The major rental companies would have been way too expensive to get a car for three weeks!

I contacted a missionary-kid friend in Alaska and asked her if there might be anyone she knew in the church or otherwise who would let us rent a car for three weeks. After checking around, she found a used car dealer who would rent to us. I called him, and as we were working out the details, he asked where we were from, and I told him the Tampa Bay area in Florida. He wanted to narrow it down to the city, so finally I told him "Largo". All of a sudden, he let out a big shout and said, "I'm from Largo!" Things took a new course from there, and he gave us an exceptional deal on a car to rent—but we were not supposed to take it on any gravel roads. After being in Alaska for just a few days, we realized that it was impossible to follow that rule. We'd be headed down the only paved road to get somewhere and suddenly, it would turn to gravel! How could we have known that in advance?

One of the great joys of the Alaska trip was to visit with Baptist Mid-Missions' missionaries and see some of the churches which they had planted over the many years of their ministries. Some missionaries had planted two or three churches in the towns or villages in addition to some camps and Bible training centers. Several missionaries were pilots of small planes they used to reach remote locations. And yes, they told us of harrowing experiences that accompanied their pioneering work. In spite of the devil's resistance along the way, God has done an amazing work in Alaska through His servants.

EXCITING MODES OF TRANSPORTATION

We flew to Anchorage, picked up the rental car, and met with my missionary-kid friend, who provided us a little cabin for a couple of nights. On our first day, we did a twenty-five-mile, all-terrain vehicle (ATV) ride to a glacier head where we had lunch and then returned. We chose a two-person ATV so one of us could drive while the other took pictures. A guide in his ATV led the way, and what a trip it was, as we had to cross a river—floating part of the way—and drive over the tundra.

PERSONALLY PLANNED TRIPS

Much to my surprise, while on the glacier, suddenly my cell phone rang! It was our son in Alabama, who had happened to punch my number by mistake. There was no real news, but I was quite shocked that my phone would ring out on a glacier northeast of Anchorage. (There were other places in Alaska, such as in deep valleys between mountains, where the phone did not work.) On the way back from the glacier, the guide took us over some very deep ruts, made by big four-wheel-drive sport vehicles, and my ATV's right front wheel slipped off a mound, tipping us over on the vehicle's right side. The guide helped us get upright again, and off we went! No one was injured since we were going slow and had our seatbelts on, but it did add to our excitement!

In Alaska, we were on almost every kind of transportation available: wheeled, float, and ski planes; white water raft; jet boat with two 300-horsepower Chevrolet inboard engines; ATV; helicopters; dog sleds; catamaran; bus; van; train; small fishing boat; and the cruise ship. Each one of these has its own interesting story, and I'll share just a couple of interesting special events.

GEE AND HAW—DOG SLED

Most tourists in Alaska take a dog "sled" ride, but it is usually a small wheeled wagon that holds about ten people and is pulled by dogs over a short land trail. We did that—but also had a much better ride! We flew in a helicopter to a dog training camp on a glacier where they trained some dogs for the Alaskan Iditarod race. Although the trip was open to anyone, we were the only two tourists on the helicopter and at the camp that day. The dog trainers took us around the camp and explained the training of the dogs and showed us the dogs' little igloo-style homes.

Then they asked if we wanted to ride a *real* dog sled and, seeing our excitement, they hitched up the dogs, which were constantly yelping and demonstrating eagerness to get moving! Betty and I each had a separate dog team and rode on a one-person sled with the dog driver on the sled rails behind the seat. Soon we were off and flying down the hill with the drivers hollering "GEE" and "HAW" to guide the dogs. The seats were small and tipping back and forth as we hung on for dear life to the sides of our sleds. We made it to the bottom of a long hill and stopped for a break for a little relief from the ride. The drivers then asked us if we wanted to "ride the rails"—or in plain English, be the sleds' dog drivers— since we were the only tourist guests that day!

been there, done that!

We sure didn't expect that, and Betty and I each accepted the challenge. They explained how to guide the dogs and use the brakes on the rails where we stood behind the seats. The drivers then sat on the sleds—and put their trust in our inexperienced abilities! Neither Betty nor I had any crashes, and the regular drivers never fell off! How fortunate we were to have that experience! If there had been a group of tourists with us, the drivers said that we would not have been given the opportunity to GEE and HAW the dogs. From the burning desert sands in Chad, Africa, to the freezing snow of a glacier in Alaska! What a difference for this missionary kid!

PARAGLIDE WEATHERED OUT AGAIN

For a long time, I have wanted to do a tandem paraglide off a mountain. I tried to do it once when we were in Switzerland, but I got weathered out. So I scheduled a paraglide off of Mt. Alyeska in Alaska. The date and time came, but about an hour before the "flight," I got a call saying that the weather cancelled my ride. I scheduled a paraglide three more times in the next few days when we would be passing near that area, but each time I was weathered out. I think Betty was somewhat relieved!

In telling others about these cancellations, people tried to warn me that maybe the Lord was trying to tell me something—that I should not do a paraglide. I'm not sure I agree with them on that! (Later, I did try to paraglide off a mountain in New Zealand but was also weathered out of that one!) Six scheduled paraglide trips have been weathered out for me. I don't know when I'll be near another mountain to try to schedule number seven, but I'm not giving up yet! Maybe seven will be the perfect number for me.

A ROUGH CATAMARAN RIDE

When we were south of Anchorage, we were encouraged to take a large catamaran boat out to see calving glaciers. The hour-long ride was quite smooth until we got to our destination in a remote bay. Suddenly, the winds kicked up and our boat captain said we had to leave the area so that we wouldn't get caught in really bad weather. In all honesty, I thought the weather right then was extreme!

We headed out away from the glacier, and near the mouth of the bay, the winds became violent and caused ten to fifteen-foot waves. Several people began to get green with sickness and were herded toward the rear of the boat. The passenger area of the boat was completely enclosed, and sometimes the waves crashed over the top of us and at other times, the catamaran would be up on its side so high that we could see one of the "pontoons" up out of the water! Neither Betty nor I got sick, but it was quite a frightful ride. As I have previously mentioned, I am not a water lover, and an experience such as this reminds me why.

BEAR WATCHING—FLOAT PLANE

We flew in a float plane to a lake where we then got into a small fishing boat to go watch the bears catch and eat salmon that were trying to make their way up some short waterfalls. Both black bears and grizzlies were in the area and impressed us as they caught fish, which were jumping up the cascading rivulet. We watched them for some time, and Betty asked our guide (in sort of a joking way) if he could catch one for us for lunch as fast as the bears caught their lunch. To our surprise, he put a baited hook in the water and literally within seconds, he had a salmon on his hook! He said he'd cook it for us, but that we would have to leave that immediate area so the bears didn't come near us while he was filleting the salmon.

On the way to a little quiet bay, he took us to a place for a potty break. The two women in our boat would go one way in the woods and the men the other. He did say that we should not go very far into the woods because of all the bears around! We heeded his warning! On his little boat, he had a Coleman stove, cooking and eating utensils, and even some different kinds of seasoning—whatever we wanted! (I assumed that he had done this many times before!) I've never had such a fresh and delicious fish dinner! He tied up all the remains tightly in a bag to carry the trash out and then we headed back to watch the bears.

Just before our scheduled departure time, one big grizzly bear came down to the water, about fifteen feet away from our little boat. He sat down in the clear water, put his head underneath, and soon came up with a big salmon in his mouth. He proceeded to eat part of it, put it down and stuck his head under for another. Then he moved over and did the same thing in front of one of the other tourist boats nearby. It was like the bear was programmed to do this for us before we had to leave. It was so interesting!

been there, done that!

FLIGHT AROUND MT. DENALI—SKI PLANE

On August 8, 2009, Betty and I celebrated the day of our forty-fifth wedding anniversary by a ski plane flight around Mt. Denali (formerly Mt. McKinley). We had previously taken a bus trip ninety miles into Denali National Park and had seen the humongous mountain from the ground. Most people in that area say they rarely see the full mountain. We hoped for a good day for flying so that we could see the mountain from top to bottom. It was a beautiful day as we climbed into the Canadian-made, DeHaviland Beaver, rotary-single-engine plane. These were old planes of the same vintage we had used in Vietnam, but now they were upgraded to meet the rigorous Alaskan environment. It brought back many memories for me as I had been in these planes many times back in 1965. Frankly, I was surprised the planes were still being used.

We circled the 20,310-foot-high mountain on this very clear day and then landed on a glacier at about the 14,000-foot level. We got out and made some snowballs and threw them at each other in memory of our first "fight" as a married couple! On our honeymoon in 1964 after being married only a couple of days, we had stopped at Snoqualmie Pass on Mt. Rainier in Washington state on our way from Chicago to my duty station near Tacoma. There we had a friendly snowball "fight" and now here, forty-five years later, we were doing it again—on another mountain—in Alaska this time! We will have to find another mountain for a snowball fight for our seventy-fifth anniversary in 2039! Will we make it until that year?

NORTH OF THE ARCTIC CIRCLE—WHEELED PLANE

The Alaskan trip was amazing in so many different ways. Out of Fairbanks, we took a van ride up the Dalton Highway to a little airstrip north of the Arctic Circle. Along the way, we had to stop every few miles to clean the mud off the windows of the van so we could see the surrounding area.

Then we flew northwest in a single engine, wheeled plane into a little village in the Brooks Range. The only way in or out of this village was by plane or by dog sled. A village guide, all bundled up in a big parka, met us and explained to us how the people survive in that harsh environment. What in the world was this missionary kid from the Sahara Desert doing in the frigid summer—north of the Arctic Circle? I don't know, but at least I have "been there, done that"!

The mountains of the Brooks Range are the northernmost peaks of the Rocky Mountains and run on an east-west axis across Alaska. They are north of the Arctic Circle.

When the caribou herds run near the beginning of the winter season—to us Floridians, it was always winter up there!—the native people get their meat for the rest of the year. We saw kids running around in flip-flops, shorts, and tank tops and we were in three or four layers of clothes! We asked the guide when they put on warm clothes, and she said they would when the temperature gets down below zero—and it was now a "warm" thirty-two degrees! I hope our guide was joking! There is only one multi-grade school in the village. Athletic teams fly to other villages for competitions since there is no bus transportation and it is too far to go by dogsled!

Almost every home in the village had a dog in their backyard, primarily to warn the occupants if a bear came anywhere nearby. Up there, it is almost all sustenance living, and most supplies are brought in by air or by dog sleds from the north. Life north of the Arctic Circle sure is different and is very difficult.

Back in Fairbanks, we had scheduled a hot-air balloon ride one evening to fly over herds of caribou, but unfortunately, the weather was too bad and that adventure was cancelled as my paraglide rides had been. One of these days, we still want to do a hot-air balloon ride over something exciting. Here in Florida where I live, the terrain is too flat, and we don't think it would be that great of an experience.

The US Army has a military base, named Fort Wainwright, at Fairbanks. (I am glad I was never stationed there in that cold weather environment.) We drove on the base and saw the unit arm patch symbol for the 52nd Aviation Battalion in front of one of the buildings near the airfield. That was the unit I was with in my first tour in Vietnam! We stopped and I went in to chit-chat with some of the soldiers who referred me to one of the officers. I briefly told him of my experiences with the unit back in 1965 and wanted to learn about the unit's history since then but he did not seem at all interested so we left his office. One of the young enlisted men heard me say that I had served with the 52nd Aviation Battalion in combat and he started asking lots of questions. He was interested in hearing about the unit's background and it was a joy talking with him. I had not been aware that my former unit was now stationed in the harsh environment of Alaska. This was an unexpected surprise.

been there, done that!

ICE HOTEL IN FAIRBANKS

We visited other unusual things while in the Fairbanks area. I couldn't believe there were hot springs flowing in that winter wonderland. People were actually in the water as its steam rose into the air around the "poolside" area, which was covered with ice. Some people were sitting there "sunbathing" beside the pool while wearing heavy parkas!

Adjacent to the pool was a hotel carved out of solid ice. Inside, the furniture was ice, the bar with juice glasses was all ice, and the beds were ice, although moose and elk skins provided the blankets. You could actually rent a room for the night at approximately $600 per room—and, no, we didn't stay there! The bathroom was out in another building which would probably hinder your desire to get up in the middle of the night. By the way, you could take your juice glass—made of ice—with you as a souvenir but it wouldn't last very long in your backpack!

In one room of the hotel, we saw marvelous and intricate ice carvings. The hotel hosts explained how, in the winter, they cut huge ice chunks from the lake and bring them into the hotel to preserve them for year-long carvings. The ice there was crystal clear and not frosty looking. I was glad we were able to visit that hotel.

At another location, we were invited to put on some heavy parkas and go into a special room, which was kept at $-30°F$ degrees, to watch a demonstration. The guide showed us how cold impacts different types of materials. Then he gave us each a styrofoam cup and said he would pour boiling water into the cup and we were then to throw the water up in the air. Upon doing so, the water froze into ice before it hit the floor and scattered ice chips all around. Amazing!

VISIT IN A "RUSSIAN" VILLAGE

One day we went to a remote "Russian" village in the southwest portion of the state. Although the people are now Americans, they are from Russia and still live as the Russians across the Bering Strait between Russia and the Seward Peninsula of Alaska. The "Russians" in Alaska do speak English! I don't think there were any paved roads, and the beautiful Russian Orthodox Church was the dominant structure in the village of about 200 people. We had been told about a little restaurant where we could eat some Russian-type food, so we tried to find it. We finally located the small building, but no one was around that we could see as we wandered around its outside. I honked the horn a couple of times to see if anyone would respond. Finally from a house down the road, a lady came out, waved, and started toward us.

She spoke a heavily-accented English and invited us to go in. We saw two or three tables out in the "sun" room and expected to eat there, but she wanted us to go into the kitchen area with her. She started rattling pans around and asked us to sit up at a counter. Then she proceeded to pull out some Russian-type clothing and put it on us. We really didn't know what we were getting into.

Soon she brought out some lacquered, wooden spoons and placed them in front of us along with some cold borscht soup. This vegetable soup was primarily made with beets and actually was quite tasty. All the while, the lady kept saying we had to eat like the Russians would eat and what they would eat. I don't remember what the rest of the meal was, but there was some kind of bread, a little meat and vegetables, and water. We had some kind of sweet biscuit for dessert. We then said we had to leave, but she wanted to take pictures first and then gave us the two lacquered spoons. I hope the pictures aren't floating around Russia somewhere! She took back the Russian clothing—which didn't look like it had been washed in quite a while—so we were glad she didn't want to give that to us! That sure was a unique "been there, done that" experience!

We had a great time in Alaska—some of it with friends who took us in and made us feel right at home. Some missionaries had some great trophies of their early pioneering days when they had to hunt and fish for much of their food. We saw some amazing moose antlers, walrus tusks, mounted fish, and other mementos like we had not seen before. One of the most interesting trophies was a narwhal's six-to-eight-foot long spiraled tusk. I am sure there are not many of those sitting around in private houses! The narwhal lives in icy waters of the north and is a whale-like mammal. Its tusk is an elongated tooth and is primarily a sensory organ and apparently not a weapon as one would suspect it to be. We also heard some unbelievable stories of God's work and God's protection as the gospel was proclaimed to the people and new churches established. Praise the Lord for these dedicated servants of the Lord!

OUR FIRST CRUISE

The last part of our four-week Alaskan trip was on a *Princess* cruise ship down the panhandle from Anchorage to Vancouver. Along the way, we pulled up close

been there, done that!

to some calving glaciers at Glacier Bay National Park, took a ride on the old narrow-gauge railroad used by miners in the gold rush era, saw the bridge to nowhere in Juneau, and enjoyed the tremendous views in and around Ketchikan. This week was a nice relaxing time, as we didn't have to pack up every day or so as we had done for three weeks on the ground in the main part of the state. In Alaska, we had many friends who invited us to stay with them. I think we only paid for one or two nights in a B&B during our three weeks on the ground before our cruise.

Except for the cruise part of the Alaskan trip, Betty and I had done the planning for all the places where we went and the things we did in that huge state. We drove about 3,000 miles in the rental car and traveled many other miles in other modes of transportation. We were not experienced travel agents, but we knew how to figure out what we would like to do on a trip and then made the appropriate arrangements to get there and fulfill our dreams. This certainly was a forty-fifth anniversary to remember.

GALAPAGOS ISLANDS

My brother, Larry, and his wife, Sallie, had gone to Peru for about four months to learn Spanish so that he could preach and teach without an interpreter in Hispanic nations. There they would be immersed in the language and culture and did accomplish their purpose. Larry had told us when the language study would be complete and invited any siblings to visit them at that time if we wanted.

Betty and I wanted to go and we found out that Dale (my youngest brother) and his wife, Debbie, also wanted to visit in Peru. Betty and I started making the plans. It so happened that we had meetings up north in the USA just prior to the desired dates for Peru. That complicated things a little as to where we would fly from and where we could leave our vehicle.

Some good snowbird friends (who come to Florida for their winters) offered for us to leave our car at their farm in Michigan, and they would take us to the Detroit airport and would later pick us up when we returned from Peru. H and D were very welcoming and showed us around their parents' homesteaded area in Michigan. We even got to sleep in the bed in which H was born "years" ago! And yes, they have changed the mattress!

Dale and I worked out an itinerary that would take us through Quito, Ecuador, and over to the Galapagos Islands on our way down to Peru. In Peru, we would spend about a week together with Larry and Sallie, visit Machu Picchu, and then break up and go our separate ways when returning to the US.

Ecuador is home to some of the highest volcanoes and mountain peaks in the world. Quito, Ecuador's capital with an altitude of around 9,300 feet, is a beautiful city and Dale and Debbie showed us how to do a Hop On, Hop Off bus tour through the city. I had been in Quito when I was in the military but did not get to see much of it at that time, so this bus tour was very interesting to me.

CRUISING THE GALAPAGOS ISLANDS

The Galapagos Islands in the Pacific Ocean are part of Ecuador but are about 600 miles west from the mainland. Their remoteness has, for the most part, kept them in their natural physical conditions with all their flora and unique fauna. Upon arriving in the islands by air, we boarded a small cruise ship and spent seven days cruising around the islands and disembarking to tour a number of them. The cruise ship held about seventy-five people, but there are no ports in the islands where it could dock. So when we wanted to go for an excursion on shore, we off-loaded into rubber zodiac rafts, which carried us the short distances to the islands.

On shore, we saw different kinds of animals and birds. The animals and birds have no predators and therefore are not afraid of any people being nearby. If any creature was on a walkway, we just had to go around it with it looking up at us and thinking about these strange creatures being on their turf! Even the seals would lie on the wooden steps leading up from the raft docking area. One seal was relaxing all by itself on a small fishing boat—I guess waiting for someone to take it fishing! Large and small birds would be nesting right next to where we were and didn't move at all. That was so surprising to me.

Some of God's creations are unique to the islands, such as the blue-footed booby and red-footed booby (birds), the frigate with its red-puffed throat, the giant tortoises, many varieties of colorful iguanas, brilliant orange-red crabs, and myriads of smaller birds. Charles Darwin did some of his major studies there, and from those, he tried to prove his theories of the evolution of the species. Thankfully, we have the Word of God that gives us the real story of creation! I love nature and a Galapagos Islands visit had been on my bucket list for years. Now that was another box to check off. I have "been there, done that"!

been there, done that!

PERU

We flew from Ecuador down to Peru and landed at the Andes Mountains city of Cuzco with its elevation of 11,150 feet. Some missionaries met us in Cuzco and drove us a couple of hours down into the valley east of the mountains to their ministry town of Urubamba.

We did some touring around there and went out to see a rescue and rehabilitation center for the Andean condor, a massive bird from that region. Some can grow up to four feet tall, weigh around thirty pounds, and have a wingspan about ten feet wide! This spectacular bird is reportedly the largest raptor in the world. We stayed in a small "resort" in Urubamba and to get around in the town most of the time, we rode in little, three-wheeled, motorized taxis. There's not much room for comfort in those!

We were in a couple of the churches where Larry preached—in Spanish! His language training had worked, and he preached several times in Spanish in his last couple of weeks in Peru. I was impressed with how fast he had picked up the language. He can now preach and teach in French, Sango (African language in the Central African Republic), Spanish, and English!

MACHU PICCHU AND INCA RUINS

Urubamba was only a couple of hours train ride away from the fifteenth-century Inca citadel and temple ruins of Machu Picchu, located 8,000 feet high on a mountain ridge. The train ride itself was quite scenic as we passed through the lush valley and a few small villages. We stayed overnight in a charming town at the base of Machu Picchu, and the next day took a small bus up the narrow, winding road to the top of the mountain where all the ruins were located. Machu Picchu, also known as the "Lost City of the Incas", is probably the most familiar icon of the Inca civilization and is a UNESCO World Heritage Site, which declares it to be "an absolute masterpiece of architecture," and we soon learned why.

Homes and agricultural areas were built into the mountainside on terraces held up by manmade walls of handcut stone. These facilities were probably primarily for the support of the emperor and the temple on the site. Over the centuries, the area became completely overgrown and was "lost" until the late nineteenth century when it was finally uncovered and opened to tourism in the mid-twentieth century. Almost all of the stone terraces and buildings use the classical Inca architectural style of polished dry-stone walls of regular shapes in which the blocks of stone are cut to fit together tightly without mortar. A piece of paper could hardly fit between the polished surfaces. It was a striking example to me of the learned and mastered skills of the local people of that era and culture.

At the time of our visit, this construction technique was explained to us. For better clarity I have copied the following from Wikipedia: "Inca walls have many stabilizing features: doors and windows are trapezoidal, narrowing from bottom to top; corners usually are rounded; inside corners often incline slightly into the rooms, and outside corners were often tied together by "L"-shaped blocks; walls are offset slightly from row to row rather than rising straight from bottom to top."

I was flabbergasted to think of the extensive and practical knowledge of the architects in that era! Like the pyramids in Egypt, I wondered how these massive stones were moved into their proper places after being cut from the steep mountain sides. This visit to Machu Picchu was another unique, unbelievable, and really unimaginable story in my life.

MINISTRIES IN TRUJILLO AND LIMA

From Urubamba in the interior, I left Betty and the group and flew to Trujillo, a coastal town north of Lima, to visit with more of our BMM missionaries. There, I was privileged to preach a couple of times in their churches. Unlike my brother, my messages were given through a missionary interpreter. In Trujillo, several churches have been established, a seminary has taught God's Word for years, and a successful camp enhances the area's church ministries.

In that region are some historic temples, which were interesting because, as one temple was destroyed by the environment and covered over with wind-blown dirt, another temple was later built on top at the same site. One place had five vertical layers of temples of which only portions of each could be excavated! To completely uncover one temple would have eliminated the temple that had been constructed on top of it. The coastal region is barren, and the sand dunes are mammoth. However, the ingenuity of the people has provided huge irrigation systems to bring the area to life and increase the productivity of crops.

I had visited Trujillo by myself and left Betty with Larry and Sallie, who flew with her to the capital city of Lima. I reconnected with her there, and we stayed with other missionaries a few days while Larry and Sallie flew on to the US. (Dale and Debbie had already departed Peru and headed for home.) Again, the

been there, done that!

Christian work in Lima had matured through missionary efforts in the planting of a number of churches, establishing a boarding school for missionaries' children, building a camp, organizing and running a nine-month long internship program for American college students, and opening a radio ministry. I was particularly interested in the school since the early years of my life were in a missionary kids' boarding school. Peru is one of the larger and older mission fields where Baptist Mid-Missions missionaries serve, so as a council member of the mission, I was delighted to see how God has worked there over the years.

SAILING PENOBSCOT BAY, MAINE

One of our volunteer staff at Moody Keswick Conference Center (MKCC) in St. Petersburg was an optometrist from Rockland, Maine. He was a fifth-generation Maine native who had broken away from the careers of his previous four generations of ship captains. They had built the Snow Shipyards, and our friend lived just across the harbor from the shipyards. He knew the history of the eastern coastline from his study of his ancestors' diaries and records and told exciting stories of their adventures on the old wooden sailing ships. Several schooners were ported in Rockland, and the captain of the schooner *Heritage* invited him each summer to be the historian aboard their weekly five-day cruises. Our friend invited Betty and me to spend a week in the mid-1990s on the schooner with him. The week fit nicely between some of our regional meetings.

SCHOONER *HERITAGE*

Neither Betty nor I are real water lovers, but we accepted his invitation. We had not been on a sailing ship before, so this would be a new experience. The *Heritage* was a large, three-mast ship with sleeping quarters for about fifteen people.

The berths were in the lower deck and were very small with two bunks hugging the curved inside of the ship, an extremely small sink, a very low wattage lightbulb, and barely enough floor space for one person to turn around—let alone two! The ship had two heads (bathrooms) up the ladder on the upper deck. The shower could only be used after breakfast if you wanted warm water, which was heated by the cooking in the galley.

All hot food preparations were done on a wood-fired stove. Our food was restaurant quality and mostly made with fresh ingredients. The baked goods were prepared right on the ship! The only power on the schooner was a one-cylinder donkey engine that only was used to pull up the anchor and charge the batteries for a little bit of electricity for lights at night. A raft, hanging off the back of the *Heritage*, was used for getting to and from shore or for emergencies since it had an outboard engine. As passenger guests, we were expected to help crew the ship by doing such tasks as raising and furling the sails, cooking in the galley, swabbing the deck, and wiping the salt off of the wood rails. Each of us even got to pilot the schooner for a while. I also had the privilege to climb up the rope ladder to the crow's nest—seventy-five feet above the water!

It was a marvelous five days aboard the *Heritage* and gave us many memories as we sailed in Penobscot Bay's salty sea air, tucked into quiet anchorages, and gazed at the brilliant stars and gorgeous sunsets and sunrises. One evening, we sailed into Camden Bay for the Windjammer Schooner Festival. It was incredible to see all the schooners maneuver and then tightly park next to each other in that quaint Maine bay.

We spotted many kinds of wildlife, explored islands, had delicious lobster bakes, visited a wooden boat factory, and enjoyed evening story hours. As Florida folks, we bundled up in layers for the cool days and evenings and were somewhat shocked to see that several of the guests from New England only wore tank tops and shorts for most of the cruise. Some of them even dove in for a swim in the fifty-two-degree water. That would not be fun for me!

Overall, Betty and I were very happy that we had accepted the invitation to sail on the *Heritage!* Such a trip wasn't even on my bucket list, but it sure was an excellent experience. Now I can say about schooner sailing that I've "been there, done that"! We'd recommend it to anyone. What a diverse life God has given to me—from the air to the sea!

SEEING THE USA!

In 1986, our family was living in a Virginia suburb on the southwest side of Washington, DC, during my military assignments at the Pentagon. Betty and I felt that we wanted the kids to have an opportunity to see much of the continental USA while we were all together. We planned a general route and then asked Phil Jr., Debbie, and Todd what they would like to see on such a trip. Phil wanted to go to Rodeo Drive in Los Angeles, Debbie wanted to see the "Little House on the Prairie" in South Dakota, and nobody remembers what Todd wanted—maybe one of the national parks.

9,200 MILES IN TWENTY-ONE DAYS

Betty and I had many friends, relatives, former co-workers, and classmates across the country. We called some of them to see if we could schedule visits with them since we would be nearby in our travels. We had a full-size Chevrolet van in which I built a "double bed" in the back at the window level with room underneath for luggage and our ice chest. Betty made curtains for all the side and back windows, we installed a fan in the rear to help the air conditioning, and off we headed for a twenty-one-day, 9,200 mile trip. Four of us could spread out to sleep at the same time with one in the middle bench seat, one in the second bench seat, and two on the double bed in back while one was driving. It was really quite comfortable! Debbie had just gotten her driver's license, so she and I drove mostly during the days while Betty and Phil Jr. drove through the nights when we weren't staying with someone. I think we only spent two nights in a motel on the entire trip.

Besides almost running out of gas in Kansas, the van overheating coming up to Hoover Dam, and getting on some wrong roads in Idaho, our overall trip plan worked out well. We drove all night one time to get to the home of some Colorado friends with whom we planned to meet and do some sightseeing in the mountains. We arrived at their house at 8 a.m., and they said we should go to bed and get some rest. But we reminded them of our restful sleeping places in the van and went right on with the day's activities.

NEAR ARREST IN LAS VEGAS

As we were going to drive through Las Vegas about 11 p.m. one evening, we came over a hill and saw all the brightly colored lights of that city and many signs advertising steak dinners for $1.99. How could we pass a good meal up—even at that hour? I was not familiar with casinos at all, and to get to the dining room in the one where we chose to eat, we had to go through the gambling area.

To teach the kids that you rarely win at the slot machines, we gave each of them some small change to use. They each pulled up a chair to a machine and started putting in their nickels and dimes and were having fun with the occasional jingle of more coins falling out of the machines. After about twenty minutes, Betty and I heard someone behind us gruffly asking if those were our kids. "Yes, officer, why do you ask?" "If you don't get them out of here quickly, I will have to arrest you. Kids are not allowed in here." We had not seen any signs, but we quickly exited that area and went to enjoy our steaks! Like most people, we left the casino with less than when we entered. Thankfully, it was just a small amount of change! The casino must use some of their profit to cover the cheap cost of the steaks and bring customers in. But the steak dinners were great!

PATIENCE NEEDED AT CANADIAN BORDER

We experienced only one time on the trip when my patience wore real thin. We were entering Ontario, Canada, from Michigan and were stopped by an agent. He told our family to get out of our van and just stand over to the side. Then

been there, done that!

security people took everything out of the van—all of our luggage, stuff that was under seats and in all the little pockets, and thoroughly checked inside, outside, and underneath the vehicle. Then they said we could load back up and go. Thanks a lot!

I asked one of the officers what that was all about, and he politely answered that they find more weapons in vehicles licensed in Virginia (like ours was!) and Texas than from any other US states. Therefore, they stop most of those vehicles and check them out. I think we wasted almost two hours there at the border. For me, that was probably the worst time on our entire trip.

Other than that, we had a fantastic trip visiting many national parks, such as the Grand Canyon (in a private plane), the Black Hills, Yellowstone, and several others; dipping our feet in both the Pacific and Atlantic Oceans; seeing the mountains and the flat plains; passing through big cities and ghost towns; being in the great redwood forest and the scorching barren deserts; seeing the devastating effects of the Mt. Saint Helens' eruption; riding the *Maid of the Mist* at Niagara Falls; and being with many friends and some relatives—even though the times were short! Betty and I had accomplished our purpose of letting the kids get a glimpse of the whole country—not every state but they had now been in every region. Later in life, they could go back and visit some of their favorite spots if they wanted. This was certainly a delightful time for us to be with our kids 24/7 and to see the marvels of our great nation defined in Irving Berlin's text: "from the mountains to the prairies, to the oceans white with foam". Indeed, with him my prayer is "God Bless America, land that I love".

GLIDER FLIGHT IN TENNESSEE

One of the items on my bucket list was to fly in a glider airplane. I was given a gift certificate one Christmas for a flight. I really didn't want to do the flight in Florida because I preferred to fly over some mountainous terrain for some interesting views and where we could pick up some nice, rising thermals in flight.

For months, we couldn't find a convenient flight. Betty and I were going to visit a granddaughter in college in Tennessee and found a glider company very near the mountains of eastern Tennessee, so I scheduled a flight while headed out from the college to a meeting in Georgia. Arriving at the small airport, I was told that the inclement weather would prevent me from flying. But the flight operations center said that the weather was supposed to be very clear the next week.

Looking at our schedule, we changed some plans and determined to go back to the airport in a few days.

When we went back, the weather was fantastic. In fact, the glider pilot said it was the best weather for flying all year! The takeoff from the airstrip was smooth as the tow plane picked up speed and the rushing air under our glider's wings pulled us off the grass runway. After circling a couple of times to get higher into the air, the glider pilot told me to pull the red handle, thus releasing us from the towing aircraft. We were now on our own—without any mechanical power! It was so quiet in that cockpit that we could hear birds outside (that amazed me!) and we followed a couple of them above the beautiful, lush-green forest below. The long, slender wings of the glider picked up some nice thermals and carried us higher and then left us to descend to find another. It really was exhilarating!

The pilot and I flew for about forty-five minutes over the countryside's hills and then headed back to the airstrip. The pilot was right on with his landing, running smoothly onto the grass until we were about to stop when he tipped the glider slightly to let a wing wheel touch the turf. We were down! Another item could be crossed off my bucket list! What a life experience this was for this missionary kid! I can say that I have "been there, done that" when asked if I had ever flown in a glider.

CHAPTER XIX

TOURS AND CRUISES

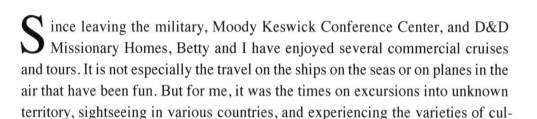

Since leaving the military, Moody Keswick Conference Center, and D&D Missionary Homes, Betty and I have enjoyed several commercial cruises and tours. It is not especially the travel on the ships on the seas or on planes in the air that have been fun. But for me, it was the times on excursions into unknown territory, sightseeing in various countries, and experiencing the varieties of cultures. Those are the things that provided the excitement.

EGYPT, ISRAEL, AND SWITZERLAND

Betty and I gave our kids a special trip in 2000. This was a big one. By now our kids were married, and we told them that we would love to take them and their spouses to Israel so that we could all be together in the Holy Land where Jesus had walked and taught. Our kids would have to make their own arrangements for travel to and from New York and for their children's care here in America, but we would pay the rest of the bill for the tour.

One of the speakers who had been at Moody Keswick Bible Conference with us was hosting a tour to Israel and Egypt, and the flight went through Switzerland. When coming back through Switzerland, our family would leave the organized tour and spend a few days in that beautiful, mountainous nation. Our kids quickly agreed to go, but Todd, being in the military at the time, said he would not be able to spend extra days in Switzerland on the way home.

been there, done that!

WONDERS OF THE ANCIENT WORLD

It was a wonderful trip! We first went to Egypt and saw the Sphinx and took a camel ride out to the Great Pyramids of Giza. The huge columns at the temple grounds in Luxor were startling and made us seem so small as we walked among them. Our guide gave us more information than we would ever be able to remember about the dynasties and tombs of King Tut and many others who ruled in that ancient land and in the Nile River valley. We took a tourist ride on the Nile in a *dhow*—an ancient, traditional style boat—used primarily for fishing and trade in that region. It all was very interesting but probably not one of my most favorite tourist spots. However, I was delighted that we were able to visit that land mentioned early in the biblical record and see those ancient and huge manmade objects as the sphinx, pyramids, temples, and some of the amazing burial spots of the former royalty of the historical Egypt.

Everywhere we went, there were people crowding around us to sell trinkets and goods of varying sorts. As soon as we stepped off the bus, they were there. When we came back to the bus, they were there, and as the bus was pulling away, they were still trying to sell us things through the windows. We just had to completely ignore them and learned to not even look at what they had. If you looked, they would hound you all the more to buy their goods.

WALKING WHERE CHRIST WALKED

Our next stop was in Israel, the land of the Bible! I had been in Israel with the military, but now this trip was different because it was more of a spiritual journey through Christ's life. We visited many places talked about in the Scriptures. We shared communion together in the garden near our Lord's tomb. We went to Masada, floated in the Dead Sea, stood in Peter's house in Capernaum, and climbed up a ruined wall of Jericho. Seated on Mt. Megiddo, we were reminded of the end times described in the Scriptures that the valley below us would be the location of the Battle of Armageddon in which our mighty God will be the victor! I was saddened to think of the many who will go into eternity in that battle without a personal relationship with Jesus Christ.

Some of our group chose to be baptized in the Jordan River near the supposed spot where John baptized Jesus. We were in the Upper Room in Jerusalem where the Last Supper was held. We stood on the Mount of Olives, went to the Wailing

Wall, solemnly prayed in the Garden of Gethsemane, and reflected on the future of the now-blocked Eastern Gate of Jerusalem. These have all taken on new meaning when I read about them in the New Testament. Walking the Via Dolorosa and on ancient streets where Jesus walked gives me great confidence regarding walking on the streets of gold in heaven where He is now and where I will be with Him for eternity. At some point, everyone should visit the Holy Land. It will add a new and historic dimension to your biblical reading and understanding. The travels in Israel were especially inspiring to me since we were there with our kids and their spouses. All of us know that we will walk in the glorious heaven throughout eternity. I pray that our grandkids and any additional family members in the future will also be in heaven with us.

JUNGFRAU IN THE ALPS

We spent just a few days in Switzerland on the way home, but that was enough time for us to enjoy that little country and its gorgeous and majestic mountains. Also, because at that time I had never been in Germany, we rented a large van, took a quick little side trip for about a half hour inside Germany, enjoyed some German food, and came right back out again!

We took a train ride up to Jungfrau in the Alps where it was extremely cold and windy. Once the train was in the mountains, all we could see were the walls of snow through which the train's tunnels were carved.

At one place where we stopped for a while in the mountains, Debbie and Betty rented some snow skis and went down a little bunny slope just to say they skied in the Alps. Phil Jr. and I were scheduled to paraglide off a mountain. I was very excited about the flight, but when we got up that morning of our flight, the fog was so thick that our paragliding was canceled. What a disappointment that was! We knew we would not have the chance to schedule another tandem jump in the Alps since we were leaving the country the next day.

Throughout Switzerland, the quietness of the valleys was broken by the multiple tones of bells worn by the cows on the hillsides. Supposedly, the bells soothe the cows and helps them produce more milk. (Someone in America was asked why the cows have bells and the response was "Because their horns don't work to let people know where they are!" I guess that could be a logical answer.) Our time in Switzerland helped us to relax and come down a little off of the tremendous

been there, done that!

emotional highs we had been on in Egypt and Israel. It also gave us time to reflect on God's wonderful goodness to us as a family.

CHINA AND HONG KONG

One of the amazing wonders of the world is the Great Wall of China, which was a major place to visit on my bucket list. Betty and I discovered that my alma mater, Wheaton College, was hosting a tour to China in 2010 and that the Great Wall was on the itinerary. By now, I was fully retired, and we decided to join the tour with other alumni. We didn't know if we would be familiar with any of the other alumni, but we all would have a common bond through the school. Much to my surprise, my Wheaton Academy high school homeroom and social science teacher from 1955–1956 was on the trip with us!

Our first stop was Shanghai, where we landed in the new airport, which very recently had been completed and opened. It was very modern and much in contrast to the surrounding countryside with all its rice fields and crude farm homes. As we sped by in our bus and headed for the city, the farmers were easily identified by their conical hats and of course, the water buffalo. The highway was very modern, and a high speed rail system connected the main city—with its millions of people—to the new airport. We were immediately impressed with the throngs of people crowding the streets and the amount of apartment-building construction throughout the city—and especially the bamboo scaffolding used in the building process on the outside of multi-storied structures. I don't think the bamboo would be approved for scaffolding here in the US!

BEIJING—PICKING UP A STONE

Beijing was our next destination. The Olympics had been held in Beijing in 2008, and the remnants of the Olympic Village were pointed out to us as we traveled around—including the now deteriorating Birds Nest stadium where most of the major Olympic events had been held. We were all excited to visit Tiananmen Square, Chairman Mao's palace, and of course, the Great Wall.

I had a snowbird friend in New York who collected little stones from different places, and I was determined to find some souvenir rocks for her from these historic places. However, everywhere we went, we were watched by Chinese soldiers. In Tiananmen Square, there were very specific instructions that we were not to step on the grass and not touch the trees. But I saw a little stone on the ground at the base of a tree and kept a watch on the soldiers so that when they weren't looking, I could quickly bend down and pick up that small rock—without stepping on the grass! It took quite a while for me to build up sufficient courage to try and get it. Finally I found an opportunity and got behind some people and picked up the little stone. Now I just hoped that I wasn't going to get frisked sometime on this tour because I wasn't sure how I could explain this inch-sized "weapon" that I was carrying.

THE GREAT WALL

The Great Wall is truly great! I can't imagine building it with manual labor in those days. It has to be one of the greatest engineering feats ever completed! It is wide and certainly did its job of keeping the hordes of the north from entering China. The guard towers (spaced every so often) ensure that no portion of the wall could be attacked by an unseen enemy. We spent a couple of hours on the wall and walked possibly 500 yards on it—which is but a minute fraction of its 13,171 miles in length! In years past, I could never have dreamed of being on that wall, but time has a way of changing things. And yes, I did pick up a small rock from there also to add to my friend's collection. I really hoped that we wouldn't have to go through some security system since I had two "weapons" now!

SUNDAY MORNING SERVICE CROWD

In Beijing, we were hosted by a Christian ministry which teaches English in several public universities in China and Mongolia. Interestingly, this ministry was given permission to build its China headquarters on a secular university campus. We were happy to share some time with the believers at that location. It seemed to me that most of the staff members were from the United States.

We were in Beijing on a Sunday morning and went to worship in a large church. We were scheduled to be in the 8:30 a.m. service and arrived about fifteen minutes before the service time. As a group, we were escorted into a specific area of a courtyard where many other folk were also waiting to get in the church building. I perceived that most of the people were not tourists but were there for regular worship. When I asked why everyone was crowded there outside, I was told that another service was already going on (before 8:30 a.m.!) and that we were in this area to be out of the way when that service ended and those people exited the church building. Sure enough, the doors opened in one part of the church and the worshippers poured out. I was thankful that we were out of their way! Immediately, those of us who were waiting started pushing through another door to take our seats inside. It was like a big one-way circle with no one blocking the movement of others.

Our Wheaton group was seated together, and each of us was handed a set of earphones to hear the translation of those on the platform. It was different to see their lips move as they spoke in Chinese and to hear a monotone, non-expressive voice speaking in English through our headsets. The service was very traditional in style. They had a choir, which sang in Chinese an anthem which I knew in English! Most of the hymn tunes were also familiar, so I could sing along in English as the congregation sang in Chinese.

The message was an excellent exposition from God's Word. However, because of tight restrictions against proselytizing, the invitation was merely a statement saying the office was open during the week if anyone wanted counsel. That was disappointing to me after such a good service and practical message, but I understood the reason.

As at the earlier service, all of us who had just been in that worship time exited out the front of the building while another group was coming in the back. I'm not sure how many services were held that morning, but I was really impressed with the numbers of people being ministered to in Beijing, the capital city of China, on a Sunday morning. I realize that this was a "recognized and authorized" church, but the Word of God was proclaimed there that day, and I thank the Lord for that.

TERRACOTTA ARMY

From Beijing, we flew to Xian to see the terracotta army, first discovered while a farmer was digging a well in 1974. This is a collection of clay sculptures depicting the armies of the first emperor of China. It is a form of funerary art buried with the emperor in 210–209 BC with the purpose of protecting the royalty in his afterlife. The terracotta, life-sized soldiers and horses in Xian remain in their original positions facing east, the direction from which the emperor's enemies would come. The military's clay soldiers and equipment were placed in big pits with protective wooden beams and dirt overhead. Over the years, the wood deteriorated and collapsed, thus breaking many of the sculptures. Carefully, many of the pieces of the figures were matched and put back together by skilled artisans. Work continues to dig out more of the warriors and other sculptures from several burial pits in the area.

Hidden for hundreds of years, archeologists have dug in three primary areas, and to this date have found an estimated 8,000 terracotta soldiers, 500 horses, and numerous formerly wooden chariots. All were life-sized and many are in battle formation with their armor and actual weapons—although many of those original weapons have been looted. What were the weapons in the emperor's army? Almost 40,000 weapons, such as crossbows, arrowheads, swords, and spears have been unearthed. Most of these are made of bronze or iron in contrast to the clay soldiers and horses. Over the years in the burial pits, most of the weapons—that have been found with the clay soldiers—have deteriorated but some have been recovered and are protected in a local museum.

The particular characteristics of the human-sculptured warriors are outstanding with uniqueness in facial expressions, clothing, hairstyle, and size. The archeological digging (in addition to the original artists' work) had to be meticulous to protect all those details. We were delighted that this historic UNESCO World Heritage Site was on our tour. The terracotta army can be viewed on the internet.

GEOLOGICAL KARSTS OF SOUTH CHINA

In Guilin in South China, we were astonished on a boat tour at the size of the towering karsts rising out of the river and the neighboring precipitous cliffs. These geologic formations are mostly eroded limestone rocks with toothy peaks and are often pock-marked by deep caves. There are karsts in other parts of the world, but these in China are unusually big and uniquely interesting in a beautiful, naturally-verdant landscape. The tropical climate produced a monsoon forest–type of environment, and the mists rising between the karsts and trees gave the area a mystical feeling as we glided along in a boat on the still water. This entire region is also recognized as a UNESCO World Heritage Site and is a wonderful example of all the unusual characteristics of land formations found in God's creation.

been there, done that!

TROLLEYS AND BUSES IN HONG KONG

This overseas tour ended in the busy city of Hong Kong. Some of our missionary friends (whom we had met at D&D Missionary Homes) showed Betty and me around the city with its defined and separate market places for flowers, leather goods, jewelry, foods, and financial districts. Their church was on the ninth floor of a big office building in the city. Naturally in that densely populated city, there was no parking for a congregation, so almost all of the people go to church on public transportation.

Riding the crowded trolleys and buses was quite the experience as people respectfully pushed and shoved to get into the doors and then pushed and shoved again to get out! One evening, we watched a gigantic light show projected on the high-rise apartments and commercial buildings across the water from our hotel. The show was almost magical. I am sure that it took a lot of computer coordination to make such an effective, wide-display of lights covering many of the waterside structures. This Asian trip gave me a different perspective of this great globe and its diversity.

CRUISING THE MEDITERRANEAN

Some of our good snowbird friends from Tennessee had been volunteers at our ministries with Moody Keswick Conference Center and then they followed us to D&D Missionary Homes. B and B had become my "go to" people when I wanted to discuss something in confidence to get alternate opinions or advice, and I really appreciated their input. They invited Betty and me to join them on a cruise in the Mediterranean, which was being planned by their church.

The potential dates of the cruise were critical to us because I had already committed to be in my brother Dale's wedding in the Dallas, Texas, area around the same time. The timing for the tour worked out just right so that we could be at the wedding, hustle back to Florida, repack our bags, and drive to Tennessee. We arrived just in time to go with their tour group to Atlanta for our flight to Rome. We would get on a Celebrity cruise ship there.

Unbeknownst to us was the unusual scheduling of all this. After Dale's wedding, he and Debbie had planned their honeymoon on a cruise from Spain to Rome. Although we didn't see them or know they were on their honeymoon on a ship in the area, we learned later that our ships were berthed next to each other in the same Italian port! Wouldn't that have made a story if we had ended up seeing them by chance in the Vatican or at the famous and stunning Trevi Fountain in Rome?

STARTING IN ROME

We had a wonderful cruise with B and B and their church friends. Seeing the sights of historic Rome, going into the prison where supposedly the apostle Paul had been held, viewing the gorgeous ceiling of the Sistine Chapel, seeing the beautiful Trevi Fountain, touring the Coliseum (picking up a stone there!) and the Pantheon, then heading out on the water toward Greece and Turkey were all very exciting parts of our tour. It is hard to describe the beauty and diverse architecture in the ancient city of Rome that has had such an important part in the history of the world.

BIBLICAL PLACES—MARS HILL AND EPHESUS

We stopped in Sicily and some of the Greek islands and sailed to Athens. There we climbed up Mars Hill where Paul had preached to the people after he saw a marker saying "To the Unknown God". Like Paul, we know who that God is! At Mars Hill, we could easily see the Parthenon on the Acropolis and then traveled there to that massive temple to the goddess, Athena, which dominates the city. Sometimes it is hard for me to grasp the age of some of the things we saw. This temple was built in the fifth century BC and is still a magnificent structure. Walking between its columns—like in Luxor, Egypt—made me feel so very small and insignificant. Regardless of how small we may seem here on the earth, in God's eyes we are very significant—so much so that He gave His Son to die for us so that we could have eternal life with Him. What did Athena do for anyone?

Hiking over the many ruins in Ephesus in Turkey taught me about the advanced culture of the days when the apostle Paul ministered there in biblical times. The flush system must have been very efficient in the large toilet rooms, which certainly offered no privacy. The huge Library of Celsus helped in the education of the young and old, and the giant amphitheater provided the forum for philosophical discussions and the platform for wonderful plays.

On the way back to Rome, we toured some of the Greek islands such as Santorini—famed for its white buildings and blue roofs—before going to the

been there, done that!

stunning and charming Amalfi coast of Italy. Then we viewed the remains of the powerful, destructive power of the volcano at what had been the thriving city of Pompeii. I was glad to see this part of the world that is so dominant in history.

SCANDINAVIA AND RUSSIA

Betty's grandmother came to America from Denmark in 1906 to be with her future husband who had previously immigrated to Chicago to get established as a carpenter and furniture-maker. Before her coming, he told her that if she wanted to see another part of the US before joining him that she should do that upon arrival in America, so she and her sister decided to visit San Francisco.

Much to her surprise as a new foreigner in the USA, the great San Francisco earthquake of 1906 opened the ground across the street from her. The odd thing about this is that we never talked with her about her impressions of the earthquake or how she got out of there—since she spoke very little English. I can hardly imagine what must have been her intense frustration trying to figure out how to leave that devastation and then travel to Chicago with that earthquake on her mind. Did she really want to stay in America after experiencing that disastrous event on the West Coast?

Why do I mention this? We had often said that we wanted to visit Denmark where Betty's maternal side came from. Betty still had a few direct, but distant relatives there, and we thought that maybe we could connect with them to show us around the old homestead and town. We were again invited to go with the church in Tennessee on a cruise to Scandinavia and Russia, which was leaving from Denmark. In planning for that, we emailed one of Betty's relatives in Denmark to try to arrange a time when we could visit them in advance of or following the cruise. We received no response until several weeks later when a friend of her relative wrote us a note saying that the family member had passed away just before our email was sent. So, we did not do the ground tour in Denmark like we had desired. What a bummer!

LOST BAGGAGE

Our flight from the United States to Denmark was delayed a few hours by bad weather. When we finally arrived, the guide from the ship met us in Copenhagen and tried to rush us through the airport's system. Somehow our bags had already arrived and were in a caged storage area in the airport. We were directed to go and try to find our bags. Most were found—except for the luggage belonging to Betty and also that of our tour director's wife. Lost baggage forms were quickly filled out while our ship's guide was frantically trying to get us to the ship so that it could depart the port on time.

We did make it to the ship, which pulled up the ramps as soon as we were on board. However, we were minus those two bags. Women do not like to travel without their packed belongings! Thankfully, Betty's carryon luggage had most of her necessities and she was invited to go to the ship's clothing store to get some new and warm clothes for the next day's trip in Norway. I guess you could say that was an advantage to having her bags lost! When we arrived back at the ship the next day after our excursion in Norway in time for the evening dinner, Betty's bag was in our room. The tour director's wife's suitcase was never located until we arrived back in Denmark at the end of our twelve-day tour.

Our trip in 2015 took us to Denmark, Norway, Sweden, Germany, Estonia, Russia, and Finland. Each place had its own unique features. Norway is known for its fjords, so we left our ship and got on a smaller one to tour a fjord. It was an excellent example of what I always envisioned a fjord to be. We also visited a maritime museum and learned of the unsuccessful efforts of a captain and his crew to reach the North Pole. A short excursion to some botanical gardens demonstrated the beauty of that rugged Scandinavian nation.

In Germany, we visited a World War II concentration camp before touring Berlin. The camp tour was so depressing as we listened to the stories of some of the prisoners and saw their horrible living conditions and the ghastly gas chambers. In Berlin, we stood on the spot near the Brandenburg Gate where President Reagan said: "Mr. Gorbachev, Tear Down This Wall"! The world is glad that Berlin is a united city again. There are only small sections of the wall left standing as a historic symbol of the past.

DISTURBED BY GAY PRIDE FLAG

I was terribly disturbed to see the gay pride flag flying on the outside of our US Embassy which faces the famous, eighteenth-century Brandenburg Gate in Berlin. We had gone through the gate and come back to the west side when I spotted that flag. I was very upset that it was right there next to our US flag.

been there, done that!

Going to the opposite side of the embassy as part of our city tour, I saw a huge gay pride flag hanging inside the big window of our US Embassy. A smaller US flag was flying from a pole over the embassy doorway. I couldn't hold it any longer. I went to the US Marine standing guard outside the embassy entrance and said: "I am a retired US Army soldier who fought for the American flag and not that big one hanging inside. Why is that rainbow colored flag there?" Hesitatingly, he replied: "I cannot comment except that the President [Obama] ordered it." The embassy is supposed to be representative of our nation, and that gay pride flag certainly did not represent the majority of our US citizens. Those two sightings of that flag at the front and back of our embassy pretty much ruined the rest of my day.

We had to get on a train at a specified time to head back from Berlin to our ship's port. All of our excursion group was there and waiting for departure. However, a couple of ladies from our ship (but not with our church tour group) stepped off to get some fresh air while waiting for the train to leave. They were only going to be off a few minutes, so they left their purses with another lady. I don't know the whole story, but the doors closed, we were off, and they were not on the train with us. Can you imagine being in that situation? I never did see those ladies to ask them how they managed to leave Berlin without their passports, credit cards, or cash. I suppose the ship worked it out for them somehow. To make a long story short, they reconnected with our cruise at the next port in Estonia. In addition to walking the narrow streets of that small nation, we visited a national maritime museum, which was very interesting.

ARCHITECTURAL BEAUTY IN RUSSIA

St. Petersburg was our primary city to visit in Russia. Stories about the czars were abundant, and the glories of those days were evident everywhere. We were in churches of every type, including the renowned Church of the Savior of Spilled Blood with its gorgeous, richly decorated, tiled, onion-shaped domes. The church's diverse architecture and internal, brightly-colored mosaics are breathtaking. The Peterhof Palace with all of its gold statues, manicured gardens, and dancing fountains was an impressive site, and the huge Hermitage museum was an exclusive attraction. For relaxation, we had a delightful night at an exquisite Russian ballet. For me, our time in St. Petersburg was a highlight of this entire cruise trip. I found it hard to believe that I was actually in Russia, a long-time, military opponent of our nation. In my military education and training, I had studied Russian military organization and strategies and had practiced tactics against its operations in case we would ever have to go to war against Russia. Now I was in its homeland!

FINLAND AND SWEDEN

In our short stay in Helsinki, Finland, we had a nice, relaxing bus tour and visited a nearby medieval town with its well-preserved buildings and fifteenth-century cathedral. In that little town, we visited a horse farm where we had a typical Finnish meal served by the family members in their century-old manor. Back in Helsinki, we went to the Rock Church where the interior was excavated directly out of solid rock. It is bathed in natural light coming through a skylight surrounding the center copper dome. The church is used frequently as a concert venue due to its excellent, acoustical-quality created by the rough, virtually unworked interior rock surfaces. The church's impressive organ has forty-three stops and over 3,000 pipes! I would have loved to hear a full concert there, but none was scheduled for the time we were in the church.

Although Stockholm, Sweden, is on the water, the cruise ship port is quite a distance away. Once on shore, we had a scenic bus ride to the city and a very informative tour at the *VASA* Maritime Museum. This museum displays the only— almost fully-intact—seventeenth-century ship that has ever been salvaged. The sixty-four-gun warship, *VASA,* sank on her maiden voyage in 1628 when she was less than a mile from shore. It was top heavy, and a slight breeze toppled it into the sea. The mighty warship was salvaged in 1961 (after 333 years on the sea bed!) and is a primary tourist attraction for the city.

EXHILARATING SPEEDBOAT FROM STOCKHOLM

To this point on our Baltic tour, I had not really found any risky or physically challenging activities until I saw a brochure advertising a RIB (rigid inflatable boat) speedboat ride from Stockholm down through the Swedish Archipelago toward the Baltic Sea. The small boat held only six guests, but I could only find a couple of others who would go with me. At the boat, we donned waterproof suits, got on board, and the captain immediately jammed the throttle forward to at least fifty miles per hour (his words), but I think he was being very conservative and

been there, done that!

didn't want to scare us! We passed myriads of little islands, a grand fort designed to protect the capital from invading navies, quaint villages with pastel-colored homes, and small fishing towns. I am not a water lover, but I wanted to sense real speed on the water while flying by picturesque landscapes. I can't say I'd want to do it again but it was a "been there, done that" experience, going that fast on the water with that salty sea spray in my face. After Stockholm, we then cruised back to Denmark, where we departed for the US.

AUSTRALIA AND NEW ZEALAND

Several years ago, the alumni office of Wheaton College set a goal to conduct tours for alumni in different years to reach all seven continents. Up to 2016, they had yet to cover Australia, Africa, and Antarctica and had set their sights on those in succeeding years. We enjoyed traveling with Wheaton College for several reasons: it was my alma mater; the tour guests were of similar faith, though with a wide variety of backgrounds; we had devotions together every day; the size of the groups was generally only twenty or thirty people; and the tours were conducted in a very professional manner with top-notch leaders and accommodations.

When we saw a tour announced for Australia and New Zealand, Betty and I signed up immediately so that we could be included on the trip. Traveling on a plane in economy class is not the most comfortable when on such a long flight as we had to Australia but we survived. I don't have any problem sleeping on a plane—or anywhere!—so for me it was not so bad. I can get on a plane and be asleep before the entry door closes, wake up when we are at sufficient altitude so I can lean my seat back a little, and wake up again when the food cart comes by! So, basically I have not had a problem with jet lag, going either way. (One year, I crossed the Pacific Ocean and back three times and never had any jet lag issues.) I am so thankful for the gift of being able to sleep anywhere, anytime, and under most any circumstance as you will read in a later chapter.

PARAGLIDE FLIGHT MISSED AGAIN

Our initial stop in Sydney, Australia, was only to transfer flights and proceed on to New Zealand's South Island. We did a couple of bus tours there and were amazed at the numbers of sheep on the hillsides. We were in the country at the end of lambing season, and it was really interesting to see all the little white dots trailing the bigger white dots in the distant, massive green pastures. In that area, the government has also brought deer into pastures. Why? The vast numbers of deer are eating so much of the forest vegetation that it has become an environmental problem. To reduce the destruction of the wooded areas, many of the deer are herded into these large, high-fenced areas. One day, we did a boat tour into one of the major fjords on the southwest side of the island.

For a different type of activity, some in our group heard about an amusement park, so we went to see what it was all about. It had a fake snow hill for sledding and a bobsled track with all its sharp curves to speed through for a thrilling ride. I saw a 200-foot-long swing off the side of a cliff at the park and wanted to try it, so I went to schedule a ticket time. But in checking with our tour guide, we didn't have sufficient time left for me to swing before we had to leave. I was quite disappointed because I had never been on such a giant swing and wanted to try it. To replace that, a few of us arranged a time the next day to paraglide off a steep hill into the valley below. Again, my desire to paraglide was foiled as weather annulled the event. That made the sixth time that I had a paraglide scheduled but canceled—once in Switzerland, four times in Alaska, and now in New Zealand. I really would like to do that someday.

Traveling around, we came to a spot where people were bungee jumping from a high bridge. One of the young alumni in our group wanted to jump, so we stopped and waited for him do that. I would have also jumped there but it was a miserably cold and rainy day, and I just couldn't get myself to strip off some of my warm layers as was required to make the jump. It was not that important to me. I don't know if I will ever bungee jump in the future since I had serious back surgery in late 2018.

GLOWWORM CAVE

We flew to Auckland on the North Island of New Zealand and again did quite a bit of touring around. In one place, we went down into this big cave and got into a rowboat for a ride on an underground lake. The interesting aspect of this was that thousands of glowworms on the ceiling reflecting in the still water provided sufficient brightness for us to see things quite clearly! The atmosphere in this large grotto was one of serene ambience as we entered a galaxy of tiny living lights radiating their unmistakable luminescence in the subterranean world. To get to the lake, we did pass through some upper grottos which were like most caves

been there, done that!

with all the stalagmites and stalactites. One area was called the cathedral room and while there, our Wheaton group spontaneously started singing a superbly harmonized version of *Amazing Grace*. It was an "amazing" sound as quite a crowd gathered around in the dimly lit cave to hear the music echoing from the solid walls around us.

RUBBING NOSES WITH MAORI PEOPLE

The Maori people group in New Zealand has its own culture as we learned when we visited one of their villages. They invited us to a special welcoming ceremony (*pōwhiri*), but they needed a person to be the "chief" for all the tourists that day. I was chosen to interact with these Maori people! I was told how to respond to certain of their actions as I led our tourists down a walkway—while picking up designated palm branches—toward a theater-type room.

A *pōwhiri* is used to welcome guests onto a *marae*. (A *marae* is a communal and sacred meeting ground that provides everything from eating and sleeping space to religious and educational facilities.) We were treated to a wonderful program of traditional music, dances, and tribal sword fighting. Their costumes were outstanding, very colorful, and very fitting to the type of music and dance. At the end of the show, as the "chief" of our group, I was escorted on the stage to give our group's mutual thanks to the dancers and warriors. What was their tradition for this? The *hongi* is a traditional Maori greeting and recognition in New Zealand. To *hongi*, you press your nose and forehead together with the nose and forehead of the person you are greeting. I did a lot of *hongis* that day with the performers who had put on a great *pōwhiri*! We really enjoyed our entire time with the Maori folks.

TOUR OF HOBBITON

We traveled to the lush pastures of a working sheep farm in the heart of New Zealand's North Island for a tour of Hobbiton, as featured in *The Lord of the Rings* and *The Hobbit* trilogies. I had not seen the movies, so this was all new to me. After the filming, which occurred over several years of the trilogies, the movie set with its forty-four Hobbit Holes was refurbished and made into a permanent tourist attraction. I was pleasantly surprised at all the features and particulars of the homes and activities of these little people—from the small, doll-type clothes hanging on a line to the miniature wheelbarrow and garden tools. Live flowers were growing in the front yards of each "home," and the big fake tree at the top of the hill looks now exactly as it does in the movies. It hasn't grown a single leaf! I was really awestruck with the level of work and attention to the tiniest of details that went into making these movies such a success.

JUMP FROM AUCKLAND'S SKY TOWER

Auckland, New Zealand, has the tallest tower in the southern hemisphere. The top of the antenna is 1,075 feet above the ground. At the six hundred and thirty feet level is a rotating restaurant with an open walkway on the outside completely surrounding the dining and tourist area. As we were eating lunch there, we slowly got to look out over the entire city as the restaurant revolved. I was particularly interested in the people on that outdoors walkway, who were tethered and had a guide with them. As we leisurely ate and circled above Auckland, I noticed that at one point, the walkway had an extension which jutted out over space, and an individual was getting ready to leap. He then jumped! We couldn't see where he landed, but I checked it out further and saw a big X on a trampoline far below.

At that point, I told Betty that I was going to go to the ground level of the tower and get a ticket so I could jump. I came back up to the restaurant to tell Betty my scheduled time, and everybody was abuzz about my potential jump. Some had asked Betty if she was going to let me do it to which she casually replied: "I expected him to jump as soon as he saw that little platform out there!" She reminded people that I had parachuted when I was in the Army.

I went back down to the tower base to get ready for the jump. I had to put everything out of my pockets and my watch in a lock box and then got into a lightweight coverall suit. An elevator then took me up to the jumping level with a special exit to the outside. In the meantime, Betty and our group went down to ground level where she was allowed to be at the landing trampoline to take pictures.

Up top at about six hundred and thirty feet, I walked out on that open grate walkway and went to the jump platform where they weighed me and fastened me up to a cable on a big winch. The winch was really big, having to hold the long steel cable. My jump would be a 100 percent freefall, but the winch and cable were to slow my descent about ten feet above the trampoline at the bottom. The height of this jump was just a little more than half of the height for military parachuting from a plane, but the landing here would be a whole lot softer!

been there, done that!

I walked out to the edge of the small platform and really thought I would develop a fear since it had been about fifty-five years since I had last parachuted. However, I had an unusual calmness as I prepared to leave the platform. Two or three times I asked the assistant if she was ready for me to make the leap, and she said she had a couple of more things to check on my harness and cable hookup and verify my weight on the winch's computer. I was pleased with her extra precautions! Also, she put a GoPro camera on my wrist for me to take pictures on my way down.

Finally, she gave the "*Go*" and without any hesitation, I jumped and was free-falling at a rapid rate without any parachute to catch air and slow me down. In less than twelve seconds, I was on the trampoline at the bottom! That is traveling at more than fifty feet a second! It was so fast that, except for the very beginning of the jump, I forgot to even point the GoPro camera at my face to checkout my expressions on the way down! Betty did get some pictures, but from her placement, a picture of me at the top showed just a speck against the sky. When I landed, I was welcomed with a big cheer from our tour group.

My risky jump became the talk of the folks for some time after that. In thinking about it, the feeling must be something like the freefall in a bungee jump except this tower jump did not have the bounce at the end of a bungee rope, and it was a much longer freefall! I'd do it again anytime! It was an exciting experience! A tower jump had not been on my bucket list of things to do in life but I am so glad the opportunity came and that I did not hesitate to jump. I have "been there, done that"!

ZIP LINES OVER THE RAINFOREST

Moving on to Australia from New Zealand, I had two more great adventures—well, actually all of them were great, but zip lining over the rainforest and climbing on top of the girders of the Sydney Harbor Bridge were unexpected highlights. One day in the northeast section of the country, along with a few others from our group, I explored the rainforest canopy from the unique perspective of zip lines and tree platforms. I think we had about ten stations with the longest zip line between stations being more than one quarter mile. We "zipped" over deep, wide valleys and between towering, flowering, lush jungle trees, all the while enjoying breathtaking views through the canopy, down to cascading streams, and out to the Great Barrier Reef. I had done shorter zip lines before in fun parks and in the Army's Ranger School, but those were nowhere near as breathtaking as this jungle canopy tour in Australia!

Also, from the city of Cairns in northeast Australia, we took a large boat out to the Great Barrier Reef where we boarded smaller glass-bottom boats to observe the brightly colored fish and the live coral reef. I have often pondered how God could dream up the great variety of colors and shapes in His wonderful creation. But He is God, so He has that incredible ability!

Exploring has always been a favorite thing for me, and I took the opportunity while on a reef island to investigate all the nooks and crannies to find the great assortment of fauna and flora species. That entire northeast region of Australia with its mountains, dense tropical jungle, white-sandy beaches, and deep blue waters abounded with a vibrant and eclectic array of plants and animals. That was another great day for this nature lover.

been there, done that!

ULURU IN AUSTRALIA'S OUTBACK

Almost everyone has heard of the Outback—and I'm not referring to that great restaurant!—of Australia but relatively few have really sensed its immensity and its unique desert beauty. Our tour took us by a plane to the Red Center of the island continent. The Outback, seemingly miles from civilization, is the major attraction of that harsh environment. One unnamed Google internet writer explained it this way: "The Red Center is an extraordinary landscape of desert plains, weathered mountain ranges, rocky gorges, and some of the aboriginal people's most sacred sites, including Uluru."

Uluru, perhaps better known to most American people as Ayers Rock, is another UNESCO World Heritage Site. Uluru is the cultural and aboriginal name for this huge, weathered, rounded rock in the middle of the desert. It is a sacred site for the native people and is to be respected that way by visitors, as it is still used for certain ceremonial rituals of the local people group. In fact, in some sacred areas, photography is prohibited by local traditional law.

As one of Australia's most recognizable landmarks, it is one of the natural wonders of the world with its almost six-mile circumference and its 1,150-foot height rising over the surrounding flat landscape. We made a sunrise visit to Uluru to watch this famous rock glow with gradients of color from vivid and intense reds, greys, ochre, dark rust, burnished orange, and all colors in between as the sun hit the different materials in its layered sandstone composition and high iron content. It was an incredible sight!

On the opposite end of the spectrum, we were served a candlelight dinner under the stars at the base of Uluru. In a sunset reception preceding the dinner, the harsh and almost haunting base sounds of a digeridoo entertained us. That is a cylindrical, musical, wind instrument developed by the local aboriginal peoples out of naturally hollowed wood (often from a eucalyptus tree). The longer (four to ten feet) the instrument, the lower its key or pitch is. It is played by a person blowing into the tube with continuously vibrating lips to produce a sustained tone and drone sound. The musician must continually breathe in while he is blowing out using a special breathing technique. Following a delicious dinner, all lights were extinguished so that we could take in the majestic and magnificent starry sky. God's creation is absolutely spectacular!

WALKING ATOP SYDNEY HARBOR BRIDGE

Sydney was next on our Australian tour. We had a quiet boat tour in the harbor, passing the stunning architecture of the Sydney Opera House and then were escorted through its multiple practice and concert rooms even while practice was ongoing.

Our son, Phil Jr., was on a tour of Australia when he was in college as part of the soccer team's ministry. While there, he met a young man in one of the churches, and later that individual toured the US. He went to Cedarville College and visited Phil Jr. who, in turn, invited him to our house in Virginia. Because we had met him, we connected with him in Sydney and had supper together in a very enjoyable evening. The Lord has given us so many friends around this wonderful world!

For an exciting adventure, eight of us from our tour climbed on top of the overhead steel support beams of the Sydney Harbor Bridge. We had to get up at 3:30 a.m. to arrive at the bridge, meet our guide, and climb on the top of its steel girders to the peak so that we could be up there at sunrise. We were tethered to a rail as we pushed ourselves up one vertical step at a time in the morning's cool hours. The darkness broke as the beginning rays of the sun poked over the horizon and soon revealed a blaze of brilliant color reflecting off of clouds, the harbor, the Sydney Opera House, and other buildings!

been there, done that!

Looking down on the white wings of the Sydney Opera House, now with shades of pink reflecting off the clouds, was an astounding picture!

With that wonderful experience behind us, the USA beckoned us home. Betty and I both agree that this Australia/New Zealand trip was the best of all our trips up to that time—partly because of the beauty of God's nature which we saw, but also because of the great variety of things we did. And for me, the jump off the Sky Tower in Auckland, zip lining over the rainforest canopy, the visit to the unusual Uluru, and the climb on top of the Sydney Harbor Bridge made it even better!

CARIBBEAN REGION

Betty and I have been on two cruises in the Caribbean area. One was with Cedarville (Ohio) University as parents of alumni, and the other was with our friends' church in Tennessee. Both of the cruises included some long days at sea, which is not my favorite part of commercial cruising. My preference is the variety of excursions offered in the countries we visit. Although the overall appearance of the people, living conditions, religion, their clothing and foods in the Caribbean nations are basically the same, the countries each have unique aspects to them. On these cruises we visited Aruba, Colombia, Panama, Costa Rica, Honduras, Belize, Mexico, and Jamaica.

MAYAN CULTURE RUINS

Mayan cultural ruins are scattered throughout the Central American and Mexican regions. We had long hours on buses to reach some of the ruins. As for the Giza Pyramids in Egypt and the Great Wall of China, I was again challenged to think of the labor that must have been required to build those massive structures and that all of this was done without the architectural tools, cranes, and heavy lift equipment we have today! Archeologists have uncovered many of the ruins and estimate that others are yet to be discovered in the jungled terrain in the different countries.

Most of the sites we visited were temple ruins used in cultural ceremonial activities. Climbing up some of the ruins, I saw altars used for sacrificing both animals and humans to their gods for different reasons. The Mayan civilization thrived for several hundred years and mysteriously and rather suddenly disappeared, leaving our archeologists and historical researchers with many unanswered questions. In some ways, it was a very advanced civilization as evidenced by the solar alignment of many of their pyramids and temples.

ENGINEERING FEATURE IN PANAMA

I had been to Panama before while in the military, and from the side of one of the mammoth locks in the Panama Canal, I had watched ships being raised and lowered while getting from one water level to another. But on this trip with the Tennessee church in 2018, we were on our cruise ship as we headed through a lock into Gatun Lake. Our time for going through the lock was early morning, so we were up with the sun to watch the big lock gates open and close in front and behind us. It gave me a whole new perspective of the locks, as we were on the water as it raised or lowered rather than watching the action from the side of the locks. We were in one of the recently constructed locks, which have been added to accommodate the larger ships being used today for international shipping.

Our ship dropped anchor in Gatun Lake, and we got into a small boat to go ashore. Here we explored the interior of Panama and visited a small, local Indian village of about ten small huts and their thatched roof "community center". Demonstrations showed us how the people survive in the jungle—how they forage for food, plant small gardens, make decorative craft items, and live in very crude structures above their goats and chickens. The rural feel sort of took me back to my days in Africa! We spent several hours on the land tour while our ship turned around and went back out to the sea where we later caught up with it and reboarded for the next segment of our cruise.

PORT BUILDING IN COSTA RICA

Costa Rica is building a huge port for international shipping. I was really surprised at the vast number of trucks and shipping containers in that small country! With that many trucks, a side industry for maintenance is required, and there are little repair shops everywhere! Some of the containers sitting in the port storage areas were refrigerated to temporarily hold bananas being shipped out to many countries of the world. We did go through a plantation where they explained how bananas are grown and harvested. We also rode into the interior of the rainforest

been there, done that!

and took a cable car tour over the lush forest, looking down on the colorful birds and flowering trees in the area.

In Aruba, I rode in an open jeep around much of the island, going up and over sand dunes, visiting some remote lighthouses, an old defense fortress, and quaint small towns along the way. It certainly is not a very big island but has many interesting views.

The port in Jamaica was quite a distance from a "touristy" spot where you could climb some waterfalls. It was interesting to watch people scramble up various levels of the low-sloping falls. They were guided as to where to place their feet and where to grab certain rocks along the way. To keep from getting all wet, I stayed on the side path going from the top to the bottom of the falls and back up where our bus was waiting for us. We also had to have some of the tasty Jamaican jerk chicken while on that island!

THAILAND

During my first Vietnam tour of duty, soldiers were encouraged to take a one week R&R (Rest and Recuperation) trip to get away from the physical and emotional ravages of that horrible war. Many took their R&R to Australia, Hong Kong, Japan, Hawaii, or other such exotic places, but in 1966, I chose to go to Thailand. I don't know why there particularly, although the country did intrigue me. I met up with another lieutenant who also was not interested in the nightlife or bars of Bangkok. Together, we wanted to see and experience the country and its culture.

We connected with a guide who had a 1956 Chevrolet for transportation. His unlikely name—for a conservative guy like me—was Mr. Porn! He really took good care of us and his car. Every time we would stop somewhere, he would get out a feather duster and rag and shine up the car.

He took us on a small boat into Bangkok's famous floating market. How many vendors in their canoes can you get in almost the same place on the water? It seemed like there were hundreds, all crowded together and yet moving from place to place around each other. Mr. Porn gave us some great suggestions for things to see and do, rather than us just trying to find brochures of interesting activities in the country.

TEMPLES AND BUDDHAS EVERYWHERE

Mr. Porn drove us to a huge temple about an hour south of Bangkok. This is the oldest Buddhist structure in Thailand and the largest in the world, with its 750-foot diameter base and almost 400-foot height. Its size and orange roof made it visible from far away.

Back in Bangkok, the royal boats used by the king and queen for ceremonial activities were remarkable with their gold covering and intricate designs incorporating dragon themes. We saw more Buddhas and Buddha idols than I care to remember. They included the mammoth, gold-plated reclining Buddha (151-foot long!), a solid gold Buddha (9.8-foot tall and weighs 5.5 tons), the emerald Buddha (located on the grounds of the Grand Palace. Its clothes are changed for each season), a large sitting Buddha (148-foot tall and 83.5-foot wide made of concrete and covered with Burmese white marble), black and other colored Buddhas (each color with its own meaning), plus hundreds of others. It was somewhat depressing for me to think of all the wasted money given in alms to the monks to try and gain favor from a mineral, stone, or wooden impersonal god.

Of all the many temples we visited, the Wat Arun Ratchawararam Ratchawararamahawihan (commonly known as the Temple of the Dawn) in Bangkok is certainly the most memorable! The temple derives its name from the Hindu god Aruna, often personified as the radiations of the rising sun. It was first completed before 1656 (but recently renovated in 2017). It is a stunning landmark, not only because of its riverside location but also because its design is so different from most other temples. Instead of the normal dome look, this one had several prangs (spires).

been there, done that!

Used by permission.
Wat Arun, 27 October, 2017.jpg: Attribution-ShareAlike 4.0 International (CC BY-SA 4.0)

Its imposing primary spire reaches to 230 feet, and its outside is artfully decorated with seashells, pieces of colored glass, and Chinese porcelain placed in intricate patterns. It is gorgeous and sparkles in the sunlight as a magnificent piece of identifying architecture for the city. The Chinese porcelain pieces were from broken pottery which the Chinese ships used as ballast, and when they came to Thailand, the ballast was thrown into the bay to allow the ships to get closer to shore. Additional spires are on the four corners of the property and huge demon-like figures guard the entrance. This was an amazing and informative temple visit.

Mr. Porn also took us to the ancient capital of Thailand, which over the centuries had become mostly overgrown by roots, vines, and trees—much like Angkor Wat in Cambodia. However, at this site, which is well guarded, is a large, gold Buddha, which in times past had been covered with caked mud to hide it from neighboring warriors. The story of it was quite remarkable. The ancient kingdom of Ayutthaya is displayed in Buddhist temples, monasteries, and ancient statues of monumental dimensions. Dating back to 1350, the city has experienced a turbulent history, rich in episodes of glory and strife. Now this historical city is a UNESCO World Heritage site,

USING TOES TO SWING HAMMOCKS

While we were out on a driving tour in the countryside, Mr. Porn pulled in to a country farmer's house in the middle of a rice paddy to introduce us to a typical Thai family. The man was in the field, and the woman of the house was sitting on the floor knitting.

Fastened to both big toes of her feet were strings leading to two small, ceiling-hung hammocks holding young children. She was multi-tasking—swinging the kids by moving her feet back and forth while doing her knitting! Did you ever see a baby hammock hanging from the ceiling in America? Just put hooks in the ceiling throughout the house and take the baby hammock or swing with you—and keep your toes free so you can swing the toddlers while you do other things!

The house was spotless with shiny teak floors and everything in place. We asked Mr. Porn if this family was a relative and his reply was: "No, I don't know them well, but I knew they would show you the genuine hospitality of our Thai people without them knowing of our coming." We would rarely do that in America! The lady then offered to serve us a simple, excellent lunch of rice and some soup. That demonstrated to me the graciousness and inner beauty of the common person in Thailand. (I did not see Mr. Porn pay the lady anything for our visit but I am sure that somehow there must have been remuneration for her kindness to us.)

INTERESTING EVENING SHOWS

One evening, we went to an outdoor arena to watch the sport of Thai boxing. It is far more than boxing! It is kicking, tripping, and some wrestling all mixed together. Out of the ten boxing matches that evening, all but three ended in knockouts! I sure wouldn't want to be in the ring with those fighters.

We were awed by going to a theater another night for a program, demonstrating the smooth, graceful, and very artistic Thai dancers. Their long, upturned fingernails were emphasized by their imaginative movements and elegant, fluid dances. Their bright costumes added to our pleasure.

been there, done that!

On the same stage that evening, Thai swordfighters came out to exhibit their skills. A wire net was pulled down between the stage and the audience so that if a sword broke, no pieces would fly out and injure an onlooker. The sharp, clashing sounds of iron on iron told us that this was not just a phony show.

We trusted Mr. Porn's recommendations on buying jewelry and other souvenirs for our families back home. I bought some nice things for Betty and other family members. Some very attractive items were called "Nielloware," which is a specialized art, combining genuine silver and a black metal into intricate oriental designs. I bought a beautiful bracelet and necklace for Betty, a brass punch set, and a dessert cutlery set—all with the Nielloware artistry in the brass handles of the spoons, forks, and knives. For other family members, I bought jewelry with embedded, black star sapphires! These were some beautiful items!

Mr. Porn had been a great guide, and upon our departure he said that he really enjoyed being with us because he didn't have to take us to bars and stay with us into the wee hours of the morning at those places. I guess that most of his foreign clients were bar-hoppers and didn't get to see all the things he took us to visit. I think I got a good glimpse of the people and the natural culture of Thailand on my R&R. That was a very enjoyable week before I had to head back to my unit in Vietnam.

THE DANUBE RIVER AND CZECH REPUBLIC

Since Betty and I were already in Europe for a medical mission trip in Romania, we decided to take time for a cruise on the Danube River. After we had completed our ministry in Romania, we spent a few days with missionary friends in Budapest, Hungary. They showed us around that bustling city and took us to an interesting place where a section of the original Roman road had been preserved—and still used! It was hard for me to believe that it still existed and hadn't been covered over or torn up. While there, I enjoyed preaching to and meeting some of the people from the church our missionary friends served in near Budapest. We then boarded a Danube River cruise ship headed north to Nuremburg in Germany.

RIVER CRUISING IS DIFFERENT

Cruising on a riverboat is so much different from a large, ocean-going vessel. There were only about 100 people on board with us. The dining wasn't as varied but very enjoyable as we ate fresh foods from the local markets every day. The riverboat was only a couple of levels high so it could get under the bridges and excursions were part of the cruise price. There were no casinos on board—that was not a disappointment to us! Entertainment was provided by folks who came on the boat in one port and got off at the next stop. We really enjoyed the intimacy of the smaller ship and highly recommend riverboat cruising.

We stopped in the Danube's riverside towns and visited quaint little shops and historic places. We were supposed to transit through eleven locks on the river. However, when we arrived at a lock near Germany, we were told that the operators of the locks had gone on strike and that we would not be able to continue our journey on the riverboat. Quick reaction by the cruise company got us on a bus to take us on to Nuremburg so that we wouldn't lose time and miss other transportation connections from there, since that was our boat's final destination. Betty and I made some arrangements so that when we arrived in Nuremburg, we were met by Baptist Mid-Missions missionary friends who gave us a wonderful walking tour of the city.

OLDEST WORKING ASTRONOMICAL CLOCK

In Nuremburg we got on a bus and took a side trip over to Prague in the Czech Republic. We thought we might like to try a Segway tour through the old town. But after trying the little two-wheelers and hearing of their expense, we decided to stay on our own two feet where we had more flexibility and didn't have to worry about the security of the Segway transportation machine if we wanted to stop and do some exploring.

The town square is home to the world's third-oldest astronomical clock—first installed in 1410—and it is reported to be the oldest clock of this type still operating. The clock tells the time, provides the date, and shows astronomical and zodiacal information. Best of all, it provides some theater on the hour when a mechanical procession of the twelve biblical apostles passes by windows in the clock's tower. Many other figurines on the clock have special symbolism. For example: a rooster, embodying life, crows at the end of the show to indicate a new hour has just begun. Interestingly, the rooster's crowing sound is made by bellows closing the windows where the life-size apostles' figures have just been.

been there, done that!

JOHN HUS'S BETHLEHEM CHAPEL

John Hus (1372–1415) was a Czech theologian and philosopher who became a church reformer preceding Martin Luther, John Calvin, and Huldrych Zwingli and their influence on Christianity in Europe. Hus was later martyred for preaching against some false doctrines of the Catholic church. He was heard praying and singing Psalms as he was burning at the stake.

In the cramped and narrow streets of Prague in the Czech Republic, we stumbled upon the Bethlehem Chapel where Hus had preached for many years. He was driven from there by the Catholic hierarchy and went to the countryside where he continued to preach and write on basic Christian beliefs to help educate the poorly trained and uninformed Catholic priests. The chapel is now a national cultural monument. It has been destroyed a couple of times over its long history but has been rebuilt in the same spot using the remains of the original walls. It is now used as a ceremonial hall for a university and venue for local events, such as a wedding reception that was being held even while we were there. I was humbled to be in this same chapel at which this great hero of the faith had ministered in spite of facing martyrdom.

UGANDA

Wheaton College planned another of their continent visits in 2019—this time to South Africa. We worked out our timing so that we could meet the tour group after spending a week in Uganda with our granddaughter, Katy, who was serving with Word of Life Fellowship International in Uganda. She was teaching in the International School, working in the children's ministry of the Fellowship Chapel, mentoring some of the Bible Institute's women students, and helping in the Local Church Support Ministries department. Her two-year internship was to end in a few months, and we wanted to visit her and encourage her in those last months in Uganda. The Word of Life property was between Uganda's two largest cities: Entebbe, where the international airport is located; and Kampala, the nation's capital city. The national language is English, so communication with the people was no problem for us, although we did have to get used to the Ugandan version of British English.

When I stepped off the plane in Entebbe, Uganda, my wife said that the first words out of my mouth were, "This smells just like the Africa I remember as a kid!" The appearance of the land, the rural feeling, and the market smells rapidly brought back many memories. We found a welcome, which felt almost royal, at the Word of Life campus.

VISIT WITH GRANDDAUGHTER IN UGANDA

Katy had prearranged some ministry opportunities for us in the chapel and Bible Institute, which we gladly accepted.

She also set us up for tours to the source of the Nile River which I had not realized that it begins in Uganda, the Tombs of the Buganda Kings at Kasubi (another UNESCO World Heritage Site), a delightful dinner and cultural show in an outdoor amphitheater, and a behind-the-scenes tour at the Entebbe Zoo where we petted a rhino and hand-fed an elephant and a giraffe. The giraffe's tongue sure was long and slimy as he took the food pellets from my cupped hands!

At the cultural show, I was really impressed with a cast of drummers. They came in with the barrel-shaped, varied-size drums balanced on their heads and beating on them as they marched around. A couple of the drums were so large that

been there, done that!

it took two people to lift them up and place them on the drummers' heads. Another interesting act was done by lady dancers who balanced small, narrow-based vases stacked on their heads. A couple of the ladies danced around with seven vases piled vertically (one at a time!) on their heads! None of the vases ever toppled, even as the dancers exited up quite a flight of steps! I'm not sure I could have moved and swayed like they did—let alone with just one vase on my head. These were very enjoyable times just to be together with Katy and to see the culture in which she was ministering.

TRICKED AT THE EQUATOR?

We also went to a spot where the earth's equator crosses a road. It has been made into a photographic opportunity for tourists, so we got our picture taken there. At that location, they have set up three, eighteen-inch diameter funnels to demonstrate the variance in the direction of the flow of water on the north side, on the south side, and right on the equator. On the north side, the water circulated down the funnel one direction, and on the south side of the equator, the water circulated in the opposite direction. When water was poured into the funnel right on the equator, it didn't spin at all but went straight down. Being quite skeptical, I tried to see if anything was done differently as water was poured into the funnels. I have heard of this phenomenon before and still don't know whether it is true or false—but I did see it with my own eyes! Was I hoodwinked or not? Someone needs to give me the honest facts—especially since the funnels were within twenty feet of each other. I really should have asked the host to let me pour the water into the funnels to find out if there is a trick to the whole thing.

SOUTH AFRICA TOUR

From Uganda, we flew into the modern city of Cape Town in South Africa to meet our Wheaton College tour group. We had a marvelous trip around the cape of Africa, visiting many attractions such as Boulders Beach with its colony of African penguins, the Cape of Good Hope which is the most southwestern point of Africa, Cape Point on the southeast corner of the Cape Peninsula, a picturesque mountainous coastal drive, and Signal Hill with its great view of the entire Cape Town area.

Because of high winds, we did not get to take the cable car to the top of Table Mountain, which is one of the city's most visited places. It is extremely flat on the top and appears to have a white tablecloth on it as clouds spread over its top and drape down the side. Also, due to the weather, we did not get to take a ferry to Robben Island, where Nelson Mandela had been held prisoner. (He was an important political and social reformer in the twentieth century.) We were disappointed that we could not get to these famed and iconic spots in the city, but at least we were able to see them from a distance!

VICTORIA FALLS

Victoria Falls is not in South Africa but we also flew to visit there while on this tour. The renowned waterfalls are between Zambia and Zimbabwe and were spectacular! They are the largest waterfalls in the world with a width of more than one mile, and in some spots the water cascades about 350-feet to the river below. We hiked on a trail most of the width of the falls and back to see all the different major viewpoints. In some places a magnificent rainbow rose above the mist generated by the falling water. More than 38,000 cubic feet of water gushes over the escarpment every second in the rainy season. We were there at the end of the dry season, so the water flow was not as extravagant at the time. However, the falls were still impressive!

I was pleased to see at the entrance to the falls viewing area, a David Livingstone monument with an engraved plaque which in part reads that people were "assembled solemnly to dedicate themselves and their country to carry on the high Christian aims and ideals which inspired David Livingstone in his mission here". The plaque was placed in 1955 on the occasion of the centenary of Livingstone discovering Victoria Falls and is a testimony to his and our Christian faith for the world's tourists to see.

From our hotel at Victoria Falls, we took a day trip to an animal preserve in Botswana. There we went in a covered but open safari jeep to see the many animals and birds in that area. Following a lunch at a little resort, we got on a sightseeing boat to see animals and birds from the waterline perspective. Because it was our first safari, we were all excited to see elephants, hippos, crocodiles, giraffes, cape buffaloes, and many impala antelopes. But the best was yet to come in future safaris.

been there, done that!

THREE DAY NARROW-GAUGE RAIL JOURNEY

A privately-owned, narrow-gauge railroad runs from Victoria Falls through Zimbabwe down to Pretoria in South Africa. Our tour host had arranged for us to spend three nights on that railroad. What a ride! The track was not well maintained in certain areas, so the cars constantly swayed back and forth and occasionally bumped forward and backward. For sleeping, we had to block ourselves in with pillows so we wouldn't roll out of bed!

Our railcar berth was very small with two narrow beds and minimal space between them. Thankfully, there was a small dresser and closet where we could store some things since there was no room to constantly be opening and closing suitcases which had to be stored overhead or under the beds so we could at least move around a little in the room. Each berth had a tiny bathroom which—depending on what you wanted to do—you had to go in forward or backward. The shower required that you almost always had to be up against one side or the other, and there was hardly enough room to bend over in there to wash your feet—especially when the train was moving!

Our berth was in a car near the rear of the train, so we had to walk through several cars to get to the dining car and the front parlor car. Going through the narrow corridors was always a challenge as we regularly dusted off the walls and windows by being jostled from one side to the other as the train rolled along. Most of our free time on the train was in its last lounge car, which had a nice open porch at the back. We did stop at one location in Zimbabwe to get off for a daytime safari.

But the trip was a lot of fun! Arriving in Pretoria, the train owner met us and gave us a great tour of the railyard and maintenance facilities. He is constantly buying older Pullman cars and old engines from around the world and restoring them to their glory days for expansion of his private rail system.

SOWETO

Soweto is a very economically-poor suburban region of Johannesburg, which does not appear to have improved itself much over the years. It was a key location of the black populace near Johannesburg and played a significant part in the fight against apartheid in South Africa. We were escorted through the area by a man who runs a community center, which provides after-school computer and feeding programs to help kids rise above their poverty conditions.

It was sad to see the conditions of the "shacks" and trashy yards of the people who live there. Most of the homes seemed to have scrap material or corrugated aluminum walls or roofs. Sometimes, only a large piece of cloth separated the homes. A community well provided fresh water for the people to get and take to their home—although they could hardly be called a home as we would define it. Toilet facilities were many porta-potties lined up on the outside fringes of the area—so that trucks could get close to empty them since there was no road space for trucks within the community. The porta-potties were kept padlocked so that only about five families with keys to their own lock could use each one. I wondered: "How were middle-of-the-night calls handled?"

We noticed the huge difference between Soweto and other parts of the well-known city of Johannesburg. There we saw many very ritzy places in the middle of the city where government and commercial buildings stand in stark contrast to the poor environment we had just seen in Soweto.

THORNYBUSH GAME RESERVE

Thornybush Game Reserve was our next destination where we spent four days in a very comfortable resort. The campus had several duplexes, meeting rooms, and an outdoor dining area. Going to our room was a new experience as we passed several wild nyala antelope grazing on the grounds and a couple of monkeys swinging through the trees. Right outside the patio doors of our room, a big kudu antelope passed by and on yet another day, wart hogs nibbled on the grass. All of these wild animals paid no attention to us even when we were near them to take their pictures.

In the early morning hours, we could hear the monkeys chasing around on our duplex's grass roof. We were told to keep our doors and windows locked when we weren't there because those little ingenious monkeys had figured out how to open them and wreak havoc in a room. When moving around the campus to go to our rooms after dark, we always had to have a night guard with us to handle any unusual situations that might occur with the wild animals.

been there, done that!

UP EARLY, OUT LATE FOR GAME DRIVES

Our schedule for each day was pretty much the same. We would get up in time to head out on a morning game-viewing drive beginning at 5:30 a.m. Coffee, juice, tea, and some kind of pastry were always available at that hour to help people wake up. We would be out in the safari vehicles, looking at animals and birds until we came back for our 8:30 a.m. breakfast, which consisted of a variety of beverages, cereals, lots of fruit, usually some kind of meat, and pastries. We did not go hungry! We had devotions together, relaxed by reading—or sleeping!—and had lunch.

Another game drive started at 3 p.m. from which we returned about 8 p.m. after it was dark. (Being fairly near the equator, the sun would rise about 6 a.m. and set about 6 p.m.) The evening meal was always delicious and varied from one day to the next. It might be kudu meat one night, beef roast the next, or pork another time, all with local side dishes. The bed—always under a mosquito net—was so welcome, and the coolness of the night made sleeping very comfortable. In fact, some mornings were cold and required a jacket as we ventured out to find animals and birds.

Our extended, jeep-like, safari vehicles were completely open with three tiered levels of seats behind the driver. He put the front windshield down for better visibility for everyone and kept a large rifle right there on the dash in front of him—just in case! The vehicle had sufficient blankets and rain ponchos if needed for each rider. Most of us used the blankets on a couple of the morning game drives! The driver's steering wheel was on the right side and a tracker sat on a high seat out over the left front headlight.

After dark, the tracker pulled out a huge spotlight that he would shine back and forth in front of us to find animals. He would always move it quickly away from any herbivore (vegetation eating) animals, such as antelope, but if it was a carnivore (flesh eating) animal like a leopard, he moved the light from its eyes to its back end. A herbivore is somewhat temporarily blinded by the light, but it does not bother a carnivore.

THE BIG FIVE AND OTHERS—UP CLOSE!

We saw so many animals, and most were fairly close! This was so different from when I grew up in the savannah and jungle areas in the south part of Chad and Central African Republic. We were told that the animals on the reserve were used to the shape and sound of the vehicles, but when we were near them, we should not make any noise or any quick moves which could alarm them. These animals had been protected for most, if not all, of their lives, and human predators were rare on this animal protected land. Of course, the natural food chain occurred every day, and the numerous impala antelope, as well as other mammals, provided plenty of meat for the carnivores and vultures. We saw the end results of efficient hunts by lions and wild dogs.

Hunters go to South Africa to see the Big Five—elephant, cape buffalo, rhinoceros, lion, and leopard—and we saw all of them several times. But we also saw kudu, sable, eland, impala, nyala, and duiker antelope; wild dog; hyena; black-backed jackal; wart hog; honey badger; civet cat; giraffe; baboon; monkey; hippopotamus; crocodile; ground squirrel; mongoose; ostrich; yellow-billed hornbill, stork, fish eagle, vulture, bee eater (a small, very colorful bird), and spoonbill birds; and a myriad of other living creatures! I loved seeing all of these in the wild without them quickly darting away from us.

FAST REACTIONS BY OUR DRIVER

A few of our safaris provided real excitement. We came across a wild dog den where we saw two males guarding their area while a female fed her nine, cute, little wobbly pups with their white-tipped tails.

We drove off-road to watch—and hear!—some hyenas chomping down on a recent antelope kill by wild dogs. We pulled up within about fifteen feet of the hyenas and they didn't even look up at us. The matriarch is larger than the males and is the most aggressive of the pack. She has priority at a feast, and we saw her chase off the smaller male hyenas (and the wild dogs) if they were too close to her food choice. These scavengers can eat up to forty pounds of meat per feeding. Hyenas basically bite and swallow after minimal chewing to pulverize bones to get the marrow and minerals they need to survive. Their stomach acids are so strong that bones and other things they consume are digested quite quickly. Hearing the hyenas crunching on bones was a little startling when we thought of how strong their jaws must be—and how close we were to them! We did not contend with them for portions of the dead antelope!

In our vehicle, we were paralleling a rhinoceros when a large bush between us blocked both the rhino's view of us and ours of him. Suddenly, it seemed the

been there, done that!

rhino became surprised as we mutually came into view while being only about twenty-five feet apart. He looked at us, started pawing the ground, and lowered his head! Our driver threw that vehicle into reverse so fast it almost gave us whiplash! Whew!

At another place, we were sitting and watching some elephants eating from the bushes and branches (they eat the bigger sticks as well as the leaves!). There were some very young elephants among them. Normally, they ignored us while walking in front of or behind our vehicle. One of the men in our vehicle turned around rapidly to try and get a great close-up picture, and apparently the elephant felt threatened as she began to raise some dust with her feet and flap her ears. That was our driver's clue to get out of there! Our driver and tracker both were always very alert and looked out for our safety as well as for our enjoyment.

Sometimes to get better pictures, the driver would go off-road and get us real close to the animals—such as when we got within ten feet of a male lion trying to take a nap. The driver was really good. Altogether, I was on eight safaris and was really happy with each one. Every game drive had its own uniqueness. I really loved being in the wild! I have "been there, done that" and highly recommend an African safari to everyone!

PART V
MISCELLANEOUS INTERESTS IN LIFE

CHAPTER XX

HOBBIES

BIKING

I don't remember when I learned to ride a bicycle, but I suspect it was when I was about six and a half years old. After my years at the Westervelt Home in South Carolina, my parents returned in 1948 for a furlough from their missionary service in Chad (which was then part of French Equatorial Africa). Our family moved in with one of my dad's sisters in South Bend, Indiana, and I recall pedaling a small bike on a sidewalk where the tree roots had raised sections of the sidewalk in places. I loved speeding over those bumps—from the right direction, of course! I don't ever remember having training wheels on my bike.

WATCH WHERE YOU ARE GOING

Upon arriving in Africa in 1949, I immediately went to a boarding school where, along with a couple of other young guys, we rode bikes over many of the local walking pathways. These were created by the Africans as they went to and from their gardens to work or gather the harvest, to the spring for water to carry back to their hut, or even to classrooms or church for education or edification.

Although these packed-dirt paths were very smooth, they were also very narrow, and often they would lead right up to a tree, then take an abrupt turn around the tree—sometimes too sharp for a bicycle to stay on the footpath. In our amateur bike riding, most of the time we would miss those trees. On the other hand, occasionally we didn't make it around the corner, and the bike handlebars would hit the tree, resulting in somewhat of a calamity! One had to watch where we were going at all times.

Another place where we had to be very accurate in our riding was at ditch crossings. Usually the ditches were beside a dirt road to aid the water runoff after the intense downpours in the African rainy season. Some of these ditches were about two to three feet wide and could be about the same depth. The Africans would just place a straight tree branch or small trunk across the ditch, walk across it, and think nothing about it.

But on a bike—well that is another story! We had to ensure that our front and back wheels were in line and our balance just perfect, or else into the ditch we would go, sometimes bending the front fork on our bikes. Of course it didn't help that the "bridge" may be a little rounded on top and only a few inches wide! After a couple of "failings" to cross a ditch and the pressure to keep up with other kids on bikes, I soon learned the mastery of squarely hitting that log bridge to get across. Those times of riding the foot paths were exhilarating and very memorable.

DAD'S GREEN BIKE—ANSWER TO PRAYER

After each four-month semester at the boarding school, we kids would travel back to the station where our folks were ministering and always took our bikes with us—usually for maintenance! I remember that during one of those two-month vacations at home, I often secretly prayed that I could take Dad's big, twenty-six-inch wheels, green, knee-action (spring on the front fork to reduce shock), Schwinn bike to school with me. I talked with Dad many times about how much I wanted it, but he never verbally agreed to let me take it. He always would say that he needed it on evangelism trips to ride to remote villages where there were no roads to get to them—just foot paths. That was a convincing reason for him to keep his bike rather than send it to school with me!

The day before departure for a new semester at the boarding school, we loaded the truck for the 250-mile/18-hour trip (yes, those are accurate numbers!), and I noted that the bike was not on the truck. Had the Lord forgotten all about my "fervent" continual prayers? That night I was really down in the dumps about the whole thing but again prayed that I could take the bike.

It was only on the day of departure—when I saw Dad's bike tied to the side of our truck—that I found out Dad was going to let me have his bike at school!

What a wonderful surprise, and oh, how thankful I was to him and to the Lord for answering my prayers. God does listen and react—even to kids' prayers! That bike was the envy of other kids who loved riding it because of its shock absorber on the front which immensely reduced the impact of the bumps and potholes on the dirt roads. I really took good care of Dad's bike so that I could take it for future semesters.

MY OWN SCHWINN BIKE

When we returned to the US in 1954 for furlough time, I prayed that I could get a bike similar to Dad's in Africa. I still remember him taking me to Albright's Schwinn bike store on Lincolnway in South Bend, Indiana. That is where he had gotten bikes as a young man, and that is where that green bike in Africa had come from. We looked at several and decided on a maroon-and-white, used bike for me. It had a wonderful leather saddle which made riding so much more comfortable, and it was really sharp looking with its white-walled tires. I really liked that bike! Dad bought it for me. It was mine!

We lived outside of town, and I soon found a couple of guys with whom I would ride. We "suped" up our bikes with streamers off the handlebar grips, lights on the front and back, mud flaps with reflectors, horns, and cardboard mounts, which made a nice motor sound when the wheel's spokes hit the cardboard. We eventually even added trailer hitches and made little trailers for our bikes. We would ride all over the area and into town, which was just a few miles away. In those days, parents didn't have to worry about the safety of their kids being out of the house for long periods of time like they have to do today.

After a year in the America, it came time for my parents to return to Africa to continue their ministry. My older sister and I stayed in the US since there was no high school available where we had lived in Africa. We went to Mid-Maples in Wheaton, Illinois, a home for teenage missionary kids (MKs) whose parents were on foreign mission fields, and of course, I took my bicycle. But now I was in high school, and it wasn't "cool" to have all that fancy stuff on my bike, so I stripped it back down to its original look.

I rode many miles during my high school years, mostly to go to places of work. Much of that was at night because of school and athletic activities, which consumed the daytime. On many Friday nights, one of the other MKs and I would ride about three miles to Wheaton College to work from about ten at night until

been there, done that!

two in the morning — sometimes that bike ride was in the rain! Another job was working on the mosquito abatement truck at night. Coming home from work was usually a seemingly long, dark ride. I had an odometer on the bike but never wrote down how many miles I rode in my high school years. Occasionally my bike riding was to various activities at church.

My parents returned on their furlough from Africa in 1959 for my high school graduation from Wheaton Academy. It had been four years since I had seen them, and it was wonderful to go back with them to our home in Indiana for the summer between high school and college. Although I got my driver's license early that summer, Dad needed his car for his deputation ministry to visit churches and report on the their recent years in Africa, so I used my bike to go to and from my summer work. I rode at least fifteen miles a day and was in good physical condition.

130-MILE BIKE JOURNEY TO COLLEGE

When it was time to go to college, Dad was on a speaking trip, and I really didn't want to use what little money I had to ride the train or a bus, so I proposed that I ride my bike those 130 miles from Mishawaka, Indiana, to Wheaton College in Illinois. My parents agreed, so I gathered twenty-six pounds of clothes, stuff, and camera—yes, I weighed it!—rigged it all on my bike, and took off in the late summer of 1959. I left Mishawaka at 6 a.m. with a carefully marked paper map. (There was no GPS in those days!) I had never done any distance bike riding before, nor am I the type of person to enjoy being alone for a lengthy period of time, so this trip was a little bit of a risk for me—and for my parents to let me go! But they trusted me and there really wasn't any other good option for me to ensure that I would get to college in time for registration. I was certain that I could pedal that far in one day.

Shortly before noon, I had ridden about sixty miles and was getting near Gary, Indiana. My bike was a one-speed, American, fat-tired bike, and I was riding west into the wind. I stopped two or three times for food and water in the first six hours, but apparently I was not drinking enough because my legs started cramping. I had no one to call to help me go the rest of the way—and besides there were no cell phones!—so I just decided to tough it out, rest, and put my legs vertically against the side of a tree for a while, drink more, and move on. I had to get to Wheaton before dark and had about seventy miles to go!

I got back on the road to get around the south end of Lake Michigan and into Illinois. By now, a stronger headwind had built up and pedaling was getting tougher! I wasn't worried about making it all the way before dark, but I knew the last half of the trip would be more strenuous. "I can do all things through Christ Who strengthens me." That verse from Philippians 4:13 encouraged me to keep pushing on.

Finally, after averaging ten miles per hour and thirteen hours of pedaling, I pulled into Wheaton! I was tired but happy!

The risk of making it all in one day paid off. I don't think there are too many people who have ridden their bike that far to college—let alone in one day on an American fat-tired bike without multiple gears! And how many college kids arrive at college with only twenty-six pounds of stuff to move into the dorm? Nowadays, it takes a truck or a big trailer to get a student to college! But to be transparent, I had packed a footlocker which Dad sent by Greyhound bus to me about two weeks later.

The bike trip to college was a major challenge that taught me that when I put my mind to a task, think happy thoughts, and demonstrate patience and persistence, I could accomplish almost anything. This philosophy and my constant reliance on God's help have carried me through a lot of events in my life.

been there, done that!

I kept that maroon bike and used it extensively while at college. When I last looked at the odometer in the winter of my senior year, it had over 17,700 miles on it! I kept it locked wherever I stopped, but one night it was stolen off the front porch where I lived even though I was sure I had locked it. However, I had not secured it to anything like a porch railing. I was very upset and in the next few days, I went all around the area looking for my bike. I guess one of the things I missed the most was that odometer that showed all my miles and the wonderful, comfortable, leather saddle, which by now had been appropriately molded to my "you know what". I could always find another good bike, but to me, those two things were irreplaceable.

On the day in 1963 that I graduated from Wheaton College, I was in the Army. I didn't get another bike until the spring of 1970 after my second tour in Vietnam. I was at another military course at Fort Benning, Georgia, and saw that someone on base was selling a pair of German-made, three-speed, gears-in-the-hub bicycles. They were in excellent condition and, like my maroon bike, they looked really sharp with their medium-weight, white-walled tires. I purchased the two bikes and quickly bought a new odometer for my bike. I tried to find some high-quality leather saddles for both of our bikes but never did find any we really liked. We kept those bikes until 2006 when I couldn't find replacement parts for the three-speed, rear-wheel hubs. I had ridden my German bike almost 15,000 miles by that time.

150-MILE BIKE TRIP ON SKYLINE DRIVE

The trip which I remember most on my German bike was a 150-mile ride south from near Front Royal, Virginia, on the Skyline Drive along the top of the Appalachian Mountain chain. I was leading a boys' battalion of the Christian Service Brigade from our church and planned a bike trip as a weekend outing. We had done our physical conditioning, and I had each boy bring his bike to me in a recent meeting to check the bike's condition to try to prevent maintenance breakdowns on our trip. And, I wanted to make sure the bike was appropriate for a long road trip. I didn't want any small bikes with a banana seat for the lengthy ride!

Twenty-four boys and two of us leaders were on this trip. We spent three days with two camping nights on the road. Only three of the group made the entire ride without getting off their bike except for defined breaks and night stops. That was quite an accomplishment for young teens who mastered the steepness of some of the hills on the road. One of those three boys was my oldest son, Phil Jr., who was only thirteen years old. He made me very proud! I had to briefly walk my bike a couple of times when my right leg (which had been severely wounded in Vietnam) began to cramp. After walking a short distance to loosen it up, I was back riding again! So, I rode the entire distance except for a total of a couple hundred yards.

We organized groups for biking, to break up what would have been a long line of bike riders, so that cars could pass if they wanted. We had to be very cautious of slippery leaves or loose gravel on the roadway—especially going down some of the hills where there were curves. At times our speeds exceeded forty miles per hour, so a spill could have caused some serious injuries. Thankfully, that never happened. We did have a chase truck in case a bike broke, to carry camping gear, and be available if a boy felt he could not ride the entire distance,

184-MILE RIDE ON CHESAPEAKE & OHIO CANAL TOWPATH

One other bike trip was very memorable. I had planned to ride with our teenage battalion of Christian Service Brigade boys on the 184-mile Chesapeake & Ohio (C&O) Canal Towpath from Cumberland, Maryland, through Harpers Ferry, West Virginia, to the towpath's end in Washington, DC. This was not an easy ride, although it was flat and slightly downhill following the course of the Potomac River—much in contrast to the ups and downs of riding the highway on Skyline Drive!

Most of the antique towpath was not paved at that time and tree roots crossed the path almost its entire distance, except in the immediate vicinity of towns we passed through. And there were many mud holes on the towpath—some completely covered the trail. After the sixty-mile ride the first day, some of our group could hardly move as we set up camp for the night. The next morning was even tougher as we got back onto those bike seats again. Ouch! Ouch! Ouch!

On the second day of our trip and about seventy miles further down the towpath toward DC, the sky let loose, and we were soaked as we arrived at our next planned campsite, which was adjacent to the Potomac River. We began to set up and try and get some fires going before dark, but as I looked out to the river, I noticed it was rising, and I decided we needed to evacuate. I didn't want to take the chance of the river flooding over the banks into our campsite in the middle of the night. We loaded up the bikes on the chase truck, got on the bus and headed for home—absolutely soaked and filthy from the tire splash while riding in the

been there, done that!

rain on the muddy towpath. That was the only time that we ever cut short one of our battalion monthly events. Most of us who had ridden the upper part of the towpath went back a couple months later and completed the ride into DC.

HOME STATIONARY EXERCISE BIKE

To allow me to ride throughout the year in Virginia, I bought a stationary bike. Supposedly, it was a good one with spoked wheel and a small polypropylene wheel on top so that by increasing its pressure, more resistance training could be accomplished. One morning while riding, I noticed a small wisp of smoke coming from the polypropylene wheel. It smelled horrible! I only had around 100 miles on this new bike and had only ridden it a few days. Investigating the pressure wheel, I saw that it was melting around its axle. I took the wheel back to the store where they gave me a replacement. I put the new one on, and it also melted. It was just not made for the type of heavy-pressure riding that I wanted to do for healthy exercise.

I remembered that we had an old pair of roller skates in the basement and knew they had metal bearings in the wheels. I put two of those skate wheels together to give increased width and replaced the polypropylene wheel on the bike. It worked and allowed me to increase the pressure on the bike wheel while I rode. But after 550 miles, the front wheel began to wobble, and in taking it apart, I realized that my pressure from the top had destroyed the hub and axle of the spoked wheel. Obviously, that was not a quality stationary bike—at least for my needs.

When I attended Harvard University in Massachusetts in 1987, I rode a stationary bike in their fitness center that had almost 70,000 miles on it. I determined that was the bike that I would get. It had a flywheel with a band around it to add the resistance. It cost a lot more, but if it was going to last at least 70,000 miles with many different riders, it would be worth it. I bought a new one like it when I returned to my home in Virginia.

In these last years since moving to Florida in 1990, most of my primary riding has been on that stationary bike in my exercise room where it is almost always considerably cooler than outside! It is better exercise because I don't have to stop at streets—if I was outside—and I can consistently push hard as long as I want. Besides, there is no coasting on a stationary bike! When you stop pedaling, it stops adding miles! At this time, I have ridden more than 66,000 miles on that stationary bike.

During my one to two-hour rides at home, I can read my military and missionary magazines or e-books and listen to the morning TV news at the same time. I would not be able to do that out on the streets. Depending on how much travel away from home I do in a year, in the last fifteen to twenty years I have normally ridden 2,000 and as much as 4,500 miles a year. I guess if one were to ask me about a hobby, biking would be my primary response. I enjoy it, and it is good for me.

STAMP COLLECTION

But I have had a couple of other lesser hobbies I enjoy. One is stamp collecting. A staff lady at the Westervelt Home (in the 1940s) was a stamp collector and encouraged many of us young kids to begin collections. Because of the many countries represented by the missionary kids at the home, there was a wide variety of stamps. I had quite a collection of worldwide stamps when I left the Westervelt Home in 1948.

Stamps were an educational thing for me. I was particularly interested in geography and where the countries were on a map, what their flowers and birds and animals were, and as with stamps today, there were historical figures or events portrayed on many stamps. Some of my stamps are unusual—such as those that the color is printed upside down on the image; some that are overprinted because of the political turmoil in the country; one that is printed on gold leaf; some that are rare and today can hardly be found except in other collections; and some that are different shapes. Although I have some new stamps, I do not make an effort to collect them, but I do have some plate-block new stamps, which were given to me.

Currently, I have around 20,000 used stamps categorized in albums, but I really haven't done much with my collection for years. I became a stamp "gatherer" rather than a "collector!" I kept saying that when I retire, I'll get back to my stamps again. I've retired three times already and still hadn't done much with stamps except soak some off their envelopes. However, the coronavirus lockdown of 2020 got me to looking at my stamps again.

In about a month's time, I sorted all the stamps I've gathered. (My wife is very happy that I've cleaned out some drawers and closet space!) In the process, I realized I had touched more than 40,000 stamps and found them to be from

been there, done that!

more than 125 countries! I gave away at least 30,000 of those as multiple duplicates while still keeping other duplicates for myself. The sorting has been very interesting as I have found envelopes which were mailed back in the early 1940s and other postmarks and stamps from as early as 1872. These old stamps often have minute variations in edge perforations, coloring, or markings from different press runs. Some of my stamps are from countries which no longer exist, and in some instances, stamps were issued by separate states/provinces/districts within a single country. This has made my sorting a time-consuming process. As of now, I probably have more than 12,000 stamps which could be catalogued into albums at some point. Who knows what will happen to this collection when I pass on? Who collects stamps these days? So far, it doesn't appear that any of my kids or grandkids are interested.

HYMNBOOK COLLECTION

I have another collection that is somewhat unusual—at least I don't know of others who collect hymnbooks. I know they are not used in many churches today, but I began accumulating them when I was the minister of music in a church in Virginia in the 1980s. A retiring lady was moving to Florida and didn't want to take her ten or fifteen hymnbooks to her new small home, so she gave them to me. They were pretty common hymnbooks, but they were all different. That small number has now grown in my collection to more than 350 hymnbooks, which are from different denominations, publishers, time eras, and countries. A few of the titles are merely different editions or colors of the covers. I also have some hymnbooks, which have special arrangements for quartets, duets, or solos. And others are unique because the notes are shaped rather than the normal round or oval look we are used to seeing.

I regret that hymnbooks are rarely used in many churches. Most church music is now sung without harmonies of the musical parts, and oftentimes, the people don't know even the main tune to the words projected on a screen. I like to sing and hear the harmonies written for or supporting the lyrics. Without a hymnbook in hand, a person cannot look back at the words (after they have been deleted from the projection screen) and review some of the great thoughts penned by the lyrics' authors. Many of the wonderful hymns of the faith are no longer sung. It is a change in worship style. Because of my love for hymnody, I prefer having words with their music in front of me and enjoy the singing of the harmonies of written musical parts.

UNUSUAL HYMNBOOKS

Although most of my hymnbooks are from the twentieth century, I do have some from earlier dates. Two are compilations of Charles Wesley's writings from the eighteenth century. He wrote the texts for about 6,500 hymns. My oldest hymnbook is a very small (2" tall by 1½" wide by 1" thick), leather-covered book of about 600 of Wesley's hymn texts. The other is about twice that size with more than 800 of his texts, bound in a hard cover. The first of these hymnbooks was published in 1833, and the other was printed in 1849—both long after the texts were written! These are treasures although the print is so small that it is hardly readable. These books have no music—just the words.

We were on a tour and in a cathedral in Greece where I saw that there were no hymnbooks in the pew racks. This was especially noticeable to me since in almost every other church building we had been in on tours, there were always pew hymnbooks. I asked a receptionist about the absence of the books. She said they were getting new ones and that all the old ones had been removed. I then asked if I could buy one of the old ones, and she said I'd have to talk with the "father" about that. She said she would get him. He came out with one in his hand, and I explained why I wanted it. He handed it to me as a gift from the church, and I was very grateful even though it was in Greek! Other hymnbooks I have are in national or tribal languages from remote places where I have been.

If I see a hymnbook I don't have when I am in a church, I will offer to buy it for my collection, and in most cases the book will be given to me. I have purchased a very few from used bookstores as I am not one to frequent those places. I could probably have a lot more hymnbooks if I were to get in more of those stores. I think my overall favorite hymn text writer is blind Fanny J. Crosby, although I find it hard to choose any one—or even ten!—favorite hymns.

I also have several books which tell the stories of hymns. I enjoy hymnody, and in my morning devotions, I usually read the story and the text of a hymn or gospel song. Many lyrics are written based on the spiritual inspiration from an experience in life—without ever thinking that the text would have music added to it later and that it may be used in a future church service. From my reading and in my opinion, it seems that much contemporary Christian music is written today

been there, done that!

for profit of the writer or publisher rather than for the purpose of encouragement in worship and praise .My dilemma will be when I pass on or have to downsize my living space, who will want such an unusual and heavy hymnbook collection? Currently my collection of more than 350 hymnbooks is in two large bookcases with each being almost four feet wide and seven feet tall!

CHAPTER XXI
WORK EXPERIENCES

HIGH SCHOOL

While I had been exposed to doing varied chores as a younger person, I had never worked for money until I was in high school at Mid-Maples in Wheaton, Illinois. With up to twenty-four teenagers in one home, we each had our responsibilities and duties to help the houseparents keep a smooth and efficient operation.

As a fourteen-year old, my first paid job was with a landscaping company where twenty-five cents an hour seemed to me like a huge sum in 1956. It was not easy work as we often prepared private house yards for their future grass. The raking never seemed to end as we leveled the ground and tried to get all of the stones out of the tractor-tilled soil in preparation for seeding or sod placement!

Another unique job at that time was riding a commercial mosquito abatement truck during the wet season. We would go to work shortly after dusk, going through neighborhoods, spraying repellents and mosquito killing chemicals with a big fogging machine on the back of a pickup truck. This was done on a rotating schedule through the neighborhoods so that people knew to close up their houses and protect themselves when we came through with the sprayer. Part of my job was to ride on the back of the truck directing the spray nozzles to take advantage of the breezes for efficient dispersal of the chemicals. We finished spraying about 11 p.m. and then went home to shower—and perhaps do a little study for the next school day! Occasionally, we were required to spray swamp areas, but that was mostly on a weekend during daylight hours.

been there, done that!

A HOMELESS PERSON IN AN UNUSUAL PLACE

In my junior year of high school, a couple of us MKs got jobs at Wheaton College. This work was at a little higher wage because the job was primarily working at night after the campus had pretty much closed down. We-rode our bikes about three miles from where we lived at Mid-Maples to the campus about 10 p.m. and many times did not get home until after 2 a.m.! This was on weekends during the college academic season. We did janitorial chores: clean buildings, strip and wax floors using a spinning buffer machine, empty trash, clean bathrooms, wash windows, shampoo carpets, and so forth.

In the summertime, we deep-cleaned the dorms! I was surprised to see all the stuff left behind by students—books, lotions, combs and brushes, some clothes, scraps of paper with phone numbers and room numbers in the dorms, and oftentimes a *big* mess! The girls' dorms always had more junk than the boys' dorms and took us a lot longer to clean.

The job at the college was actually quite interesting for several reasons. We interacted with the campus cops and often got the "inside scoop" on some of the happenings at the college! Also, during our cleaning jobs, we sometimes "investigated" unusual places on the campus.

One of those places was the space underneath the balcony and above the first floor ceiling in the old chapel building. It was sort of spooky there, and one night we found a man making his home in that secluded spot. He got away before we could get the campus cops—no cell phones then!—but he sure left a lot of clutter behind of things he had pilfered over time. I am not sure how he got in and out of the building because the doors were locked at night but I am sure he had his timing figured out so that he didn't get locked out of the building when he wanted to be in it. We also occasionally investigated crawl spaces for utilities between floors of some other buildings on the campus, and I am sure that there were very few other students who ever explored some of those as we did on our night cleaning jobs! Life was fun, and sometimes risky, but I wouldn't trade the experiences of those days for anything else.

LANDSCAPING AT THE COLLEGE

On many weekends and part of the summers, I also worked on the grounds of Wheaton College and did a lot of landscaping to help keep the campus looking great. The beauty of the campus was accredited to a man named Mr. D. He had retired from the Botanical Gardens in Chicago and really knew a lot of detail about plants. He chose many kinds of flowering plants and shrubs and knew just when to plant them to make the campus beautiful. Mr. D, in coordination with the head of the Biology Department, also oversaw the campus greenhouse—both for science purposes and for growing flowers for some of the offices. He was the boss over those of us who were the groundskeepers and taught us excellence in the care of the landscaping. He was meticulous in his landscaping maintenance and taught us about using the right tools for the job and paying attention to the smallest details.

For example, Mr. D wanted all the trees and shrubs to have the right natural look with their trimming and very sharp-looking edging at their base. To please him—and keep our jobs—everything had to be just right! We did all that work by hand since we did not have some of the great electric, battery, or gas-powered tools available today. Some days, we mowed all day and didn't dare allow the grass clippings to get inside the circle around the base of the manicured trees and shrubs. I continued to work sometimes with Mr. D after I started going to the college.

But Mr. D also had some weird ideas. He often talked about how the insects and bugs were going to take over the world someday. He shared lessons learned from certain bugs, such as the ant and how industrious they were to carry food and store it for future use. If the ant couldn't carry the load, a bunch of others would come to its aid and move the load to where it should be in the ants' nest. So, if we couldn't accomplish work by ourselves, we should seek others to help get the job done but not to leave a job undone just because it was too big for us. That is still a good lesson for all of us.

Through my high school years, I learned the value of a strong work ethic and the importance of loyalty to a job, my boss, and the employing organization. Sometimes the work was hard, but if I was going to go to college, I would need to pay my own way, since my missionary parents would not be able to help with expenses. There were very few scholarships at Wheaton College in those days. In college, there would be little time or money for me to participate in many outside activities because of the necessity for me to work. I became very frugal and saved most of the small amount I earned.

been there, done that!

UPHOLSTERY AND CARPET CLEANING

After graduating from high school in Wheaton, I lived that summer with my parents in Indiana. That is when I got my driver's license, as Dad taught me to drive his 1955 gray-and-white Chevrolet sedan. What a beautiful car! But because he was gone on deputation and speaking away from home much of the summer, I primarily used my maroon bicycle for transportation. I got a job across town in a carpet cleaning and upholstery shop. We cleaned carpets and furniture in homes, and in many cases, we pulled large area carpets and took them to our shop and spread them out on large cement pads for cleaning. It is amazing how much dirt can accumulate under an area carpet and in its fibers! We also reupholstered furniture. That was very interesting to pull the old upholstery off—finding money and all sorts of things—get new fabric approved, and then put it on the furniture. My boss was a master at his work and taught me a lot about that business. Like Mr. D at Wheaton College, he was meticulous and wanted the final product to be the best! I worked that job six days a week to help save money for college.

COLLEGE

LUMBER YARD—PHUZZY PHIL'S NAILS

During the summer months following my freshman and sophomore college years, I worked in a lumber yard in Elkhart, Indiana. (After my junior year, I went to ROTC summer camp.) I probably did not weigh much more than 120 pounds in the 1960 summer, and my job on the first day was to unload a semi-trailer full of ninety-pound roofing rolls and stack them in the proper bay! Oh, was I ever tired that night and sore the next couple of days! On other days, I would unload (by hand) railroad boxcars of lumber, which held everything from 2"x4"x8-foot studs to 2"x12"x20-foot planks. The latter were very heavy and awkward to handle, especially getting them out of the boxcar, which sometimes had been "humped" in the railyard and the lumber inside all jumbled up!

I was also put in charge of the nail department of the lumber yard with its heavy boxes of nails. My boss put up a sign calling that section "Phuzzy Phil's Nails". My hair was very kinky and wiry, so I guess I deserved the title! By the end of the summer, my muscles had begun to bulge, and I was in really good shape! I really enjoyed working at the lumber yard and the interaction with the staff, independent customers, and contractors. Much to my surprise, about thirty years later, I again met one of the contractors we had served in the lumber yard. He had retired and now lived in Florida where we had moved after my own retirement from the military.

HEATING PLANT SHIFT WORK AND DATING

I believe it was the second semester in my freshman year that, in addition to continuing the college campus landscaping, I started to work a few hours in the heating plant at Wheaton College. The heating plant was centrally located on the campus at that time and was in the basement of the graduate school building. The three huge boilers provided most of the steam for heating the buildings on the main part of the campus.

Two of the boilers had been converted to gas, but the third was still an oil burner. Thankfully, that was our backup boiler if one of the others was down or if we needed extra steam. We had to constantly monitor gauges and dials to ensure steam pressures were maintained and water levels kept at certain levels so that heat was flowing throughout the campus in underground pipes. We also had to regularly test the water for softness and alkalinity and add appropriate chemicals or regenerate the machines if the numbers were out of range.

My shift hours at the heating plant were generally 5 p.m. to 1 a.m. or the second shift was 1 a.m. to 8 a.m. A full-time employee worked the daytime shift. Often, I would work forty-hour weeks between the heating plant and landscaping. About thirty of those hours were on the weekend so I could give more attention to my studies through the week.

In my last couple of college years, I had met Betty at the West Suburban Hospital School of Nursing (West Sub) in Oak Park, Illinois. The nursing school was affiliated with Wheaton College. Even though her school was twenty-five miles away, I determined to spend maximum time with her, but I had to remember that I also had to work to pay my bills at the college!

For most of my last two years of college, I averaged a little over four and a half hours of sleep a night. Why? Because of so little sleep or study time on weekends (as described below), I often had to stay up late on weeknights to get my studying done.

Usually I went to work in the heating plant from 1–8 a.m. on Friday morning, went to class and studied the majority of Friday, then went in to West Sub in the evening for a date with Betty. I had to have her back in her dorm by midnight and then hustled back to my room at the college just in time to change clothes to get to the 1 a.m. heating plant shift on Saturday morning. That ended at 8 a.m. on Saturday, and I went right to work in landscaping on the campus. Upon finishing that day of work, I changed clothes and headed back in to West Sub to be with Betty, and again, she had to be in by midnight. I then drove back to Wheaton, changed clothes again and went to the heating plant for the 1–8 a.m. shift on Sunday. At 8 a.m., I showered and put on a suit and tie—that was a different era!—and four or five of us from the college drove to Naperville, about twenty minutes away where we were helping to start a new church. When morning church was over, the pastor or another church member normally invited us to their house for lunch, and then I crashed! That was approximately sixty hours without ever lying down to sleep! I was up again in time to help with the youth group of the church on Sunday evening.

When I finally got back to my room after church, I immediately went to bed and got a full night of sleep! I really don't know how I did all that, except to say that I was really in love with Betty and that I really had to work to pay my bills to stay in college! Love can make you do amazing things! I also think that the Lord was preparing me for some of the long hours I would have to endure in Army training and combat operations. The Lord was also giving me training in ministry by helping in the new church.

The work in the heating plant didn't stop when the weather warmed. That was the time to de-scale the inside of the boiler tanks. The boilers were probably fifteen to twenty-foot long and inside, they were five to six-foot in diameter. To de-scale, I had to crawl through a hole about eighteen-inches wide to get inside the massive, cavernous boiler, taking with me an air-hammer chisel, electric light, and some smaller hand tools. I wore ear plugs, nose and mouth mask filters, and goggles as I chipped the solid water scale from the entire inside of the boiler.

The dust sometimes was so thick that occasionally I had to go to the entrance hole to get some fresh air—and drinking water! Of course, the scale debris then had to be cleaned up, causing more dust. Working inside the boiler was hot, and I sweated profusely, causing the black dust to cling to my coveralls and any bare skin. It was not a fun job but it was necessary for the efficient operation of the boilers. When I finally came out of the boiler each day, I was completely black.

NIGHT SWITCHBOARD

The heating plant was also the location of the night telephone switchboard for the college and the communications center for the campus police. The day switchboard was transferred to the heating plant at 9 p.m., and we then handled all calls to the campus. Some of those were fascinating and somewhat intriguing.

We learned a lot about some of the students—not by eavesdropping but by answering questions and seeing who was calling whom in the dorms! We handled emergency calls in coordination with the campus cops and heard a lot from them about some of the unusual activities—some good and some bad—on the campus. That aspect of the heating plant job was very interesting.

Let me tell you about one incident. Each year in the springtime, the senior class would plan a Senior Sneak to some place out of the state. While the seniors were gone from campus, the junior class usually pulled some kind of prank on the seniors. Because of the roar of the boilers, we often could not tell what was going on outside the building.

The heating plant was very close to the central fountain and its pool on the campus. Late one night, the campus cop came to the heating plant and asked if I knew who had floated a lot of car wheels with tires in the fountain pool. I did not but found out later that some of the juniors had pulled wheels from a bunch of the seniors' cars in the parking lot while they were on Senior Sneak. These wheels and tires were put in the pool!

Surprise! When the seniors came back, they could not move their cars until they could find their car's wheel(s) at the fountain pool. Think about this: do you know your car's wheels well enough to be able to distinguish yours in size, style, and brand from a bunch of others? I would doubt it for most people. Many of the seniors didn't either and had to try on a couple of different wheels before they found their own. The seniors displayed quite a bit of aggravation over the whole thing, but the rest of us sort of leaned back and snickered. Fun, Fun, Fun! Unfortunately in today's era, such pranksters may be taken to court. How our world has changed!

CHANGING THE FLAG IN THE TOWER

One aspect of our work at the heating plant was to occasionally change, lower to half-mast, or raise the flag in the tower of Blanchard Hall, the old original building on the campus. This was the highest point on campus and required us to go above the fifth floor and climb across some planks, over rafters, and up some rickety stairs to get up to the point where we could physically handle the ropes and get to the flag. Very few people have had that privilege. And what a wonderful view it was from up there—especially raising the flag at sunrise! I have "been there, done that."

One Easter Sunday, I decided to have my own personal sunrise service in a place that I felt no one else had held one. I went to the Blanchard Tower, climbed up to the base of the fluttering flag hanging high above the campus, quietly sang a few songs, read some Scripture, and talked with my risen and living Lord before going back to the heating plant. That was a very special time for me.

A large church bell was a couple of landings below the flag pole in the tower structure. Once, I was asked to replace the rope to the bell. In addition to announcing other major events on campus—such as a major athletic victory—the bell was used by newly engaged couples to publicize their engagement. After gaining permission and getting a key to the trap-like door, the couple would climb steps up in the tower and pull the rope from a landing just below the bell. When the bell pealed out its sound across campus, everyone knew that an exciting event had just occurred, and in the spring, the bell would be rung quite often—mostly by senior students. I regret that Betty and I never rang the bell announcing our engagement, even though I had popped the big question to her on the campus front lawn just below the bell tower.

OTHER WORK EXPERIENCES

My work experiences had a couple of other variations. In 1977, I left the active Army and joined the Army Reserve. I thought the Lord was possibly leading me into some type of full-time Christian ministry. By now, I had a lot of church platform and choir-directing experiences, plus I had worked with youth quite a bit. I submitted applications and, in some cases, interviewed for youth and/or music positions in several churches, but the Lord did not give me peace about pursuing any of those, so I continued to volunteer my music leadership in our church.

In the meantime, to provide income for my family, I did some miscellaneous maintenance at our church, worked part-time with an appliance repair and maintenance company, and became the general manager of a biomedical equipment maintenance company with which hospitals and doctors' offices contracted for our

24/7 services. Our technicians inspected, evaluated, and repaired or replaced electric or electronic pieces of hundreds of items of medical equipment. I learned a lot about medical equipment and devices through this company and our employees.

During those years, I also was serving as an officer in the Army Reserve which helped somewhat with our family finances. My military duties are discussed earlier in this book. All of these interim jobs made me trust more in the Lord and in His provisions for my family. The Lord was gracious and always provided for our needs. On one occasion, a friend left a wonderful donation in our mailbox so that our family could go out and eat somewhere. How grateful we were for that special gift.

US ARMY'S PROFESSIONAL ASSOCIATION

Later, in 1980, I accepted a position with the Association of the United States Army (AUSA) with its headquarters right there in Northern Virginia. AUSA is the Army's privately-run professional association, although most of its key personnel are former Army personnel. It has chapters around the globe, helping to educate communities about the Army and its people. AUSA chapters were also great supporters for Army personnel on military posts and with government organizations.

My primary responsibility was with these chapters and AUSA's program for college ROTC cadets. I was privileged to be on many college campuses and to see the enthusiasm of these potential officers for their future assignments in the Army. I really enjoyed working with AUSA since I was continually connected with current events happening in the Pentagon and meeting people who strongly supported our military forces.

INDY 500 TRACK'S BRICKYARD

I visited several of the AUSA chapters each year, and the majority of them were near Army posts. One particular visit to the chapter in Indianapolis is very memorable. The chapter president was on the Indianapolis 500 Speedway board.

After a day's luncheon at a National Guard armory where I won a small plastic Indy 500 race car, we were taken to the racetrack and given a small bus trip around the big oval. When we got to the brickyard—the finish line for the race—I asked the driver of the bus to stop. I got out and pushed my plastic racecar hard enough so that it sailed across the finish line! I still have that car. I don't think that too

been there, done that!

many people have a toy race car that has zipped across the Indy 500 brickyard! That evening at a huge AUSA banquet, I was on the dais with all the VIPs from the city and was seated next to Miss Indiana of that year. What a life! It was always full of fun, excitement, and unexpected variety. I have certainly "been there, done that" by traveling on and around the Indianapolis 500 track and meeting important people. I thoroughly enjoyed it!

CHAPTER XXII

INTERESTING BIRTHDAY FACTS

DON'T BLAME ME!

I am often "accused" as having started World War II since I was born on December 3, 1941, just four days before the bombing of Pearl Harbor! I can assure you that I was too young to have anything to do with that horrible conflict for our nation. But that war certainly changed things in our family as policies developed by the US government during the war's early years impacted major decisions for missionaries. My parents were on furlough from their missionary ministries in Africa and lived in northern Indiana at that time. The war caused our family and many other missionary families and their children to be separated for several years as explained earlier in this book.

I have never been a big birthday celebration person. This could be because as a young missionary kid who spent a lot of time in boarding schools, any gifts were normally quite meager, and so it seemed there was not much reason for a big celebration. One gift that does stand out to me was a pint jar of homemade strawberry jam that my Aunt Helen—Dad's dear sister with whom we lived in 1948–1949—gave to me each year as a birthday present. The jam was sometimes early and sometimes late for my birthday, but she faithfully gave it to me, even up into my college years. It was the best strawberry jam I ever ate, and I hope that when I get to heaven, she will also have some there for me!

been there, done that!

RED CROSS NOTIFICATION IS WRONG

In my first tour in Vietnam, my wife and I had only two phone conversations. It is hard for military personnel overseas today to envision a world without instant communications—either by cell phone, WhatsApp, Skype, Facetime, or all these other modern-day digital and social media wonders! It was a different world.

About two months after arriving in Vietnam in 1965 for my first combat tour, Betty gave birth to our firstborn. When I arrived home after my year of combat duty, I was met by our ten-month old son, although I still struggle to get his birth-date correct. Why? In Vietnam, I had received a radio notification from a man at the Red Cross on September 14 announcing the arrival of Philip Ray Fogle Jr. on September 9, 1965. He had no details except that mother and son were doing fine. My wife regularly wrote letters, so I eagerly waited for her to tell me about details of the birth. These letters often arrived a couple of weeks after they were written and mailed. Remember, we didn't have email or texting back then!

I anxiously opened her letter dated September 9 only to read that the baby had not yet made his appearance. The letter of September 10 was the same and I began to wonder if the Red Cross had given me some "fake" news. The Red Cross caller had said Philip was born on the ninth but Betty's letters from the next two days said nothing about going to the hospital. Finally, her letter of the September 12 came and said Philip Jr. had been born the previous day. But in my mind the Red Cross's report of the birth on September 9 made a permanent mark since it arrived first. Slowly, I am getting the birth date correct since both of our daughters-in-law have birthdays on September 9. As I think of their birthdays, I am reminded that Phil Jr's is two days later!

When I came back to the US, Philip Jr. was already ten months old, and this was my first time to see him. His hair was long and curly, and I told Betty that I thought we had a boy! Betty had wanted me to have a "first" with him and wanted me to give him his first haircut. As a military guy, it didn't take long for us to get out our hair clipping set and get that issue resolved! I should really have been more sensitive to my wife's concerns at that point.

THANKS FOR A SPRAINED ANKLE

While telling about birthdays, I should also tell you the unusual circumstances regarding the birthdays of our other two—Deborah Lynn in June of 1967 and

Todd Andrew in March 1969. I was stateside for Debbie's birth since I was in the middle of an Army ROTC teaching assignment at Wheaton College in Illinois. I was scheduled on orders to go to Fort Riley, Kansas, for Wheaton cadets' six weeks of military summer camp training, and it looked like I was not going to be with Betty for Debbie's birth.

I regretted that I had already missed our first child's birth, and now I would probably miss our second baby's birth as well. I did not expect the Army to make any change to the situation. However, in ways that only the Lord could arrange, a few days before I was to depart, I severely sprained my ankle while playing basketball. The military doctor put me in a lower leg cast for ten days and restricted me from going to camp on the scheduled date. Sometimes, an adversity in life can turn into a real benefit!

On the sixth day in the cast, my wife woke me up and said if I was going to get shaved, I'd better do it quickly because she needed to get to the hospital! It didn't take long for me to get ready before we took off. Betty kept saying to hurry because her contractions were getting closer and closer. Believe me, I sped down the road and while crossing some railroad tracks, she let out a big groan. I began to wonder if I should stop for a "roadside" delivery! The hospital was only about five more miles away, and I asked her if I should keep going to which she replied, "Just go faster!" She said go straight to the emergency room where I dropped her off into a nurse's care, and I went to park the car.

I'm not sure that I realized the urgency of the situation as I took my time getting parked and into the waiting room since I had heard about long, anxious stays there. I had no sooner sat down in the waiting room among a few other men when a doctor came in asking for a Mr. Fogle. That was me! He said that I had a new daughter! I told him that I had just dropped my wife off, so he must have the wrong person. I wonder what those other waiting dads thought about me not having to wait even a few minutes when some of them had probably been there for hours.

The doctor went on to say that they barely got my wife into the labor bed when the baby arrived. Betty's own doctor had not even gotten to the hospital yet although Betty had called him before leaving home to tell him she was on the way to the hospital, and it wouldn't be long until the baby would arrive. So, our daughter Debbie was safely delivered, and I didn't have the long waiting room experience of so many dads. It was to be my first and only time of being present at the hospital for one of my children's births.

been there, done that!

After Betty came home a couple of days later from the hospital, I went back to my doctor to get the cast removed and was sent to Fort Riley, Kansas, the next day. I think I had only a couple of nights in my house with a newborn, and then I didn't see my wife or my new daughter for more than six weeks. Now while I was away, Betty had a twenty-one month-old boy and a baby girl to care for by herself. Her inner strength and support from local friends and our church kept her going in those days.

ANOTHER WRONG BIRTH ANNOUNCEMENT

So what is the story about our third child's birth? At the end of nearly two years at Wheaton College, I was ordered back to Vietnam. We made some trips from the western suburbs of Chicago to Indiana and soon purchased a house in South Bend where Betty would stay with the two young ones while I was overseas for another year. Now she could live independently in our own home, which was near my sister's family with similar age kids, my parents, and my home church family. They would all be a great blessing and assistance for Betty. She would be away from the big city of Chicago but near enough to visit with her folks and our kids' grandparents.

In August 1968, after I had been in Vietnam for about a month, I received a letter from Betty saying she was pregnant again. Oh my! This was a shock which neither one of us had anticipated! Obviously in those last few days before my deployment, we had some wonderful times together! We had no computers in those days and communications were by letter, cassette tape, or with a rare phone conversation via ham radio.

We had plenty of time to determine a name for a boy or a girl. How did we do that? We each made lists of potential child names and mailed them to each other. Betty then compiled our two lists—one for boy's names and one for girl's names. As the letters went back and forth, each of us would cross off names we did not want and after some months of communications, we narrowed our choices—one for a boy and one for a girl. The name chosen for a boy was Todd Andrew, but I don't remember the girl's name we had selected—nor does it matter.

March 1969 was the expected delivery and while on a combat mission in the highland's jungles of Vietnam, near Cambodia, I received a telegram notice from the Red Cross announcing Todd's birth. But—the telegram information was wrong again! It read that Todd Alexander was born on March 10. I thought:

"Where did Betty get that second name? It had been crossed off the list very early in our letters". Since Betty wrote letters every day, I waited anxiously to hear her story about the name change. In Betty's next letter, she confirmed our original choice of Todd Andrew. I guess the lesson in all this is to not believe all the news we receive.

These were times when we wished so much that we could talk together, but I was out in the boonies and had no way to even get to a phone. Bottom line: both times when my boys were born while I was in Vietnam, the Red Cross had given me wrong information! I have long since forgiven them since the facts were eventually revealed, and the news from them came much faster than snail mail. At least I knew that the boys' births were successful!

One of the unique characteristics about the birthdays of the three males in our family is that all three of us were born in the same place—Memorial Hospital in South Bend, Indiana—with many years, miles, and places where we had been between our births. The boys were both born while I was in Vietnam, and it so happened in God's timing that I also was born in South Bend while my missionary parents were there on furlough from Africa.

THE KIDS TODAY—2022

Phil Jr. works for an insurance company in Alabama, and is married to Bunny who is a health care administration and nurse educator with an earned PhD. Their kids are Brooke, who is attending Cedarville University in Ohio, and Nick, who is a junior in high school.

Debbie and her husband, Jim, live near us in Florida. Debbie is a medical assistant in a doctor's office and Jim is an instructional technology provider with a local program dealing with preschool children. Ethan is an entrepreneur in the eco-agricultural field. Katy is a missionary appointee to Uganda (where she has already served as an intern for two and a half years). She works in a department store while generating her missionary support. David is with a retail fishing outfit in Nicaragua.

Todd is a brigadier general in the US Air Force and has had special operations assignments across the globe. His wife, Johanna, is a great military wife who has supported Todd in his continuous moves and during separations caused by combat duties. She works in an oral surgeon's dental office. Nathan is employed by an optics company in Michigan, Claire serves as a theater stage manager in various

been there, done that!

places and Adam has graduiated from high school and plans to attend Cedarville University starting in 2022. Betty and I are proud to have such a wonderful family.

CELEBRATING BETTY'S FIFTIETH BIRTHDAY

Now, I don't want to forget about one of Betty's birthdays. At the time of her fiftieth birthday, I was the director of the Moody Keswick Bible Conference in St. Petersburg, Florida. The center had a nine-foot Steinway grand piano in the chapel that was used extensively for concerts, regular services, and occasionally by the Christian school co-located on the campus. The piano showed considerable wear and its strings were breaking—even in the middle of a concert! I decided to have it refurbished and contracted with a Steinway dealer in the area for the project. The dealer explained that it was a valuable piano and that it was built in 1894. It was 100 years old! But it needed new strings, hammers, and other parts as well as a complete refinishing inside and out.

The restoration of the piano was complete for the beginning of the Bible conference season, and I invited a concert pianist friend to come and play for a special rededication of the piano for our ministry. We had an afternoon concert at 3 p.m. and another at 7 p.m. on a Saturday. Although I had not pre-planned it on purpose, the concert date also happened to be Betty's birthday.

At the halftime intermission of each concert program, I gave some comments about the history of the piano and that the piano was now 100 years old. But I also announced that this was Betty's birthday and that she was "half again as old as this piano," intending to mean that she was fifty. The snickering suddenly told me something was wrong! What I had said actually would have made her 150 years old! Oh, did I ever hear about my 150 year old wife—but I'll say that she looked much better at her age of fifty than that newly refurbished piano we were celebrating, even though it was like new! Betty never let me forget that faux pas!

But to help her remember that birthday, I asked that both concerts' guests sing *Happy Birthday* to her. There were more than 1,000 people in the two concerts that day. Plus, more than 100 people sang to her in the dining room of the conference center that evening and another 100 or so at the afterglow following the evening concert. Betty does not like to be up front and be recognized but this was a birthday she will never forget! How many people have had about 1200 people sing *Happy Birthday* to them? She was an extra special celebrity that day!

BLACK BALLOONS COVERED MY CEILING

I guess that I should also mention something about my fiftieth birthday. Our son, Phil Jr., was an advanced-level mathematics teacher in St. Petersburg, Florida, at Keswick Christian School, co-located with the Moody Keswick Conference Center where I was the director. I was sitting in my office in the chapel building when a young person in a black choir robe came to my office carrying a helium-filled, black balloon and said "Happy Birthday". Then she left. I passed that off as a greeting from the school. Soon, in comes another person (dressed the same) carrying another black balloon, then another, and another, and another! Altogether in the end, fifty of those black balloons were floating all over my ceiling covering the lights and making my office very dark. My son had been up to one of his tricks. He had arranged for all of this making my fiftieth birthday very special and memorable!

I have often said that I wish I had been born at Kyabe par Fort Archambault in French Equatorial Africa! Why? I could have raised a lot of eyebrows filling out forms for the US Government since the length of the names of my likely birthplace wouldn't have fit in the government allocated spaces. And besides, that country (French Equatorial Africa) no longer existed after the early 1960s at the

been there, done that!

time when I was filling out forms for the Army! I'm not sure I would have been granted any security clearances if I had used those actual place names!

CHAPTER XXIII

SPORTS

AFRICA—KICKBALLS MADE FROM INTESTINES

I have always enjoyed sports—both watching and playing. In Africa at the boarding school, we had very few organized sports. Yes, we played some touch football, but it was just run and get open and hope that the ball would be thrown to me, and if it was, run for an end line before a defensive person tagged you. We did play some softball, but again, we didn't necessarily have all the positions filled and we didn't have ball gloves, so it made the game a little interesting if a ball was hit hard at you or if someone threw a fast ball to you. I guess we got used to doing what we could if the ball came our way—sometimes even with our feet!. The bottom line was that I had no information on the real rules of any of the games.

Out in the village at our home in Kyabe, I would play whatever the other kids were playing. One little game was spinning a snail shell on the hard ground and try to get certain points by flipping it upside down with your hand into certain circles before it stopped spinning. In other games, sometimes we had a ball but other times we did not, so we would improvise! Most parts of an animal Dad killed were either edible or in some manner usable.

One animal part which I used with boys from the village was the intestines. After a hunt, we would wash some of these parts well and then tie one end very tightly. We would then blow into the stretchable intestine until it formed a fairly "round" ball and then tie off that end much like we would a balloon to prevent the air from escaping. Now we had a nice and really soft kickball! We always tried to play in an open, sandy area so that our "ball" would not get punctured by a

been there, done that!

stick or a thorn. But if it did, we would just make another ball—since we didn't have any duct tape to seal the hole! We did learn that some animals' intestines were thicker than others, so for example, it was better for us to use a wild boar's intestines rather than those from a young antelope!

We had a croquet set, which we introduced as a game to the village kids. They occasionally would try to kick the ball through the wicket instead of using the mallet, but soon discovered that the croquet ball was a little harder on the feet and not as soft as an intestine ball!

HIGH SCHOOL

For high school, I was at Mid-Maples in Wheaton, Illinois, and we missionary kids went to Wheaton Academy, which was probably one of the best things that ever happened to me! I really wanted to learn sports, having come from Africa where we didn't have American organized sports. Because the academy was small (under 250 students), I had a much better chance of getting involved in its sports program. I would not be competing for a team spot against many other students who had been playing organized sports much of their lives.

FOOTBALL—UNDEFEATED 1957 TEAM!

Football season was right at the beginning of my freshman year, and I attended every game that I could get to that fall. I just wanted to be involved somehow. In my sophomore year, I managed the football team's equipment room and began to learn the fine points of the positions and the rules of the game.

In my junior year of high school, I made it on the varsity football team as a kicker (not punter) and a third-string quarterback on offense. I also played as a defensive end on the first team even though I was quite small. I seemed to have the right knack for aggressively playing that position and containing outside running by the opposing team. At times, I was moved to a cornerback slot.

That year, 1957, was an unbelievable year as our team won every game and to this day, it is the only undefeated football team since the school's founding in 1853! Team members were invited back for a special recognition in 2012 for our induction into the Academy's Hall of Honor. I was there as part of that weekend celebration!

Undefeated 1957 Football Team

In the fall of my senior year, we again had a great football team—but not undefeated. I injured the thigh of my kicking leg and could no longer do the kicking but still played first string defense and was "promoted" to second string quarterback.

A sad thing happened in one of our practices that year. I was playing a defensive cornerback position and a running back broke past our defensive front line. Our defensive safety, D, and I tackled the ball carrier at the same time. After helping the running back up, he went back to the offensive huddle and was getting ready for the next play when he suddenly collapsed. Medical personnel attended to him, and he was rushed to the hospital where he remained for about nine weeks. As I remember, he had sustained a broken blood vessel in his brain. He eventually returned to school but had severe speech and cognitive problems. D and I have reminisced sadly about this tackle but know in our hearts that we were not in any way at fault. It is a hazard of sports.

BASKETBALL—A GREAT BENCH WARMER

I figured that a good way to learn sports was to manage a team because I would be there for all practices and games. The coach accepted me as the manager of the basketball teams when I was a freshman. In the fall of my sophomore

been there, done that!

year, I tried out for the basketball team and at least made it to the bench! I only got in toward the end of games if we had a substantial lead on the opponent. But I continued to learn more about playing the game and did really enjoy the time with the team—especially traveling to away games and getting to miss some school classes.

I did not play basketball as a junior or senior and in fact did not even try out for the team when I realized that we had some excellent players who had been dribbling and shooting basketballs since they were little kids. I knew that some of them could keep that bench just as warm as I had kept it!

TRACK—TEAM CAPTAIN

Track season was in the winter and spring. I determined that there really weren't any significant rules to learn. You just strip down to a flimsy pair of shorts and a tank top, put on a pair of lightweight, spiked shoes, and run around a loop on a wood or cinder track (in those days!) as fast as you can!

I was not a speedster, but I seemed to have good endurance and ended up running the half-mile and the mile individual races and in most of the long-distance, four-person relays. In my freshman year, my times came down in a fairly consistent manner and I was having fun—although I sure didn't like taking off my warm-up, sweat clothes when it was so cold outside in the early spring!

Each year, I continued to improve and felt that I was an asset to the team. One little quirk to this is that in our sophomore biology class, we had measured our vital capacity (lung volume) and I had the smallest capacity of the entire class, yet I was a primary distance runner on the track team!

I was on the track team all four years and tried desperately to get my mile time down to five minutes and finally succeeded near the end of the track season of my junior year. I was really happy to meet that goal.

Our team participated in some indoor track meets in Chicago in the winter and early spring. Some of the indoor arenas were quite small, and for the mile race at one place, we had to go around the wooden track sixteen times! That almost got dizzying! Most of those smaller indoor tracks had banked curves, which made running a little different. Thank goodness for our coaches on the sideline who held up signs telling me how many laps I had to go because I lost count almost every race on those small indoor tracks.

Track practices were after school as for most sports, and they could be grueling. Our coach wanted me to reach my peak performances and really pushed me with a variety of distances—being monitored constantly against the stopwatch. In addition to the afternoon practices, the coach wanted me to have a good distance workout in the mornings.

Our Mid-Maples missionary kid (MK) home was five miles from Wheaton Academy. In the morning, I would give my schoolbooks to another MK who was riding the bus to carry them to school for me. I would then run the five miles to school to be there in time for a shower and then to my first class. On days when the snow was too deep, I rode the bus with the other kids. I started this morning run routine in the mid-winter of my junior year and continued the same training in my senior year when I was selected as the track team captain.

Our team did very well in our league and in regional competitions. We participated in some significant track meets against large public and many private schools in the greater Chicago area. One meet was at Stagg Field—which had been Chicago University's football stadium. However, we were told not to go to certain sections of the stadium because that is where some of the work on the atomic bomb had been done and radioactivity still remained in the structure. That was interesting to learn about, but to us teenagers, that really didn't have much meaning at the time. We were there to run—and that we did!

In the state competition at the end of my senior year, I ran my best mile ever. My time was four minutes and thirty-six seconds! I had run a few other races under five minutes that year but never dreamed I would get that good of a time. However, I still only placed fifth in the state meet. Some guys were just plain fast!

SLOW PITCH SOFTBALL

I did not play any sports in college because I had to work to cover all my own costs of tuition, room and board, and miscellaneous fees. I sort of wished that I could have been on the track team, but there just wasn't time for even the intramural sports. After college, I did play some softball with church teams.

I had played fast-pitch softball in Indiana when I lived with my folks in the summer of 1959. The church was in a teenager's league for churches and city teams. It also had an adult men's fast-pitch team in a combined church and industrial league. I loved to watch those underhanded pitchers whip that softball over the home plate and decided that I wanted to fast-pitch for the teen league and did so for quite a few games before I had to head off to college.

Slow-pitch softball was very different, and in later years, very few churches or even cities had fast-pitch teams and leagues. Fast-pitch now seemed relegated to girls' and women's teams and some of those ladies can really put some speed on that ball! As I moved in my military assignments, I had the opportunity to join church teams and slow-pitched for them. Occasionally, I would also play catcher, but I enjoyed the pitching much more. My greatest fear was always about that ball being hit back at me—probably because I had gotten hit pretty hard a couple of times in other games.

One season for our church team in Virginia, my batting average was in the upper .300s. Our team coach felt that was pretty good for a guy who did not have extensive experience playing the sport as a young person. I certainly was not a long-ball hitter but seemed to be able to get the ball just beyond the infielders' reach and short of the outfielders' ability to get to the ball. The fellowship with other ball players was one of the great aspects of playing on a team, and I did enjoy the sport.

Although now I don't play any sports due to some physical limitations, I do like to watch college and professional football games. Except for cheering on home teams, I usually pull for the underdog team in whatever sport I am watching. I am really happy when that team has an upset victory. When watching a track meet on TV, I almost get out of breath while "mentally running" with the people on the track. I know what it feels like since I have "been there, done that"!

CHAPTER XXIV

MY VEHICLES

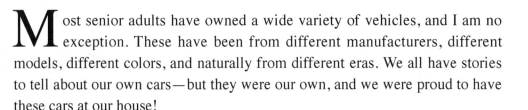

Most senior adults have owned a wide variety of vehicles, and I am no exception. These have been from different manufacturers, different models, different colors, and naturally from different eras. We all have stories to tell about our own cars—but they were our own, and we were proud to have these cars at our house!

BEES IN THE BACK SEAT

During my parents' furlough from their missionary service in Africa in 1959–1960, our family lived again in Mishawaka, Indiana. Following my high school graduation, several of us in the church youth group were quite active in the county Youth for Christ ministry's weekend rallies. One of the older teens had the idea of getting an old car and using it as an attraction while driving around to invite kids to the Saturday night Youth For Christ rallies. I liked the idea and said I would help him.

We searched around and found a 1931 Model T Ford in a junk yard and thought it could be fixed up and used for our purpose. The body was solid and the motor was complete but not running, so we decided to pull it to my house and fix it up in our alley garage. The brakes didn't work well but the emergency brake was there when needed. We hooked up a chain to his car, and we headed down the road toward home—about ten miles away. I was "driving" the Model T, and because there was no battery in the car, I had no horn to contact the lead vehicle nor did I have any brake lights to warn people behind me. I had learned and had to use basic hand signals for turning or stopping.

As we rattled and shook going down the road from the junk yard, bees awoke in their previously unseen hive under the back seat of the Model T! Fortunately the windows were all down and the wind coming in the front by my driver's window tended to keep most of the bees in the back of the car unless they flew out the window. I don't know what kept them away from me, but thankfully I didn't get stung while I was "driving" for over a half hour.

When we stopped the car in the alley behind our house, I got out and slammed the door which really alarmed the bees and instantly, they were everywhere. I ended up with a few stings as I sprayed them, but it did take a few days for us to garner courage to get in the car to clean the hive out. Little by little, we worked to get the car in shape but by the end of the summer, our rallies had stopped and the car just sort of sat and I left for college. I don't know what happened to the car! My friend must have taken it to his home. We did have a lot of fun trying to get it ready for a ministry usage. That was my/our first car!

COAL ASH COVERED THE CAR

My parents were home for my high school graduation in 1959, and I spent that summer with them in Indiana and got my driver's license. After working in various summer jobs, I bought a sedan from a lady who paid me to care for her yard, wash windows, and do other jobs around her house. She lived next to an alley where all the clinkers from the coal furnaces were dumped and naturally, there was a lot of black dust on windows, her outdoor furnishings, and on the garage which was accessed from the alley.

Near the end of the summer while washing the garage windows, I peered inside the dark garage and saw something big, but in the dim light filtering through the two windows, I couldn't figure out what it was.

Being real curious, I asked the lady about it. She told me about this car which her husband had bought just before he died about five years earlier. She had never learned to drive, so after his death, the car was initially left out on the street in front of her house. One day someone ran into it and dented the rear door so she decided to have the car moved into the garage where it sat for about four years! She had forgotten all about it and had not even been in the garage in a long time. The car had a heavy coat of coal ash all over it. It was a black, four-door, Deluxe model, 1948 Chevrolet.

I needed a car, so I asked her if I could buy it from her. She said she didn't know if it would even run. I said my dad could get it going since I had seen his mechanical abilities in Africa, and he also had a brother who worked as a mechanic at the South Bend Gates Chevrolet dealership. She told me she would think about it. I went home and talked with my dad, who immediately said we should pray for a couple of days about whether I should buy it. That was good counsel!

Going back to the lady, I asked her what her price was and she said she would sell it to me for $200. I thought that was a steep price for something that we didn't know would run, and besides I was a missionary kid without much money and was headed off to college. She asked what I thought I could afford and I offered her $50, thinking that there was no way she would sell it for that! My thought was that the car was already eleven years old and had been sitting for four years so it shouldn't be worth too much. I feel that she took pity on me and agreed to my offer! Again I realized that God still answers prayer, and this was my first effort to really "bargain" for a deal! I was very excited and immediately rode home on my bike to solicit Dad's help to get the car home.

He got some tools to pull spark plugs and check the distributor. Then we bought a new battery and a couple gallons of gas on the way over to get the car. We also took a tire pump because I had noticed the tires were a little low but not flat! (I realized later that the tires were real rubber and when they sat on an immobile car or in cold weather, they would develop a "flat" spot. That spot would round itself out when the car was driven for a little while.) Believe it or not, after

been there, done that!

Dad checked a few things, the car started right up, and we decided that I would follow Dad home with me driving my "new" car!

We pulled out in the alley going very slowly and headed toward the street. He stopped at the sidewalk to check on traffic and I pushed on the brake pedal in my car. Oh, Oh! The pedal went all the way to the floor and the car didn't stop. Fortunately, I was only going a couple of miles per hour, but I then had my first accident and bumped into the back of his car! The bumpers matched, and there was no damage, but I really felt bad since I should have known enough to pull the emergency brake. I had hardly owned the car for half a day and already had an accident with it!

Dad gently drove the car back to the lady's garage, using the hand brake to stop it, and we then went out to get some brake fluid—the one thing we had failed to check. Finally, we got the car home, and I began the work of cleaning it up and evaluating what I had just bought. In talking with my uncle at the Chevrolet dealership, he said that my car model was the top of the line in 1948. It had vacuumatic transmission, a quality radio for that era, velour-type upholstery (which was in great shape), carpet, real chrome on the outside and inside, and the body was heavy-gauge metal. When I polished it up, the deep black body and chrome really shone, and I was one proud car owner—even with its dented door!

I was not permitted to have it at college my freshman year, so I left it in the care of a friend in the church youth group and his dad. He could start it and drive it occasionally and keep the piles of snow off of it. That "kid" eventually became a long-term pastor of our home church in Mishawaka, Indiana.

I did take the car to college in my sophomore year, and it was a real asset. Every Sunday, I took four or five of my college classmates to Naperville, south of Wheaton, Illinois, where we were involved in a church planting ministry. Most of the car's mileage that year was driving to and from church twice each Sunday, Wednesday evenings, and occasionally for youth functions or visitation. I never did have the dent in the door fixed.

CLUNK, CLUNK, CLUNK ON THE HIGHWAY

The summer after my sophomore year of college, one of my high school classmates from Mid-Maples—the MK home where we lived during our high school years—was getting married in Pennsylvania. I offered to drive several of us kids from Wheaton out to the wedding. About 2 a.m. while driving on the Ohio turnpike, my eyes suddenly caught the dial of the oil pressure gauge drop rapidly down to zero. Then there were some clunk, clunk, clunk noises, and I pulled off to the side of the road. I remember looking under the hood and seeing oil all over the engine. A quick prayer meeting ensued. Then a vehicle stopped behind us and offered to take me to the next exit to an all-night garage. They had a tow truck and took me back to where the car was and all of us piled in the car—I am not sure that would be legal today!—and rode behind the tow truck to the garage. There we were told that the rubber oil line from the pan to the filter broke under the pressure and heat of the engine. I had owned the car for two years by this time and as a very amateur mechanic, I never thought to check the rubber hoses in the engine compartment. It was obvious that they had begun to rot.

Now, what were these young college students going to do? One girl said she would call her dad and after explaining our dilemma, he said we could use his station wagon to go on to the wedding. There was only one problem. How would we get it? We were half way across Ohio, and the station wagon was in north central Indiana. A couple of the kids said they would hitch hike back to pick up the car. It was now beginning to get light, and they were successful at getting a ride. About eight hours later, we had transferred things from my Chevy to the station wagon and were off to the wedding. We left my car at the garage in Ohio and would work on getting it later.

ENGINE REBUILT FOR $67

That summer, since my parents were back in Africa, I was living with the pastor of our home church in Indiana. He had a son, D, who was my age. A couple of weeks after the wedding, D and I took the pastor's car out to Ohio and towed my car back to Mishawaka. Because the pastor had been a missionary in Africa prior to becoming the pastor of the church, he liked to fix his own vehicles and had constructed a car pit in his garage. This was similar to the car pits in oil-change businesses here in the US.

D and I pushed my car over the pit and determined that we were going to take the engine apart and fix it ourselves. Mechanics told us we could never do that without pulling the engine completely out, but we proved them wrong! For $67 worth of parts, we rebuilt the engine. We pulled the crankshaft out, had it ground to new specifications, put in new oversized piston bearings, pulled the engine head and installed new piston rings, added new carburetor parts, and basically

been there, done that!

fixed all parts we could find. The car started up with the first turn of the key! D and I, as amateur mechanics—with expert advice of my uncle at Gates Chevrolet and from the pastor—were pleasantly surprised at the end of our work! Where could one get an engine rebuilt for $67 today?

In the meantime, for me to get to work at a lumberyard about twenty miles away, I had bought a 1952 Chevrolet which I decided to take back to college in my junior year. I then sold the 1948 Chevrolet for $100—twice the cost of what I had paid for it, but it now had an almost-new engine in it. I would sure like to have that car now!

VW BUG MEETS A DEER

Betty and I bought a number of cars over the years, moving from one vehicle in 1964 until in the late 1980s we had five cars—one for each of the three kids, plus Betty and I each had one. With two other college classmates, Phil Jr. was taking our 1971 VW (Volkswagen) Super Beetle from Springfield, Virginia, back to Cedarville College (now is Cedarville University) in Ohio after a winter break when the car hit a deer in Pennsylvania. Thankfully, no one was hurt, but the VW bug was severely damaged.

The boys managed to pull the fender out far enough so the tire wouldn't rub on it and sort of taped a headlight in place and headed on to school. The accident had buckled the hood of the car which opened it up to let cold winter weather in with the boys. Phil Jr. needed a car at college, so we ended up taking another of our cars to him, and I would drive the damaged VW back home. Because the engine was in the rear, the motor was not disabled, so it ran fine.

When I got in the car in Cedarville in January 1985 to bring it back to our home in Virginia, it wouldn't start. The battery had frozen in the night, and when we checked the temperature, it was minus 46°F. Yes, that is minus 46°F with a news report of the wind chill bringing the feel-like temperature to minus 62°F degrees! That is too cold for this African jungle bunny! But we had to get back home to Virginia, so we took the battery inside to thaw, got the car started, bundled up by wrapping blankets around our legs, and took off. I had two high school boys and our youngest son in the car with me.

Because of our breathing, the windows quickly frosted up, so I pulled out credit cards and had the boys scraping the frost off the inside of the windows so I could see to drive. For some reason, I didn't have an ice scraper in the car.

If you know anything about that vintage of VW beetles, you are aware that the heaters did not work very well, and it took a long time and many miles before we could get enough heat to come from the rear engine to eliminate the window frosting problem. We stopped at a friend's house (still in Ohio) on the way home and pulled the battery and took it inside so we could be assured of the car starting in the morning to finish our drive home. We had the car repaired and used it for quite a while after the accident.

THE RALLY-RED DASHER

One of my cars was a new 1974 VW Dasher. In my eyes, it was a bright red-orange, but VW called its color Rally-Red. I really liked that car, and it got great gas mileage—especially when drafting behind big trucks. On a trip from Virginia to North Carolina, I got sixty-three miles per gallon and was I ever happy to broadcast that around! However, none of my kids ever liked the Dasher. It had a stick shift on the floor and was the car I used for teaching each of them to drive. I wanted them to know how to drive a stick shift car in case they would need that skill sometime in their future.

One evening, Phil Jr. used the Dasher for a date and was just a few blocks from delivering the girl back to her home. When in the process of shifting gears, the gear shift stick came out of the floor with him holding it in his hand. Now what? I don't remember how the date ended, but I sort of jokingly "accused" him of trying to delay getting the girl home. At least he wasn't out on some distant road with her because if he had been, my story may have been more plausible. Probably, in using the gear shift in previous months, it had become unscrewed from the base and at the inopportune moment, it came out in his hand. Maybe that's why Phil didn't like the car, and the other two kids may have been adversely influenced by Phil's dilemma that night.

MY "TOYS" GO TO THE KIDS

I had recently bought a new 1985 blue Honda CRX HF model. It was my mid-life "toy", but I ended up giving that to Phil to take to college in his junior year since unintentionally he had gone through two of my other cars. I had gotten to use my CRX for only a few months and really liked this little compact car. So I began to look for another and bought a used white CRX a year later. I ended

been there, done that!

up giving that one to Debbie, who needed a car after her college graduation. I still didn't have a little two-seater hatchback which I really wanted. After some extensive looking, I ended up finding a red CRX just like the other two, but soon that became Todd's to take to college. I guess I wasn't supposed to have such a nice "toy".

I tried to find a time when all three of these cars would be together so I could get a picture of my red, white, and blue CRXs and send it to the Honda company. But one of the cars was always somewhere else. I really hadn't intended to be so patriotic with my cars. It just ended up that way!

Later, we traded our Honda Accord to Debbie in Illinois to get the white CRX back and knew that Todd with his red one would be home before long on college break. Phil Jr. was in Florida with his blue one, so this was going to be my chance for the picture since we were in the process of moving to Florida. Unfortunately, only a week or so before we moved, Phil's blue car was totaled in an accident and we never got the picture. Why do some things never turn out as planned?

We have had several other cars and used them extensively for our ministry trips for Moody Keswick Conference Center and for D&D Missionary Homes. In recent years we have owned vans, which are much more convenient for long-term travel.

CHAPTER XXV

WILDLIFE VIGNETTES

ANIMALS

Every couple of weeks when I lived at Kyabe in Africa, Dad would have to go on a hunt to get us some fresh meat to eat, and I was delighted to go with him. There was a river about five miles behind the mission property, and we would often go there early in the morning or to a natural watering hole and try and get some kind of animal.

We had many animals and birds in the savannah-like area—several kinds of small and large antelope, ostrich, turkey-like birds, wild buffalo, guinea hen, giraffe, occasionally an elephant, and wild boar. Monkeys were abundant. Sometimes we would find an abandoned baby animal, so as kids we did have monkeys and antelope as pets—in addition to cats, dogs, and goats. The wide variety of the area's wild animals provided meat for us and for natural predators. Usually we came home from a hunt with some type of game. We rarely killed to get a trophy. Rather, hunting was to get meat for our table, and whatever we saw first was what provided our dinner. Since we didn't have a freezer to hold meat for long, our African friends also benefited from a successful hunt. Sometimes we would see a pack of wild dogs or hyenas, but we never ate them, so we never shot them. You would think that we would see lions but that was rare. We could hear them back by the river, but in five years in Africa, I only saw one wild lion and that was from a great distance.

Because there was such a wide variety of big game in our general area, occasionally an individual from the US would contact us and ask if we could accommodate them for a big game hunt. Dad could help them get appropriate permits and take them out in our truck for their hunts, but Dad would not let them shoot any animals just "for fun". It had to be for their trophy animal from which most of the meat would go to our people in the village.

One group of these "hunters" was a professional photography team. They wanted pictures both during the daylight and in the night hours. They brought huge spotlights, which Dad temporarily mounted on the truck for their night photographic shoots. I went out with the photographers a couple of times. Early in the mornings, they could usually get good pictures of several kinds of wild animals at a watering hole and also some hippos in the river. At night, they got movies of a pack of wild dogs chasing and killing an antelope. I can still picture in my mind the piercing eye reflections of the wild dogs as the spotlights shone on them.

During our hunting, the Africans would teach me how to track animals, and in places where we needed it, they taught me camouflage techniques. I didn't realize it then, but those informal lessons would play an important part of my future Army career as a Ranger.

Some special animal memories come back to me. Dad had shot a large antelope through its front shoulders, and it immediately went down. We came near it and were waiting for one of the Africans to spear it and finish it off—since Dad didn't want to use another bullet—when suddenly it kicked hard with its hind legs, shoving it forward with its head at ground level, and its foot long horns headed right for me! He missed, but I was one scared boy for a few minutes! And I learned to never stand in front of a wounded or "dead" animal!

Our main source for lard in the southern Chad was from a hippopotamus. Under its outer skin is a thick layer of lard. But since it was such a large animal, you didn't want to shoot it in the water lest you couldn't get it on shore. You can only roll a hippo so far before its legs stop you from moving it farther! It is just too big and heavy! We ensured that the Africans who were skinning the hippo would be very careful so that no dirt got into the lard while we were down at the river. From one hippo, we got a fifty-five-gallon barrel full of lard that lasted all of us on the mission station a long time! Obviously, the fat under the outside skin was quite thick, and the tough meat provided great eating—for the villagers! We got some of the meat but I am not sure what part of the hippo it came from.

At the dorm at our boarding school, we often heard about some of the wild animals in the nearby jungle. One of the fiercest and most dangerous animals out there is the cape buffalo. Often the nurse in the dispensary would tell us about another African who had been attacked and seriously gored while on a path to their garden or between villages. These people would be brought to her dispensary for treatment, but all too often the patient didn't survive. Apparently, the buffalo becomes aggravated by just seeing a person in its territory. I have heard that cape buffalo kill more people in a year in Africa than any other animal.

DON'T LOOK IN THOSE HOLES!

In the early 1950s, a new missionary couple moved to Kyabe to help my parents in the ministry. Their shipped baggage was slow in arriving. That was not an unusual thing for where we lived, so they learned to live for several months with the luggage they had carried with them.

When their barrels and crates finally arrived, Uncle B first wanted to see if his big elephant gun (.375 magnum) for hunting was there and if it worked. Unexpectedly, at our house about fifty yards from theirs, we heard a loud "POW"! We rushed over to their house to find the new missionary laughing and commenting on how well his gun worked. He had stood in the back door of his house and shot a chicken about twenty-five feet away! With that size gun and ammunition, nothing was left but some scattered feathers! Normally when we killed a chicken, it was because we wanted something to eat, but we were now with one less dinner! Uncle B had some things to learn about using that gun and what it should and should not be used for.

Not too long after Uncle B arrived at Kyabe, Dad and some of the Chadians took him on a hunt. I was also on this trip. We had parked the truck and had begun to quietly track an antelope by its fresh hoof prints when we came upon a large hole in the ground. All of us (except Uncle B) had previously seen these holes and knew to stay away. Wild boars dig these as their "nests" and to escape some of the burning sun's heat.

The boars were big, powerful, and dangerous with their curved tusks. (In fact, one missionary had his vehicle turned on its side by a boar charging it and rooting under it to flip it.) This new missionary "hunter" was forewarned: "Don't look in those holes" to see if it was occupied. But you know the power of curiosity! Uncle B lagged behind the group a little and decided to check out a hole. Then we heard a loud bang from his elephant gun. A large boar had rushed out of the hole, ran between his legs—fortunately spread in time!—and upended Uncle B into the dirt as he accidently pulled the trigger. That was a lesson learned, and

been there, done that!

thankfully, no one was hurt. As I recall, we did not have a successful hunt that day. The sound of his big gun must have chased away all the animals!

MY RED RYDER BB GUN

Much in contrast to that powerful elephant gun, I had been given a Red Ryder BB gun for Christmas, and for practice, I would often get up early in the morning to go out and shoot some of the big, colorful lizards which seemed to be everywhere. I guess they were out for their morning breakfasts. I got pretty good at picking them off from fifteen to twenty feet away, and some days would end up with more than ten in a little bag which I gave to some of the workmen who, I assume, ate them.

That BB gun might have been enough to get an eight to twelve inch long lizard, but it sure didn't have sufficient power to put down a small antelope. The smallest adult antelope in our area, called an *ouia*, was no taller than about twenty-four inches. A group of boys from the village went out on a "hunt" with me one day, thinking I could get some mice or lizards or maybe a bird for them to take back to their huts for a meal. I was the big white hunter with my BB gun!

We saw a young ouia that I was going to shoot for them, but they said they wanted to try and catch it. So we formed a circle, and as it tried to escape, we would try to grab it. They had done this before, but I thought it would be easier to shoot it. My little BBs must have bounced off of it because when the BB hit it, the ouia would just flinch a little and head another way in the circle. The BBs never even broke its skin. It finally escaped and proved to me that this young hunter wasn't as good as he expected to be.

FUN INSIDE AN ELEPHANT

Probably the most exciting animal story during my years at the school in Africa was when one of the missionaries shot an elephant. There was going to be a big conference for the African pastors and church leaders, and rather than shoot several animals to get sufficient meat for the week, the missionary shot an elephant. All of us kids at the dorm were invited to go out to see the elephant before it was butchered up into pieces so it could be brought back to the mission compound.

Picture courtesy of David Watkins

It was huge as it lay there on its side. As the Africans began to "gut" the animal, we kids were running up over its extended trunk and head to the top of its rib cage and played King of the Mountain! Then, for those of us brave souls, *after* the intestines and other parts were pulled out, we were allowed to get inside the huge hollowed-out cavity where the stomach and intestines had been. How many other people can say they have "been there, done that" <u>inside</u> an elephant?

It was a little creepy being inside that mammoth body, and we didn't get to stay in there very long so that the butchers could continue their work with axes and machetes. We remained and watched until the elephant was all cut up with just scraps and the stench left for the buzzards and hyenas. That unusual experience sort of made me think a little about Jonah in the belly of the great fish. At least I wasn't under water and in a stomach with everything else! Now you can see why I say this was an exciting story. It's true! Do you want to know how to eat an elephant (besides "one bite at a time"?) See the chapter in this book on "PHIL WILL EAT ANYTHING!"

been there, done that!

WHERE'S OUR BUDDY? ASK A TIGER

Part of the war mission of my unit in my second combat tour in Vietnam was to establish listening posts (LPs) across a wide swath of terrain to give us early warning of the enemy's intentions. These LPs would be out for several days and consisted of three to four soldiers. With this number, one or more could always be on the alert when the others were sleeping. They were required to check in with us in the operations center at designated times by a certain code on the radio so that they could remain silent.

One night, the designated signal was not received from an LP. We waited and waited and then tried to contact the LP but to no avail. The next morning, we had to send out a patrol to the LP site to determine what had happened. Maybe it was a bad radio or dead batteries.

Apparently the soldier who was supposed to be alert fell asleep and a tiger (or some type of large jungle cat) killed him instantly and quietly dragged him off while the other soldiers were sleeping. He had the radio fastened on his uniform so the remaining soldiers could not check in when they woke up and their first thought probably was: "Where's our buddy?" Carefully looking around, they could tell by its footprints that a large jungle cat (assumedly a tiger) had been there, and eventually our men did track and find the mangled remains of the soldier. In all of my field time in Vietnam, I never saw a live tiger, but there was evidence of their presence. (President Roosevelt had built a hunting lodge in the general area—and one of his desired trophies was a tiger.) We did not have tigers in Africa, but this was substantiation that they were in Vietnam. What is the main lesson out of all of this? Don't fall asleep while on duty!

RATS IN THE MARKET

I have been in many open markets around the world. In a number of countries some of these have walls between vendors but in other places it may be a light curtain or no divider at all. Most of the major city markets will have many merchants under one expansive roof with additional sales spaces on the sidewalks outside. I was in the meat market section in one nation where all the dealers were hollering to get your attention and have you buy from them rather than one of the other sellers. One particular market had three-foot-high cement walls between the vendors' spaces. I noticed big five-inch holes at the base of the little walls and wondered about the purpose for them. I was told it was for cleaning the cubicles and to come back in a half hour and watch.

Did I ever get an eye full? The merchants were gone and men with boots and firehoses were there hosing down the floor and cubicle areas. The water ran out through the holes under the walls but with the water were these huge rats scurrying ahead of the water from the hoses! The rats seemed to know where the getaway holes were under the walls.

Some of the well-fed rats were so big that they could barely make it through an escape hole, and if it was "occupied," the rats would head for the open "doorway" space where we were. And of course, the men with the hoses would try to hit them and make them jump or move faster! I had to make sure I was behind those men as they drove the rats (and dirty water) out the end of the building! Actually, it was sort of fun to watch. I must have seen more than 100 of those oversized rats that afternoon. My guess was that they were hiding in corners of those booths, feeding on scraps of meat that were either accidently dropped or intentionally thrown on the floor by the sellers. I don't know where the rats went after being "hosed," but one man said they came back every day. The things that can entertain a missionary kid are interesting.

The large open markets contain all sorts of things for sale: hand-made jewelry, shoes, clothes, vegetables and fruit, small appliances, furniture, hats, and meats. One of the unusual meat products seen are the full heads of hogs lined up on a rack or table! Sometimes the ears will be standing up and other heads will have the ears flopped downward. I never thought to ask which head would taste better.

LEOPARD

Shortly before our furlough from Africa in 1954, a missionary in the US wrote and said that he wished he had killed a leopard so that he could have it tanned to use as a rug or a wall-mounting in his home. He asked that if we saw one, could we kill it and bring the skin home to him?

Dad had recently shot an antelope and hung it from a high tree limb overnight before cutting it up. The next day, we saw leopard tracks on the ground below where the antelope was hanging. (This was about seventy-five feet from my bedroom!) Dad determined to get the big cat, so he set up an unusual V-trap between two big mahogany logs. (See picture below.) Near the point of the joining logs, he penned a goat. He then rigged up a pulley system on his shotgun so that as the

been there, done that!

leopard tried to go through the logs' small opening at the other end to get the goat, his head would push against a string which then pulled the trigger on the vertical shotgun. The leopard would be shot in the back of his head—if it all worked.

I don't know where Dad got this idea, but it was a great one! The next night, the leopard came back again—and WHAMO! We all stayed in the house while Dad and the night watchman got in the truck and went to look for the animal. They found it very near the trap. Dad's trap had done its job, and we had a beautiful trophy for the missionary back in the US! My twin brothers and the rest of our family got to see the large leopard the next day in front of the ingenious log and shotgun trap. The leopard missed his evening dinner—both the antelope and the goat!

OH, DOES IT STINK!

But now comes the "rest of the story". We were only a couple of weeks away from leaving the country for our furlough, and we had to get this skin "tanned". Our helpers skinned the leopard and scraped as much of the flesh from it as they could and opened the skull to clean it out. Then they salted everything to draw out all liquids and laid it out in the sun. They did this over and over again in the next few days but it reeked. Oh, did it ever stink!

Dad tried to figure out how we were going to get the big skin with the skull back to America. A couple days before departure, one of the locals said to get some African perfume and heavily douse it on the skin and the smell would disappear. That did help, and Dad rolled the skin up in some heavy-type paper and told me to be responsible for it while we traveled. Thanks, Dad!

Off we headed in a few hours to get to the airport. I carried that roll on the plane, and it really did not smell too good—even with all its perfume. I put the wrapped skin in the airplane's rack overhead. We stayed on that plane from Africa until we stopped in Newfoundland where we had to change planes. When we opened the overhead bin, the horrible stench escaped! I pretended it wasn't what I was carrying and got off the plane but, of course, everyone completely avoided getting near me while we waited inside the airport for our next flight.

Later when we arrived in Chicago, the terrible stench had only gotten worse! The African perfume was not doing its job, and people in America were not used to that almost-sickening fragrance. When they got a whiff of my "package," the customs people were very hesitant to let the skin go through, and we had to untie the wrapping a little to prove what this stinking package was. They closed it quickly and got some plastic wrap which helped contain the odor. I don't remember how we then got the skin to the missionary, but I sure remember the flight with it. I can almost smell it as I write this portion of my memoirs! As Paul Harvey would say: "And that's the rest of the story".

SNAKES ALIVE!

It's not that I like snakes, but I am not really afraid of them either. They are in many parts of the world, and I have seen them in their native habitats. Some are small—although their venom is very deadly—while others are large and are constrictors of their prey. And then, of course, many are completely harmless to humans.

I have seen one of the large ones, which was killed by the Africans shortly after it had swallowed a medium-sized antelope. A snake's skin can stretch fairly easy and its jaw is not hinged allowing it to swallow large dinners. I suppose this one was resting and trying to digest the animal so it could move more easily. I could see where the antelope's horns and a couple of its knee joints and hooves

been there, done that!

were pressing against the inside of the python's skin. A couple of our helpers killed it, fastened it to a pole, and carried it between them back to the village.

I have a skin of an African Rock Python that my dad got when we lived in Kyabe in Chad. The skin is seventeen and a half feet long and that is without the head (which likely would have added about eighteen more inches)! Dad purchased the skin from a camel caravan passing through our Kyabe village. Most of the time, the skins had been cut up and made into shoes, sandals, book covers, belts, purses, hats, or other common sales items. Dad asked one of the caravan guys to bring him a full skin when he came again, and Dad would buy it. That is where my snake skin came from. I have had a lot of fun telling people "stories" (i.e. "tall tales") about the skin!

SNAKE IN THE BEDSPRING COILS

At our school at Fort Crampel in the Central African Republic, the teacher reached over from her bed one night to get her flashlight and felt a snake on her bedside table. Can you imagine how her heartbeat must have jumped? She quickly got another light from the other side of the bed and then hollered out her window for help. One of the boys in our dorm—which was about seventy-five yards away—heard her and woke up our houseparent. In the meantime, the snake slithered off the table and went into the open coils of her bed's springs.

Our heroic missionary took his small-caliber rifle and an African guard, went to the teacher's apartment, and carefully lifted the mattress off of the springs to find the snake wound in the metal coil springs. He shot the snake but its muscles continued to contract around several of the springs. Finally, they had to cut the snake up to remove it and of course, there was a cleanup required after that before the missionary lady would go back to bed! She was a brave lady to go back to her bed after that encounter with a snake! We kids in school sure heard about that story the next day.

Although the snake was initially thought to be a very poisonous one, it later was identified—based on its triangular body shape and color—as a file snake, which is not poisonous. Whatever it was, you don't want to be surprised by touching it in the middle of a dark night!

THE SPITTING COBRA

At Kyabe, I woke up one morning to a bunch of exciting noises and loud talking outside our house. The workmen were coming to work and now were pounding on our door for my dad to bring his rifle. He wasn't even in the house but was out in his little prayer house at the time. They went and got him and told him there was a spitting cobra snake near our house. From about six feet away, the snake had killed a thirty-four-inch lizard by coating its nose and face with the cobra's saliva. The snake was now probably dreaming about consuming its next meal and it wasn't going to leave even with all the people looking on!

Dad shot the snake. He had heard that if you leave a dead snake alone that its mate may come to it. Sure enough a couple of hours later, the mate came, and a workman killed it. Not far behind the mate was a small young cobra. The first cobra was sixty-two inches long, and the Africans said they had not seen one that big. We got rid of three dangerous snakes in just a few hours.

MALA, MALA CORAL SNAKE

Betty and I were in Colombia, South America, in 1973 with a mission team to build a house for a pioneering missionary in the jungle. Early on a balmy morning, one of our team's men and I were going to get water from a spring, which was our only source of fresh, clean water for drinking. The spring was in the jungle about twenty minutes from our construction site. We carried a couple of five-gallon jugs on a pole between us as we headed down the newly cut trail through the jungle. Walking casually but constantly on the alert, I looked ahead of me and there was a yellow and black and red striped snake lying across the path. Immediately I thought it was a very dangerous coral snake, which reportedly has the second most potent venom of all snakes.

I told my buddy that we had to kill it since we could see it now and may not see it when we returned. I rummaged around beside the trail and found a long, forked stick. Carefully, I pulled the leaves away from atop the snake's head and pushed the fork right behind its head. As you would expect, it started thrashing its body around, so I asked my friend to hold the forked stick on the snake while I got out and opened my Ranger knife. I then grabbed the snake's tail and reached down to cut the head off—just in front of the forked stick.

been there, done that!

Just as I had my knife near its head, somehow, the snake pulled its head from under the forked stick. Now, here I was holding a coral snake by its tail as it was vigorously wiggling and trying to get away! But thinking it may come back to attack, and rather than throw it down, I lowered it so that it could try and slither away on the ground. Was this a wise move? I'll let you decide! I told the other guy to fork it again which he successfully did as I was still hanging on to the tail. I then cut its head off, and we left the body beside the trail to pick up and take to the village when we returned from getting our water at the spring.

I wanted an Indian to skin it for me so I could take it back to America. But when I showed it to the villagers, they backed away and all they could say was "Mala, MALA!" meaning "Bad, VERY BAD!" They would not touch it. They further said that in the woods you couldn't normally tell which end was the head and which was the tail because both ends are blunt. That is true of coral snakes. I ended up skinning it myself, and I did bring it home with me. It was thirty-two inches long—which is very long for a coral snake. After coming home, I called the Smithsonian Institution, which said the longest coral snake they had on record was thirty-four inches. I'm glad we got it rather than it getting us!

CROCODILE HUNT

Also in Colombia, the missionary, D, had previously arranged with some Indians to take a couple of men from our missionary work team on a night hunt for crocodiles. In exchange, D would bring flashlight batteries, some canned food, and more bullets for the Indians' guns. They had no calendar, so D had to tell them he would come back in so many days after a new moon and that they needed to be on a straight stretch of the river so he could land and take off in the float plane. D could take only two people in the plane with the extra weight of the provisions for the Indians. I excitedly volunteered to take the place of one of our ten mission-team men who was scheduled for the trip but decided at the last minute that he didn't want to go. The Indians would hunt from their canoes on and along the river for crocodile skins, the pelts of other animals, and colorful bird feathers.

OH, OH! WRONG GROUP OF INDIANS

We arrived at the distant river in D's float plane around 4 p.m. and saw a group of boats which D assumed to be the group of Indians with whom he had made the arrangements. Looking down from the plane, D commented that the Indians sure hadn't picked a very long stretch of river for him to use as a runway but in assessing the situation, he figured he could make it. We landed and pulled up to their boats. D didn't recognize any of them! In fact, they did not seem friendly. They were probably quite surprised about this "bird" landing on the river and coming to them. Upon realizing that this was the wrong group of crocodile hunters, D decided to leave to find the correct group before the sun went down.

D calculated where the longest stretch of water for take-off was and pushed the throttle forward. Halfway down the "runway", he knew he would not be able to get off the water because of our total weight. He reduced the throttle speed, and we went back to the Indians and made an unexpected donation to them of batteries, bullets, and canned goods to make the plane lighter. I'm sure the Indians were thankful for that! I was also glad that D didn't offer to leave me and my weight there with them so that he could lift off the river!

Then we tried to take off again. We barely got off the water before a major river bend where D had to tilt the plane between the trees on the river banks so much that I thought he would catch a wingtip on the water and we would soon be swimming. But his pilot skill was superb, and we made it. He later said that he had also been concerned about making it safely away from that area. I'm sure that someone was praying at that moment, but it wasn't me because I was watching with my eyes really wide open!

SNAKE INSTEAD OF A CROCODILE

We flew in the missionary's plane upriver until we saw another Indian group on the water with a nice long and straight "runway" and landed just as the sun was setting. I don't know what D's plan would have been if this was another hostile group. He pulled up near them and tied the plane to trees on the bank. These were the correct and friendly tribal folk! There were three or four small dugout canoes fastened to a larger open boat on which they kept their supplies and some crocodile skins and pelts from their earlier hunting. There were about ten to twelve men who had been out there for over a month already.

been there, done that!

Several hammocks were draping from the boat's roof. I am not a hammock-type guy and immediately knew that this would be pretty much of a sleepless night. A couple of men were cooking on the shore, and in between the boat and the bank was a large catfish. I mean it was big! They estimated that it weighed around 200 pounds! They were keeping it alive so they could have fresh fish later in the month.

About 11 p.m., D said it was time to leave the primary boat and get in a dugout canoe to go hunt for crocodiles. He explained that the three of us in the dugout would each have a flashlight. When the light was focused on the eyes of a crocodile in the water, the eyes would shine red, and there would be a reflection of their eyes in the water. This would give us a target between those four red dots. We would take turns shooting.

So, I got in the middle of the canoe and was given a rifle. One Indian got in the front and another behind, but D didn't get in as I had anticipated! I didn't speak the Indian language or Spanish, and they didn't speak English. This could be an interesting situation! However, with certain sounds we would communicate. Off I went with the two Indians paddling softly in the smooth river water in the Colombian jungle! Not being a water lover and sitting in a canoe with the top edge of the canoe's sides being only about two inches above the water in a jungle river, I definitely felt at risk! This was going to be a new adventure!

The man in front fired at the first crocodile we saw and immediately jumped in to drag the crocodile into the canoe. As he jumped, the canoe swayed and water poured in over the side. As the water came into the canoe, I thought sure I was going out! He came back empty handed, and again when getting back in the canoe, we took on more water! My shoes were now full of water! I quickly grabbed a little bucket and started bailing! I didn't want to be sinking in that river!

I also missed when it was my turn to shoot. Next we saw only two eyes shining instead of the four I expected, but the man in the rear shot at them anyway. (Keep in mind that it is only a couple of days after the new moon and it was very dark—except for the dim light from the stars.) To get to the presumed kill, the men paddled further into the branches of a mangrove thicket. I am thankful that no snakes fell out of the mangrove bushes into our canoe while we worked our way through the vines and branches! Again, the man in front jumped into the water—really rocking the canoe—causing me to almost lose my rifle as I grabbed the sides of the canoe! After a few minutes he came back and as he quietly talked to the other Indian, he opened his arms real wide a couple of times. I didn't know for sure but I assumed he was showing us that the target was a big snake rather than a crocodile. My supposition was confirmed when we finally got back to the mother boat and I got a translation of his story. We didn't bring back a crocodile that night, but there was a lot of buzz about that snake our man had shot. That could have been quite a wrestling match if the other Indian had grabbed that big snake and tried to get it into the canoe!

SILENCE BROKEN DUE TO A BAMBOO VIPER

The green bamboo viper is a dangerous venomous snake. In Vietnam, I was moving my company of men to an objective and had been quietly tromping through the triple-canopy jungle for a couple of hours. I wanted to give the men a break, so we found an area where I could put out good perimeter security with one of my platoons while the other platoons took a short rest in the middle. A dense bamboo thicket on one side of the perimeter aided our temporary security plan.

Everyone was to maintain silence so that we didn't attract enemy interest. As did most of my men on break, one soldier sat down with his rucksack still on to use as a backrest. He apparently sat down on a snake hiding under the vegetation on the jungle floor and suddenly, he was hollering. I turned toward him and saw his legs and arms flailing in the air as he was trying to get up. I noted that a green bamboo viper was quickly slithering away. My soldier said he had been bitten on his bottom. My medic quickly checked him out and found two holes in his pants but the fangs had not penetrated the skin. That was a real relief to the soldier!

But now I had to get our unit up and moving since our silence had been broken. Our rest break was immediately concluded. We rarely knew where the enemy might be and whether he could possibly have heard the commotion. Our enemy was twofold: one was the North Vietnamese or Viet Cong soldier, and the other enemy was nature itself.

LEARNING TO HANDLE A SNAKE

I worked with a teenage boys' battalion in the Christian Service Brigade program at our church in Virginia in the 1970s. One year, we emphasized survival skills where we taught the boys the "hows" of trapping, fishing, skinning, identifying edible plants, and preparing things to eat when in a survival situation.

been there, done that!

On a campout in the early winter, we found a large, non-venomous black racer snake settled down for its hibernation in a hollow log. After I recognized what it was, I reached in and grabbed it, showing the boys how to hold a snake behind the head and for those that wanted to hold it, I carefully handed it to them. The snake itself was quite lazy in its fattened condition just prior to winter. At one point, a boy grabbed it too far behind the head and it reached around and scratched the back of his hand. The poor kid thought he was going to die right then, and it took quite a bit to calm him down. Later, I showed the boys how to skin a snake, and after cutting it into small pieces and cooking it, each boy could sample a real survival meal!

DONE IN BY ITS OWN GREED

We had a chicken coop at our mission station at Kyabe in Africa. The chickens provided fresh eggs for us as well as an occasional great chicken dinner. When we closed the coop at night, the chickens were quite safe from any predators. However, there was a small—maybe about a half inch—opening under the door. One morning, I went to get eggs from the hens' nests and felt some resistance in opening the door. A snake had gotten into the coop under the door and had swallowed three eggs. It was trying to get out through that little slat through which it had entered, and now the eggs inside it were preventing it from fitting under the door. As I opened the door, one of the eggs got crushed but the other eggs were still good, as we discovered after we killed the snake. Yes, we later ate those eggs! They were still fresh! The greedy little snake had done itself in by swallowing our eggs.

CHASED BY A SNAKE

One fall season, I was in a mission conference representing D&D Missionary Homes in our local church. The pastor had a preliminary dinner meeting with the missionary guests regarding administrative things during the conference and the general sequence of the next few days. On that first night, he said that he would introduce each of us and wanted us to tell a story from our life. I proceeded to share the following, which did not relate to my present ministry at D&D but was from my days as a missionary kid (MK) in Africa.

As a young fifth grader at the boarding school's dorm, the houseparents would occasionally take all of us MKs out to a meadow-like place where we could play. One of the games was tag, and the safe base would be certain of the two-foot high, mushroom-shaped ant hills dotting the area. Running around, I jumped up on this long six-inch thick log and taunted others to come get me.

All of a sudden this "log" moved, turned, and slithered quickly toward me as I ran. Now I had a snake chasing me instead of another MK! It seemed to move as fast as I did. Thinking that it could not climb a tree, I ran for the nearest tree and crawled up into it. The snake soon arrived at the tree and to my horror began winding itself around the tree trunk and working its way upward toward me! I moved up into the branches until I could go no higher, and in sheer fright I saw that it kept coming. (The story was very dramatic and animated, and at that point some in the audience were holding their hands over their mouths with breathless expressions on their faces.) I continued to tell my story of how I tucked my legs up as tightly as possible as I watched the snake move slowly toward me.

Suddenly, it snapped at me and grabbed my leg and started pulling and pulling. At that point I took a deep breath and paused in my story and then said, "Just like I'm pulling your leg." Betty, my wife, was on the platform watching the people's reactions, and when I said "just like I'm pulling your leg", the people let out a variety of expressions of relief and Christian anger that they had been taken by a big joke.

Maybe that wasn't the kind of story the pastor was anticipating—but it was a "story"! If the people had rotten tomatoes available at that point, I'm sure I would have been pelted! As a kid, I'd been told not to tell a story—or in other words, a lie—but in this case, the pastor had told me to tell a story. After the service and for days later, people would come to me and comment on my story-telling and how they had been on the edge of their seat, hoping that I could escape the snake. Of course, I was right there in front of them, so why would they question my escape that day? At my display table, I had my big seventeen and a half–foot long snake skin to show that snakes can get big!

There is a sequel to that event. A few weeks later, I was nominated to be a deacon at the church. Before the congregation votes on the nominees in our church, each potential deacon shares a testimony. In introducing me, the pastor gave my name and then said he really hesitated putting me before the congregation because I had told such a story (lie) about a snake at the mission conference. My response was a genuine apology to any who had been offended, and

been there, done that!

then I shared a *true* testimony of God's gracious work in my life. I was accepted as a deacon.

ANOTHER "TALL TALE"

In my office at D&D Missionary Homes, I had draped my seventeen and a half–foot long African rock python snake skin on the wall. Occasionally, people (mostly women!) did not want to stay too long in the office when they noticed the skin. Even little kids' eyes would warily view it on the wall, and I would tell them a little "story" about my snake skin. I told them that I had grown up as a missionary kid in Africa. This huge snake had been my pet and that each day I would have to put a leash behind its head (really, where is its neck?) and take it out for a crawl. (You can't "walk" a snake!)

While out on its crawl, it would see a pretty little girl and try to go over to her and just hug (squeeze) and wrap itself around her. Of course, I had to pull on its leash to bring it back under control. By now, the little kid's eyes were getting bigger. One day, the snake lunged so quickly to get to a child that I yanked on its leash and its head came off, and that is why my snake skin does not have a head! You should have seen some of the expressions on the faces of both parents and kids when I told this story—which I then confessed that it was not true. But, I always warned them to be careful going out the door because my snake's mate was still looking for it and wanted to come in my office. I knew missionary kids could handle a tall tale such as this.

HAWKS AT MY HOUSE

I knew very little about red-shouldered hawks before moving to Florida in 1991. In some places they are called chicken hawks. The large hawks were beautiful birds with a dark brown back, reddish tinted shoulders, and a beige chest speckled with dark brown feathers. They were almost majestic as they soared and floated high in the skies, taking advantage of the thermals in the Florida air. These hawks normally return to the same general nesting area when they arrive back in Florida each year. After they build their nest and raise a couple of young hawks in the spring, they and their offspring fly away, and the parents return to either rebuild the previous year's nest or make a new one in the same immediate area. The offspring do not come back to that area to raise their own families.

At the Fogle house in the Tampa Bay area of Florida, we had a very large, sprawling, oak tree in the front yard. These are not at all like northern oak trees! Ours have small, one-to-two inch-long, oval-shaped leaves with no large indentations as most larger-leafed oaks in the north. One year, a pair of hawks built their nest on a large branch extending far out over the middle of my yard. It was twenty or twenty-five feet off the ground. Their nest was skillfully built with some sticks about an inch in diameter and smaller twigs and seemingly almost anything they could find to soften the nest interior. Soon, we assumed that eggs had been laid since one of the hawks would regularly be in or near the nest.

GET IT BACK IN THE NEST

Betty and I were traveling for a few weeks, and when we came home, some of the neighbors and their kids came over and excitedly told us about our hawks. Apparently there were three chicks and one of the very small babies fell out of the nest. Not knowing how to get it back up in the nest so high above the ground, our neighbors carefully picked it up in a towel and took it to the local bird sanctuary. It didn't appear to be hurt and the caretakers at the sanctuary said that the only way the bird would survive would be to get it back in the nest with its parents. The sanctuary would not take it.

Rushing back to our house, the neighbors contacted the Fire Department to ask if they could bring a ladder truck to get the baby bird back in the nest. They would not do that. Then one of the families remembered that a friend of theirs was an arborist who had some long ladders. He agreed to come and try to place the bird back in the nest. All of this had an urgency to it since the bird needed the nourishment and warmth only its parents could provide.

Gently holding the little baby hawk in the towel, the tree man worked his way up the ladder, which was extended to its limit to reach the branch with the nest. Just as he was nearing the nest, the parent hawks decided to come and protect the other two small babies. Obviously, this was not a comfortable situation for the man carrying the baby bird, but he continued to climb. He quickly "dumped" the baby out of the towel into the nest as the parents swooped at him in an attack mode. People on the ground held their breath in fear the arborist would fall off the ladder or the ladder might slide off the branch it was leaning against. Thankfully, he got down safely even though the mature hawks continued to squawk and

been there, done that!

"attack" while the ladder was being removed. All ended well, the babies grew, and the hawk family eventually left the area—for a few months anyway.

FEEDING THE BABIES

That wasn't the end of our hawks. They came back year after year. One year, the hawks built their nest high up in the tree branches hanging over the peak of our garage roof. I enjoyed watching the two babies grow and the parents as they brought food to the hungry young ones. It was very interesting to observe the feeding. The babies never fought for the food being provided from the parent's beak, and the parents seemed to know which of the birds to feed first. The other baby in the nest would wait patiently for its turn to widely open its mouth and accept what mama had to offer.

What did the adult hawks bring to the nest to feed the little ones? I have seen them carrying wiggling snakes up there and geckos (lizards) they had snagged on the ground, and I've seen the end results of other birds they have caught.

One day I saw the hawk sitting on our backyard fence and eyeing something on the ground. Soon it swooped down and caught a young rabbit. I didn't realize that rabbits could squeal so loudly, but this one sure did as it was carried up to a branch. As the rabbit squirmed and squealed, the hawk firmly kept hold of it with one claw while gripping the branch with the other before finally doing it in and taking the baby rabbit to the nest. That must have been quite a feast for the hawk family! And now, they could have a fur-lined nest!

REMEMBER, I'M BIGGER

Speaking of the young birds' patience while waiting to be fed, the adult hawks also have patience. Blue jays do not like the hawks, and sometimes when an adult hawk is sitting on a branch a good distance away from the nest, the jays will make a nuisance of themselves and flitter around the hawk. They would fly at it and peck at it to try to drive it away. Perhaps the hawks had been raiding the jays' nests which obviously would be perturbing.

But as the blue jays are flying back and forth around the hawk and making a horrendous noise, the hawk calmly sits there turning its head and occasionally flapping a wing or twitching its tail. This must irritate the jays immensely as they keep getting louder and louder. Why won't the hawk go away?

Perhaps the hawk wants to keep their attention on him instead of letting the blue jays head toward the eggs or babies in the nest. He also must be wishing he could tell the jays, "Remember, I'm bigger" and warn them that he could have any one of them for a meal if he wanted! In fact, every now and then I would find a bunch of blue jay feathers on the ground, which made me assume that one of them had become too much of a bother to one of the adult hawks!

HAWK IN THE FIREBOX

As the babies grew, they soon seemed to be about the size of the parents—but they could not yet fly. They would hop up on the edge of the large nest and eventually on to some nearby branches. At one point, one of the two young birds fell more than ten feet onto our roof and hurt its leg. It was hopping around on the roof for a couple of days, and then we noticed that the other young sibling was also on the roof.

Our large fireplace chimney had a cement roof cap over it, leaving about a six-inch opening all the way around to let the smoke out. As I was watching the birds, one jumped up into that opening and although we were unaware at the time, it must have fallen down into the firebox just above the fireplace inside our house. That night, we heard the soft screeching of a bird but didn't know where it was. In the morning, my wife chased down the sound and realized that it was coming from the fireplace. We sort of thought that perhaps the bird was still at the top of the chimney and we were hearing the echo down through the chimney chute.

Then we heard the other bird outside "talking" with the one in the fireplace. What a surprise it was to us to see the sibling sitting on the bay window ledge outside our living room. The two birds were communicating! The one outside seemed to be empathizing with its sibling caught in the firebox. We could get up close to the window on the inside near where the bird was outside, and it didn't seem a bit concerned with us looking at it. It was like he couldn't see us through the glass. Somehow it must have known that we could not harm it since the window pane was between us.

The one outside was the one that had hurt its leg coming down on to the roof and could not move very quickly since it still could not fly. We again called the bird sanctuary to see if they could rescue the bird in our firebox. Initially, they said they could not help, but then one of the workers agreed to come to our house after hours and get the bird. We wondered if the bird would survive the rest of the day as its screeching seemed to be getting softer and weaker. The sibling bird would come occasionally through the day, hop up on the outside bay window sill, and "talk" with the poor bird inside our house in the firebox. The birds could obviously hear each other even through our double-paned glass windows even though their screeching was not very loud. We hoped the hours would pass quickly so that it could be rescued.

In the early evening, a man came and said he would have to open the flue to get the bird. I hoped that the bird wouldn't fall out and cause us to chase it around the house to capture it. But the man carefully opened the flue into the firebox and reached up with his heavily gloved hand to grasp the bird and pull it out. He hugged it tightly to his chest and said that it was very dehydrated and he would have to take it to the bird sanctuary hospital. He had originally thought he could release it outside so the parents could feed it but realized it was too weak to survive outside.

We also asked him to look at the other bird to see if it also needed care because of its hurt foot. After chasing it for a short distance, he concluded that it could heal on its own, so he would leave it in our yard where the parents could nourish it. He said that when the first bird was well enough, he would bring it back to be with its sibling and be cared for by the parents.

Almost a week went by. The bird in our yard seemed to be doing well, and we would see the parents calling it to locate it and feed it. It still could not fly. We would see it in different places in our yard but stayed away from it because almost every time that we were anywhere near it, the parents would loudly let us know that they were watching their baby!

Then one day we didn't see the juvenile bird—although it was nearly the size of the adult hawk—and we wondered if it had flown away. Sadly, I found it dead under one of our bushes. Because it could not fly and defend itself, some animal had apparently caught it and killed it. Now the parents did not hang out nearby as it seemed that they realized the loss of both of their young ones.

Another week went by when the bird sanctuary called and said they were ready to bring the hospitalized bird back to its parents. We had to tell them that the sibling had died and the parents were no longer around. They then said that when it could fly, they would take it elsewhere and release it. That was a sad ending to that year's hawk family.

ATTACK! YOU LOOKED AT MY BABIES

But that still wasn't the end of our hawks. They came back the next year and refurbished their nest to lay their eggs and try and raise more babies. In a short while, we could hear soft noises from the nest high above the garage. There were only a couple of spots in our yard where we could look up through the leaves and branches to watch action in the nest and the babies' development. It was an exciting day when we could see small, fuzzy, light-yellow heads peering above the edge of the nest.

One time while watching the activity in the nest, I could see one of the parents standing on the nest's side near the babies. All of a sudden, it dove down at me. I ducked and waved my hand to scare it away. It flew and landed in the tree behind me, and I thought no more about it as I looked back up at the babies in the nest.

Sensing some movement behind me, I became conscious that the hawk was headed toward me a second time. So again I ducked and waved my hands at it. I thought: "The parents don't like me watching how they raise their babies, so I'll go inside for now." I headed around the house to come in the side garage door. About fifteen feet from the door, I felt something hit my head and saw the hawk fly off in front of me. My initial reaction was: "What is going on? I haven't done anything but look, without any intent to do any harm to the little birds, and here I'm being attacked!"

I came inside and told Betty about it. I put my hands on my head to show her how the hawk had attacked me. In bringing my hands down, I saw that they had blood on them and I realized the hawk's claws had dug into my scalp! I guess it couldn't pick me up even though that shiny, nearly bald head may have been something to take back to the nest—probably to eat! Or maybe it just wanted to help me get up there to get a closer look at her beautiful babies!

Betty, being a nurse, carefully cleaned *five* puncture wounds on my scalp and wisely suggested that I wear a hat whenever I would go outside as long as those hawks were around. They really didn't like me for whatever reason. That afternoon when I went out to the end of our driveway to get the mail, the hawk swooped down over me again. I guess that was just to remind me of its presence and its protection for its young. Almost every time I would go out of the house for a few weeks after that, the hawks would start hollering at me. Betty could always tell when I was outside because of their distinct noise.

been there, done that!

The hawks nested in that tree out in front of our house for a number of years. Many times I had wished that they would nest somewhere else because of the terrible mess they made on the garage roof and on our driveway. One year, I had to remove that huge oak tree where the birds had nested so long because it was dying. I think the hawks were a little confused when they came back the next year. But they did end up building a big nest in a tree in our back yard. Now we had the mess at the back of the house rather than the front!

For the last few years, they have moved into a cluster of oak trees across the cul-de-sac from us and above a small retention pond there. The neighbor over there "thanked me"—well not really!—for sending the noisy hawks and blue jays over his way. Unfortunately, they have swooped him a couple of times—he has a head that looks sort of like mine! Apparently, they like big, shiny, flesh-colored balls!

Most recently they nested in a big oak tree where a widowed lady lives kitty corner from our house and across our cul-de-sac. The hawks also tried to attack her when she was out in her front yard. It was interesting to see her on her riding mower wearing a construction helmet! At other times she would be walking out in her yard and constantly waving a stick over her head to keep the hawks away. I think my neighbor learned a lesson from my experiences.

PROUD HAWK HUNTER

One other hawk event comes from my life as a ten-year-old boy at our home at Kyabe in the southern Sahara Desert area in Chad. I had received a BB gun for Christmas and practiced with it quite a bit around the mission station. One morning I saw a fairly large hawk sitting on a branch a short distance away. It probably was waiting for a young chicken to emerge from our chicken coop! We were raising the chickens for us to have eggs and an occasional dinner. I thought that I could at least scare it with the "pop" of my BB gun. I aimed and fired!

Much to my surprise, the hawk fell to the ground, flapping one of its wings vigorously and running on the ground. I chased it around for a while as it tried to find a hiding place. I wanted to put it out of its misery. Finally, it seemed to wear out and hopped up into a bush. I got closer and closer to it and shot it in the head a couple of times before it went limp. I carefully pulled it out of the bush and looked it over and saw that my first BB had hit it in one shoulder or wing joint and had disabled it.

I held it up, blood dripping from its head and shoulder, and put my BB gun over my shoulder as any proud hunter would do! But who would believe my story? I had to show it off, so I excitedly carried it into the house to show my mother—who was still in bed! She didn't seem to think much of my bleeding trophy and let me know in no uncertain terms to "Get that thing out of my bedroom!" Needless to say, I had a cleanup job afterward from the front door, through the dining room, into her bedroom, and out the back door! Who would have ever thought that I could get a hawk with a little BB gun? And, why didn't I think about the blood dripping on the floor *before* taking it into the house? Good lesson learned for later in life!

CHAPTER XXVI

"PHIL WILL EAT ANYTHING!"

I don't know how many times I have heard someone say: "Phil will eat anything!" Well, that is almost a true statement because I have eaten so many things that some people would consider strange, weird, or not edible. In survival training in the Army, I've eaten snake, alligator, and turtle—the latter which I also had in a bigger variety in Colombia and the Cayman Islands. Of course, I've eaten the entire variety of the Army's C-rations and the dehydrated MREs (Meals Ready-to-Eat) which can be rehydrated or eaten straight out of the bag. And I have eaten an earthworm and a goldfish on a dare! Normally, if another living being will eat something, I might also eat it—and enjoy it!

AFRICAN FOODS—RANCID BEEF

I can think of only one time that I really had a problem eating what others were also eating. I was with my brother, Larry, teaching a seminar in a village in the northwest portion of the Central African Republic in 2012. The seminar was for about 100 national pastors and church leaders and was to last five days.

On Monday, the first day of the seminar, a cow was purchased and butchered to feed the attendees. Portions were set aside to eat each day. Keep in mind there was no refrigeration in the remote village. The meat and sauce was still good on Tuesday, but by Wednesday, it began to have a smell and seemed a little spoiled.

On Thursday, Oh my goodness—it had really turned! The smell was very strong, but the Africans were eating it, so I started eating what they brought to me. It was just plain *rancid*! I didn't see any little worms crawling around in it, so I figured it would be all right since it had just been reheated. I took a bite of the beef, washed it down with some warm water—there was no cool water in the

been there, done that!

village!—took a spoonful of rice and greens, and started over on the next piece. After a few pieces of meat, I finally decided I was full and said I couldn't eat more.

Thankfully, I did not get sick—but what a taste, and did I (along with everyone else) ever need some mouthwash! Of course, there was none out there in that remote area! We ended up closing the conference at noon on Friday since we didn't have food to feed Friday's lunch to the conferees. Normally, we went through the afternoon with our teaching.

ANTS OFF THE WALL

As a missionary kid growing up in central Africa, I really did like what the local people ate. They even enjoyed picking the flying ants off the wall and eating them fresh as a snack, so we did also! You had to grab the ant by the wings and just eat the body—because the wings would stick on the inside of your cheek—and you had to chew quickly, lest it start crawling or sting you. One of the missionary kids missed getting the ant between his teeth and it crawled into his throat. Fortunately, it didn't sting, but he couldn't get it up or down regardless of trying to drown it with water or push it down with some bread! It just hung on to the inside of his throat until it died. That was a miserable time for my friend!

OTHER DELICIOUS AFRICAN MENUS

Although the mashed manioc/cassava/yucca—we called it gozo—drying in the sun out on the ground had quite a sour odor to it, it was still very good when cooked. Gozo was a root and a regular staple much like a potato would be in our American diet, and the Africans grew a lot of it. In our own garden, we grew the majority of vegetables we ate, but when out in a village, we would be served other things found in the jungle or the greens of peanuts or the gozo plant.

Boule was made from millet or maize grain and some gozo all mashed together in a very thick, dough-like mush piled in a bowl for a community meal. To eat, you just dig in with your fingers, grab some boule, dip it in some sauce and some greens, and stuff it in your mouth. The sauce may be made from mashed greens, crushed and cooked palm nuts (which was also a good topping for boiled rice) or it may be some meat juice. Sometimes the boule was formed into a two-or-three inch diameter roll and wrapped in a banana leaf to take with you when you traveled. When on the road we also ate a lot of canned Spam as a good American treat—and I still like it!

We hunted most of the meat we ate in Africa. Occasionally, a person from the village would bring us a hind quarter of a goat or maybe a nice fat porcupine for us to enjoy. To me, porcupine was one of the best meats! When we did shoot an antelope, we ate most of its parts—brain, tongue, liver, heart, and kidneys in addition to the roasts and steaks.

In fact, rice and kidney gravy was a special meal that we kids always looked forward to having for breakfast! Back here in the US when we had a family reunion, my sister would make that for our family, but all of the spouses would head out to a restaurant for their breakfasts! We adult Fogle siblings were glad they left because it meant more for us! One other breakfast from Africa that I continue to eat at least once a week is hot cooked rice with milk and peanut butter. Super crunchy peanut butter is best and nearest to the chopped peanuts that we put on our breakfast rice in Africa.

I never did try eating bat. We had a bunch of bats in the attic of the dorm at our boarding school and the houseparent went up there with a blow torch to singe their hair/fur so they couldn't fly. A helper would pick up the bats as they dropped from hanging on the rafters and throw them out the gable window where other men below would gather them and take them a little distance away. There, they put them on a spit over a fire for cooking and eating. I probably didn't eat any because they didn't offer some to me. Additionally, there is not much meat in a small bat's wings!

I've eaten most any meat or fowl found in the savannah or jungle areas—monkey, ostrich, giraffe, many kinds of antelope, cape buffalo, camel, guinea hen, wild turkey-like birds, elephant, caterpillar, crocodile, hippopotamus, grasshopper, a wide variety of fish—we would almost fight to get the delicious fish eyes!—and you name it! We only killed for meat and not for trophies. What we didn't take for ourselves, we gave ample portions to the African villagers.

HOW TO EAT AN ELEPHANT

Sometimes when mentioning foods which I have eaten, a person will ask: "How do you eat an elephant?" You eat it one bite at a time just like any other food, but there is something special about eating elephant. Its meat is very tough, and we only ate portions cut out of the trunk.

been there, done that!

Because the meat is so tough, you put a section of the skinned trunk in a pressure cooker and let it go for a few hours. An elephant's trunk has cartilage in it to divide the nostrils like in our noses, so when a round slice is put on your plate, it is like a divided dish and you can put potatoes and gravy in one "hole" (i.e. nostril) and your peas in the other side. Then you cut around the cartilage so it is separate from the meat, and cut bite size wedges of the meat as you eat. You just hope the elephant doesn't sneeze while you are eating! The eating part is true—but the sneezing is just my add-on!

LIZARD IN THE GRAVY!

We had some important guests at our house for a few days, and Mother always served them special meals. One evening, all of us sat down for our dinner, and Mother had a roast, *babalos* (a white sweet potato-like root), gravy, vegetables, and dessert. We had prayed and were passing the food around when suddenly a lizard on the ceiling lost its grip and plopped right down lengthwise in the elongated gravy bowl! The gravy was hot and splattered all over the tablecloth and other plates of food. We kids laughed—almost uncontrollably! But it didn't seem so funny to Mother. Dad got up, picked up the gravy bowl with the squirming lizard, and got rid of the gravy and lizard quite quickly.

We were used to seeing the lizards on the walls and ceilings as they chased and ate the bugs flying around the lights, but we had never seen one fall. However, it really was unique to see how this lizard fell lengthwise right into the gravy bowl in such an acrobatic way without even touching the bowl's sides! You just don't know what a day may bring forth when living in a tropical and rural environment. I still giggle when thinking about the shock that little four-to-five-inch-long lizard must have felt when it lost its grip on the ceiling, went airborne without a parachute, and ended up in a fancy gravy bowl. I doubt it survived! I do hope that it got to at least enjoy a taste of Mother's delicious gravy on its way out of this world!

I LIKE VARIETY

One of my characteristics is that I enjoy great varieties in my eating. I rarely eat the leftovers from one day on the next day; however, we do put them in the refrigerator for a delicious lunch or dinner later on. And, I normally keep several open breakfast cereal boxes, instant grits, cream of wheat, or steel-cut oats in the cupboard in order to have something different every day! As Betty and I travel locally or internationally, we often hear people say: "Phil will eat anything!"

BANQUET FOOD FROM EIGHTEEN COUNTRIES

I was the speaker at a mission conference in the Cayman Islands in the Caribbean Sea in 2003. As I remember, the congregation members were from eighteen countries! One evening of the conference included a banquet, and each nationality was to bring a special dish from their country. Probably by mistake in one of the meetings, I announced that I would sample some of the food from each motherland—primarily the Caribbean Islands and Central America.

At the dinner buffet, I tried to take small portions from the great variety of foods. Those who prepared the dishes were all standing around to ensure that I took some of their cooking, and almost all insisted that I take more for a "real good taste". They all wanted to make sure that I fulfilled my promise to eat some of their country's food. My plate was very full, but I had no idea what I was eating or where it was from! Then the people would come to me afterward and asked how I liked their specialty. How was I to know who prepared what? I tried to be very diplomatic in my responses so that I didn't offend anyone. Actually, I did enjoy it all but just didn't know what the food was, how it was prepared, or the nation it represented.

DOG AND STINKY NUOC MAM

I spent almost two years in Vietnam, so its foods deserve special notice. I was checking a tribal military outpost in my area early one morning. Coming up to the location, I smelled the terrible odor of burning hair. Getting closer, I noted a fire with a small animal carcass laying on it. The soldiers had killed it during the night when they sensed some movement in front of their position and randomly fired at the noise area. At daylight, they checked in front of their position and found that they had shot a dog.

While I was with them, they pulled the dog's carcass off the fire, scraped the ashes, hair, and skin off with a machete and started eating the meat. There wasn't much meat on that skinny little dog, so it was good that there weren't many people there to enjoy the breakfast! I was offered some of the meat—and ate it and it was

been there, done that!

not bad—especially cooked over an open fire! A little BBQ sauce would have enhanced the flavor! Not much was thrown away except the bones.

Vietnam food is known to most of us soldiers primarily for its *nuoc mam* fish sauce. I venture to say that most Americans who were in Vietnam never tasted it because of its horrible stink. The real flavor (and smell) comes from the process of fermenting fish for anywhere from a couple of months to a longer time. *Nuoc mam* is really part of Vietnam's identity and is characteristic of their cuisine and culture. Personally, I like it, but it is tough to initially get by its powerful odor. You just have to get used to it!

"YOU ARE A TRUE INDIAN BROTHER!"

Other countries have their own specialties. In India, they serve both the red and the green curries, which are absolutely wonderful. I really like hot peppers, and in India they have some very hot ones that they serve with their meals.

While teaching in a conference in Northeast India, we were served a buffet style meal, and my interpreter warned me that if I eat one particular kind of chili pepper, which they really liked, that it will take my spirit away since it is so hot. I asked how I would get your spirit back after eating it, and he said that a certain green paste will help. When I ate the chili pepper without a problem, he immediately said: "Pastor Fogle, you are a true Indian brother!"

We ate with our fingers in India as they did. I will say that the hot pepper in the curries made my fingers burn for a while until I could get them washed with some soap and water.

OTHER NATIONS' UNUSUAL FOODS

I have eaten *balut*, which is a fertilized and boiled developing duck egg embryo specialty in some Asian countries. There is a certain way to eat it by cracking and taking the top of the egg shell off and working your way down through the egg. It doesn't look so appetizing, but the taste is very good and supposedly very healthy for you.

When I was in Thailand, our guide took us in a canoe-type boat to the floating market where there were seemingly hundreds of vendors in their canoes, selling all types of goods: fruits and vegetables, fish, red meat, fowl, flowers, small furniture, clothing, pots and pans, and almost any item you may want. The vendors were constantly and slowly paddling their little boats around among other salespeople and potential customers on the river. Our guide kept asking if someone would sell us some Thai eggs, and when he finally found some, then he wanted to find a certain kind of banana. Now with these in hand, he told us to crack the egg and peel the shell. The whole thing was a dark, yucky-yellow-green color with no definition of a yolk or the white! We were to take a bite of the egg along with a bite of the banana. Really? Once I got over the thought of eating a fermented egg, it went down quite easily! Yes, "Phil will eat anything!"

A Korean staple dish is *kimchi*. I first had *kimchi* when I was working with a Korean military unit in Vietnam and was served it in their dining hall. Some varieties of kimchi are spicy hot and, based on the spices in it, it can also be somewhat smelly. It is normally made of a fermented, aged cabbage and can be eaten as a side dish or as the main dish in a Korean meal. I enjoy it as a side dish and will occasionally even find it in a US grocery store and bring a jar home. But that variety is not nearly as good as fresh, home-cooked kimchi by a real Korean cook!

The Cayman Islands in the Caribbean are not big enough to have pasture land for grazing mammals, so the primary meat on the island comes from turtles. These are caught from the sea and kept in huge vats of water and sold to the restaurants and individuals. Each vat would hold hundreds of turtles, which probably averaged more than fifteen inches in diameter. Most eating places and many homes have highly polished, beautiful, turtle shells hanging on the walls. However, it is illegal to sell the fancy shells to tourists to take off the island.

A common food for the village people in Peru is the guinea pig. Going through one of the villages in 2016, we spotted some guinea pigs being cooked on a spit. I had to stop and get a picture but unfortunately for the vendor, we did not buy any since we were just passing through. Later, one of the missionaries served us guinea pig for dinner. There's not much meat on a guinea pig, but the taste was great! The taste is nothing close to pork, squirrel, rabbit, or even chicken! It is uniquely different and delicious.

In Newfoundland, cod cheek is served in fast food places, and "ard" bread is a standard with fish. Water is served there with iceberg chips.

On Prince Edward Island in Canada we enjoyed seaweed pie. Also, their fresh, steamed mussels are probably the best mussels on the market. They were extra good with a nice hot sauce. While on the island, we also enjoyed a couple of their famous lobster dinners! The lobster rolls in those Atlantic Provinces are also outstanding!

been there, done that!

In Honduras we saw many large iguanas, and our bus guide said that iguana meat is somewhat of a delicacy in the country. Upon arriving back to our cruise ship from a tour, I asked the guide if there was a place nearby where I could try the iguana meat. She took Betty and me to a small hole-in-the-wall "restaurant" and asked the lady there to cook some for us. Not bad! But beware because there are many, tiny bones chopped up in the meat!

In Cambodia, prepared dishes out in the village included chicken and pig. It was a little odd to look at the platter of food and see the bright yellow feet of chicken and the two holes of the pig's snout staring up at you. But they were good!

In Argentina, we had mammoth, freshly-cut beef steaks on the grill. I don't think that God makes better steak than we were served down there on that mission trip in 2012.

Betty and I went to a dumpling restaurant while on a tour in China. The waitress brought out several varieties of dumplings in bowls and put them on a lazy susan turntable at our table of eight. She explained the content of the dumplings and right away some of our group decided they wouldn't even touch this kind or that kind. I enjoyed them all! After that, some of our tour group jokingly said they didn't want to eat at my table because "Phil will eat anything!"

"NO, PHIL, FROM A BULL"

On a mission trip in 1973 to Colombia, South America, we had a *barugo*—which really is like a big river rat and is really delicious eating. Also down there, we had a night in Bogota and went to a restaurant to eat. I don't read Spanish and am one of those who will just point to something at a reasonable price on a menu and order it without knowing what it is. The missionary translator also didn't know what it was I ordered.

When the meal came, there were two good-sized, oval-shaped, very tender pieces of meat covered in a red sauce on my plate. It was really good, and others at the table wanted a taste so the plate went around the table and no one could figure out what the meat was. We all wanted to know, so the missionary asked the waiter, and hearing the answer he turned a little red in the face. Finally, the missionary translator slowly and quietly said it was testicles. I now wanted to know what kind of animal they were from and asked: "From a cow?" (thinking of beef versus pork or venison). Suddenly and with a lot of laughter, the missionary loudly responded: "No, Phil, from a bull!" Now I was the embarrassed one with the red face!

AN EXPENSIVE FISH HEAD

In my last military assignment in the late 1980s with the Reserve Forces Policy Board, we conducted a study that took us to Korea and Japan. On our last night in Japan, I really wanted to go into town and eat local food, but some of the generals and admirals on the board asked me to stay and eat with them in the big hotel. They all had to have the menu translated and made their choices. However, as I have done in many restaurants, I just pointed to one of the lesser-priced items when ordering.

My first course was a little two-inch diameter woven basket with some greens in it and some wasabi sauce. I didn't know that the basket was to be eaten also, so when the waitress came by to pick up the appetizer dish, she motioned for me to eat the basket before she would take the plate. Interesting! I think it was seaweed. My next course was some miso soup, which had some tofu and green onion pieces in it. My main course came out and—it was a blackened fish head! I'm thinking that no wonder the price was cheaper than the other items on the menu. There's not a whole lot of "meat" on a fish head, but I think that I cleaned it up pretty well. Dessert was a small bowl of pudding.

Now it was time to pay. The senior officers individually paid first and asked for a conversion to US dollars. "$160, $130, $140" were answers given to them. They had some wine with their meal, so I was sure mine would be lower—but it was still $80. I'd never had a meal that expensive before, and when I got back to my room, I immediately called Betty and told her not to be shocked when she saw the credit card statement. That is still the most expensive meal I've eaten—and I'm really not sure that I got my money's worth out of a fish head!

FRESH SEAFOOD—RIGHT FROM THE WATER

Betty and I both enjoy lobster. It seemed that each time we were with friends in New Brunswick, Canada, it was the beginning of lobster season. They would take us out to the wharf to be there when the first lobster boats were coming in to sell their catch to commercial enterprises.

been there, done that!

After bargaining with the captain for several lobsters, we took the treasures to our friends' camping trailer. We have never had such a feast as we had there after throwing the lobsters with a little seaweed into a large pot of boiling water on an open camp fire! You don't get a meal much better than that!

It was also similar in Maine with friends who were lobstermen (and women!) We actually went on their lobster boat where the captain pulled traps that had our supper in them! I had the "pleasure" of filling the traps' bait bags with leftover parts after the fish cleaning process. Fortunately, they gave me some nice big rubber gloves to do that job! The fresh lobster catch of the day was cooked outside in a propane-fired pot, piled on a plate, and brought in to eat with corn on the cob and tomatoes just picked from our friends' garden! My mouth is almost drooling just thinking about that feast!

Also in Maine, we had lunch on a little island where we had homemade, stone crab claw sandwiches and lobster rolls along with wild gooseberries found near where we ate. Seeing some little breathing holes in the beach sand, we dug down and pulled up fresh clams. The boat captain waded out into the water, washed and opened the clam shells, and he and I enjoyed the clams right there while standing in the ocean water. That is what I call fresh seafood! Some of the others who were with us on the island wouldn't think of eating raw clams. In other places I've eaten raw oysters on the half shell — sometimes as a real delicacy in a fancy reception in Washington and other times at an oyster bar in Louisiana. I think they are great and will order them where I can—and they are even better with some good hot sauce!

I'LL NEVER SAY THAT AGAIN

When Betty and I were first married and living in our little 8x35-foot house trailer in Washington state, Betty was developing her cooking skills and wanted to please my tastes. One day, I brought an eggplant home from the grocery store. In Africa, we grew these in our garden, and I thought she could fix it for supper. Apparently she had never seen one and asked how to cook it. I really didn't know "how", so I suggested she look for a recipe in the cookbook.

She couldn't find anything there except a recipe for an eggplant casserole, which didn't sound that inviting to me. She then went to a neighbor and asked her if she had any good recipes for eggplant, but they couldn't find any in her books either. So, we decided that she could make the casserole. This early in our marriage, I didn't want to be telling her "how" or "what" to cook. At least I had some smarts—but not enough!

The casserole turned out to be absolutely horrible! I tried to be kind and ate some but finally told her that "it didn't taste like the way my mother had fixed eggplant—usually in a frypan". I'll never say that again! I quickly learned that I should never bring my mother's good cooking into any kind of comparison with my wife's cooking! That was the wrong thing to say to a young bride who was trying to please me. We look back on that casserole and laugh now about it, but it wasn't a laughing matter then.

LIPSTICK ON MY COFFEE CUP

I don't remember that my parents ever drank coffee in our home. However, some of the places where I lived, the houseparents seemed to be almost addicted to it. I sort of liked the smell of coffee brewing, but I never really wanted to drink it. Even while I was in the Army, I didn't drink it except on very rare occasions, such as at a social event. Coffee's bitterness just did not appeal to me.

After I retired from the Army, I would drink coffee a little more often but rarely at home. I always doctored it up with cream and sweetener. Betty didn't even know how to make coffee until our kids urged us to get a coffee maker for

been there, done that!

their benefit, and then they showed her how to make the beverage the way they liked it. As they had some with dessert at our house, I would also have a social cup of coffee with them. At Moody Keswick Conference Center, I began to have a couple of cups a week but can't say that I really enjoyed it and certainly didn't crave it like other people.

While in the leadership of D&D Missionary Homes, a pot of coffee for the staff was always made when I arrived at the office. At break time, I would join some of the staff in our little office kitchenette and always used my special Army 4th Infantry Division cup. (This was the division I fought with in my second tour of Vietnam and I was with that division before going to Vietnam for my first tour.) Because it was a common snack area, sometimes I would go there, and my cup would be missing. Guests or volunteers would come in and just use it as another mug from the cupboard. But I wanted to use my cup! Soon, some of the volunteer ladies in the break room would intentionally hide my cup from me, and once they even put their red lipstick on the rim. My cup soon became a big jokester thing.

To prevent my cup from being hidden, I developed a little habit by coming to the office in the morning and immediately getting my cup of coffee to take with me while wandering to greet my staff people in their work areas. Only occasionally would I take a sip from it before I finally arrived in my office. By mid-afternoon, I would see my coffee sitting there on my desk, gulp it down cold, and take my mug into the kitchenette to wash it and put it in the cupboard. I am not sure that I really like coffee yet, but I will admit to drinking it more often—especially since there are unproven reports in the news that it is good for a person's health.

NORMAL FOODS?

I don't know for sure that I have eaten anything in the cat family such as lion, leopard, or tabby cat. But I probably have since I have eaten in a lot of Chinese restaurants around the world and the US. I never see any cats wandering around them like I have seen at other places!

What are some of my eating quirks? Is there anything that I don't like? Not much, except the yellow crispy cardboard cone that many people use to hold their ice cream and the same yellow crispy cardboard of a Nabisco wafer sandwich. Why that? When I came home from Africa in 1954, someone wanted us to have an ice cream cone as a treat. In eating it, I cut the roof of my mouth with the cone. I've never liked those since. But I do like a waffle cone!

I love beets. However, I don't like beet juice flowing on my dinner plate into other foods. It just looks bad to me to have beet juice mingling with my mashed potatoes or turning my corn or chicken into that deep red-purple color. My wife knows to serve my beets in a separate bowl. If I am at a guest's house, I will try to pick the driest beets out of a serving dish before putting them on my plate. It's just a quirk of mine!

In addition to international foods, you should know that I also like anything American, such as Louisiana gumbo, Alabama coon stew, Florida alligator tail, Alaskan king crab and elk and moose, Midwest Mulligan stew, Boston baked beans, Maine lobsta', North Dakota quail, Iowa pork, Michigan silver-queen corn, DC escargot, and everything else American—even grits and fried mush! Phil will eat anything! Let me tell you this in closing out this section on food—it does not all taste like chicken! What a marvelous world we live in with all its great and varied foods and tastes!

CHAPTER XXVII
PLACES WHERE I HAVE SLEPT

Sleep has never been difficult for me. I have often said that I can sleep anytime, anywhere, and under any conditions—and my wife can verify that! I've slept on hard beds and too-soft beds, short beds, skinny beds, and no beds! I have even slept in church pews—although I was probably just meditating! But I've noticed that many people have done that, so I won't take up space to talk about that snoozing. I am not really proud to announce my sleeping there but it is one of the myriad places where I have slept. However, I have always been grateful to get sleep most anywhere. Some examples of my sleeping places are described below.

PINE COTE CABIN

My earliest recollections of a sleeping place were as a very young boy at the Westervelt Home (mentioned earlier) in South Carolina. There were several of us little guys (ages eighteen months to five or six years) packed into one small room where one could hardly get around the beds. There was really nothing so unusual about that, except the crowded condition and the scheduled times for all of us to get up and go to bed each day. We slept in a little cabin named Pine Cote on the edge of the main campus. In 1947, the Westervelt Home moved back into Columbia, South Carolina, into a large, mansion-like house where our bedrooms seemed expansive in comparison to our former place in Pine Cote.

BRICKS IN THE BED

As life progressed to my parents' 1948–1949 furlough from Africa, our family stayed with an aunt in an old house in South Bend, Indiana, which had a big

been there, done that!

coal-fired furnace in the basement. My aunt was quite poor and my parents, being missionaries, also did not have much money, so joining in one house was beneficial to my aunt and to our family.

To preserve the coal in the winter, it was used very conservatively at night times with just enough so that the furnace could be restarted easily in the morning by using the coal chunks, which were still warm. As a result, our bedroom on the second floor was very cold. Like many people did in that era when we went to bed, "upholstered" bricks were heated and put near our feet under the blankets in the bed. Early in the night, you didn't want to touch those bricks because they were so hot, but as the night wore on you wanted to absorb every bit of heat that may be left in the bricks.

My dad and aunt's mother would occasionally come to spend the night with us. She would sleep in our bed with my sister on one side of her and me on the other. In the winters in our upstairs bedroom, we would snuggle up to her to absorb some of her warmth but in the summers, we wanted to be as far away from her in the bed as possible!

DORM IN AFRICA

Shortly after I arrived in Africa in 1949, a new dormitory building was completed enough to move into by two other boys and me, along with two single missionary lady houseparents. Initially, in our end of the building, there was no running water in the bathroom—except the bucket shower—there was no ceiling over the rooms, and there was no electricity. We were used to not having electricity, and used kerosene lanterns and pressure lamps with those fragile mesh globes after dark.

We had bunk beds, but the top bunk was not quite high enough to be able to look over the wall into the adjacent bedroom. Every afternoon, we had to take a siesta, but what boy likes to take a nap in the middle of the day? A bed check ensured we were in bed for siesta at the designated time, but I can assure you that a lot went on between then and the time to get up! All sorts of things went flying over the walls between the rooms, and wrestling matches were sometimes held in the middle of the floor. But if we heard the houseparents stirring around, we seemed to always be asleep in our proper beds! We had a pretty good lookout system to give us warning. Boys will be boys!

Some of my best "sleeping" memories were when the rains came and beat upon the dormitory's corrugated aluminum roof. It was so loud that we could hardly hear each other talking. But when it was bedtime, the hammering by the rain on that metal roof seemed to be very soothing, and it put me right to sleep. Even after a wood ceiling was put later in the dorm, the sound of the rain was muffled somewhat but the sleeping was still great! I still like that sound of rain at sleeping time!

THE CLOCK THAT COULDN'T KEEP TIME

Each year in Africa, we were at the boarding school for four months, went to our homes for two months, back to school for four months, and the last two months we were at home again. Our home at Kyabe in the southern Chad was a masonry house with a thick grass roof when we first moved there, but then my dad put an aluminum roof on it. I liked that since I could hardly hear the rain through the foot-thick, grass roof! My bedroom was at one end of our back porch, and at the other end was our inside kitchen, with the cooking kitchen in a separate building out back. My room had a screen door out to the porch and one screened window.

Because of the extreme heat, everyone took afternoon siestas, but I never got much sleep. I was constantly de-winging flies on the window screen, capturing wasps, and active in reading or playing games. Much to my dismay now, I also would often sneak out into the living room and "adjust" the mantle clock to make the siesta shorter. It was a clock that rang its bell to denote the hour change and a ding at the half-hour time when we could get up.

Years later when my parents were retiring, after forty years of their missionary service in Africa, they asked if there was anything any of us kids wanted from our home out there. I immediately told them that I wanted that mantle clock. Mother asked why I wanted that since the old thing didn't keep time very well! I had to admit my siesta prank and ask forgiveness. I am quite surprised that no one figured out that the clock was wrong only at the end of siesta time! Fortunately, they got a good laugh about why I wanted the clock. The clock still works! It is now more than eighty years old!

been there, done that!

HYENAS AND ELEPHANTS REALLY CLOSE

At night, I always locked my bedroom screen door that opened to the back porch at our Kyabe house, but that didn't stop the noises of animals which came on the porch. Sometimes, the hair on my neck would stand on end when the hyenas would come on the porch and do their hideous "laugh". That could go on for fifteen minutes or so—although it seemed like an hour—and all that was between them and me was a screen door and my mosquito net! Thankfully, they didn't like living meat. They are primarily scavengers.

One night in that same bedroom, I woke to hear rumblings and branches breaking from the trees right outside my window. I felt the ground shaking a little and crawled further under the covers, having no idea what was going on. The noise seemed so close! The next morning, the night guard told us that a herd of about ten elephants had tramped between our house and the kitchen building which was only about forty feet from my room. A big tree in the middle was almost ruined with most of its lower branches broken. Footprints showed that some of these enormous animals were less than five feet from my bedroom window! Yikes!

Earlier in these memoirs, I mentioned how hot it was there in the southern Sahara Desert area. The thermometer often read 130–140°F or hotter during the day. At night, the temperature may drop down to around 80°F and because of the drastic contrast to the daytime, we would have to cover up with blankets! It really did seem cold after being out in the searing heat all day. And when the hyenas were on the back porch, just outside my screen door, the blanket was an extra measure of perceived security.

HIGH SCHOOL AND COLLEGE BUNKS

At the Mid-Maples home for teenage missionary kids in Wheaton, Illinois, our rooms were reconfigured each year, according to the number of boys versus the number of girls in residence. One year, we had ten teenage girls and fourteen teenage boys in that one house! That year, the girls slept in the second floor rooms. To accommodate all the boys, a room in the basement was changed from a game room into a bedroom, and six of us boys slept down there on three bunk beds, with the younger teen boys sleeping in four bunk beds in the two rooms on the first floor. In spite of the closeness of the bunks, we all seemed to get along quite well.

College life in my first year had two of us in a room in a dorm with a common hall bathroom for about twenty boys. Of course, typical college pranks were played on some of the boys. I am thankful that my bunkmate and I never had our beds turned upside down, mattresses removed or soaked, limburger cheese hidden in the closet, or any such prank. By today's college dorm standards, our rooms were very small and without all the amenities that college kids have today. There certainly was no room for small refrigerators, computers, electric hotplates, and such luxury items, by the time you put in a bunk bed, a built-in closet, and a couple of dressers and small desks. I'm not sure the old dorm's electric system could have handled all of those niceties kids have in their dorm rooms today.

Starting in my second year of college, I moved with a buddy into a professor's house where we lived in an upstairs bedroom. We shared a bathroom for six of us—which was much better than the dorm bath which accommodated many more. The bed was much more comfortable for what little time I spent in it. During much of my time in college, I worked some night shifts in the heating plant at the school. I must admit that occasionally, but rarely, I took a brief snooze even in the midst of all the racket and activity in the heating plant. I have the ability to wake up quickly if there is any unusual noise. Most of my life up through college was on bunk beds.

HANGING IN A TREE TO GET A NAP

After college, I was in the US Army as an officer. Oh my, there were certainly some unusual sleeping places in the woods in addition to the small pup tents we were issued! In my early years in officer basic training and in Ranger School, I learned the value of a sleeping bag with an air mattress. My Ranger class was from October through December—the beginning of the cold season. To sleep warmly, we were taught to fasten two sleeping bags together and crawl in next to our Ranger buddy to get the warmth of each other's bodies. I doubt that is being taught in today's era with its potential sexual overtones. It did work for us—especially in the North Georgia mountains in the ice and snow—although I can't say it was the most comfortable sleeping.

Three weeks of our Ranger training was in the panhandle of Florida, where we focused on waterborne operations, river crossings, rope bridges, and operating in swamplands. It was not easy to find a sleeping place in the swamps. On more than one occasion to get a little nap, I would climb up in a tree, loop my equipment harness over a branch, and just hang there snoozing. At least, my feet were up out of the water so that "swamp critters" could not nibble on me. I did have to make sure my harness was tight enough so that I would not slip out of it in the middle of the night! I have "been there, done that"! I am sure that others have slept in a tree, but were they hanging there—or in a tree house?

SCRITCH, SCRITCH—MATTRESS DEFLATES

For most of my first tour and almost half of my second tour in Vietnam, most of the time I slept on a cot with about an inch-thick pad and got very used to that. However, as a company commander out in the field for the last half of my second tour, I carried an air mattress. I'm not too sure why I carried the extra weight because the mattress didn't seem to last more than a couple of nights when we slept on the jungle floor. Ants with big pincers seemed to be everywhere under the leaves and debris covering the ground where we wanted to set up our night position, but you couldn't see any of them.

At first, most of us put the mattress right on the ground and the ants seemed to know right when I would fall asleep because I would soon hear "scritch, scritch, scratch" through my air mattress. Within a half hour or so I heard the scratching noise change to "shhhhhh" as the air began to leak out of my mattress, and then it went completely flat. The ants had bitten holes in my comfortable air mattress, and I was not happy! At another night position, having gotten new air mattresses for most of my troops, I put my poncho on the ground before putting my air mattress down. It took longer for the ants to get to my mattress, but they finally made it through my poncho and flattened that new mattress also!

I figured the only solution to our dilemma was to thoroughly spray the area where we would sleep. But that had its own problems with having to carry the extra weight of cans of ant spray and to get resupply as needed. Also, the enemy may be able to smell the spray or at the least know that we had been there after we had left that overnight spot. I sure didn't have any idea of the viciousness of the ants and their capability to puncture a poncho and the vinyl of the air mattress. Their little pincers were quite strong and also left us with leaky ponchos that we needed when it rained!

One of our missions for a few days was to provide security for some of our big artillery cannons. The 8" howitzer fired a round weighing over 200 pounds and a 175mm howitzer's round weighed 150 pounds. It took a lot of explosive powder to get those big rounds out of the tubes and toward targets fifteen to twenty miles away! Can you imagine the loud sound of those when they are fired? Try sleeping near them! They would cause a shock wave that bounced you and your air mattress when they went off. That was not conducive to sleeping! Thankfully, I was in the infantry and not the artillery, so I was not around the big guns that much.

AN AIRCRAFT CARRIER AT SEA

Earlier in these memoirs, I wrote of flying onto an aircraft carrier at sea for a study by the Reserve Forces Policy Board. It was exciting to land in a fixed-wing aircraft and to be abruptly halted on touchdown by the arresting cable. We were on board for a couple of days, and my berth was an officer's single room, which was quite comfortable—except for the horrendous loud noise above.

My berth was one deck below the location of the aircraft carrier's arresting cable, and when a plane came in to land, the cable caught it—that is if the pilot adequately lowered the plane with its tail hook. Down below in my bed, I heard the squeals of the aircrafts' tires hitting the deck, the tail hook's screeching as it dragged on the carrier's deck, and the cable's winches as they unwound to slow and then stop the plane. Then the winches would rewind the arresting cable. What a racket!

When a plane wasn't coming in to land on the carrier, maintenance was being done on the winches and the cable, thus generating additional noise as the cable bounced on the carrier deck. On top of all that clanging was the constant noise of the jet engines because as an aircraft came to land, it was at full throttle just in case its tail hook missed the cable and the plane had to take off again. I guess the sailors and officers get used to all that noise, but for me it made for a couple of nights with minimal sleep. How many missionary kids (who were not in the Navy) have "been there, done that" trying to get some sleep on an aircraft carrier?

HIDING OUR "EVIL" DOINGS

When Betty and I were traveling for Moody Keswick Conference Center and D&D Missionary Homes, we appreciated the opportunity to spend nights in the private homes of some of our snowbird friends or members of churches where I was speaking. We always enjoyed the social interactions of being with other people, rather than being confined to a motel room. Some of the homes' rooms were huge and classy—well above our normal accommodations! Others were very average and comfortable while a few—well, I'll be kind and just say it this way—were different.

In one house, we were in a remodeled attic room that had a low-sloped roof. The three-quarter size bed was against the wall and the edge of the roof came right down to the edge of the bed. Betty had to get in bed first to sleep next to the wall since she rarely moves at night, but I'm like a rotisserie—constantly rotating. I knew if I slept over there, I would be banging against the roof all night.

In another place, Betty had gotten in bed before me, and when I got into the bed, we both rolled right into the middle and crashed into each other. That mattress had a problem!

I spoke in a church in another place, and we were invited for the night to a family's house on a farm. It was very cold and had been snowing and now the ground was very muddy. We pulled up to the house and found a slippery plank laid out for us to walk on to get into the house. We were all bundled up, and the kids in the house were used to the cold and in light pajamas and bare feet and seemed eager to have us with them. Kids always seemed to want to hear an unusual and exciting story, but I had to be careful that my stories didn't scare them or cause them to stay awake at night.

Eventually, we were escorted to our room where we noticed many, many pillows of different sizes and shapes on the bed—which we could hardly even see! What would we do with all of the pillows so we could get in bed? We piled them over in a corner and got in bed. Oh, what a bed! Laying on our backs, it felt like our knees were being folded up to our chests. Now we knew what to do with the pillows! While I held the mattress up, Betty put many of the pillows on the middle of the broken springs beneath, and when I let the mattress back down, it almost stayed level. The next day we had to reverse our actions to make the room look normal again.

We have often slept on sofa beds in a spare room. Most of those beds have a fairly thin mattress which hardly allows for good sleeping because of the horizontal support rod in the folding bed frame. If you have slept on an old sofa bed, you have felt that support bar. More than once, we have pulled the mattress off the bed, folded up the sofa bed frame, and put the mattress on the floor to get a good night's sleep. Again, the next morning required us to remake the room to hide our "evil" doings. However, we were still very thankful for the hospitality of people and our opportunity to get to know them better!

TWO IN A NARROW BED—WITHOUT ROACHES!

Probably our most memorable sleeping situation was on a mission trip in Colombia, South America. I wrote earlier that after flying in to La Pedrera on a small float plane, Betty and I were going to sleep in an abandoned military barracks building with no electricity. It was dark, and Betty had not been in such crude conditions, so she was tightly hanging on to me as we walked along the river's edge to the barracks area. Shining our flashlights into our room, large cockroaches began to scatter everywhere. We saw two very narrow beds with inch-thick, straw mattresses held in place by 2x4=inch frames. Immediately, Betty emphatically told me that she was *not* going to sleep there that night. She said she would just stand up all night, and if the batteries in her flashlight wore out, she would take my light! Remember, she is from Chicago, had never been in a jungle environment, had said originally she was *not* going on this mission trip, and probably had never seen more than one or two roaches at the most! This would be her second test of the meaning of *"not going!"*

I tried to show bravery and told her I would get rid of the roaches, which by now were scurrying into unknown places—perhaps down the cracks in the rough flooring. I gave Betty my flashlight and reached over, grabbed one of the inch-thick straw mattresses from one bed and shook it vigorously to knock off and scatter the cockroaches and then pounded it on the edge of the bedframe until no more roaches were moving anywhere. Then I did the same to the other mattress. I told Betty that I would pile the two mattresses together and that we would sleep together in one bed that night. I don't know how much sleep we got as we lay head to toe so we could fit on that skinny bed that was only about two-feet wide—but at least with two mattresses, it was two-inches thick and didn't seem quite so hard! She did survive! The next day, we moved to a more comfortable bed.

BACK OF A PICKUP TRUCK IN A MUD HOLE

How many people do you know can say they have slept in a mud hole? For transparency, I will admit that I wasn't in the muck. I think that I did get a little sleep that night we were in a pickup truck that was stuck in a mud hole on our way back to Chad from our school in the Central African Republic. It definitely was not a bed, and it certainly was not comfortable. And, it was not very quiet with the mosquitos buzzing around and all the other strange night noises from the

been there, done that!

jungle! The story of that night is earlier in this book (See page 36). I am thankful that sleep has never been a problem for me. If it had been, I'd probably be in a permanent "sleep" now.

CHAPTER XXVIII
CHRISTMAS CELEBRATIONS

THE BIG COLORING BOOK

The first Christmas I remember was at the Westervelt Home in Batesburg, South Carolina. I was probably three or four years old, and I'm not particularly thrilled with the details of my recollection. We had just eaten lunch, and some of us little kids were doing little craft items. It was just a few weeks before Christmas, and we were making some Christmas items by drawing on paper with red and green crayons. We also had the opportunity to color some mimeographed pictures. At that age, the lines of the pictures didn't mean too much to me, as there were probably more crayon marks outside the lines than in them.

My great mistake was that I had seen a big, fat, library-style dictionary on a high stand in the large sitting room near where we were coloring. I remember dragging a chair over to the stand and climbing up on it to be able to see this *big* book and turn its pages. Why I would be looking at the dictionary at that age is still a mystery! Anyway, I saw a lot of little black and white pictures—next to the printed definitions of the words in that book. Not realizing that the dictionary was *not* just an enormous coloring book, I took a red crayon and proceeded to "color" those little pictures on many of the pages—and of course, I didn't stay in the lines very well, if at all, as I held the crayon in my tightly-fisted, little hand!

Unfortunately for me, someone in authority saw me standing up on a chair at the dictionary. I don't think they were concerned about my safety on that chair. You can guess what happened when they saw my beautiful coloring! To give you a hint, I could not sit down without significant pain for quite a while, and probably my back side was the same color as those newly-colored red pictures in the

been there, done that!

dictionary. I deserved what I got, but I do wish they had given me that giant coloring book for Christmas after the "authority" realized how talented I was with only one little red crayon! To be truthful, to this day, I am not a big fan of art works. Maybe my mind just goes back to my earlier artistic experience and the end result.

POPCORN, CRANBERRIES, AND RAISINS

At another Christmas at the Westervelt Home when I was a year or so older, all of the missionary kids had gathered in the big dining room with us little kids mingled in with some of the teenagers at huge tables. Every year, we had a popcorn-popping evening, and on each table were big cooking pots full of popcorn; other bowls had bright red cranberries; and yet others had raisins. The older kids threaded some large sewing needles with heavy-duty thread for us and then we made long strings of popcorn, cranberries, and raisins for decorating several Christmas trees and for hanging garlands in the dining room, a common living room, the schoolhouse, and even for a little nicety in our cabin.

I will admit that not all of the popcorn was put on the strings. Some ended in our little tummies and much of it ended on the floor as some kernels broke when we tried to poke them with the needle! As I look back, we must have spent hours and hours stringing that popcorn. We actually even used a small artist's brush to paint some of the popcorn for added color. I'm not really sure that kids would be entertained by that in these current days! I don't remember getting any packages or seeing any under the Christmas trees, although I am sure that some of us must have received something each year. Christmas at the Westervelt Home was simple but very enjoyable for all the missionary kids—at least for us younger ones who were separated from our parents serving in so many nations around the world.

UNIQUE CHRISTMASES IN AFRICA

Christmases in Africa were unique. There were no nicely shaped pine trees to buy in the village or even to cut from the jungle! So, we had to find something that we could hang a few ornaments on. The best we could find was a branch of our lemon tree. It was fairly straight with a lot of one- to two-inch thorns and smaller branches growing off the sides. With a lot of garland and other homemade accessories, it turned out to be reasonably festive.

We were always very careful to not tear paper when we unwrapped our packages. We could not buy wrapping paper in the village markets, so some of the paper would be reused year after year. We sort of played a little game in trying to remember what was last wrapped in that used and wrinkled paper! My parents wanted to give us kids as much of an American Christmas as possible.

ONE-PAGE, SPIRAL NOTEBOOK GIFT

Often we would have Christmas at the regular time of the year, but then we would have a second Christmas in the next year's late spring when packages from the US would finally arrive—and when we were home from four months at boarding school!

One year, my nicely wrapped package from America contained a small 3x5-inch spiral notepad. When I opened it, I saw that the little notepad had only one sheet of paper in it, and there was the stub of a pencil pushed into the spiral top of the notepad. The pencil had no eraser, and no lead was visible. It was too short to even sharpen in a typical manual, rotary, pencil sharpener. Someone in America thought that this would be a great gift for a poor missionary kid out in Africa, and their heart was probably right in their effort to support missions. But to this kid in the southern Sahara Desert, it was difficult to be grateful for a gift like that.

USED TEA BAGS AND MELTED CANDY

You have probably heard stories of missionaries getting dry, used tea bags. I can verify the stories as I watched my folks open a package with approximately ten of those used tea bags, which certainly were not worth the Christmas wrap or cost to send them to Africa. How many used tea bags does it take to make an eight-ounce glass of tea? Other memorable gifts were chocolate bars—which had been completely melted by the desert heat—oozing out of the wrapping and beginning to turn powdery-white from age.

There were also gifts of the tall tin cans of hard, brightly-colored, Christmas candies. It was almost impossible to get out a full piece of candy because all the candies had melted together. But we did learn that an icepick came in very handy to chip fragments of candy out of the can! I really did like the candy, even if we

been there, done that!

only got chips rather than a whole piece! If a small chip fell on the floor, it wasn't long before a bunch of ants were also enjoying their Christmas.

IN EVERYTHING, GIVE THANKS

Having received these varying gifts in addition to nice things as clothes and toys, Dad constantly reminded us that "in everything, give thanks" and that it is the "thought that counts". Regardless of our age, those can be difficult principles to follow, but they are maxims for each of us to try and achieve. The people who had sent the gifts were at least thinking of us and probably were good prayer and financial supporters for which we were very thankful. Some of them may not have had much for themselves and gave what they could.

I am reminded that God told Adam and Eve they could eat from all the trees in the garden, except one. So what did Satan do? He got them to focus on the one tree and its fruit they couldn't eat. God wants us to be thankful for all that we have and not focus on the things we don't have or didn't want.

SIXTY-TWO-INCH WAIST USED PANTS

For one of the Christmases at Mid-Maples in Wheaton, Illinois, during my high school years, more than 500 gifts from individuals and church groups were "under" the tree for the twenty-six of us in the house! As teenagers, most of the gifts were clothes. To know what clothes belonged to whom for laundry sorting assistance, we had to hand-sew our own name tags in each piece of clothing—or try to get the girls to do it for us. If a guy had a "girlfriend" in the house, it was easier to get the name tags sewed in!

Sometimes the clothing was used! The giver's thinking may have been: "You know that MKs have nothing, so used clothes at Christmas are better than nothing!" One of these gifts was a *big* pair of trousers! Two of us boys got into them and buttoned them at the waist. As I recall, the pants had a sixty-two-inch waist—for a teenage boy! I am sure many missionaries could tell similar stories.

SHOOTING OUT OUR CHRISTMAS LIGHTS

Our big front porch at Mid-Maples was decorated with strings of Christmas lights with the large, pointed, colored bulbs. Some boys from the neighborhood decided that our lights would make good BB gun targets, and one night we heard the bulbs breaking. A couple of us boys snuck out the back door of our house and surprised the culprits. What were we thinking? They had BB guns, and we had nothing! But anyway, they ran and we chased—racing through people's yards, over fences, into cornfields, and through a swampy area.

Eventually, they got back to their neighborhood, thinking that they had lost us. In reality, we held back and hid to see which house they would go to. We gave them a few minutes and then went up and rang the doorbell. A man came to the door and seeing our wet and muddy clothes was about to close the door when we asked to talk with the boys who had just gone into the house.

He asked what it was all about, and we told him about the boys shooting out our Christmas lights and how we had chased them to this house. He seemed sorry to hear that and called the boys who had to admit in front of their dad what they had done. Confrontation is never fun but is often necessary. We said that they needed to pay for a couple of new strings of lights, and we would let the matter go. The father agreed and said that he would pay, and the boys would be dealt with later. We never saw the boys around our house again! Hopefully, they were still living when their father finished with them.

LONELY CHRISTMASES IN VIETNAM

I spent the Christmases of 1965 and 1968 in the combat zone during my two tours in the Vietnam War. In 1965, the battle in the Ia Drang Valley had diminished, but the role of my unit had increased as I sent out more patrols around our Camp Holloway Army Airfield. Christmas being a holiday, the enemy forces may consider that our security would be lessened. However, much to the opposite, I remained in the combat operations center much of that Christmas day, monitoring the progress of my additional external patrols and strengthening our internal security.

We did get a wonderful Christmas dinner, which made it different from the standard menu. Thankfully, none of my men suffered any casualties that day while they were on duty, and every one of my men did get to enjoy the Christmas feast, although for some of them, it was later after they returned from their patrols. Special efforts every year are made to give fantastic feasts to the military forces around the world—whether they are in a garrison environment or in the field at Christmas and Thanksgiving time. The menu includes everything (and more!) one could expect at a home-cooked dinner. These holiday dinners with their desserts were absolutely amazing!

The Christmas of 1965 was only the second Christmas for Betty and me since our wedding, and here we were a continent and thousands of miles and an ocean apart. She would celebrate in her own way with our three and a half-month old son whom I had not yet even seen—except for pictures! In those days, we did not have Skype or Facetime or WhatsApp—let alone cell phones to call on. I could not call her but certainly thought a lot about her in Indiana.

I spent Christmas of 1968 in Vietnam mostly sleeping since I got off duty in the morning. My daily duties in the division's combat operations center were from 7 p.m. until about 9 a.m. the following day. We did have a Christmas Eve gathering on our Camp Enari base for all soldiers at 11 p.m., and then the group divided into separate Protestant and Catholic services. Someone relieved me so that I could get off duty to attend the programs and share in a communion time. The service was very quiet as I think most of us were thinking of our loved ones in the US, rather than the service being conducted. I had to hold back tears of loneliness a couple of times as I sat there. I wanted to be home with Betty, Philip Jr, and Debbie so very much. It was tough going back to work about 12:30 a.m. after that Christmas Eve service.

I did get up on Christmas afternoon to share the special Christmas dinner prepared for all the troops. But outside of that, the day was like any routine day for me. Usually, the mess hall fixed sandwiches for those of us who worked through the night, but on this Christmas night in 1968, we had our favorite midnight meal: C-Rations! Ha, Ha! Something had gone wrong in the kitchen, and the cooks couldn't make sandwiches for us. Oh, well, the cooks did need some time off also.

In 1968, communications were not much improved from my Christmas in 1965. Letters had to suffice, although Betty and I did use cassette tapes more often so we could hear each other's voices. That Christmas, Betty was six months pregnant and had a three-year-old boy and an eighteen month-old girl to care for at home. She helped them enjoy Christmas without Daddy. In Vietnam, I could only dream of being with my family and their celebrations. Thankfully, communications for our troops with their families is much better now, and they can be in contact—and even see each other—almost any time their tactical situation permits.

However, I do remember the loneliness in moments of those two Christmases, although I could not dwell on it because of the pressing responsibilities in the operations center—when I wasn't sleeping or enjoying the Christmas meal.

Christmas had no special meaning for the North Vietnamese or Viet Cong soldiers, so the war continued as on any other day.

IN A CAST AT HOME FOR CHRISTMAS

Christmas of 1969 was more joyous because I was with Betty and our three children. However, I was somewhat hampered in what I could do. In Vietnam, I had been wounded severely in May of that year and had been wearing a full-body spica cast for a few months. It covered me from my chest down through my hips and all the way down my right leg to the ankle. The cast was hinged at the knee to give me more flexibility, but to get around, I had to use crutches to maintain my balance.

Just before Christmas, I was so happy to get out of the full-body cast but now was put in a long-leg, hinged-knee cast from my upper thigh to my ankle. Now, I could bend at the hips but was still restricted because I had limited range of motion in my knee and stiffness in my hip that hadn't been bent since the middle of May. I was just thankful that I could be home from the hospital on convalescent leave through that Christmas holiday season! Since then, Betty and I have had all our Christmases together.

CHAPTER XXIX

CLIMBING EXPERIENCES

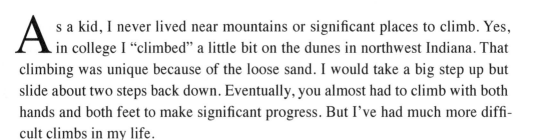

As a kid, I never lived near mountains or significant places to climb. Yes, in college I "climbed" a little bit on the dunes in northwest Indiana. That climbing was unique because of the loose sand. I would take a big step up but slide about two steps back down. Eventually, you almost had to climb with both hands and both feet to make significant progress. But I've had much more difficult climbs in my life.

RACING UP THE WASHINGTON MONUMENT

I do remember climbing the steps inside the Washington Monument while on a history class trip to our nation's capital in my senior year of high school in 1959. Being on the track team as a distance runner and in good condition, a sprinter on the team challenged me to a race up the almost 900 steps to the top of the monument. He thought that since the monument was only about 555 feet tall, he would win. Some have estimated the stair climb to be the equivalent of climbing forty-six stories in a hotel. I accepted the challenge as an endurance race, thinking his "juice" would run out before he got to the top.

At the halfway point, he was a couple of flights of stairs ahead of me. I finally passed him about two thirds of the way up and was waiting for quite a period of time for him at the top landing. Endurance won over speed, but both of us knew we had really accomplished an unusual feat by racing to the top—but our thighs and knees were really aching!

We had assumed that we could ride the elevator down to the bottom of the monument but were told by the elevator operator that we had to have a ticket to ride. Talk about a "downer" for two teenage boys with very tired legs! We had to

been there, done that!

walk back down, and that was tough! Our legs were like rubber, and we had to give them a good massage and rest before we could go anywhere else. For me, this climb was one of the toughest physical challenges I met and achieved early in life.

REAL MOUNTAIN CLIMBING

I learned about real mountain–type climbing in the Army Ranger School near Dahlonega in northeast Georgia. There we were introduced to ropes, knots, belays, prusik climbing, overhangs, pitons, snap links (carabiners), rope seats, rappelling, and mountain evacuation techniques (piggy back and litter/stretcher). All of that was new to me.

I found rappelling to be the most fun, and the prusik and overhang climbing were the most difficult for me. The face of Yonah Mountain was our learning and practice field. My confidence in myself and in my fellow soldiers increased immensely during this period of mountaineering training. I had never done anything like this before, and I proved to myself that I can accept and overcome very difficult challenges. Fear and doubt constantly lingered and I had to overcome these while on the face of a vertical cliff and push myself to keep moving toward my goal of reaching the top. We used this training to learn technical skills and to build confidence.

In our patrolling up and over the Tennessee Valley Divide, it was sometimes ten to fifteen degrees colder on the north slope when cresting the ridge in late November. I am glad that the Army never assigned me to posts where I would have to endure extreme cold weather.

CLIMBING IN VIETNAM

Ranger training was excellent preparation for me—both in my military career and my teaching opportunities in civilian endeavors. It emphasized small unit operations and skillful application of mountaineering techniques. In both of my tours in South Vietnam, I was in the central, west side of the country where the mountains were. They were more like the Appalachian Mountains than the Rockies. After the rains, the slopes of the hills became extremely slippery and made operations more difficult. We never had to use real mountain-climbing techniques with pitons and snap links, but on a couple of occasions we did use ropes to help pull ourselves up or down the slopes.

In one mission, we were fighting the North Vietnamese Army (NVA) on some steep slopes while following our artillery barrages higher up the hill as we climbed. That is when the first man of my company was killed in combat. When recovering his body on the steep hillside, we had to continue to fight the NVA while our artillery and mortars brought heavy, indirect-fire on the hillside above us. But it also was raining the enemy's artillery shrapnel on our advancing forces. Climbing mountains or steep hills in battles is arduous and treacherous—but is sometimes necessary to fulfill a mission. It reminds me that in life we will face many difficult, uphill situations where we may have to use "helps" provided by someone else for us to be overcomers and achieve victory.

AGONY ON THE TEMPLE OF THE DAWN

During my first tour in Vietnam and nearing its end in 1966, I took my rest and recuperation (R&R) week in Thailand. I met up with another lieutenant who wanted to go with me to many of the tourist sites and events. Being in pretty good shape, we decided to climb up the outside of the Temple of the Dawn in Bangkok.

The temple is not that tall, but it was the steepness of it that made it a real challenge. At times for the climb, I wished that I had mountaineering pitons, snap links, and a rope to use—as I had learned in Ranger school—while we climbed higher and higher up the outside of the temple.

Lots of the people in the plaza around the temple were just watching other climbers but they were not going to go up. So, when two foreigners came forward with tickets to climb, they all wanted to see if we could do it. The steps up were very narrow and tall and in a very few spots at the lower levels, there was a very rickety railing that I really didn't trust! Most climbers went only as high as there were railiings but we continued up to the top level where we were permitted to climb and took time to look around the city from that height. There was nothing to hang on to except the stone material used in construction, and it was rather frightening as we clung to the near vertical wall. Wow, it was a great view outward over the river and city—but it was a scary view to look down the steep walls where we had come from!

Slowly we started our descent, but soon our calves and thighs were telling us that they were being overused and were ready to cramp! In some places, I found that it was best for me to come down backwards, using both feet and hands for the steeper parts. There was no place to sit and rest because the steps were so narrow. Believe me, I began praying pretty hard that I could keep going and not fall down from that height.

To the cheers of some watching, we finally made it down to level ground, but our legs were like rubber, and we could hardly walk over to a bench. I don't think I will ever forget the physical agony and mental fear of potentially falling that I experienced at that temple. Why did I ever want to climb the temple in the first place—especially with no ropes or other climbing assistance? I guess it was just the challenge of seeing others succeed in a very difficult task that urged me to make the climb. (I understand that the temple exterior has been recently upgraded, broken rock steps have been repaired, and sturdier handrails have been installed in places to aid people in their climbs. But I don't think that I'll go back and climb it again—now that I am a few years older!)

MOUNTAINEERING WITH TEENAGE BOYS

In the 1970s, I was the captain of a battalion of the international Christian Service Brigade organization when we lived in the suburbs of Washington, DC. The battalion for teenage young men was sponsored by our church. The theme of one of our years was mountaineering techniques and skills. I taught the information for climbing and rappelling to the boys at our Wednesday evening programs, and then put it all into practice out in the Shenandoah Mountains to our west. I had all of the appropriate paraphernalia and safety equipment needed, but the boys had to get their own hardhats. Parents had confidence in my training and leadership. Although we had some close calls, we never had a serious accident as we climbed and rappelled in the mountains. It is true that these were not huge mountains, but the techniques and fears are basically the same—just on shorter but still dangerous cliffs.

A favorite climb was an all-day trip up Old Rag Mountain in the Shenandoah National Park in the west part of Virginia. Although the mountain is only 3,284 feet high, it can be strenuous nine-mile hike for young, teenage city boys with its switchback trails and occasional rock scrambling. However, the view from the top gives a 360-degree panorama of the beautiful surrounding Blue Ridge Mountains—particularly in the fall season. We climbed the mountain in all seasons and in varying types of weather. Since our climbing Old Rag in the 1970s, I understand that a decent trail has been built and maintained, and it has become a popular tourist spot in Virginia.

A significant result of mountaineering training is the increased confidence instilled in individuals. We always emphasized the importance of teamwork and safety when climbing or rappelling. One should be constantly checking another (or be checked by a team mate), whether in the proper use and correctness of knots, the security of anchors, or the effective knowledge of a person handling the belay rope for someone else. Stepping over the edge of a cliff or climbing up vertical rock faces takes a lot of courage and faith in others who are there to help. I noticed big differences in the boys' confidence following our practical application in the mountains of what they had been taught on Wednesday evenings.

Climbing and rappelling teaches the importance and value of gratitude. One should never climb alone. When your teammate aids you in any fashion, it should generate a deep spirit of thankfulness. Their support may reduce the potential of severe injury. It is like that throughout life in whatever endeavor we may attempt. Appreciation is an important characteristic to carry and express to others in all ventures in life. Gratitude encourages continuing support—whether in times of stress or when a great victory has been achieved.

been there, done that!

VIEW FROM THE CROW'S NEST

Betty and I were invited to go on a five-day sailing cruise on the Schooner *Heritage* in Penobscot Bay in Maine in 1996, right after the closing of the Moody Keswick Conference Center. One exciting thing for me was a climb up the rope ladder to the crow's nest. I had watched two from the paid crew go up there to lower the tallest masts when we had to go beneath a bridge and seeing that, I asked the captain if I could climb to the crow's nest. He said they didn't normally allow passenger guests to do that because of the strength it took to go up and down but also because the sway and tilt of the ship may make a person sick.

I explained that I had been an Army Ranger and that heights didn't bother me. To further convince him, I told him that I had used rope ladders in obstacle courses and over the side of a ship and that I could make the crow's nest climb even though it might be a little risky. The captain hesitatingly agreed to let me go up. The rope ladder was about two feet wide at the bottom but only about eight inches wide at the top.

It was an interesting climb as the boat leaned from one side to the other in the wind. At times, my chest would be pressing against the rope ladder and just a few moments later, I would be laying back and hanging on the "rope rung" of the ladder. But I made it and enjoyed sitting in the crow's nest for a while! What a view!

The crow's nest was seventy-five feet above the water line and as the ship tilted, I could look straight down to the water with no boat underneath me! That was a little scary! My legs were a little shaky by the time I got back down on the deck, but I was sure glad that I had that fantastic experience. I have "been there, done that!" The captain of the *Heritage* said that I was the first non-crew member that he had let go up to the crow's nest during all the years he had been sailing!

SPIRITUAL CLIMBING

Climbing up to and back down from the high point of the ship reminded me so much of our spiritual walk in life's journeys. Sometimes a climb or descent can be very rough, but we always have our Lord with us. When we arrive at a peak in our life and look out or up, we see the beauty of the horizon and the brilliance of a sunset or sunrise—just as I did at the top of the Sydney Harbor Bridge! However, looking down, we can become very discouraged when there is no boat below and all we can see are the rough waves of the sea, the steepness of the downward slope, and the difficult aspects of life which we may go through. But like almost all of our physical climbing, we must come back down from the delightful heights into the reality of daily living. Isn't it great to know that wherever we are in life, Jesus Christ will never leave or forsake us—on the special heights or in the deepest valleys! He is our aide, offering us words of His wisdom and guidance, giving us comfort when we may be hurt, and giving us rest after a difficult moment in life.

Psalm 23 reminds me that "though I walk through the valleys...I will fear no evil: for thou art with me." It is in the valleys that "He makes me to lie down in green pastures" where I can look up and see God's beautiful creation and enjoy the glistening rivulets of water streaming down the mountain's side into the water below. It is there in the valley that "He leads me beside the still waters." Praise the Lord for those places of peace and restoration of my strengths to be ready to move on to my next challenge in life. My compassionate God will walk with me up the strenuous mountain side or through a difficult valley—whether in the bright sunlight or in the darkest of nights. I trust my faithful Shepherd to always lead me in all trails (and even trials) of life.

Because of my love for Christian music, it seems that whenever I was climbing something—whether it was high or low—I would think of a song. Some of these songs were: "Climb, climb up sunshine mountain"; "We are climbing Jacob's ladder"; "I'm going higher, yes higher someday, I'm going higher to stay"; "Zacchaeus climbed up in a sycamore tree" (just to see Jesus!); "Rock of ages"; "I'm pressing on the upward way, new heights I'm gaining every day"; "On Christ the Solid Rock I stand": "Faith is the victory that overcomes the world"; and there are many more. I am challenged to focus on reaching the top but in almost all situations, there are lows and valleys which I will have to descend into and pass through in order to get to that next mountain top. Hiking in the mountains of life is a constant challenge we all must learn to accept!

Just as it takes strength to climb something physical, it takes spiritual strength and endurance to reach spiritual heights in our journey in life. And there will be times when we may have to use the help of others in our spiritual climbs or walking on a rugged path. On the other hand, we may have to assist someone else in their climbing efforts. I have had to do both. Our service to others will often be based on experiences God has allowed us to endure. We cannot effectively benefit others if we have not passed through similar trials and have leaned on our

been there, done that!

Father to help us be an overcomer. As I close these memoirs, I am truly thankful for all those that have "thrown me a rope" in my times of need to help me progress upward in my spiritual journey. But, looking back, I am also very grateful to the Lord for opportunities to pass a rope or a hand to a struggling friend. It has been my privilege to hold the belay rope to give additional encouragement to those who are still climbing or plodding on the rough rocks in the valley. God has been so good to me throughout my life and I want to be a channel of blessings to all those around me.

CHAPTER XXX
A BRIEF LIFE SUMMARY

This book has given details of some important portions of my life, but I cannot begin to write about every aspect of others. What a life I have had! I reflect back with much joy on the places and events where I have "been there, done that"! I thank my God for the unique and unbelievable stories surrounding every opportunity I've had as a missionary kid. I believe that more is still ahead.

In summary, here is a quick listing of some of the privileges in spiritual ministries which God has let me enjoy. For some of these, I have provided narrative and given some of the details in previous chapters but for others, there is just not room to explain. These have all enriched my life! They are not in any order of priority or levels of excitement: Captain for many years of teenage boys in a battalion of the Christian Service Brigade; director of Moody Keswick Conference Center; president of D&D Missionary Homes: minister of music and director for youth and adult choirs in several churches; church planting team member for churches in Illinois and Virginia; mission trip director to Colombia; guest on Christian radio and TV programs; team member on four (two medical and two construction) mission trips; speaker at Vesper Services in retirement communities; men's chorus director; deacon; mission conference speaker; Veterans Fellowship leader; church senior adult activities coordinator; Adult Bible Fellowship class leader; Sunday School teacher; international seminar and Bible school teacher; mission agencies' board member; facilitator for Christian organizations' strategic planning; devotional speaker on cruises and tours; patriotic event speaker in churches; consultant and advisor for mission agencies; and missions committees member.

Just since my military retirement and direct ministry involvement beginning at Moody Keswick Conference Center in the early 1990s, at this writing and according to my records, I have preached or made presentations 478 times in 179 cities and in 273 separate ministries. These numbers do not include devotionals for my staffs and I am sure that some presentations were not recorded. I trust that God has been honored in all of these events even though I am not formally trained as a preacher. I enjoy sharing what God has taught me. In addition to my twenty-six years in the military, this has been a unique life for a missionary kid! Please praise the Lord with me that I can say that I've "been there, done that" in so many parts of His world! I am a blessed and privileged person and still waiting for more opportunities to serve my Lord!

I have learned the value of courage in all aspects of life. It is a necessary characteristic when facing unusual risks—whether these are voluntary or involuntarily forced upon me. I once read the following from an anonymous author: "The next time you find your courage tested to the limit, lean upon God's promises. Trust His Son. Remember that God is always near and that He is your protector and your deliverer. Remember that God rules both mountaintops and valleys—with limitless wisdom and love—now and forever." How true! One of my maxims in life has been that if I don't have the courage to lose sight of the shore I am currently on, I will never be able to experience the exciting worlds or events elsewhere. I have left behind the known shores in life many times and have willingly taken required risks which have resulted sometimes in failure or injury. But more often, taking risks has resulted in unforeseen increased potential and success! I am thankful for where I have been, what I have done, and my confidence in where I am going for eternity in heaven with my Lord and Savior, Jesus Christ!

All of my experiences could not have occurred if I had not been born into a missionary family, raised in homes led by godly parents and houseparents, accepted Christ into my life at an early age, and let Him have dominion in my life. The Lord has changed the course in my life from what I and others wanted, to that which He planned for me. His course was definitely for my benefit, and I trust also for the enrichment of other people's lives. I am thankful and happy and hope to always be an encouragement to others in my words and presence. May the Lord be honored and glorified by all who read about these stories of my life. It has been and continues to be a wonderful and fun journey.

My prayer is that if the apostle Paul were here today, he would be able to say of me as he said of Stephanas in I Corinthians 16:15 that my life has been addicted to, devoted to, and consumed by a passion of ministry to the Lord's people—and to others not yet in my Lord's family.

May my unique and unbelievable stories be used in your life to give you courage and an understanding that if God can take me through all these experiences in my life, He can and will do the same for you!

APPENDIX A

Phil Fogle's Core Values—(Philippians 4:8)

Honor God—in all things at all times wherever I am. Love Him with all my heart. Be dedicated (fully committed) to Him. Follow the examples of my parents.

Love my family—leave a heritage that will be remembered in positive ways. Ensure financial security for my wife and if possible for our three children.

Honor my country—continue to fight to retain the freedoms it has afforded to me. Promote patriotism in speech and by example.

Encourage others—locally, nationally, and internationally. Be involved in missions programs. Be addicted to the ministry of the saints (I Corinthians 16:15c).

Rejoice evermore—let my inner joy be reflected in my outward appearance. View life through a lens of gratitude. In everything, give thanks. Reflect on God's goodness in my life.

Earn trust and respect—not praise—of all whom I meet. Do all things with excellence and integrity. Carry out my word. Hold myself to a high standard that others may see and want to follow.

Make wise decisions—motivate others through my life by supporting these decisions.

Be a positive, happy, people person—express optimism, meet new people, enjoy wit and humor, and accept opportunities to explore the unknown.

been there, done that!

Exercise regularly—to attain body, mind, and soul fitness. Study to show myself approved unto God (II Timothy 3:15). Be informed on issues in the spiritual and secular subjects of life.

Communicate effectively—choose my words carefully. Voice my concerns tactfully. Provide or recommend solutions where difficult situations exist.

In summary, may I have the passions of Christ and the consistent grace to adhere to these values and live for His glory in all aspects of my life.

APPENDIX B
MILITARY BIOGRAPHICAL SUMMARY

Name: Fogle, Philip Ray

Rank: Colonel, Infantry, US Army—Retired

Date and Place of Birth: 3 December 1941, South Bend, Indiana, USA

Retirement Date: 31 August 1989

Home Address: 13377 Pine Bark Court, Largo, Florida 33774

Last Military Assignment: Staff Director, Reserve Forces Policy Board, Office of the Secretary of Defense, Washington, DC

Source and Date of Commission: Wheaton College (Illinois) Reserve Officer Training Corps (Distinguished Military Graduate) 10 June 1963

Years of Commissioned Service: More than twenty-six years (10 June 1963 – 31 August 1989)

been there, done that!

Military Schools Attended:	**Year Completed**
The Infantry School, Infantry Officer Basic Course	1963
The Infantry School, Ranger	1963
The Infantry School, Airborne	1964
Military Equipment Readiness Course	1964
The Infantry School, Republic of Vietnam Refresher Course	1968
The Infantry School, Infantry Officer Advanced Course (Honor Graduate)	1971
The Infantry School, Nuclear Weapons Employment Course	1971
Defense Information School, Information Officer Course (Distinguished Honor Graduate)	1971
Defense Information School, Public Affairs Seminar	1972
University of Wisconsin, Public Affairs Advanced Course (Distinguished Graduate)	1972
Industrial College of the Armed Forces, National Security Seminar	1972
Command and General Staff College	1980
National Defense University, National Security Management Course	1982
USA Readiness Group Meade, Training Manager's Workshop	1983
Defense Information School, Senior Public Affairs Seminar	1984
Harvard University, Senior Officials in National Security Studies	1988

US Decorations/Badges:	**Year Awarded**
Defense Superior Service Medal	1989
Legion of Merit	1989
Defense Meritorious Service Medal	1989
Armed Forces Reserve Medal	1988
Office of the Secretary of Defense Identification Badge	1985

MILITARY BIOGRAPHICAL SUMMARY

Army Meritorious Service Medal with Oak Leaf Cluster	1984
Army Service Ribbon	1982
Joint Service Commendation Medal	1978
Army Meritorious Service Medal	1977
Department of the Army General Staff Identification Badge	1976
Army Commendation Medal	1973
Bronze Star Medal with V Device	1969
Bronze Star Medal (Meritorious Service) with Oak Leaf Cluster	1969
Purple Heart Medal w/ Oak Leaf Cluster	1969
Purple Heart Medal	1969
Vietnam Campaign Medal (5)	1966 and 1969
Valorous Unit Award (3)	1966 and 1969
Combat Infantryman Badge	1969
Meritorious Unit Citation	1969
Bronze Star Medal (Meritorious Service)	1966
Vietnam Service Medal	1966
Air Medal	1966
National Defense Service Medal	1966
Expert Infantryman Badge	1964
Expert Qualification Badge (Rifle, Pistol, Grenade, Bayonet)	1964
Parachutist's Badge	1964
Ranger Tab	1963
Retired Service ID Badge	2019

Other Decorations/Awards:

Vietnamese Cross of Gallantry with Palm	1966
Fifth US Army Certificate of Achievement	1968
Vietnamese Unit Honor Medal	1969
Tailhooker's Certificate	1989

been there, done that!

National Guard Bureau Eagle Award	1989
Special Recognitions from: Office of the Chief of Army Reserve, Association of the United States Army, Reserve Officers Association, National Guard Association, and The Retired Officers Association	1989

Chronological List of Appointments:

Second Lieutenant	10 June 1963
First Lieutenant	10 December 1964
Captain	10 June 1966
Major	02 February 1971
Lieutenant Colonel	15 November 1982
Colonel	15 November 1987

Chronological Record of Duty Assignments: From—To

ACTIVE DUTY

Student, Infantry Officer Basic Course; Ranger; Airborne	Jun 63—Feb 64
Rifle Platoon Leader, Company B, 1st Battalion, 22nd Infantry, 4th Infantry Division	Feb 64—Jul 64
Weapons Platoon Leader, Company B, 1st Battalion, 22nd Infantry, 4th Infantry Division	Jul 64—Dec 64
Heavy Mortar/Davy Crockett (Nuclear) Platoon Leader, Headquarters Company, 1st Battalion, 22nd Infantry, 4th Infantry Division	Dec 64—May 65
Detachment Commander, 52nd Security Detachment, 52nd Aviation Battalion, 1st Aviation Brigade, Vietnam (Combat)	Jun 65—Jun 66
Assistant Professor of Military Science, US Army Senior ROTC Instructor Group, Wheaton College	Jun 66—Jun 68
Assistant G-3 (Plans), 4th Infantry Division, Vietnam (Combat)	Jul 68—Sep 68

MILITARY BIOGRAPHICAL SUMMARY

Assistant G-3 (Operations), 4th Infantry Division, Vietnam (Combat)	Sep 68—Jan 69
Rifle Company Commander, Company D, 2nd Battalion, 35th Infantry, 4th Infantry Division, Vietnam (Combat)	Jan 69—May 69
Patient, Valley Forge General Hospital, (Wounded in Action)	May 69—Feb 70
Instructor, Ranger School	Feb 70—Apr 70
Student, Infantry Officer Advanced Course; Nuclear Weapons Employment Course	May 70—Feb 71
Student, Defense Information School	Feb 71—Apr 71
Administration/Management Officer, Command Information Unit, Department of the Army	May 71—Jun 73
Briefing Officer, Office of the Chief of Staff, Department of the Army	Aug 72—Oct 72
Public Information Officer, News Branch, Office of the Chief of Information, Department of the Army	Jun 73—Jun 76
Community Relations Officer, Office of the Chief of Information, Department of the Army	Jun 76—Apr 77
Public Affairs Officer, News Branch, Assistant Secretary of Defense (Public Affairs), Department of Defense	Apr 77–Feb 78

US ARMY RESERVE—NOT ON ACTIVE DUTY

Individual Ready Reserve	Mar 78—Aug 78
Public Affairs Officer, Office of the Chief of Public Affairs, Headquarters, US Army Training and Doctrine Command	Aug 78—May 82
Public Affairs Officer, 97th US Army Reserve Command, 1st US Army	Jun 82—Oct 84

US ARMY RESERVE—ACTIVE DUTY (SADT or AGR)

Public Affairs Officer, Interallied Confederation of Reserve Officers (CIOR), Office of the Chief of Army Reserve	Jun 82—Aug 82

been there, done that!

Assistant for Public Services, Office of the Assistant Secretary of Defense (Reserve Affairs), Department of Defense	May 84—Sep 85
Staff Director, Reserve Forces Policy Board, Office of the Secretary of Defense	Sep 85—Aug 89

Civilian Education:	**Degree Received & Years Attended**
Wheaton Academy, Wheaton, Illinois	Graduated 1955–1959
Wheaton College, Wheaton, Illinois	BA (Social Science) 1959–1963
Graduate Work, University of Wisconsin, Madison, Wisconsin	1972
Graduate Work, Catholic University, Washington, DC	1978
Graduate Work, Harvard University, Cambridge, Massachusetts	1988

Civilian Employment:	**From—To**
Heating Plant Operator, Wheaton College, Wheaton, Illinois	Feb 60–Jun 63
General Manager, METER, Inc., (Biomedical Equipment Repair Company), Alexandria, Virginia	Aug 78–Dec 79
Operations Manager, Association of the United States Army, Arlington, Virginia	Jan 80–May 84
Licensed Insurance Agent, Mortgage Broker, Securities Representative, PRIMERICA, Fairfax, Virginia, and St. Petersburg, Florida	Aug 89–Jul 93
Director, Moody Keswick Conference Center, Moody Bible Institute, St. Petersburg, Florida	Apr 91–Jun 96
President, D&D Missionary Homes, Inc., St. Petersburg, Florida	Jul 96–Nov 08

Teacher, Pastoral Enrichment Program, Baptist Mid-Missions, Cleveland, Ohio   Oct 99–May 13

Family:

Married to Betty (Becker) Fogle, a registered nurse from Chicago.

Son, Philip Jr., is a risk mitigation specialist senior consultant for an insurance company. His wife, Bunny, is a registered nurse with a PhD in Health Administration and Nursing Education. She is a nursing education specialist. They have two children: Brooke, Nick.

Daughter, Deborah, is a medical assistant. Her husband, Jim, is an IT director. They have three children: Ethan, Katy, David.

Son, Todd, is a brigadier general in the US Air Force. His wife, Johanna, serves in an oral surgeon's office. They have three children: Nathan, Claire, Adam.

APPENDIX C

General Biographical Summary

PHILIP R. FOGLE

13377 PINE BARK COURT, LARGO, FL 33774–5438

E-MAIL — phrfogle@gmail.com TEL: 727–596–5936

EMPLOYMENT HISTORY:

Served more than twenty-six years in the US Army, retiring as a full Colonel of Infantry in 1989.

Highlights include training as an Airborne Ranger, two tours of combat duty in Vietnam (being wounded twice in the second tour); seventeen and a half years of duty in the Pentagon in the Department of the Army and the Department of Defense, performing public affairs duties and policy development for all military services and their reserve components.

Served as the director of the Moody Keswick Conference Center in St. Petersburg, Florida (April 1991–June 1996). Responsible for a thirteen-week winter Bible conference and for year-round retreats.

Served as president of D&D Missionary Homes, Inc., St. Petersburg, Florida (July 1996–November 2008). Responsible for the quality provision of fifty-two homes and support services for active missionaries and pastors in transitional periods.

been there, done that!

MINISTRY PRIVILEGES:

Assisted in the establishment of two churches in Naperville, Illinois, and Springfield, Virginia.

Served as deacon in several churches, taught Sunday School classes, directed choirs and sang in others, served as volunteer minister of music in churches.

Achieved a Herald of Christ badge (compare to Eagle Scout) in Christian Service Brigade and served as junior leader in the organization as a teenager. As an adult, led a Christian Service Brigade Battalion program for teenage boys for more than ten years.

Directed a two-week mission trip for sixteen people to jungle areas of Brazil and Colombia, South America. Participated in mission trips and missionary ministries in Cambodia, Thailand, Hong Kong, Germany, Netherlands, Argentina, Hungary, Peru, Romania, and Ukraine.

Team teacher for Pastoral Enrichment Program (PEP) in India, Nepal, Myanmar, Andros and Eleuthera Islands in the Bahamas, Central African Republic, and Chad.

Speaker at seminars, men's conferences, missionary conferences, and represented both Moody Keswick Conference Center and D&D Missionary Homes in numerous venues.

Served as facilitator for strategic planning for Christian organizations.

Served on the Elected Council of Baptist Mid-Missions and have served on boards of other nonprofit ministries.

Served as the adult Missionary Kids Coordinator for Baptist Mid-Missions.

Coordinated senior adult activities for more than five years at local church.

Established and coordinated a Veterans' Fellowship at church.

Served on missions committees in several churches.

CHURCH MEMBERSHIP: Starkey Road Baptist Church, Seminole, Florida.

FAMILY: Married in 1964 to Betty. We have three married children and eight grandchildren!

DATE AND PLACE OF BIRTH: December 3, 1941, in South Bend, Indiana, to missionary parents who served a total of forty years with Baptist Mid-Missions in the heart of Africa. I lived in Chad and Central African Republic for five years.

EDUCATION:

Graduated from Wheaton Academy, Wheaton, Illinois

Graduated from Wheaton College in 1963 with a BA degree in Social Science (with a concentration in Geography) and a commission as a Second Lieutenant of Infantry in the US Army.

Graduate work at the University of Wisconsin and Catholic University.

Graduated from the Senior Officials in National Security Program at the John F. Kennedy School of Government at Harvard University.

Graduate of numerous military schools including the US Army Command and General Staff College and the Industrial College of the Armed Forces at the National Defense University.

PROFESSIONAL ASSOCIATIONS:

Association of the United States Army

Reserve Officers Association

Military Officers Association of America

Disabled American Veterans

APPENDIX D
MAPS

Central African Republic and Chad

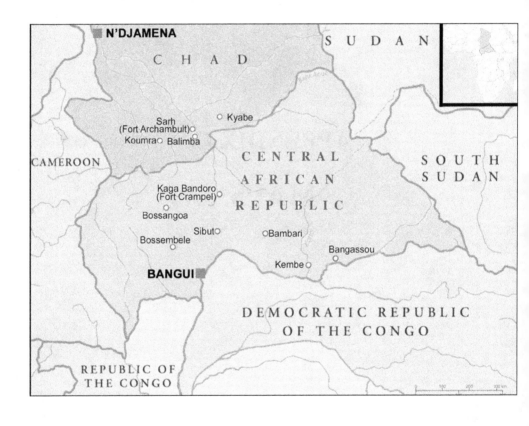

Vietnam

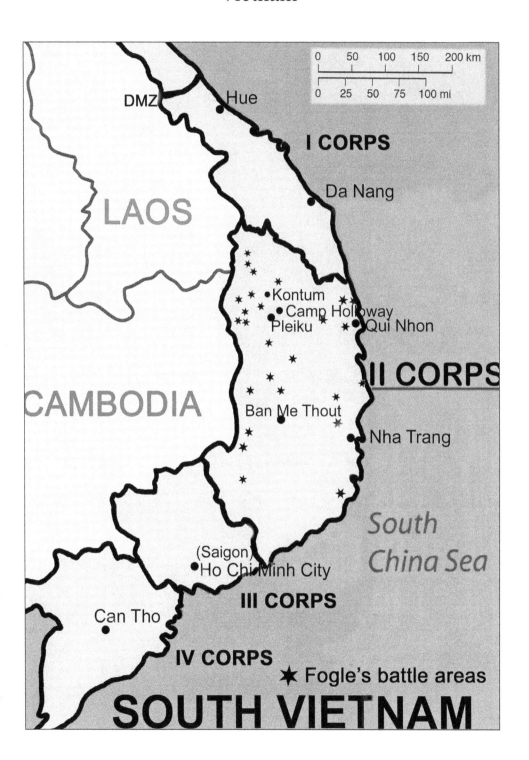

CPSIA information can be obtained
at www.ICGtesting.com
Printed in the USA
BVHW012050190822
645023BV00004B/82